THE GOLD RING

ALSO BY KENNETH D. ACKERMAN

Young J. Edgar:
Hoover and the Red Scare, 1919-1920

Boss Tweed: The Corrupt Pol Who
Conceived the Soul of Modern New York

Dark Horse: The Surprise Election and
Political Murder of President James A. Garfield

WWW.VIRALHISTORYPRESS.COM

Kenneth D. Ackerman

THE GOLD RING

*Jim Fisk, Jay Gould,
and Black Friday, 1869*

VIRAL HISTORY PRESS, LLC
FALLS CHURCH, VIRGINIA

The Gold Ring
Jim Fisk, Jay Gould, and the
Black Friday Corner, 1869

Viral History Press, LLC
Falls Church, VA 22044
www.viralhistorypress.com

Copyright © 2011 Kenneth D. Ackerman

Dodd, Mead & Company, Inc. edition 1988

Library of Congress Cataloging-in-Publication Data is available.

ISBN-13: 978-1-61945-005-9

Designed by Zaccarine Design, Inc.
Printed in the United States of America

Dedicated to Karen,
for still being a good sport.

CONTENTS

Author's Note ix

Part I: The Ring 1
1. War 3
2. "Fort Taylor" 12
3. The Money Lock-Up 17

Part II: Golden Visions 31
4. Alliances 33
5. Trial Balloons 43

Part III: The Fix 49
6. The Politico 51
7. Savior of the Nation 61
8. Propaganda 68
9. A New Stooge 73
10. The Plunge 77

Part IV: Shoulder To Shoulder 87
11. Coming Undone 89
12. Shoulder to Shoulder 96

Part V: Bears 99
13. Bankers 101
14. The Bold and Brilliant Plan 110
15. A Done Deal 115
16. Twisting Arms 120
17. Resistance 129
18. Messages 131

Intermission: Photo Insert 139

Part VI: Bulls 155

19. Sneak Attack 157
20. Bad Blood 164
21. Change of Plans 166
22. Center Stage 171
23. Putting Heads Together 178
24. Foreboding 182
25. Eye of the Storm 189

Part VII: Outlaws 205

26. High Old Times 207
27. Falling Out 213
28. Wreckage 222
29. Behind the Barricades 228
30. Family 236
31. Bears Regroup 239
32. Lawyers 243
33. Coup d'Etat 248

Part VIII: Dirty Laundry 255

34. Astounding Revelations 257
35. Politics 266

Part IX: Fortunes 273

36. Evasions 275
37. Light of Day 281
38. Bygones 288

Afterthought: "Israel Freyer's Bid For Gold" 297

Bibliography 301

Reference Notes 309

Acknowledgments 351

Index 353

AUTHOR'S NOTE

They say that every good storyteller is a good liar. In the case of Jim Fisk, Jay Gould, and their 1869 gold spectacular, however, I found no need to stretch reality. Fogging the authenticity of the narrative with manufactured dialogue or characterizations would only diminish it. The story of the 1869 gold corner is fascinating because it is true; Gould and Fisk, two real people, actually said and did all the seemingly outrageous things that are portrayed in these pages. The fact that they got away with them, that they made sense in the context of their nineteenth-century world, speaks volumes about this formative stage of our national psyche.

I have kept lying to a minimum. All statements, events, and situations depicted are as "truthful" as the materials cited in the "Notes" section.

The writing of this book was largely completed before the stock market crash of "Black Monday," October 19, 1987. Still, any similarity between this story and the events of Black Monday is hardly coincidental, and 1987 doubtless was not the last time.

Ken Ackerman, March 1988

• PART I •

The Ring

• • • • •

• 1 •
WAR

O N MONDAY MORNING, March 2, 1868, *The New York Times* carried a dispatch from Galveston, Texas, on the western frontier. A desperado named D. McKinney had shot a man named Clay Sharcy in nearby Navasota. McKinney had been drinking that morning and had drawn his pistol on saloonkeepers who refused to serve him free liquor. The sheriff arrested McKinney and set out, along with deputies on horseback, to deliver the prisoner to nearby Anderson to stand trial.

But the people of Navasota took unkindly to outlaws in their town. That night along the road, the posse carrying McKinney was stopped by sixty armed men, "disguised and blackened." The vigilantes disarmed the sheriff and deputies and then took McKinney and tied him securely, and hung him by the neck to a tree limb. The rope broke, so they hung the outlaw again to a sturdier branch that was more than ten feet from the ground. This time the rope held. The armed men dispersed, leaving McKinney's body dangling in the wind.

No further arrests were reported in the case.

On that same morning in New York City, Cornelius Vanderbilt, the seventy-four-year-old "Commodore" and master of the New York Central Railroad, sent shudders through Wall Street by declaring war on his chief competitor, the Erie Railway Company. After months of legal sniping and maneuvering, Vanderbilt now threatened to gobble up Erie just as he had already gobbled up the New York Central, the Hudson, and the Harlem River railroads in stock "corners" that had made heads spin. Backed by a personal fortune estimated at $30 to $60 million, Vanderbilt ordered his brokers on the Stock Exchange to buy Erie shares by the fistful. At the same time, his lawyers obtained decrees from friendly New York judges that prohibited Erie from issuing any additional stock or convertible bonds.

Then as now, stock-takeover wars gave smart operators an opportunity to get rich. Vanderbilt's reputation for ruthless competition over the course of sixty years fueled their anticipation. His name had long been a household word. Vanderbilt—tall, physically tough, and handsome—had made his original fortune in steamships, running passengers first from Staten Island up the Hudson River and later to Europe. In 1856 the Commodore almost single-handedly organized the overthrow of the government of Nicaragua to preserve his exclusive right of transit across the isthmus to the Pacific. Years earlier, he had committed his own wife to an asylum until she agreed to live in a new mansion on Manhattan Island.

Long before government securities regulations, antitrust laws, the Federal Reserve, or any effective controls in the United States, big-money stock operations were bare-knuckle affairs. Wall Street after the Civil War was an untamed frontier, like Texas and the Wild West.

Organized finance in New York dated back at least to 1792, when brokers had gathered under a buttonwood tree to trade real estate and old U.S. Continental money. But the Stock Exchange remained small potatoes. Then the Civil War and the rise of the railroads launched a speculative fever in America. In December 1865 the Exchange moved from a small room on "Change Alley"—off Broad Street, near Wall—to a grand, hundred-foot tall marble palace on Wall Street.

The men who now gambled their fortunes on the Exchange moved with swagger and bravado. "[S]tockbrokers are a jolly, good-hearted, free-and-easy class of men," wrote observer Kinehan Cornwallis, "who spend their money fast when they are making it fast, and sometimes even when they are not doing so."

But Vanderbilt's assault on the Erie Railway surpassed anything yet seen.

Vanderbilt was the biggest shark in this sea; the smaller carnivores smacked their lips at the coming feeding frenzy.

Opposing the Commodore was an old rival, Daniel Drew, the Erie Railway Company's seventy-one-year-old chairman and treasurer. A notorious stock manipulator, Drew veiled his shrewdness behind a country-bumpkin Bible-quoting front. Years before, when he was a cattle drover, Drew had fed his cows salt and let them drink gallons of water before weighing them for sale—the original "watered stock." A trustee of the Methodist Episcopal Church and semiliterate, like Vanderbilt, Drew became Erie's treasurer in 1853 and thereafter bilked the line mercilessly. As treasurer, Drew knew company secrets and could control or foresee every jiggle or waggle in Erie stock prices. Unhindered by today's legal bars on insider trading, he made money every time.

"I got to be a millionaire before I hardly know'd it, hardly," "Uncle Dan'l" said. He had no intention of letting Vanderbilt walk away with his cash cow now.

When it was first built twenty years earlier, designers had considered the Erie Railway a technological marvel. Stretching from Jersey City westward across New Jersey, Pennsylvania, and Southern New York to Buffalo, it was the first rail link to the Great Lakes. There it connected to points west. But by the late 1860s, although still one of the United States' corporate goliaths, the Erie had deteriorated from years of neglect. Engineers jokingly called the aging rails and roadbed "two thin streaks of rust." Drew's corrupt management of the company had earned Erie a reputation as "the scarlet woman of Wall Street."

Vanderbilt saw the Erie Railway as competition. By the early 1860s the Commodore had changed his business vision. He had sold his steamship empire and cast his lot with the United States' newest transportation medium, railroads. Starting from scratch, Vanderbilt had built an empire of steel rails that would ultimately increase his fortune from $10 million to an unheard of $100 million during his last fifteen years of life. By 1867 the Commodore had dazzled the financial world by capturing and consolidating three moribund lines into the New York Central system, which now stretched from New York, north to Albany, then across to Buffalo, where it connected, like the Erie Railway, to points west.

With Erie in his pocket, Vanderbilt could control all rail traffic between New York and the western frontier. No federal bans against regional monopolies would be imposed for decades. So the Commodore, the self-proclaimed "friend of the iron road," began buying up Erie shares and soon he controlled several seats on the board of directors.

Confident and vain, Vanderbilt forced the issue in November 1867. He proposed a merger under which Erie and his own New York Central would set joint freight rates and pool their profits. To Vanderbilt's surprise, the Erie board rejected the plan. Daniel Drew had corralled enough allies to outvote Vanderbilt's directors. In February 1868 the board added injury to insult by agreeing with the Michigan Southern Railroad, the primary link from Buffalo to Chicago, to build a special narrow-gauge line from Chicago that would connect with Erie in the east, diverting traffic away from the New York Central.

The Commodore steamed. The Erie Railway Company had deceived him.

Throwing a tantrum, Vanderbilt announced that he would simply buy Erie and set policy as he pleased: no bother with tender offers, waiting periods, disclosures to the Securities and Exchange Commission, or other legal mumbo jumbo.

It seemed the fight would be over before it began. Who could resist an onslaught of Vanderbilt money and clout? Keen observers, however, knew that Vanderbilt and Drew had been banging heads for forty years in business wars over steamboats and railroads. And this time, Uncle Dan'l seemed oddly serene. Old Cornele could bluster all day long, but Brother Drew had two aces up his sleeve. In anticipation of the fight, Drew had elevated onto the Erie board two obscure young protégés cut from his own mold of fiscal connivance. They were quick, arrogant, and unscrupulous; to Drew's mind, the smartest young men on Wall Street.

So it happened that Jay Gould, thirty-one years old, and James Fisk, Jr., thirty-two, entered the annals of Americana.

At first, Gould and Fisk were nonentities in the conflict—"Mr. Fish" or "Fiske" or "J. Gould" to the newspapers. Jay Gould, quiet and fidgety, with intense eyes and a brilliant mind for numbers and detail, already had a purple reputation on Wall Street. In 1858 the twenty-two-year-old Gould had convinced an elderly New York millionaire named Charles Leupp to invest $60,000 in a tannery business that Gould managed. After a falling out, Leupp shot himself in the head with a revolver. Gossip, true or not, had it that Jay had cheated the old man and driven him to suicide.

Psychoanalysts would have marveled at Jay's upbringing. Born in 1836 to dirt-poor dairy farmers in rural Roxbury, New York, his mother had died when he was five years old. His father, John Burr Gould, outwardly ridiculed the boy, telling him he was "not worth much" around the farm. When Jay complained about going to school, his father locked him in the cellar for days until Jay's five sisters raised a ruckus. A frail youngster, Jay had learned to survive by bending rules. He sometimes cheated at wrestling with his boyhood friend John Burroughs.

When Burroughs complained, Jay had said, "But I'm on top, ain't I?" One night when Jay was eight years old, a gang of fifteen gun-toting men dressed as Indians broke into the family farmhouse and dragged his father from bed.

The men, part of a terrorist wave during the so-called "Rent Wars" in upstate New York, threatened to tar and feather John Burr Gould unless he joined their anti-landlord movement. He refused. His little son, watching from behind a door, admired how his father stood his ground. "Conscious of right, he shrank from no sense of fear," Jay wrote.

Jay went on to invent a mousetrap; he wrote and self-published a 450-page *History of Delaware County* and ran the ill-fated tannery with Leupp. Then he came to New York in 1858 to make his fortune. There he joined two other brokers in 1862 to form Smith, Gould, Martin & Company and started buying railroad stocks. Like other young men of destiny—J. P. Morgan, John D. Rockefeller, and Andrew Carnegie, among others—Jay avoided military service by purchasing a $300 replacement under the eminently unfair Civil War conscription acts.

By 1867 he had accumulated a stake in the Erie Railway big enough to be courted by the embattled company treasurer.

James Fisk, Jr., by contrast, was a chubby, outgoing showman who spent his money on women, diamond stickpins, and good times. A year older than Gould, Fisk first learned his business smarts as a teenager, when he worked as a barker with Van Amburgh's traveling circus. Later he peddled housewares with his father through small towns in Vermont's Green Mountains. When business was slow, James Junior persuaded his father to decorate his merchandise carts like circus wagons with bright colors and glittering harnesses and ride into town at a full gallop, handing out pennies and candies to children. The customers loved the spectacle. The business became so successful that Boston's Jordan Marsh retail firm hired Jim as its Washington sales agent early in the Civil War.

During the war, Jim distinguished himself in the cloak-and-dagger cotton smuggling trade. He bought cheap contraband cotton from Confederate warehouses, sneaked it past Union lines, and shipped it north for Jordan Marsh to weave into uniforms for Lincoln's army.

Jim's mother died when he was an infant, but his father and stepmother doted on him. When a schoolteacher whipped Jim for pulling a prank, his father was so indignant that he kept the boy home for months.

Jim told a story about a woman who came to him one day when he was peddling with his father. She complained that Fisk Senior had cheated her on a handkerchief. The handkerchief had cost nine pence—a few pennies in the then-local New England currency.

Jim thought a moment, then stuck up for Dad. "No! The old man would-n't have told a lie for nine pence," said he, "though he would have told eight of them for a dollar!"

Jim Fisk migrated to New York in 1864 and proceeded to lose all his money in the stock market. Before he left town broke, he gave fair warning of his return. "Wall Street has ruined me, and Wall Street shall pay for it," Jim said. He refueled his bank account in Boston and returned to New York the next year. He soon charmed his way into the good graces of Daniel Drew by doing favors for the Erie treasurer and acting as the old man's agent on secret stock trades. By the time he needed to plant an ally on the Erie board, Uncle Dan'l had been much impressed by young Jim Fisk's peculiar talents and his loyalty to him.

Jay probably considered Jim Fisk a loud-mouthed buffoon when they first met on the Erie board in late 1867. Fisk likely shared the general view of Gould as a sinister manipulator. On the surface, they differed as night from day. But underneath, powerful forces bonded them. Both had experienced grinding rural poverty in the uncaring society of the mid-1800s; both had clawed their way up to affluence by their wits. Fisk and Gould shared a self-confidence that bordered on arrogance, a disdain for public opinion, and mountains of ambition.

Prudent young men would have avoided a blood battle with the likes of Cornelius Vanderbilt. But Gould and Fisk had watched Uncle Dan'l Drew enrich himself from Erie. Now, given the chance of a lifetime, the two pro-tégés wanted their own turn at the trough.

First, Drew's lawyers found a friendly judge who issued decrees to nullify Vanderbilt's decrees. Vanderbilt's judges responded by decreeing the new de-crees null and void. As the legal eagles sparred with injunctions and counter injunctions, Fisk and Gould discovered a more potent weapon in the base-ment of Erie's Wall Street offices—a printing press.

Wasting no time and ignoring Vanderbilt's court decrees, Gould, Fisk, and Drew got secret approval from their friendly board majority to issue $10 million in bonds convertible into shares of Erie stock, supposedly to purchase new steel rails and equipment for the Erie line. Saturday night and Sunday, March 8 and 9, the printing press cranked out page after page of fresh Erie stock certificates. On Sunday they issued 50,000 shares and parceled them out in two 25,000-share blocks to Fisk's and Gould's personal brokerages: Fisk and Belden, and Smith, Gould, Martin & Company.

Jim Fisk explained the strategy: "If this damned printing press doesn't break down, we'll give the old hog [Vanderbilt] all he wants of Erie."

As the Stock Exchange prepared to open on Monday morning, March 10, the Erie directors lay in ambush. In these stressful moments, Jay Gould steadied himself by tearing corners of newspaper pages into confetti.

Trading in railroad stocks on the New York Stock Exchange took place in the Long Room, a large, high-ceilinged chamber with tall windows that looked out onto New Street; it was unfurnished except for an elevated dais at the Wall Street end, and it had an upper gallery for spectators. It also had a separate gallery for telegraph operators, who flashed the latest prices almost instantaneously to brokers' offices miles away. At ten o'clock every morning (including Saturdays), the chairman, standing on the dais, banged his gavel and called the first stock to trade for ten minutes, then the next, and so on down the list.

When he reached Erie that morning, Vanderbilt's agents grabbed the stock as fast as it was offered. The roomful of brokers raised a clamor. After the allotted ten minutes, the speculators rushed outside into the street to continue the frenzy, leaving the deserted Exchange floor behind, oblivious to the winter cold. Mobs formed around the Drew and Vanderbilt brokers on the sidewalk as the price ran from $78 to almost $83 per share.

Shortly after noon, the tide turned. Brokers allied with Gould and Fisk suddenly offered Erie stock in blocks of a hundred or five hundred shares. The mob sensed danger. An apparently unlimited supply of Erie stock was flooding the street. In a "violent panic," the price dropped from $83 to $71. Vanderbilt brokers learned that one brokerage was delivering crisp, new certificates signed only the day before. The "bull clique" was "demoralized," wrote a *Herald* reporter.

Vanderbilt's agents ran to the Commodore's office with news of the watered stock and asked what to do. "Do?" Cornele roared. "Buy all the stock the sons-of-bitches offer to sell! They think they can pick my pocket, do they? Well, by God, I'll show 'em that there's such a thing as law in this State!"

Vanderbilt kept buying, but theatrics aside, his raid was dead. After spending $8 to $10 million on Erie stock, he was still no closer to controlling the company, and the value of his newly acquired shares was falling fast.

Fisk, Gould, and Drew were elated. Flushed with victory, they met the next morning in their West and Duane Street offices. Stock Exchange messengers carried in bags of money—the proceeds from Vanderbilt's purchases of funny stock. Like a medieval warlock and his two sorcerer's assistants, the three men amused themselves by sorting the money and tying it into bundles.

But Vanderbilt found no humor in the situation. Not only was the Erie raid a public embarrassment, it had become expensive. Even his own deep pockets felt the pinch.

Vanderbilt wielded power beyond the sheer weight of money, though, particularly through his relationship with William Magear Tweed, the reigning boss of New York's Tammany Hall, who in 1868 controlled the New York judicial system.

Vanderbilt turned to George Barnard, a justice of the New York Supreme Court. Barnard had been handpicked, nominated, and sustained by Tweed and was widely known as a "slave of the [Tammany] ring." Barnard was very helpful.

New York State had only one level of courts at that time. New York Supreme Court judges held trials and issued orders with no appeal short of the United States Supreme Court. After a hastily called hearing, Judge Barnard found that Drew, Fisk, and Gould had violated the earlier injunctions by issuing the Erie convertible bonds. He declared them in contempt. Even as the trio then celebrated their victory over Vanderbilt's stock raid, news arrived in their suite that New York police were en route to arrest them.

Erie's top directors had to choose between spending time in the Ludlow Street Jail, New York's pen for civil cases, or getting out of town.

By nightfall, Drew and a dozen other Erie officials had packed their money, stocks, bonds, and records—including the $8 million in cash fleeced from Vanderbilt—and were heading across the Hudson River. They would set up Erie-in-exile at Taylor's Hotel in Jersey City, New Jersey—beyond the reach of New York justice.

Fisk and Gould only narrowly escaped the law. They left Drew, and before leaving New York, they stopped at Delmonico's restaurant at Broadway and Chambers Street to further celebrate their victory with steak and champagne. A messenger interrupted their meal with news that the police were heading over to their table at that instant. Leaving dinner half finished, Fisk and Gould raced outside into a waiting carriage that took them down to the foot of Canal Street. There they hired a small lifeboat with two deckhands to attempt to cross the river.

The fog that night was so dense that they almost collided with a steam powered ferryboat. After rowing in circles for hours in the cold, they landed in Jersey thoroughly drenched.

Two other Erie directors who dawdled in New York were arrested by Barnard's police and spent the night behind bars.

· 2 ·
"FORT TAYLOR"

THE "GREAT ERIE WAR" became a major public spectacle for newspaper readers across the country. Jim Fisk entertained reporters in a well-stocked bar at Taylor's Hotel—"Fort Taylor"—by portraying Gould and himself as protectors of the common people against arch-monopolists like Commodore Vanderbilt. They waged their fight "in the interests of the poorer classes especially," he said.

New Jersey authorities embraced the renegades, hoping that Erie-in-exile would attract business to the Garden State. The New Jersey legislature passed a law making Erie a New Jersey corporation, and Jersey City provided police protection for them when boatloads of toughs landed on Jersey shores threatening to assault "Fort Taylor" or kidnap Uncle Dan'l Drew.

Fisk hired gangs of "detectives" to guard the hotel. Asked how he thought the affair would end, Fisk joked: "Can't tell just yet, but it'll either be inside of marble halls in New York or stone walls in Sing Sing."

Back in New York, Commodore Vanderbilt fumed at his opponents' getaway. Judge Barnard placed the New York Erie company under judicial receivership, naming Peter Sweeny, a Tweed crony, as receiver. Barnard threatened to hold Drew, Fisk, and Gould on $500,000 bail apiece if his troopers ever caught them.

Weeks went by. The stalemate continued. To pass the time, Jim arranged for his romantic interest, "actress" Josie Mansfield, to join him at Taylor's Hotel.

Finally, Gould conceived a plan.

If the original watered stock ploy violated Judge Barnard's injunction, why not go over Barnard's head to the New York State legislature? The Erie directors agreed. Gould headed for Albany with a suitcase containing half a million dollars to convince state lawmakers to pass a bill that would legalize the convertible bonds and reverse Judge Barnard's order.

It is difficult today to conceive of the ensuing contest between Gould and Boss Tweed for the hearts and minds of the state legislature. Tweed, as state senator (among other offices), personally represented Vanderbilt in the fight. Gould and Tweed reportedly distributed over a million dollars each as the Albany lawmakers debated the Erie legislation. They took suites on different floors of Albany's Delavan House hotel, tending bar and doling out largesse. One state senator, A. C. Matoon, reportedly championed Erie's side after receiving $15,000 from Gould, switched to Vanderbilt's after taking $20,000 from Tweed, then supported Erie on the final vote. "The wealth of Vanderbilt seemed pitted against the Erie treasury," wrote Charles Frances Adams.

At one point, when a Vanderbilt agent arrived from New York with fresh cash, Gould reportedly paid him $70,000 to disappear.

Judge Barnard tried to stop the chicanery. He ordered Gould arrested when he first arrived in Albany, but Jay raised bail and found a doctor to testify that ill health prevented him from traveling to a hearing in New York.

Vanderbilt steamed at the spectacle. "[I]t never pays to kick a skunk," he told friends. The Commodore ordered Tweed to cut off the bribes at once; he knew a bad investment when he saw one. Albany legislators now discovered that their fountain of easy money was dry. Senators and assemblymen who had demanded a thousand dollars for their votes days before now offered their support for a mere hundred. To Adams, the mood among Albany lawmakers was reminiscent "of the dark days of the war when tiding came of some great defeat. ... the lobby was smitten with despair."

The legislators passed the Erie bill by a vote of 101 to 6; they had rejected it 83 to 32 when Vanderbilt money was being offered.

Jay Gould told the press that he was "perfectly astounded" by suggestions of bribery in the affair.

Another factor guided the Erie victory behind the scenes. One Sunday, as Gould was doing battle in Albany, Jim Fisk crossed the Hudson River back into New York armed with a letter of introduction from Albany journalist Hugh Hastings, and made a pilgrimage to Bill Tweed. Civil summonses could not be served on Sundays.

Tweed, a hulking man in shirt sleeves with a wide face, red beard, and twinkling eyes, received the Erie fugitive at his law office on Duane Street, near the Tombs prison. Except for the governor, Tweed wielded more political authority than any man in New York State. His titles tell only half the story—chairman of the New York County Democratic Central Committee, school commissioner, assistant street commissioner, state senator. His new Tammany Hall building, an elegant brick "wigwam" on Fourteenth Street, would house the upcoming 1868 Democratic National Convention.

Tweed listened for half an hour as Jim Fisk plugged the benefits of an Erie link. Beyond pay-offs and profits, chemistry sparked between the peddler's son from Vermont and the Boss of Tammany Hall. At the end, they shook hands. Tweed's a man I can do business with, Fisk later told Gould.

Gould and Fisk suddenly stood on rarefied ground. They had squarely beaten the Commodore in back-to-back contests on Wall Street and in Albany.

The war, however, was not yet over.

Vanderbilt saw a weakness in the Erie camp. Old Daniel Drew was tired of fugitive life and wanted to go home. A Vanderbilt spy slipped into Taylor's Hotel and passed Drew a note saying, "Drew: I'm sick of the whole damned business. Come and see me. Van Derbilt [sic]."

Without telling Fisk or Gould, Drew slipped across the Hudson one Sunday and negotiated with the Commodore.

Fisk and Gould seethed when they learned of Drew's betrayal. Jim got a New Jersey court order attaching Drew's personal fortune and threatened to hold it hostage against the old man's returning to New York. But on reflection the two protégés realized that the game was lost. Drew and Vanderbilt held the power. The two men potentially could settle the affair and divide the spoils between themselves, cutting Gould and Fisk out entirely if they refused to go along.

Jay Gould and Jim Fisk had learned a lesson: In the heat of battle, trust only each other. Outside of their private alliance, the world was a den of snakes.

Not wanting to be left out of the talks, Gould and Fisk crossed the Hudson themselves early one Sunday and without an invitation sought out the Commodore at his 10 Washington Place home. A servant showed them to an upstairs foyer, but Fisk had no mind to wait. Leaving Gould behind, he barged into Vanderbilt's bedroom where the old man was putting on his clothes. Vanderbilt, nonplussed, nonetheless wasted no time getting down to business. Sitting half dressed and buckling up his shoes, he demanded that Erie buy back the printing press stock. Vanderbilt "said he had got his blood-hounds on us and would pursue us until we took that damned stock off his hands—he'd be damned if he'd keep it," Fisk later testified.

"I was grieved to hear him swear so (laughter)," Jim said. "But being obliged to say something, I remarked quietly that I'd be damned if we'd take it back (great laughter)."

The Commodore then asked if a "trade" for the stock "could be slipped through our Board," Jim explained. "I told him I wouldn't agree to anything of the kind; that I wouldn't submit to a robbery of the road under any circumstances; and that I was dumbfounded—actually thunderstruck, to think that our directors, whom I had always esteemed as honorable men (great laughter), would have anything to do with such outrageous proceedings!"

Thunderstruck Fisk might have been, but the honorable Erie directors signed a peace treaty with Vanderbilt in July 1868. The terms were generous to all. Erie paid Vanderbilt $4,750,000 for half of the printing press shares that he had bought during the mid-March stock raid. In return, Vanderbilt dropped all his claims against Drew, Fisk, and Gould. Other directors took handsome pay-offs; Drew kept his years of Erie booty, and Peter Sweeny, the Tweed crony who had served as receiver during the court fights, received $150,000 for his trouble. Richard Schell and Frank Work, Vanderbilt's agents on the Erie board, fattened their wallets by $429,250, plus another $25,000 for their lawyers' fees.

All together, the combatants walked away with $9 million in loot from the Erie treasury to heal their wounded feelings and pockets.

At first, everyone seemed to have come out rich except Gould and Fisk, who got not one penny from the July "settlement." The two young speculators were left instead to become the new president and vice president of the Erie Railway Company, that venerable property which the whole battle had been fought over in the first place and which all now considered a spent wreck.

"There ain't nothin' in Airy no more, C'neel," Drew reputedly told Vanderbilt in sealing the deal.

"Don't you believe it," the Commodore replied.

As the dust settled, a deeper meaning of the affair emerged. Jay Gould and Jim Fisk, a pair of nobodies just months before, now stood at the helm of one of America's mightiest corporations. The Erie Railway, despite the embarrassments, still comprised an empire with 8,000 employees, 714 miles of track, and a capitalization of over $50 million—and more money available through smart financing.

In late July, the new titans unveiled their tie with Tammany Hall by nominating Boss Tweed to Erie's board of directors. The next time the law was needed, Judge Barnard and the other New York magistrates would be in Fisk and Gould's hip pocket, not in Vanderbilt's or anyone else's.

Things looked bleak for the time being. The Great Erie War between Drew and Vanderbilt had ravaged the Erie treasury. Vanderbilt still wanted to see the Erie closed down, and other challengers hoped to steal the company from its new masters. Gould and Fisk would have to fight to keep it. Months later, Jim Fisk claimed that he always remembered the exact date when he had become an Erie Railway director—October 13, 1867. "It forms an episode in my life! ... I had no gray hairs then," he said. Soon he had "Plenty of them! And I saw more robbery during the next year than I ever dreamed of as possible!"

Then again, Fisk had the best of vantage points to see robbery going on. Such are the beginnings of great dynasties.

• 3 •
THE MONEY LOCK-UP

NO BANDS OR PARADES GREETED the Erie fugitives—Jay Gould, Jim Fisk, and Daniel Drew—on their return to New York after seven weeks of exile at "Fort Taylor." Once the peace treaty with Vanderbilt was signed, Judge Barnard settled his contempt charges against the renegades with fines of $10 apiece. Life returned to normal. Drew resigned as Erie treasurer, and the board of directors, meeting on July 10, elected Jay Gould to fill the old manipulator's shoes by a 9-2 vote.

The recipient of the two votes, long-time director Dudley S. Gregory, promptly resigned and left the room. Three weeks later, on July 30, the board formally elected Jay president and unanimously seconded Jim Fisk's nomination of Boss Tweed as a director.

The formalities completed, Jay displayed his management style by shoving the board aside. Blithe legalisms like "corporate democracy" held little appeal for Fisk and Gould. They had a railroad to run. Aside from one formal meeting in October 1868 to rubberstamp the prewired annual company elections, President Gould saw no need to convene the board again until October 1869. Meanwhile, the Erie bylaws delegated day-to-day power to a five member executive committee composed of Gould, Fisk, Tweed, lawyer Frederick Lane, and an in-law named Miller, who never came to a single meeting.

The inner cabal of the Erie-Tammany ring could now hatch its plans in an eminently respectable private venue: the boardroom of the Erie Railway.

Once back in New York, Jim Fisk also had time to court the alluring Josie Mansfield. He rented rooms in the Clarendon House for Josie and then leased her an apartment at 18 West Twenty-fourth Street. What had started as a fling now blossomed into love.

Jim had first met Josie, an impoverished, unemployed "actress," at the home of Annie Wood, a well-known madam. Josie had wormed her way into Jim's heart and charmed him into buying her clothes, jewels, furs, and servants. Jim called her "Dollie." She called him "Sardines" or "James." She was voluptuous, with raven-black hair, full red lips, and pearl-white skin.

Josie sometimes even embarrassed Fisk with her good looks. She visited Jim's Erie office one day decked out in magnificent clothes and jewels, which caused no small wave of office gossip. Afterward, Jim scribbled her a chastising note: "Strange you should make my office or the vicinity the scene for a 'personal.' You must be aware that harm came to me in such foolish vanity, and those that could do it care but little for the interest of the writer of this."

More than just a backroom mistress, Jim made Josie a second spouse. He called her his "power behind the throne." Her parlor became the favorite meeting place for Jim's business friends. Jim hosted a private victory party at Josie's after the Erie board elections in October 1868. "James McHenry, the partner of Sir Morton Peto, the largest railway builder in the world, Mr. Tweed and Mr. Lane will dine with us at half-past six o'clock," he wrote her. "I want you to provide as nice [a] dinner as possible. Everything went off elegantly. We are all safe."

While Lucy Fisk, Jim's wife of fourteen years, lived quietly in faraway Boston, Josie lived like a duchess in New York off the tab of Fisk and the Erie Railway stockholders.

Jim's private life contrasted totally with Jay Gould's. The socially timid Jay lived quietly with his wife Helen and two sons George, four, and Edwin, two, in a four-story Fifth Avenue townhouse. There he indulged his private passion of cultivating orchids. Whatever controversy rocked his business dealings, he kept his family life a safe harbor, strictly private and conventional. Jay, the family man, bit his tongue plenty at Jim Fisk's revelries.

Meanwhile, Fisk and Gould were facing a fundamental problem at Erie: no money. Saving Erie from bankruptcy and defending it against stock raids would take cash—lots of it. But after paying out $9 million to Vanderbilt, Drew, and the other leeches to end the Great Erie War, Erie's cupboard was bare. The "settlement" price tag came to two-thirds of the company's $14.3 million total revenues for 1868.

To replenish the treasury, Jay and Jim decided to try something special, something worthy of their bold new leadership style.

There was a trick on Wall Street called a money "lock-up." Only big fish could perform it, it took loads of ready assets, plenty of nerve, thorough planning, tight secrecy, and a thick skin. Like any "bear raid," the goal was to push down stock prices so that ring members could profit by selling stocks "short"—that is, by promising to deliver stock in the future at today's price.

If prices dropped in the meantime, say from $20 to $10, "short-sellers" could buy the stocks at $10 and still sell them at the agreed $20—pocketing a neat profit.

This speculative "short-selling"—selling what you don't own yet—carried an especially sinful onus for puritanical Americans in the 1800s, who saw Wall Street "stock jobbing" as devil's work to start with. They felt that short-sellers risked their fortunes hoping to see evil triumph, stock prices fall and values diminish. In 1812, the New York State legislature had fretted that speculators were using short-sales to manipulate stock prices and practice immoral gambling; it voted to outlaw the practice altogether. This unenforced statute was not repealed until 1858. A similar law in Massachusetts remained in force into the twentieth century.

The New York Stock Exchange and the SEC to this day have rules barring short sales after a "downtick," adopted in response to abuses uncovered in the 1930s.

In a lock-up, bears went further. They helped the stock collapse by temporarily crippling the local banking system. They withdrew so much money from the economy that credit disappeared and an artificial depression resulted.

Sound far-fetched? In 1988, yes. In 1868, not really.

The United States after the Civil War was not unlike a less-developed country in Africa or Asia today. It had no telephones or retail electricity and barely a dozen companies big enough to trade on the nation's major stock exchange; the currency was eroded by inflation; and there was no central bank and only a few fledgling labor unions. Almost half the country had been devastated by the war and was under military occupation. The weak civil executive branch was swamped with debt and was overshadowed by a large, popular army. President Andrew Johnson had just barely escaped impeachment; General Ulysses S. Grant sat as Johnson's heir apparent. People traveled almost exclusively by foot, saddle, steamboat, or horse-drawn wagon, and rapid inter-city overland communications were limited to a skeletal system of railroads and telegraphs.

The United States sat on the verge of a sweeping industrial boom unleashed after the Civil War, but by 1868 that ship had still barely left the harbor.

Scarce money, another lingering hangover of the war, made the banks especially weak. The nation's money supply in 1868, including currency and bank deposits, was less than $1.28 *billion* compared with $2.5 *trillion* in 1985— a two-thousandfold difference. By contrast, the population grew only eight-fold, from about 38 million to 240 million, during this same period. Bank deposits coast-to-coast in 1868 totaled less than $800 million, with only a fraction of this amount in New York.

Take $20 or $30 million from the small circle of banks catering to the stock speculators of Wall Street and watch the sparks fly.

Every autumn—harvest season—money from the New York banks moved west and south to pay transportation costs for the newly harvested grain and cotton crops. This made credit tight. Suppose a group of investors aggravated the shortage by pulling money from the city's banks. The banks would have to cut off new lending or call in their existing loans to raise cash. Brokers and speculators carrying stocks on margin would sell to avoid paying high interest rates. Falling prices would make the stringency worse.

Stock values would tumble, and the bears holding short-sales contracts would have a field day as legitimate commerce chafed under extortionate credit costs.

People have been tarred, feathered, and jailed for less.

No single man, even in 1868, wielded a purse big enough to squeeze the local banking establishment by himself, except maybe Vanderbilt. But if a combination of millionaires whose members also controlled the funds of a great corporation like the Erie Railway and a great city like New York suddenly withdrew its cash from the banks—pulled it out of the economy and locked it up—the effect could be drastic.

President Jay Gould and Comptroller James Fisk, Jr., chose this ambitious plan for their debut in the public limelight at the helm of Erie.

In early July 1868, only days after becoming company president, Jay Gould started selling Erie stock. In September, without telling the public, the stockholders, or even his own directors, he issued bonds that were convertible into more than 200,000 new stock shares, worth $20 million at par. Working through his own personal brokerage firm—Smith, Gould, Martin & Company—he sold the stock discreetly in small lots over a period of weeks. To minimize suspicion, he offered much of it to investors in far-away England, marketed through the international banking firms of Joseph Seligman and August Belmont.

British bankers, aware of but not comprehending the gory details of the Drew-Vanderbilt war, still saw Erie as a solid investment in transportation and a vital link to the American West that was bound to yield dividends some day. By early August, Seligman alone had sold fifty thousand shares to unsuspecting British investors.

Overall, Jay issued $23 million in new Erie stock between July 1 and October 24, 1868. The company's capitalization ballooned from $34 to $57 million. Together with the funny stock that had been issued to kill Vanderbilt's raid the previous March, this amounted to a 138 percent increase in Erie stock in eight months. Nineteenth-century railroaders hardly blushed at the practice of stock watering to raise cash, but the scope and daring of Jay's expansion moved Charles Frances Adams to call it "perhaps ... the most extraordinary feat of financial legerdemain which history has yet recorded."

As the new Erie stock glutted the market, the price started to slide. Quoted on the New York Stock Exchange at almost $70 in July, it dropped by August 19 to $48.

That day, Jay Gould closed the company transfer books. Only stockholders of record on August 19 could vote in the upcoming annual board election scheduled for October 13, two months thence. With Boss Tweed at their side, Gould and Fisk had learned the art of fixing elections. They were satisfied that they controlled enough stock at this point to re-elect themselves to the board.

In October, like clockwork, money from New York banks began to leave the city for harvest season and moved west to finance the new crop. About this time, Fisk and Gould invited Daniel Drew to join them in a plan to get very rich, or richer, very quickly: locking up all the available cash in New York City and launching a bear raid on Erie.

Gould and Fisk bore no special love for Uncle Dan'l after the old man's betrayal during the "Fort Taylor" episode. The Erie Railway had purposely severed all ties with its twenty-year treasurer after Jay Gould took control. It had paid Drew $300,000 to buy out his fleet of Lake Erie steamships instead of maintaining an ongoing lease. After settling in July, Drew retired from Wall Street to sit on his fortune. He hoped to grow old peacefully, occupying himself as a church elder with revivalist prayer meetings and Sunday school classes.

But both sides now needed each other. Uncle Dan'l still controlled one of New York's biggest bankrolls, estimated at $13 million at its peak. Gould and

Fisk, still newcomers, had few allies to choose from. Drew was better than no-body. As for Uncle Dan'l, after decades as Wall Street's consummate insider, he found retirement boring. The smell of fresh action tempted him like sin.

So the old master and his two former pupils decided to bury the hatchet for one last fling at the Stock Exchange.

Nobody knows the full extent of the Fisk-Gould-Drew lock-up plan. Gould and Fisk agreed, for their part, to withdraw $12 million in cash from New York bank accounts, most of it Erie money. Drew agreed to lock up an-other $4 million.

Beyond this $16 million lump, Erie's Tammany Hall partner, Boss Tweed, committed city funds to the plan to help tighten the screws. At any given time, New York municipal accounts held $6 to $8 million, which were under the control of City Chamberlain Peter Sweeny, Tweed's confidant and an Erie Railway director since early October. Late that month, Sweeny threatened to pull $3 million from the Broadway Bank, a major city depository. Sweeny needed the money, he said, to pay quarterly interest on city revenue bonds.

To meet Sweeny's demand, the Broadway Bank called in $3 million worth of loans from other customers, mostly stockbrokers.

Tweed, working with Sweeny and Jay Gould's brokerage partner Henry Smith, withdrew as much as $20 million from accounts under their control. Smith held his $4.1 million share under lock and key in his house.

Erie stock kept falling. It hit $41 on October 29, 1868, and touched $40 on October 30. Gould, Fisk, Drew, and the other ring members sold massive short contracts on Erie to profit from the price decline.

Tight money, falling prices, and rumors of backroom company finagling sent Wall Street into a tizzy. On October 26 the Stock Exchange board, alarmed over reports of secret, possibly illegal Erie Railway stock issues, ap-pointed a delegation to demand an explanation. The next morning, five dis-tinguished Exchange directors knocked on the door of the president of the Erie line.

Wall Street hardly knew what to make of newcomers Gould and Fisk.

Jay, knowing his advantage, played his role like a Shakespearean actor. Seizing the opportunity to further undermine his own company's shares, he painted a wonderfully dismal picture. He told the Stock Exchange delega-tion that, yes, Erie had issued $5 million in new shares to pay for steel rails and equipment, and that another $5 million waited in the wings for "certain contingencies."

Erie might even default on paying certain acceptances that were due January 1.

The Stock Exchange delegation, shaken by Gould's bleak assessment, reported back immediately to the Exchange that Erie stock was multiplying like rabbits. The news hit the Wall Street grapevine. The *Herald* published details of the interview within hours, describing Gould's revelations as being of a "very damaging character."

Prices sank lower. On November 5, Erie touched $38.

Finally, the truth leaked out. Weekly public bank statements confirmed that what the *Tribune* called "an unscrupulous crowd of speculators" had "locked up" $10 to $15 million in currency. The markets panicked. Interest rates skyrocketed from 7 to 50 to 150 percent, dragging prices of all commodities into the gutter. Government bonds dropped 4 percent in two days; wheat prices fell 25 cents per bushel, and cotton 3 to 4 cents per pound. Stocks took steep losses. Wall Street became irate as brokers and bankers sweated under the manufactured credit squeeze. Nervous appeals from politically smart bankers like Henry Clews and Philadelphian Jay Cooke reached Washington, D.C., and Hugh McCulloch, secretary of the Treasury under lame-duck President Andrew Johnson.

Federal officials cared little about warfare among Wall Street factions. But ripple effects of the money lock-up were spreading far beyond New York. The money scarcity "threatened to cut off the winter food of the poor, to rob the farmer of the fruits of his toil, and to bring ruin upon half the debtor class of the community," explained Charles Frances Adams. "The very revenues of the government were affected by the operations of the gamblers."

Washington had no choice but to step in.

On Saturday, November 7, 1868, McCulloch telegraphed word through the New York Subtreasury that he was prepared to release $50 million in currency if needed to relieve the pressure. A crack appeared in the well-laid plans of the Erie operators. Even if the government never actually released a penny, the threat of federal cash en route meant that the lock-up would soon break apart.

◎ ◎ ◎ ◎ ◎

Something inside Daniel Drew snapped. He was not satisfied with making a killing along with his two protégés. Maybe he hated playing second fiddle to Fisk and Gould and wanted to call his own shots. Pride has destroyed greater men than Daniel Drew. But Uncle Dan'l now decided that Erie stock was due for an unprecedented fall. By breaking with the pool, he could make a second fortune overnight.

Drew had cheated on the pool from the beginning. Instead of the $4 million he had promised, Drew had withdrawn only $1 million of his fortune for the lock-up. Now, seeing Erie sink to new depths, he threw honor to the winds. Using another $1 million, Drew bought more short contracts, thinking that Erie would fall indefinitely.

By Friday, November 13, when Erie bottomed at $35, Drew held short commitments to deliver seventy thousand shares at an average price of $38.

Word of the betrayal reached Gould and Fisk. Drew had cheated them again. But this time, things were different. Although an insider for twenty years, Daniel Drew operated now as lone wolf, ignorant of the Erie Railway's inner councils. Drew no longer had "the privilege of pulling the wires, nor the wool over other people's eyes," wrote Henry Clews. Rather, by his own doing, he "was to be one of the puppets that should dance to the music of Fisk and Gould, and let them pull the wool over his eyes."

Jay and Jim changed the tune. With Washington committed to breaking the lock-up with government cash, they decided to ride the tide in dramatic style. On Friday, November 13, only hours after learning of Drew's slight-of-hand, Fisk and Gould released their own $12 million to the banks and bought all the Erie stock available at bargain prices. In a flash they transformed themselves from bears to bulls. Instead of locking up money, they locked up Erie, covering their short-sales commitments and betting on a big price rise.

With money now plentiful, the market rallied. Erie led the pack with an emphatic surge; on Saturday the price jumped from $35 to $61 per share before settling at $53, "an unprecedented advance of 50 percent within twenty four hours," reported the *World*.

For Drew to cover his seventy thousand short contracts at $53 would cost him $15 per share—a total loss of over $1 million.

In the chaos Fisk and Gould had created a perfect squeeze. Drew needed Erie stock to deliver on his short sales, and the only people with Erie to sell were Fisk and Gould. The law demanded that Drew pay Gould and Fisk over $50 per share for stock that they had bought at $35 and then sell it back to them for $38. Should he default, Drew faced bankruptcy and perhaps jail.

Uncle Dan'l once wrote a poem about speculating on the short side:

> *He that sells what isn't his'n*
> *Must buy it back or go to pris'n.*

After forty years as a leading Stock Exchange operator, though, Drew still had friends on Wall Street. The lightning-fast swings in Erie had caught many speculators off guard, and a growing circle besides Drew faced huge losses from the Fisk-Gould maneuver.

That Saturday night, lawyer Edwards Pierrepont—who had represented Commodore Vanderbilt in earlier rows—called a meeting in his Manhattan townhouse. Pierrepont brought together a diverse group of victims to vent their anger at the new Erie management. Some of their names were familiar from earlier episodes: Drew; Frank Work and Richard Schell, Vanderbilt's two former agents on the Erie board; and current Erie directors Henry Thompson and Frederick Lane.

An unlikely sufferer joined the group—August Belmont, banker, socialite, U.S. agent of the House of Rothschild, and chairman of the National Democratic Committee. Belmont had sold large blocks of Erie stock to his British customers, probably including the Rothschilds themselves. Belmont's customers had panicked and sold out at depressed prices at the bottom of the lock-up. Now they felt cheated as values rebounded.

Despite their differences that Saturday night Pierrepont's group agreed on one point: Fisk and Gould, the two renegades who had created this mess, must be ousted from the Erie Railway. The group cloaked themselves as reformers. Only by deposing the sinister Gould and his loud-mouthed comptroller, argued Pierrepont and Belmont, could they return honest management to the company. Other bears in the group couldn't have cared less about honest management, but they hoped that the confusion caused by fresh rounds of bitter infighting might drive Erie stock prices back to the basement.

After hours of talk, they decided to appeal to the courts.

First thing Monday morning, lawyer Pierrepont would file suit before Judge Josiah Sutherland, claiming fraud and mismanagement at the Erie Railway. He would ask Sutherland to place Erie under judicial receivership, the surest way to remove Jay Gould and Jim Fisk. Belmont himself would lend his name as primary plaintiff, suing on behalf of himself and his British customers. Drew would buttress the lawsuit by providing a sworn affidavit revealing the past sins of Fisk, Gould, and Erie during the "Fort Taylor" episode.

Instead of signing the affidavit on the spot, however, Drew asked to take the hastily drawn document home until Monday morning. Secrecy was essential, but Belmont, Pierrepont, and the others trusted Uncle Dan'l. Well past midnight, this odd assortment of speculators and money men ended their meeting in Pierrepont's parlor and went their separate ways into the November night.

When Sunday morning came, Daniel Drew could not rest. He had just betrayed Fisk and Gould to this new cabal under Belmont, but he still fretted for his money. Worse, he imagined the embarrassment he would suffer by disclosing his affidavit, rife with confessions of fraud, stock watering, and bribes—not the stuff to please Methodist elders. Drew decided to appeal to his former protégés for sympathy; he hoped that young Jim and Jay would still bail the old man out.

After church, a distraught Uncle Dan'l walked his tall, lanky body down to the Erie Railway offices. Just his luck—the company president and comptroller were both in.

Josie Mansfield was visiting Jim Fisk's office that morning when a messenger came to the door with news that Daniel Drew wished to see him. "Run along, Dollie," Jim told her. "I've got to attend a funeral now." Josie smiled sweetly at Drew while making her exit. Drew acted as if he didn't see her.

The interview in the privacy of Jim's office between himself, Drew, and later Jay Gould reeked of the cheapest melodrama. As Jim later described the scene, Uncle Dan'l said he had come to "make a clean breast of it, and to throw himself upon our mercy. "Drew admitted to being short Erie stock by thirty thousand shares; Fisk shot back that he knew Drew was short at least seventy thousand shares. Drew "complained bitterly" of his position. He "begged and entreated that I should go and bring Mr. Gould."

Jim hardly sympathized. "I told him that his disposition and his nature were so vacillating that I should not trust him," he said. "I tried to convince him that this was one of his old tricks, and that he was the last man who should whine at any position he had put himself in with regard to the Erie. "Jim relented and sent for Jay Gould, but where Jim had brashly mocked Drew's predicament, Jay simply let the old man sweat under an icy stare.

Uncle Dan'l asked Jay to issue convertible bonds, to loan him stock—do anything to help. He got nowhere. Finally, he tried to win back his old comrades by betraying his new ones. He had met the night before with "the enemy"—Pierrepont's bears—said Daniel Drew. They planned to bring suit on Monday morning to throw Jay and Jim out of the company. August Belmont's name would appear. Lawyers were busy drawing up papers.

Uncle Dan'l did not mind sharing this information with Jim and Jay, he said, because all he "cared about was to look out for number one."

All Drew's begging fell on deaf ears. Jim, sick of the scene, promised to meet Drew again at ten o'clock that night with a clear answer to his proposition. This was just a ploy to get the old man out of the office.

Not even a sharpster like Uncle Dan'l fully realized how badly his Sunday confessional had harmed Belmont and his other erstwhile allies. Warned in advance of the coming lawsuit, Gould and Fisk now had time to launch a preemptive strike. Immediately after Drew left their offices that afternoon, Jay sent for his lawyers, Thomas Shearman and David Dudley Field. They worked all Sunday night preparing a masterstroke of litigation.

Judge Sutherland, who conducted regular chambers sessions on the Supreme Court that month, did not normally open his doors for business until ten o'clock on Monday mornings. This gave the Erie Railway lawyers time to strike first by filing suit before a different judge, one who opened earlier and was friendlier to their side.

Jim Fisk waited until eleven o'clock Sunday night to rendezvous with Drew at the Erie Railway offices, making Uncle Dan'l cool his heels for over an hour. Trying to keep the meeting short and sweet, Jim led Drew through the deserted building to his office. They sat face to face across Jim's wide desk, their faces illuminated by gas lamps.

Jim got straight to the point. He told Drew in no uncertain terms that there would be no deal, no bailout.

Drew begged for sympathy. "Then if you put this stock up I am a ruined man," he said. He pleaded with Fisk to lend him stock for just fifteen days at an interest rate of 3 percent per day—about $100,000. He threatened vengeance. If Jim refused, he—Drew—would publish a damning affidavit revealing all the inner crimes of the Erie Ring. "I swear I will do you all the harm I can do you if you do not help me in this time of my great need."

They talked for more than two hours, until about one o'clock Monday morning. At each turn, Fisk gave Drew the cold shoulder and rejected every offer.

Dejected and humiliated, Drew finally had had enough. He stood up, took his stovepipe hat from the desktop, and showed himself to the door. "I will bid you good night," he said, and walked off into the winter darkness.

The first thing Monday morning, Fisk and Gould sprang their ambush.

Hours before Judge Sutherland opened his chambers, the Erie Railway lawyers were knocking at the Manhattan townhouse of Justice George Barnard of the New York Supreme Court.

Sitting at Barnard's breakfast table, the lawyers presented papers for a lawsuit filed by Charles McIntosh, an Erie ferryboat operator who owned two hundred shares of stock. The suit claimed that a "combination" of "speculators"—Belmont et al.—threatened to file "harrassing" suits against the company for the purpose of "impairing and depreciating the market value of the stock."

Barnard sympathized completely.

Yes, this was the same George Barnard who had literally run Fisk and Gould out of the state and threatened to imprison them on $500,000 bail apiece only months before, when Commodore Vanderbilt had called the tune. Mere consistency mattered less on the New York bench under Tammany than Barnard's fine skill for reading political winds.

Now those winds had shifted. The reason was simple: its name was Tweed. Barnard owed everything to his mentor, William Magear Tweed. As a Union College graduate from Poughkeepsie, Barnard had come to New York in the mid-1850s without friends or money, after years of drifting in California. Tweed had recognized Barnard's flair for politics and had nominated him for city recorder in 1857. Barnard, tall and commanding with wavy black hair and a dark moustache, won the seat easily. Tweed then nominated him for the Supreme Court in 1860, over objections from almost every sitting judge. Barnard's own brother had said, "George knows about as much law as a yellow dog." But with Tweed's support, Barnard's election was assured.

After ten years as Tammany's boldest henchman on the city bench, Barnard now lived well. He lunched at Delmonico's, commanded a private box at the theater, and nursed a fortune estimated at $5 million, held mostly in his wife's name.

Sunday afternoon, sometime after Drew's confessional, Jay Gould had sent Tweed a message about the pending Erie lawsuits and asked him to grease the wheels with Barnard. Tweed had happily agreed. "I asked [Barnard] to do it as an act of friendship to me," Tweed later conceded. "I was the best friend Barnard ever had in the world; he owed his position entirely to me, and I risked my life to nominate him."

After hearing the arguments Monday morning at his breakfast table, the justice promptly issued an order to enjoin the Belmont group from bringing any legal action against Erie, place the Erie line under receivership, and name as receiver the most qualified individual money could buy—Jay Gould. As bondsman for the receiver, Barnard chose the equally qualified Erie comp-troller, James Fisk, Jr.

Later Monday morning, the Belmont group, as yet ignorant of Barnard's decree, went to court and got an injunction from Judge Sutherland appoint-ing ex-Judge Henry E. Davies as Erie receiver. Wall Street took two days to untangle the legal morass caused by the two orders, but victory clearly be-longed to Gould and Fisk. Barnard had issued his decision first. Technically, this nullified Sutherland's subsequent action, and Gould was the receiver, not Davies.

Pushing their advantage to a flourish, Gould and Fisk appeared once more before Barnard to ask for a special favor. Barnard naturally agreed. Two days after his first order, Barnard issued a second decree. This one authorized Jay, as Erie receiver, to buy back all the 200,000 shares of Erie Railway stock is-sued since last summer, paying market prices of up to $100 each.

In effect, Gould and Fisk could now take the oceans of Erie shares they had bought days before at $35 per—the bottom price during the money lockup—and sell them back to the company at now-buoyed prices of almost $50. The money game had come full circle, and Fisk and Gould had won every turn. Drew ate losses estimated at over $1 million.

It was Uncle Dan'l who later said of Jay Gould: "His touch is death."

◎ ◎ ◎ ◎ ◎

The impact of these financial-legal maneuverings on the growing reputations of Jay Gould and Jim Fisk was immense. The *Herald* tempered its outrage with a backhanded compliment. "However questionable these schemes may be," it said, "their skill and success exhibit Napoleonic genius on the part of those who conceived them." The Wall Street grapevine magnified the legend, spreading stories about the powerful Erie Ring. The *World* reported on Friday, November 20: "The rumors in the street are that the Erie clique intend to ob-tain possession of the New York Central [Vanderbilt's line] and, with that and Erie, to control the Albany legislature, and work them both as political machines."

If it were only so, Jay and Jim must have thought.

Within days, the New York dailies had printed the sworn affidavits of Fisk, Gould, and Daniel Drew, given in court proceedings, that detailed all the dirty laundry: Drew's humiliating meeting with Fisk and Gould the previous Sunday, the lock-up scheme, the Belmont lawsuit, and all the rest. Drew was exposed as a deceitful cheat. The *Herald* satirized Drew's ostentatious religiosity by composing a special Wall Street version of the first commandment: "1. Steal largely or not at all; for is it not preached in Gotham that he who steals largely and gives donations to the Church shall enter the kingdom of heaven, while to him who confines his stealings to modest peculations shall be open the doors of Sing Sing."

Lawsuits and countersuits from the lock-up ensnarled the New York courts for months. Judge Sutherland overturned Gould's receivership; Judge Barnard reinstated it; Judge Albert Cardozo found no basis for *any* receiver being appointed in the first place and returned control of the company to its officers. By then, the passage of time had made the whole proceeding irrelevant.

In January the Stock Exchange, angry at Jay Gould's stock watering, adopted a rule that companies had to register their shares with a bank or neutral agent before their stock could be traded on the Exchange floor. Jay refused, and the Exchange promptly barred Erie from the Long Room.

The saga of the Erie Ring, even without exaggerations, struck fear into many hearts. Gould and Fisk combined skill and boldness with disdain for law and public opinion. "The alliance between Tammany and Erie was equivalent to investing Mr. Gould and Mr. Fisk with the highest attributes of sovereignty," wrote Charles Frances Adams. It "shot out its feelers far and wide; it wielded the influence of a great corporation with a capital of a hundred millions; controlled the politics of the first city of the New World; it sent its representatives to the Senate of the state, it numbered among its agents the judges of the Courts. Compact, disciplined, and reckless, it knew its own power and would not scruple to use it."

With such clout, young Jay Gould and Jim Fisk—ambitious, jaded, and suddenly very rich—scanned the financial horizon as kids scan candy store shelves and wolves eye flocks of supple lambs. Everything looked delicious; nothing was too big or too expensive for them. The United States was entering the Gilded Age, a period of unbridled greed, conspicuous consumption, casual corruption, and ruthless acquisition. At the same time as General George Armstrong Custer and his Seventh Cavalry were roaming the western plains picking fights with the Indian nations, the new masters of the Erie Railway leisurely scouted their next target on the other untamed American frontier, the embryonic, unregulated financial bazaars of Wall Street, New York.

• PART II •

Golden Visions

◎ ◎ ◎ ◎ ◎

· 4 ·
ALLIANCES

I N THE PEACE THAT FOLLOWED the Great Erie War and their victory in the November money lock-up, calm settled over Gould and Fisk early in 1869. After almost a year of nonstop fighting, the two now sat securely atop the Erie Railway, their company coffers filled, their enemies disorganized, their link with Tammany strong and profitable.

New York's newest financial celebrities were free to enjoy life each in his unique fashion.

Jim, dubbed "Prince Erie" by the newspapers, promoted himself to "admiral" by purchasing the Narragansett Steamship Company, which ran elegant liners across Long Island Sound to Massachusetts, Connecticut, and Rhode Island. Many afternoons found him strutting about the Chambers Street pier in his custom-tailored admiral's uniform—a collage of navy blue embroidered with gold buttons, bars, and stripes—choreographing every detail of his ships' loadings and unloadings. His two biggest boats, both three-decker steamers almost two hundred feet long, he named the *James Fisk, Jr.* and the *Jay Gould.*

To liven up the trips on the Sound, Jim stocked his liners with two hundred and fifty singing canaries. He named each after one of his favorite celebrities: Commodore Vanderbilt, August Belmont, Tweed, General Grant, Hamilton Fish, Jeff Davis, Robinson Crusoe, himself, and Gould—the list went on and on. Conspicuously absent were feathery namesakes for Daniel Drew or any of Jim's lawyers.

But nothing fixed the Fisk-Gould regime at Erie in the public eye more dramatically than their moving the company headquarters from drab Wall Street to the palatial premises of the Grand Opera House. Jim fancied himself a producer of opera bouffe. He coveted the newly constructed Pike's

Opera House on West Twenty-third Street and Eighth Avenue. In December 1868 he and Gould purchased the fantastic structure for $820,000. Erie footed the bill, although Fisk and Gould recorded the deed in their own names and rented the upper floors back to the company for $70,000 per year.

Writer Meade Minnigerode described Erie's new domicile as "The most fantastic offices ever occupied by a business corporation—a splendor of marble, and black walnut inlaid with gold, and silver name plates, and crimson hangings, and painted ceilings, and washstands decorated with nymphs and cupids—in the midst of which Prince Erie throned in his corpulent shirtsleeves. "Colorful frescoes by the Italian artist Garibaldi, who also painted New York's Academy of Music and Booth's Theatre, decorated the interior.

Jim completed the splendor by "not infrequently opening champagne and oysters for the gay ladies of the opera." Sounds of sopranos and baritones rehearsing echoed through the hallways, punctuating business meetings and amusing company clerks, bookkeepers, and officers.

As a final touch, Jim paid $44,000 for an adjacent townhouse for Josie Mansfield. He himself took a small bachelor's apartment next door, but he moved in with Josie and they began to live, as they say, as man and wife.

Adultery did not go unnoticed by New York society in 1869. Despite his reputation for womanizing with opera singers and ladies of the night, Jim until now had kept up appearances with his wife Lucy in Boston. He had voted and paid taxes in Boston since the late 1850s, although he had been living in New York since at least 1864, renting rooms at the Hoffman House or the Grand Central Hotel.

Conceding the obvious, Jim now moved his legal residence to New York and set up housekeeping with his paramour.

Jim visited Lucy at their Boston home on spare weekends even as he was sharing Josie's bed. Lucy never complained publicly about the duplicity. She understood that Josie had captured her husband's passion and made no pretense to compete.

Some respectable New Yorkers considered it scandalous to be seen or even mentioned at the Fisk-Mansfield household. Still, many prominent business, legal, and political figures accepted invitations from Jim and Josie to attend their lavish dinner parties and receptions.

Nothing Josie did could shake the gossip that she was an adventuress, using her charms to manipulate cash and good living from the strong-headed but weak-hearted "Prince Erie." Josie had had no money, no home, no job, and only one silk dress when Annie Wood, a well-known madam, introduced her to Fisk in late 1867. By mid-1869, in addition to the house, furniture, a stock trading account, and a weekly allowance of $200 to $300, Jim had supplied Josie with a stable, carriages and horses, diamonds, a closetful of dresses, and a private box at the Opera House.

Josie's past would have put anyone on guard. Her mother went though three husbands before Josie reached womanhood. Josie's father, Joseph Mansfield, a Boston newspaperman, had abandoned the family in 1849 for the California gold rush. Three years later, he was shot dead in an Old West-style gunfight in Stockton, California, after a political argument.

Even as a preteen, Josie had cut a striking figure, and she had been a schoolgirl flirt. A pamphleteer pictured prepubescent Josie "With dark eyes, and dark brown, wavy hair, ruddy cheeks and a plump, finely developed figure, set off to best advantage by the style of costume then in vogueshort dress, high-heeled boots, and the never-to-be-forgotten 'tilting skirt.' "

Short of money, Josie's mother soon moved in with Dr. Charles Mansfield, her slain husband's brother. The brief marriage ended in divorce when Charles discovered his wife's affair with another man.

Charles had shipped Josie off to a private boarding school, but Josie packed her bags to join her mother, who had moved out west after the breakup.

On reaching San Francisco, a wide-open, saucy seaport in the late 1850s, Josie found that her mother was married again, this time to a con man named Warren. Warren decided to use his attractive new stepdaughter as bait for "roping in" rich men. The blackmail scam worked fine until one victim, a wealthy middle-aged lawyer named D. W. Perley, fell so head-over-heels in lust with his young temptress that Warren twice had to chase him away with a loaded pistol.

To escape her parents, Josie befriended a roving actor named Frank Lawlor who was then performing in the San Francisco Opera House. Lawlor proposed marriage, and she accepted. The young couple left California and headed back east, living in Washington, D.C., and Philadelphia before landing in New York. There, Josie followed her mother's example and started playing the field on the sly. Lawlor found out and filed for divorce.

Alone and penniless, Josie tried acting. She took bit parts on the New York stage, but she had no talent and the offers soon dried up. She also probably tried to earn cash by plying her charms at Annie Wood's house of pleasure but without much success there, either.

Fortunately for Josie, luck walked into her life at about this time in the form of the pudgy, vivacious comptroller of the Erie Railway Company.

Whatever Josie's true motives were in regard to Jim Fisk, he was no blushing innocent. If Josie manipulated Jim, he showed every sign of enjoying the process and loving his tormentor.

Among Jim's close friends, only Jay Gould never accepted Josie. From the very beginning, when Jim had first brought her to "Fort Taylor," Jay, the conventional puritan, had seen Josie as a distraction. If Jay ever thought Josie was playing Jim for a sucker, or if he was ever offended by Jim's loose morals, though, he held his tongue. Jay sometimes joined Jim and Josie for dinner to keep up friendly appearances. When Jim and Josie started fighting later on, they called on Tweed and even Judge Barnard to mediate—never Jay.

Fame had its drawbacks, they found. The *Springfield* (Massachusetts) *Daily Republican* published a scathing expose in November 1868 that touted Jim's adultery with Josie, identified Lucy Fisk of Boston as his wife, and disclosed that Jim's father, James Senior, had been committed to an insane asylum in Vermont.

At this, Jim's good nature disappeared. Samuel Bowles, the editor of the *Republican*, visited New York with his family a few weeks later, staying at the Fifth Avenue hotel. Jim filed libel charges and, three days before Christmas, asked Judge McCunn, another Tweed creature, to issue arrest papers. Within hours, a deputy sheriff appeared at the Fifth Avenue Hotel to escort Bowles to the Ludlow Street Jail.

The New York press howled at Jim Fisk's high-handedness, and libel suits blossomed like wildflowers.

As Jim dabbled in these high-visibility antics, Jay used the quiet months of early 1869 to indulge his own favorite passion: work. Nothing distinguished Fisk and Gould more than their attitudes toward money. Fisk's pleasure came from spending it on gaudy frivolities; Gould's came from figuring out new ways to make more. J. P. Morosini, an Erie Railway auditor, once painted a warm picture of the company president working long hours in a sparsely furnished office at Fisk's Opera House. "[Jay] was affable to every employee from the high strung head of Department to the humblest track layer on the road," he wrote.

Always looking for angles, Jay hatched a plan to tighten his and Jim's lock on Erie.

New York State law required corporations to hold annual elections so that stockholders could choose the board of directors. Then the board was to appoint company officers. Jay, Jim, and their circle controlled most of the Erie stock in the United States, but overseas investors, mostly British, held about two-thirds of the total shares. The British stockholders had already shown impatience with the Fisk-Gould management and had nearly struck a fatal blow with the August Belmont lawsuit.

Jim and Jay knew that if the British ever organized effectively, they could stage a coup on some future company ballot. The solution? Why not put off the shareholder elections? True, this would require convincing the state legislature in Albany to amend the law, but Erie counted on its board the master of the political fix. For the delicate task, Jay turned to the Honorable State Senator Tweed.

Boss Tweed was enjoying his tie with Fisk and Gould at the Erie Railway.

Being an Erie director fattened his wallet substantially. Since he joined the Erie board in mid-1868, the company had paid Tweed "legal expenses" of over $105,000, plus gifts of free stock and another $150,000 in fees to his ally, City Chamberlain Peter Sweeny. His access to Erie secrets allowed him to make money in operations like the November lock-up.

In May 1869 the Boss gave Jim Fisk a personal check for $100,000, presumably to play the market.

Boisterous and outgoing, Tweed hit it off especially well with Jim Fisk.

He became a favorite at Josie Mansfield's dinner table. The "playboy side of Fisk … appealed to Tweed," wrote Tweed biographer Denis Tilden Lynch. "[Tweed] was accustomed to associating with men always on their dignity, pretended or natural, and the change amused him."

Tweed, forty-five years old, reached his zenith in early 1869. Born to working-class Scottish parents in 1823, he had spent his early years working in his father's chair-making shop and then as a clerk-salesman in a hardware store. He saved his money to attend an academy in Elizabeth, New Jersey. But Bill Tweed had a dream. Like any red-blooded American boy of his time, Big Bill really wanted to be a fireman.

The New York volunteer fire department held a special place in the community of the 1800s. Engine houses opened their doors and became clubrooms for neighborhood men. The firemen were local heroes. Tweed, a natural leader—tough, strong, and decisive—rose through the ranks and became foreman of the "Americus" fire house, nicknamed the "Big Six" for its dashing exploits. His fame as the local fire chief opened doors to him in politics.

Elected in 1852 to the New York Common Council—the "Forty Thieves" —Tweed discovered that he had a talent for working the quagmire of patronage, graft, and kickbacks of city government.

Modern New Yorkers would have felt comfortable in Bill Tweed's city; then as now, it was a dizzying collage of contrasts, energy, and ceaseless novelty, by far the biggest, brashest metropolis in the United States. New York's population exploded during the nineteenth century, from 312,710 in 1840 to 940,290 in 1870, fueled by waves of Irish and German immigration. Brooklyn, then a separate city across the East River, held another 400,000 people. Tweed estimated that immigrants or immigrants' children made up two-thirds of New York voters in 1868.

Garish wealth on Broadway and Fifth Avenue existed side by side with crushing poverty. Broadway, New York's proudest avenue, vibrated with life. Horses, carriages, and swarms of people crowded the street and spilled over into P. T. Barnum's museum, A. T. Stewart's giant shopping emporium, Matthew Brady's photographic studio, and the dozens of shops and businesses in between.

Trinity Church's steeple towered over rooftops from the Battery to as far uptown as Forty-second Street. In 1860 ambitious designers started laying out Central Park, starting in the countryside at Fifty-ninth Street and stretching uptown another two miles. Hundreds of steam- and wind-powered ships from around the world clogged New York's harbor waiting to unload exotic cargoes.

High society revolved around formal balls at the Astor House and concerts at the Academy of Music; lower-class revelry played at the hundreds of dance halls, drinking saloons, and houses of prostitution dotting Canal Street, Greene Street, and the Bowery.

Just blocks away from Broadway, the notorious Five Points—a crowded slum with streets named Murderer's Alley and Cow Bay—epitomized the city's seamier side. "The streets and alleys of the Five Points lay deep in filth," writes historian Lloyd Morris. "They were lined by ancient tenements and low clapboarded houses in an advanced stage of decay. In cellars ten feet below the street there were 'lodging houses' without ventilation or windows, overrun by rats and vermin. Tiers of bunks covered all four slimy walls."

An estimated 100,000 homeless children roamed the city.

Sometimes the city's teeming human cauldron erupted into violence and bigotry. Two major slum gangs, the Dead Rabbits and the Bowery Boys, vented their anger in pitched battles with guns, rocks, and bricks. One time they set up street barricades until the state militia restored order. The 1856 saloon shooting of pugilist Bill Poole sparked rising anti-immigrant resentment into a boomlet for the bigoted Native American Party, the "Know Nothings," who came within inches of capturing City Hall several times in the 1850s.

During the Civil War, New York became the "Richmond of the North, a center for antiwar and anti-Negro "Copperhead" agitation," capped by the bloody 1863 anti-draft riots, which killed over a hundred people.

Tweed sided with the immigrants. He supported state financial aid to Catholic schools, city-supported hospitals, and Irish faces in high-profile jobs. After a lackluster term in Congress, Big Bill returned from Washington in 1854 to reclaim his old New York Alderman's seat. The Know Nothings challenged him by running Charles Fox, a nominal Whig who rode the prevailing tide of prejudice to victory. Tweed's old congressional seat also fell to the Know Nothings.

Despite this setback, Bill Tweed's distinctive profile made him popular among Irish and German voters and a power at the Tammany Society, the social-political club that had dominated "regular" New York Democratic Party politics since the days of Aaron Burr.

A big man—six feet tall and 300 pounds with a protruding belly—who had a wide, bearded face and swaggering gait, Tweed was energetic, good natured, and loyal. He served on the Democratic Party nominating committee and piled up IOUs and greenbacks from anxious office-seekers. Peter Sweeny's nomination as City Chamberlain netted Tammany a reported $60,000 in cash.

Tammany nominated Bill Tweed in 1857 to join the powerful Board of Supervisors, which approved all payouts from the city treasury. The Supervisors commanded a well-organized system of civic graft. Any contractor filing a claim—be it for street construction, printing, painting, or providing pencils or real estate—padded his bill by 15 percent before presenting it to the Board. The Board members then divided the 15 percent cut among themselves.

Recognizing talent when they saw it, the Supervisors elected Tweed their president four times.

As school commissioner and deputy street commissioner, Tweed soon controlled hundreds of patronage jobs and awarded million-dollar city contracts. On January 1, 1863, the same day that Abraham Lincoln issued his Emancipation Proclamation freeing the slaves, the New York Democratic General Committee unanimously elected Bill Tweed—now known simply as "Boss"—its permanent chairman.

Most remarkable for pure graft was the county courthouse. The project was started in 1862 for a projected cost of $250,000. The city had poured $5 million into this rat hole by 1868; most of it went straight to the grafters. The building lingered unfinished years behind schedule.

In mid-1868, as Fisk and Gould consolidated their hold over the Erie Railway, the Boss was dreaming of extending his machine beyond the metropolis. Democrats that year nominated New York's six-term Governor, Horatio Seymour, to run for President against Ulysses Grant. This left the Albany seat empty. Tweed used his clout to nominate New York City's popular Mayor John T. ("Toots") Hoffman, a long-time loyalist, to take Seymour's place.

If Hoffman were in the Governor's Mansion with Tweed in the State Senate, Tammany could milk the entire Empire State just as it now milked the city.

For the 1868 election contest, Tweed produced a masterwork of vote fraud that in its bold, inventive tactics rivaled anything yet produced by Fisk, Gould, Vanderbilt, or Daniel Drew on Wall Street. The vote totals tell the story: Votes counted in New York City that year exceeded the total number of registered voters by 8 percent.

To exploit better its strong support among recent Irish and German immigrants, Tweed's City Hall had ordered 105,000 blank applications from the Tweed-owned New York Printing Company and had set about mass producing citizens. In the month before Election Day, Judge George Barnard alone gave the oath to 10,070 new voters, often by platoons; Judge John McCunn naturalized another 17,572. All together, Tweed's judges had processed over forty thousand new citizens in time to support the Tammany ticket, including thousands of fresh-off-the-boat illiterates and minors, often registered under fictitious names, sometimes after forcibly removing spectators from the courtroom.

Tweed hedged his bets further by organizing armies of repeat voters, compiling fake voter-registration lists, and bribing inspectors. Most brazen were the vote counters. A. Oakey Hall, New York's pliable district attorney, sent a letter to upstate Democratic poll-watchers, instructing them to contact Tweed by telegraph with an estimated vote count as soon as their polling places had closed. At the bottom of the letter, he forged the signature of the state party chairman, lawyer Samuel Tilden.

With this advance warning, Tweed's vote counters in New York City could create—by fiction, if necessary—as many extra votes as they needed to overcome the normally pro-Republican upstate turnout. To keep upstaters ignorant of the Manhattan vote, Tweed hogged the telegraph lines so that no messages could go north. His agents literally telegraphed the Bible from beginning to end over the wires.

After receiving the upstate returns, Tammany's counters then announced that their slate had received as many votes as they needed to win, often without even counting the ballots. Tweed later explained that in New York, "The ballots made no result; the counters made the result."

Congressional investigators later estimated that "the total fraudulent and illegal votes cast in the State of New York" that year "were not less than, and probably exceeded 50,000 votes." For Tweed, the effort was well worth it. After the dust settled, John T. Hoffman had carried New York City by a whopping 60,678 majority, more than overcoming his upstate deficit of some 50,000.

Ulysses Grant had captured the White House, but Tammany had won the Empire State. With Hoffman as governor, Tweed was re-elected state senator, and within weeks, A. Oakey Hall, "Elegant Oakey," became Mayor of New York City. In March 1869, New York Democrats paid homage to the architect of their great triumph by electing Tweed Grand Sachem, the Tammany Society's highest honor.

Early in 1869, Jay Gould gave Tweed a chance to exercise his newly won power. He asked him to put a bill through the Albany legislature called the Erie Classification Act. The Classification Act gave directors of certain New York railroad companies five-year rotating terms. That way, only one-fifth of the board would have to stand for election each year. Jay planned to give Fisk, Tweed, and himself the longest terms so that they would be untouchable by angry shareholders for at least five years.

For fast results, Senator Tweed turned to his favorite legislative technique—bribery. State lawmakers of the late 1860s expected nothing less from their New York colleague. Vote-buying was so prevalent that Albany legislators had made it a science. One group of twenty-odd assemblymen organized a sub rosa compact called the Black Horse Cavalry. The group regularly bartered its votes as a bloc, big enough to break most bills in the 128-member body, in order to extort higher pay-offs.

Tweed played Santa Claus to the newspapers as well. He paid the *Albany Evening Journal* up to $5,000 for each favorable article while arranging sweetheart deals for the *Albany Argus* on almost $800,000 in legislative printing from 1868 to 1875.

Tweed's pay-off total may have topped several hundred thousand dollars for the Classification Act; the money came from Jay Gould's "India Rubber Account" for "legal expenses." Tweed got results. The bill passed the legislature easily on May 1, and Governor Hoffman, Tammany's stalwart in the statehouse, signed it into law promptly.

With his tenure at Erie now safe, Jay turned to deeper subjects of railroad high finance: expanding the Erie line westward, competing with Vanderbilt's New York Central, replacing metal rails with steel, and wooing business from the Pennsylvania coal fields. And a new fetish also began to tickle Jay's mathematical instincts, teasing his fancy for intrigue and drawing his attention like a fresh face in an old crowd.

As Jim Fisk occupied himself with fast living and as Tweed hatched his plans of political hegemony, Jay focused his own considerable mental powers on that peculiar institution of the late 1860s, the New York Gold Exchange— the "Gold Room."

· 5 ·
TRIAL BALLOONS

J AY GOULD'S PREOCCUPATION with gold began as a little-noticed aspect of the November 1868 money lock-up. At the height of creating a Wall Street panic with their Erie Railway stock manipulations, Gould and Fisk had also tried to corner the gold market.

Gold prices had slumped as Jay and Jim were tightening their lock-up that fall by withdrawing $12 million from the local banks. The price of gold had dropped from $145 (*per* $100 gold coin) on September 2 to $132 on November 6, the day Treasury Secretary Hugh McCulloch announced plans to release federal funds to break the pressure. Scarce paper money had made gold relatively cheap. When Jay switched sides and suddenly released his own oceans of money to send Erie Railway stock soaring, the gold market snapped to attention, too.

Starting that Friday, November 13, Jay and Jim bought millions of dollars of gold through Gold Room floor brokers and locked them up. Sure enough, the gold price jumped from $133 on Friday to $135 on Saturday and $137 the next Monday. The corner collapsed within hours as gold trickled in from banks and other speculators. Jay quickly dropped the venture and went back to the more amusing work of squeezing Daniel Drew.

Still, an idea had jelled in his mind.

Gold speculation in New York, like the scores of crippled veterans lining the streets begging for handouts, was a product of the recent, bloody Civil War. To finance Abraham Lincoln's army, Congress had suspended the gold standard in December 1861 and had floated almost $450 million in paper money while selling over $2 billion in long-term bonds. A new dual-currency system resulted, with "greenbacks" as legal tender for domestic debts and claims, while gold coin—specie—remained the currency of the world, needed for foreign trade, tariffs, and customs duties.

Without government backing, the value of paper against gold floated freely.

A brisk gold trade arose along Wall Street in early 1862, driven by inflation and the political chaos of the war years. Every Confederate military victory sent gold soaring and greenbacks plummeting. Speculators, stock traders, rebel and Union sympathizers, and Washington officials with access to battlefield news had dominated the gold trading dens, far outnumbering the bankers, exporters, importers, and other commercial gold users. Daily price fluctuations affected the national war effort, since rising gold prices eroded the value of the federal Treasury.

Bankers like Philadelphia's Jay Cooke called the New York gold traders "General Lee's left flank."

The New York Stock Exchange had refused to allow "unpatriotic" gold trading under its roof during the war, which forced gold speculators to form a separate Gold Exchange on nearby William Street. Gold prices peaked in July 1864 at almost $300 in paper per $100 in gold—a two-thirds devaluation of greenback money—as General Ulysses Grant's army sat stalled outside Petersburg, Virginia. Congress had closed the Gold Exchange in late June 1864, but this only made matters worse, encouraging hoarders and fueling the panic.

The gold price skyrocketed by almost $100 before frantic appeals from New York merchants convinced Congress to repeal the Gold Act and reopen the Exchange ten days later.

Only General Sherman's capture of Atlanta in August 1864 broke the bull market and cooled the fire. When Robert E. Lee surrendered to Grant at Appomattox Courthouse on April 9, 1865, the gold price sagged to $144—less than half its wartime high.

By the time Jay Gould began tinkering in 1869, the Gold Room had calmed down from its Civil War days, but the basic equation remained the same. Gold and greenbacks sat at opposite ends of a seesaw. When one went up, the other went down, and the fortunes of the nation rode on the balance.

History can plant funny clues about people. Jay's family tree in America stretched back to 1647 and included Connecticut jurists and Revolutionary War heroes. The original family name until 1806 was Gold. Thirty years later, Gould's parents had named their son Jason after the mythical seeker of the Golden Fleece. His name was later shortened to Jay.

Now Jay, an adult, preoccupied himself with the yellow metal, drawn as if by fate.

Jay waited until April 1869, five months after the lock-up episode, before trying his next flier in the gold market. That month, Jay decided to buy $7 million in gold. Henry Smith, Jay's brokerage partner since 1862 at Smith, Gould, Martin & Company, cloaked the transaction in secrecy. An experienced operator with strawberry-blond hair and a full beard, Smith broke the purchase into three smaller orders and assigned them to three separate brokers in the Gold Room, telling none of them of each other nor the identity of their ultimate customers.

Any hint that Jay Gould, the newest kingpin of New York finance, was behind the buying spree could cause panic and push prices to the ceiling.

It took Smith almost a full week to fill Gould's order. For Jay, the result was intriguing: the price of $100 in gold coin (about 4.8 troy ounces) rose from $132 to $140 in greenback dollars. Other Gold Room speculators followed suit, and by May 20 the price topped $144. Jay sold his gold in late May for a profit, and prices slumped to about where they had started, reaching $136 in July.

Watching the movements day to day on his "ticker" machine, Jay marveled at how easily he could push the gold price up and down. The investment was dirt cheap. Using a popular technique, Jay had had Henry Smith lend out the $7 million in gold to bankers or merchants in exchange for cash collateral of about $9.5 million in paper money ($7 million gold at $135 paper). He then used the collateral to pay the original purchase price. As a result, the gold had cost him almost nothing. Only if values fell drastically would Jay have had to pay margin on his account.

Most Wall Streeters looking into their crystal balls saw gold prices trending down to the $120s in late 1869 because of a big U.S. trade surplus and few prospects for the kind of political crisis that always favored the yellow metal. Most dismissed the Gold Room in 1869 as an economic quandary, a gambling casino, a risky venture.

But Jay had a vision. The gold market, he thought, could be used as a lever to tilt the international financial structure into a river of riches that would flow to the pockets of the Erie Railway, Jim Fisk, and himself. Excited, Jay buttonholed Jim at the Opera House and made a beguiling proposal.

Jay could be very convincing, especially face to face, when his soft voice and deep eyes accented his command of detail and financial minutiae. Suppose he and Jim "bulled" up gold prices from the mid-$130s and held them at $145 or $150 through the fall harvest season, Jay said, drawing pictures with his nervous hands. Scarce gold would mean cheap money, which would help U. S. farmers sell grain overseas. Export grain prices were set in London in gold. If gold were more valuable compared with U.S. greenbacks, then farmers could charge the same gold-based prices to Europeans but reap higher paper-money profits at home.

Bigger profits would mean more exports. More exports would mean more business for the Erie Railway as growers in the West sent their produce eastward to load aboard Europe-bound ships.

Scarce gold would be good for farmers, good for factory workers, good for exporters, good for railroads, and good for America. And incidentally, Jay argued, a gold run-up would be good for him and Fisk, since they would be the insiders speculating on a price rise.

The Gold Exchange was a sitting duck.

Jim Fisk may have laughed out loud on first hearing Jay's plan to corner the gold market. Even after having taken on Vanderbilt and Uncle Dan'l Drew, a proven market buccaneer like Prince Erie had to have flinched at gold. In fact, Jim saw an obvious flaw in Jay's design.

Ever since the Civil War, the U.S. Treasury had been hoarding gold.

Only about $15 million in gold coin was circulating around New York in late 1869, compared with the Treasury's reserves of almost $100 million. Certainly, a circle of rich speculators could easily buy control of the public supply and create a corner, but the Treasury could break the corner anytime it pleased. Not even their good friend Tweed could help them, Jim argued. Nobody could control gold without also controlling the federal government.

Success would require spinning a web around Ulysses S. Grant, the newly elected President. Grant, inaugurated only a month before in March 1869, had promised to put America back on the gold standard. He favored hard money and cheap gold, as did the bankers who financed the Republican Party.

There was no doubt in anyone's mind that General Grant, the "savior of the nation," could not be bought.

"The country's against you," Jim told his partner. "Folks don't want gold to go up; they want it to come down. It's too dangerous." To a friend, he confided, "Gould's a damned fool. ... The government isn't going to let him get away with it."

Jay certainly appreciated the dilemma. The November lock-up had even dramatized it. When he and Jim squeezed the banks too hard, the bankers had squealed to Washington. Treasury Secretary Hugh McCulloch had broken the lock-up with promises of federal funds. Should Jay ever dare to try seriously to corner gold, the same bankers would once again holler to Washington, and as sure as day, Washington would step in. Gold touched too many nerves in the national economy for the Treasury to stand by. According to E. L. Godkin's *The Nation*, national policy in April 1869 required the Treasury secretary to hold his gold reserves *"in terrorem* over the heads of the naughty gold speculators. When the fellows were running the premium too high, he was to come into the market, and sell out like mad, as the boys say, and frighten the wits out of them."

If only Jay could tie the Treasury secretary's hands ... but that was daydreaming.

The debate about gold, particularly the Treasury's hoard, took center stage in U.S. politics during the late 1860s. Four years after Appomattox, American credit still suffered from an unpaid Civil War debt, including over $2 billion in government bonds plus $450 million in unredeemable greenback dollars. President Grant made a campaign promise in 1868 to repay the war debt in gold, which brought joy to the bankers who had footed the original bill for Lincoln's army. "To protect the national honor, every dollar of the Government indebtedness should be paid in gold," Grant announced in his March 4 inaugural address. "Let it be understood that no repudiator of one farthing of our public debt will be trusted in public places."

Grant's new Treasury secretary, the radical Republican and former U.S. Congressman George Boutwell, pledged himself to buy back U.S. bonds and to sell Treasury gold as the first steps to returning to a national gold standard.

The chorus for "hard money" carried the day. It would be a cold day in hell before Jay Gould would be able to convince the likes of Boutwell to stand still for a gold market corner.

Gould saw no solution to this problem. Still, gold fascinated the ambitious president of the Erie Railway. It tempted him, engaged him, and teased him like a puzzle with no solution. Then one day, on a trip to New Jersey to buy some land, Jay encountered another American adventurer of the 1800s—in Gould's words, a "very shrewd old gentleman." This man offered to give the Erie-Tammany Ring a foothold in the door of President Grant and the key to the gold conundrum.

Jay Gould, meet Abel Rathbone Corbin, the President's urbane brother-in-law.

• PART III •

The Fix

THE POLITICO

THOUSANDS OF JUBILANT AMERICANS thronged Washington, D.C., in March 1869 to witness the inauguration of Ulysses S. Grant, General of the Army and conqueror of Robert E. Lee, as President of the United States. Ambitious men scrambled for plum jobs, appointments, and favors from the new administration. George Boutwell captured the Treasury department, and Hamilton Fish became secretary of state, but Abel Rathbone Corbin walked away with the biggest prize of them all: the President's sister.

Corbin had had the good luck to meet Miss Virginia Paine Grant, the President's second-youngest sibling, during the rounds of inaugural balls and receptions. Their eyes met, and something clicked.

"Jennie," thirty-seven years old, unmarried, shy, and inexperienced, had been living at home with her father Jesse in Galena, Illinois, in 1869. In February, just weeks before her brother's inaugural, she had wondered whether she would go to Washington at all to see Ulysses's big moment. But by May 1869 she had transformed her life like a rags-to-riches fairy tale. She packed her bags and moved to New York City as Mrs. Abel R. Corbin.

The marriage surprised everyone. Corbin's previous wife, Elizabeth, an amiable woman popular around New York, had died suddenly the April before, leaving him a widower at sixty. Now at sixty-one, Corbin was almost twenty-five years older than Jennie Grant and hardly a physical specimen. The *Sun* described him as "very tall, somewhat slender, stoops slightly, has grey hair and light brown eyes." Jennie, by contrast, radiated youthful beauty. Julia Grant, the President's wife, had first met Jennie in 1850 and wrote a moving description: "Next came Jennie, the Captain [Grant's] favorite, with her golden hair and dark dove-like eyes. Her complexion was exquisitely fair with just a tinge of pink, and this sweet girl was as good as she was beautiful. I say everything when I say that she was like her mother."

His physique aside, Abel Corbin appealed to women like Jennie Grant and men like her brother Ulysses with his intellectual gifts, his articulate speech, his amusing stories, and his deft analytical powers. "Mr. Corbin was a good talker, original, versatile, and well-informed," a *Times* reporter wrote. "In politics he was remarkable for his fertility of resource." A confidential advisor to Abraham Lincoln, Stephen Douglas, and Andrew Johnson, a newspaper publisher, a writer, a politico, and a financier, Corbin exuded the polish of a wealthy man in late life.

No one doubted Abel Corbin's true motive for marrying President Grant's sister. Maybe they loved each other, but even a blind man could see the interests at work. Corbin gave Jennie a ticket from her father's house in backwoods Illinois to high society New York. And Jennie gave Corbin, a lifelong politico, the ultimate inside connection.

In the romantic swirl Jennie seemed to ignore the known blemishes on Corbin's reputation from his long years in politics—particularly the bribery scandal that had ended his Washington career.

Corbin's tie to the Grant family went back thirty years. Born in 1808 in rural Otsego County, New York, and educated at Bacon Academy in Colchester, Connecticut, and at Hamilton Academy (now Hamilton College), Corbin had headed west around 1834 to find his future on the frontier. He had stopped at the outpost of St. Louis, Missouri, a rough-and-tumble place with "but few respectable persons," as teenager Jay Cooke, the future banking king who also spent his formative years there, described it. "It is dangerous for a person to go out after dark," Cooke wrote of St. Louis in the late 1830s, "for persons are often knocked down at the corners of the streets and robbed and frequently killed."

There Corbin found work teaching high school and became friendly with a student named Julia Dent—the future Mrs. Grant.

Corbin soon demonstrated a talent for journalism, particularly political debate. He became a favorite contributor to St. Louis newspapers, sometimes taking both sides of apparently heated arguments through off-setting anonymous articles.

Local politicians asked Corbin to organize a Democratic mouthpiece in the city, and he took the opportunity to found the *Missouri Argus*. A lively weekly, its columns brimmed with politics, drama, poetry, humor, and community gossip. He was soon co-editing the paper with his new bride, Eliza-beth. Fame as *Argus* editor won thirty-one-year-old Corbin a seat on the St. Louis City Council. His editorial work frequently took him to Springfield, Illinois, where he became friends with the rising political stars of his day, young Abraham Lincoln and Stephen Douglas.

Corbin sold the *Argus* in 1842 and headed east to Washington, D.C., to take a job as clerk to the U. S. House of Representatives Committee on Claims. Washington certainly had drawbacks: it was a sleepy southern town with mud streets, unbearable summers, and scant culture. President John Tyler, a Whig, sat in the White House, and Whigs held thin majorities both in the 52-member Senate and in the 141-member House—the last time any political party besides the Democrats or the Republicans controlled Congress. For sixteen years Abel Corbin occupied a niche in Washington, enjoying the city as an outlet for his two keenest appetites—rubbing elbows with famous men and selling his influence to high bidders.

Corbin's Washington career had honorable high points. He helped Samuel B. Morse gain federal support for the telegraph, for one. But the smear of a corruption scandal colored the rest.

Corbin's position as Claims Committee clerk carried major influence. Fewer than a dozen staff aides serviced the entire House of Representatives in marked contrast to the swollen twenty thousand-plus congressional staff of the 1980s. Corbin enjoyed ready access to key congressmen and senators, plus an insider's fluency in Congress's complex parliamentary rules and political coalitions that was valuable to anyone wanting to sway legislation.

Power tempted Abel Rathbone Corbin, and Corbin happily yielded to the temptation.

Although plenty of mediocre politicos bought votes in the New York State legislature and in the city board of supervisors during the 1850s, it took a special arrogance to circulate bribes in the U.S. Congress, where men like Charles Sumner, Hamilton Fish, and William Seward walked the hallways. In early 1852, Abel Corbin convinced a Boston textile firm called Lawrence, Stone, & Company that it would save a million dollars each year if Congress were to reduce tariffs on its major imported raw materials, coarse wools and dyes. For $7,500, Corbin offered to shepherd the statute through the national legislature.

The plan failed in 1853, but Corbin offered to lead another charge in the 1855-56 session. This time he demanded top dollar. In a bold letter Corbin told his patron, Lawrence, that railroad men had already agreed to pay him "$10,000 if you will carry our measure, and you may expend $40,000 more" presumably to payoff friendly lawmakers. Corbin now told Lawrence to ante his share. He demanded that Lawrence "pledge the payment of from $15,000 to $25,000 *in cash* the moment the bill making wool and dyes duty free has been signed by the President," he wrote. "Of course, I mean in addition to the $25,000 heretofore agreed upon."

Corbin's plan backfired. Not only did Lawrence refuse to pay more than a $1,000 gratuity, but Corbin's threatening letter fell into the hands of a congressional committee investigating legislative corruption. Summoned by Committee Chairman B. Stanton, Corbin denied the letter's plain meaning, saying that he had only wanted to sap the corruptors. "This was a scheme, originated by me, by which these people would forever be benefited, per annum, one million of dollars, if the bill succeeded," he testified. "And, in that event, what would it be for them to pay me $50,000, which would make me competent for life."

The Committee's public report stopped just short of calling Corbin a liar. Corbin, fifty years old, promptly resigned his congressional staff job.

Whether Abel Corbin had already masterminded other such adventures, nobody knows. Still, he had enriched himself enough to buy an elegant house on I Street, becoming a neighbor of his friends Stephen Douglas and John Breckinridge. Even after the bribery scandal, Corbin still counted among his friends Andrew Johnson, Douglas, and journalist William Cullen Bryant. President Lincoln asked for Corbin's help in dealing with recalcitrant Missouri politicians during the Civil War to prevent that key border state from bolting the Union.

In 1863, Corbin left Washington for New York City, presenting himself as a "retired" diplomat, journalist, and lawyer, and he speculated in New Jersey real estate and railroads.

After the war, Corbin sold his I Street house to General of the Army Ulysses S. Grant, the future President and his future brother-in-law.

From his New York exile Corbin stayed close to Washington politics. He gave President Andrew Johnson advice on handling his budding war with the radical Republicans, cautioning him against political inroads by General of the Army Grant. In 1866, Corbin urged Johnson to avoid appointing "Grant men" to high administration posts, fearing Grant as a threat to Johnson's 1868 re-election prospects. "If we create a large corps of noisy 'Grant men' " in government jobs, Corbin wrote in a "personal & private" letter, "they will try to perpetuate themselves in office by striving to make him [Grant] run [for President] even against his interest."

Ulysses Grant openly backed the senators who screamed for Johnson's scalp in the ugly 1868 impeachment affair, and the bad blood was still flowing at Grant's 1869 inaugural. The incoming President snubbed the outgoing by ignoring Johnson's invitation to ride together to the official swearing-in ceremony. Johnson then snubbed Grant in turn by refusing to attend the inauguration, pretending that paperwork tied him to his Oval Office desk during the final hours of his Presidency.

Nobody suspected that Corbin's loyalty to Johnson might prejudice his feelings toward his bride's older brother. "[A]t least [Corbin] was now no longer engaged in any active occupation," wrote Henry Adams, "and he lived quietly in New York, watching the course of public affairs, and remarkable for an eminent respectability which became the President's brother-in-law."

What could have been more logical—like combining nitro with glycerin—than that Abel Rathbone Corbin should cross paths and become fast friends with Jay Gould?

Corbin first met Gould at the summer resort in Saratoga, New York, in 1866 or 1867. But their friendship blossomed in the spring of 1869, just as Corbin was growing accustomed to the pleasures of life as husband to the lovely Jennie Grant. He enjoyed the summers at Saratoga and Long Branch, New Jersey, the rounds of fashionable New York dinners, the nights at the theater, and the days spent fending off envious socialites while entertaining their favorite house guests, the President of the United States and his First Lady.

Corbin's New York home, a five-story, high-stooped brownstone mansion on West Twenty-seventh Street, befitted a President's sister and retired man of affairs. "The furniture is Paris made. Elegance, but not sumptuousness marks the interior," reported the *Sun*.

Jay Gould visited Abel Corbin in early 1869, at about the time he was starting to dabble in the gold market. The Erie Railway wanted to lay track across a piece of Corbin's New Jersey land, and Jay came out to negotiate the deal. Maybe Jay deliberately sought out Corbin as the President's brother-in-law, or maybe Corbin sought out Gould as the sharpest operator in New York. But the two found a common language. Corbin, through his wife, had the best connection money could buy and no visible scruples about using it. Jay, barely half Corbin's chronological age, had concrete ideas and enough cash to translate Corbin's political contacts into a gold mine.

"[A]s I had heard that [Gould] was a Wall Street operator, I always improved the opportunity to talk with him," Corbin later explained.

Jay's memory matched perfectly. "[Corbin] came to see me; wanted to make some money in some way, and asked my opinion, as one gentleman would meet another."

Except for Jim Fisk and his broker Henry Smith, Jay Gould had shared his musings about the New York gold market with no one since his April trial balloon. Jay had had no good answer to Jim Fisk's argument that the U.S. Treasury's gold hoard made the plan too dangerous. But Abel Corbin's presence cast a whole new light on the situation. To keep the federal government from interfering with a gold corner, why not make the President a partner?

Jay took a leap of faith with his new friend Corbin. He told him he had an idea to save the U.S. economy. By letting gold prices rise, Jay said, President Grant could spark an export boom for American farmers and factory workers and enjoy great political popularity. Abel took the bait. "[Corbin] saw at a glance the whole case, and said that he thought it was the true platform to stand on," Jay explained. "He was anxious that I should see the President, and communicate to him my view of the subject."

Corbin actually had little reason to risk his position over a wild scheme. Most likely, he genuinely wanted to help his brother-in-law succeed as President; he certainly savored the role of presidential confidant. "I had a natural desire for the success of the administration of the brother of my wife, especially during its first year," he later explained, and probably meant it. By every indication, Corbin was enjoying a happy marriage with Jennie Grant. The President's family treated him well, and he had no desire to hurt anyone.

Still, whatever bug it was that had got Corbin to try to extort bribes from Massachusetts wool makers in the 1850s had bit him again now.

Putting their fertile minds together, Jay Gould and Abel Corbin thought up half a dozen ways to profit from Corbin's celebrated family tie. For starters, the job of assistant U.S. treasurer for New York's SubTreasury had come open. The Treasury conducted virtually all its transactions through New York markets. Whoever held the SubTreasury job would know in advance every time the government bought or sold gold, bonds, currency, or stocks—a speculator's dream.

Corbin's choice for the job was Robert Catherwood, a New York industrialist and his own son-in-law. Corbin summoned Catherwood to a meeting in early June in which he and Jay proposed a straightforward quid pro quo: Corbin would use his influence with Grant to win Catherwood's appointment if Catherwood would agree to share secrets about upcoming government gold and bond purchases with them, so the two speculators could "operate in a legitimate way and make a great deal of money."

Catherwood balked. Jay and Corbin had to find another pawn.

However, Jay's plan for the gold market intrigued the aging politico more than anything else. To Corbin, Gould's "crop theory"—that high gold prices would stimulate farm exports—made perfect sense and fit well into the brewing public debate on the economy. The gold question was a major irritant to General Grant's administration; it was a time bomb that threatened to undermine the North's postwar industrial boom.

Before 1862, the United States had only twice issued paper money that was not immediately redeemable into gold: during the Revolutionary War and during the War of 1812. Both times, fiscal chaos had resulted as the fiat money became worthless. At the opening of the Civil War, U.S. currency still functioned under Alexander Hamilton's Coinage Act of 1792, which had established a U.S. dollar equal to 24.74 grains of pure gold ($19.39 per troy ounce) or 371.25 grains of silver, a silver-gold ratio of 15 to 1. Congress changed the ratio slightly in 1834 to produce $20.67-per-ounce gold. (This value remained constant until 1932, except for the 1862-78 "greenback era.")

Aside from minting metal coins or "specie," the national government stayed out of money-making. State banks freely issued their own notes or private currencies, each redeemable in gold by the individual bank. Bank reserve requirements varied from state to state. Only sharp financiers could keep track of the dozens of different banknotes, weed out counterfeits, and know which "wild cat" or "shin plaster" notes to avoid.

When a bank failed, its notes became worthless. In emergencies like the War of 1812 and the 1857 stock panic, some banks closed the specie conversion windows on their own notes.

The outbreak of the Civil War created money needs that were decades beyond the capacity of the gold-based currency system. After the Union's 1861 debacle at Bull Run, Abraham Lincoln's government had faced a fiscal dilemma as dangerous as its military one. As Congress conscripted hundreds of thousands of Union boys into soldier's uniforms, Secretary of the Treasury Salmon Chase floated $50 million in "demand notes" to finance the mushrooming war effort, then saw needs for another $50 million, and then another $150 million in cash. By February 1862, he confessed to Congress, "The Treasury is nearly empty. I have been obliged to draw the last installment of the November loan, as soon as it is paid. I fear the banks generally will refuse to receive the United States notes."

Virtually every state bank had by then suspended specie convertibility, as had the U. S. Treasury. Congress feared that borrowing huge sums from northern capitalists would subject the government to "shinning," that bankers would extort usurious interest rates from Uncle Sam.

Despite the misgivings of Secretary Chase and the New York bankers, Congress adopted the Legal Tender Act in February 1862, which authorized the Treasury to issue paper greenback dollars to be recognized as legal tender on all domestic obligations except customs duties and interest on the national debt. Unredeemable into gold or silver, only Washington's edict separated the new greenbacks from scrap paper. Federal printing presses started rolling, and soon Uncle Sam was paying all debts in paper. It had saturated the country by the war's end with over $428 million of the fiat currency.

The inevitable result of pouring all this new money into the economy—the greenbacks plus over $2 billion in government bonds plus huge increases in state banknotes and national banknotes under the new national banking system—was rampant inflation. Amid the grim carnage of war, the United States sat elbow-deep in cheap cash. Wholesale prices more than doubled between 1861 and 1864, from 89 index points to 193 (1880 = 100). Greenbacks fell from their original par with gold ($100 paper = $100 gold specie) to 33 cents on the gold dollar by mid-1864.

Still, people liked the greenbacks, particularly small farmers, debtors, and laborers, for whom inflation—more money in circulation—meant more money in their pockets.

After the war, Washington faced a grim choice. Gold and greenbacks now circulated side by side as competing forms of money; their relative values shifted constantly. As peace set in, gold traded at $130 to $140 in paper dollars (per $100 gold). With such a big gap, an immediate return to strict gold convertibility would be disastrous. Every paper dollar held by Americans would shrink by 30 to 40 percent in value. Meanwhile, if gold became too cheap compared with greenbacks, speculators and bankers would hoard paper money, making credit tight and perhaps causing a depression. If gold became too expensive, greenbacks would grow plentiful, sparking inflation.

The fact that Wall Street operators were skulking at the fringes trying to make a fast buck from the government's dilemma infuriated President Grant as well as "respectable" bankers and businessmen.

Everyone had an opinion on the gold-greenback debate. Susan B. Anthony and Elizabeth Cady Stanton, who launched their tabloid *The Revolution* in late 1868, tiraded against the "high art swindling" policy of restricting greenbacks "which cost only the paper and printing." "[W]e want more money, more greenbacks, to give confidence and facilities to commerce, agriculture, and cotton-growing in the Southern States," they argued, along with women's rights and tax reform.

The Kentucky State Court of Appeals in *Hepburn v. Griswald* had declared the Legal Tender Act unconstitutional. The U.S. Supreme Court, hearing the case on appeal, was preparing to hold greenbacks invalid to pay debts predating the 1862 statute. Chief Justice Salmon Chase, the same political animal who had designed the greenback system when he was Abraham Lincoln's Treasury secretary, now denounced the unredeemable paper currency.

Democratic politicians, hoping to exploit public prejudice against big-city money men, suggested that the government repay its $2 billion-plus in war bonds with paper instead of gold. This idea horrified bankers and their Republican allies. "If the Repub'n party is to turn *repudiators I will desert them,*" wrote an alarmed Jay Cooke, the country's richest financier. "This whole matter must be *at once understood before I give any money,*" he said. "The scoundrels deserve hanging for the irreparable injury they are doing to our glorious nation."

Ulysses Grant had advocated "hard money" in his speeches and a return to the strict gold standard as soon as possible "without material detriment to the debtor class." This left plenty of flexibility, even as his Treasury secretary, George Boutwell, started selling gold from the Treasury's stock-pile regularly each month and buying back bonds to payoff the national debt.

Jay Gould's bright idea, which so delighted old Abel Corbin, promised to make everyone rich from the gold dilemma.

Since the gold-greenback disparity existed anyway, why not use it to get a better deal for American exporters, especially farmers, who still constituted half the nation's workforce? Every European country operated on a gold standard and set their prices for imported wheat, cotton, and factory goods in gold. By letting the gold premium over greenbacks rise from about $130 to

$150, farmers could sell the same amount of wheat to Britain and charge the same price of, say, $100 in specie but be paid $150 in greenbacks instead of $130. Better still, these same farmers could cut their price, say from $100 to $95 in specie, undersell the competition, and still increase their paper-money profit.

Exports would rise as U.S. farmers edged out foreign competitors, and the profit would benefit the whole country, especially the railroads carrying produce from the West to harbors back east.

Jay's voodoo economics exquisitely married his public interest and selfish conniving. To convince President Grant to stand aside while a Wall Street clique "bulled" the price of New York specie, he needed to give the President a political excuse to support expensive gold. If all went well, the "crop theory" would be that excuse, making Grant a hero while earning fortunes for Jay Gould, Corbin, and "Prince Erie."

Corbin thought the "crop theory" might even win Jay grudging public affection. Well aware of Jay's reputation from his escapades at the Erie Railway, "a railroad which was very much stigmatized," Corbin later explained, "I told him I thought the true road to popularity lay through the field of usefulness." Whatever doubts Corbin had that his brother-in-law might accept Jay's solution to the nation's fiscal ills, Corbin now thought it his civic duty to bring Grant together with the conceiver of this great idea.

· 7 ·
SAVIOR OF
THE NATION

THERE THEY STOOD—Ulysses S. Grant, President of the United States, and Jay Gould, president of the Erie Railway—together in the foyer of Abel Corbin's New York brownstone. Corbin introduced the two men, but all the people and the excitement made conversation impossible. Grant, while traveling from West Point to the Peace Jubilee in Boston, had stopped off in New York to leave his family with the Corbins. From New York, the President would ride the steamer *Providence*, flagship of Jim Fisk's Narragansett line, to Boston.

Grant would travel as the honored guest of Fisk and Gould.

Corbin had been bragging to Gould for weeks about his influence with his brother-in-law the President. Now, on Thursday, June 15, 1869, he produced the *corpus*. For twelve hours, as the steamer floated across Long Island Sound, Grant would be a captive audience to Jay's performance on the crop theory and the virtues of scarce gold.

Corbin may have noticed a certain physical resemblance between Gould and Grant as they stood side by side. Grant was a few inches taller; Gould was skinnier. Both had dark beards, although Grant's was shorter and better trimmed. Grant's level gaze and bearing lent him an air of resolution. Most strikingly, they both looked ordinary. Neither had the larger-than-life quality of a great personage. Grant, standing five foot eight in his black broadcloth suit, his shoulders slightly stooped, seemed nervous around people and fumbled at small talk—odd for a politician and General of the Army.

After a few minutes, Grant and his distinguished coterie filed out of Corbin's house onto West Twenty-seventh Street to meet a military guard, which escorted them to the Chambers Street pier.

Eager New Yorkers crowded along the wharf and the nearby streets behind lines of uniformed police to watch the celebrities board the *Providence*. Jim Fisk commanded the dockside carnival, directing every detail of the boarding. He cut a dashing figure as the chubby "admiral" of the Narragansett line, marching across the gangway in his bright uniform, which one observer described as a military-style tunic "with a broad gilt cap-band, three silver stars on the coat sleeve, lavender gloves, and a diamond breast-pin as large as a cherry."

Jim had doubts about Jay's gold scheme, but for the President's visit he nonetheless had the *Providence* washed, painted, and decorated stem to bow with gaily colored streamers. Dodsworth's band played music for the crowd as passengers sipped champagne from the ship's bar. A *Herald* reporter, much taken by the colorful sight of "ladies in their brilliant costumes, the bright uniforms of the military and the semi-naval dress of the steamboat officers," complimented Fisk on his "admirable" arrangements and the "great credit they reflect on his management." Prince Erie knew how to throw a party.

A military brass band on the wharf struck up "See the Conquering Hero Comes" to announce the presidential carriage. A cheer went up as a well dressed, unassuming man passed from the carriage to the boat, bowing slightly to his admirers. Jay Gould followed close behind. The circus atmosphere reached a crescendo as the *Providence* pulled off into the Hudson River at 5:00 P.M. for its overnight journey to Fall River, Massachusetts, its twin smokestacks belching clouds of white steam.

Dodsworth's band started a lively tune, wrote the *Herald* reporter, while the military band on the wharf played "something of a national character, the absolute identity of which is rendered uncertain by the discord of the two, which is further increased by the letting off of a cannon."

With Grant onboard, Jay Gould savored the moment. Just over a year before, he and Fisk had been renegades, fighting the combined power of Commodore Vanderbilt and Boss Tweed, threatened with jail if they even set foot in New York State. Now their influence reached almost to the President of the United States.

For now, Jay wanted to learn whether Grant would favor higher gold prices for the sake of American farmers and railroaders.

For the longer term, Jay envisioned something bigger. The Erie Railway already had an arrangement with Tweed that was making them all rich.

Maybe they could reach terms with Ulysses Grant as well. Anything was possible.

Grant must have had suspicions about his hosts. He had to know of Fisk and Gould's reputations. Only weeks before, the *Times* had castigated Jim's Wall Street operations as "more curious than the performance of Alladin, Blue Beard, and Signor Blitz put together." A New York State legislative committee had recently headlined Jay's payola attempts in Albany during last year's Erie takeover war, and everyone knew that Gould and Fisk shared a political bed with Tweed.

Grant had agreed to the trip for only one reason: Abel Corbin had told him it was a good idea. Grant trusted his shrewd brother-in-law. And why not? Corbin bad well served the great leaders of ills era—Lincoln, Douglas and Andrew Johnson. Why should Ulysses Grant not expect the same loyalty from a family member?

Jay Gould had probably heard a story that followed Grant throughout his career. One day when Grant was a boy of eight in the frontier town of Georgetown, Ohio, his father Jesse had sent him to buy a horse from a local man. Young Ulysses took along some money, found the horse trader, and made him a proposition: "Papa says I may offer you twenty dollars for the colt," he said, "but if you won't take that, I am to offer twenty-two and a half, and if you won't take that, to give you twenty five."

Things didn't improve much for the first thirty-nine years of his life. His boyhood friends jokingly called him "Useless," although young Ulysses did have a talent with horses. At West Point he graduated Twenty-first in a class of thirty-nine, with a four-year total of 290 demerits for improper conduct. As a commissioned colonel, Grant had served in Mexico during the 1848 war as army quartermaster—a glorified bookkeeper. In 1852, after he spent two happy years stationed near Detroit and St. Louis, the army had ordered him to leave his wife Julia and two infant children for the Pacific coast, where he spent at least two years at the wilderness outpost in Humboldt Bay, California.

Isolated, bored, and frustrated by army brass, he turned to the bottle and became seriously alcoholic while waiting for orders to return east. Grant finally quit the army and headed home to Galena, Illinois, where he failed at fanning and business. His father-in-law refused to loan him money. A younger brother hired Ulysses as a part-time store clerk just to feed the family.

After this bleak start, who would have expected thirty-nine-year-old

Ulysses Grant ultimately to become the most honored American of his time, praised more than Lincoln and credited with winning the bloodiest conflict ever fought on U.S. soil? Great events can change people; for Grant, war was the catalyst that produced a remarkable transformation.

Grant had hungered for a military commission at the outbreak of the Civil War, but military brass knew his reputation from Mexico and California. Despite fifteen years of regular duty and a West Point degree, the army had no room in Ohio or Illinois for Grant. He turned for help to General George McClellan, his West Point classmate and now a major general commanding all Ohio volunteers. But "Little Mac" let Grant sit for two days in a waiting room at his Ohio headquarters without receiving him.

After three months, the Illinois militia chose Grant to replace a derelict colonel whose intoxicated fits had destroyed morale among his one thousand badly disciplined troops. Grant took command and within months dazzled the country. While other Union military leaders sat on their hands complaining about inadequate troops and supplies, Ulysses Grant engaged the enemy on the battlefield and won.

Acting without orders, Grant besieged and captured the Confederate garrison at Fort Donelson in February 1862, demanding the unconditional surrender of the fifteen thousand rebels inside. At Shiloh, an obscure Tennessee crossroads, Grant's troops withstood vicious attacks and suffered thirteen thousand casualties but held their ground. In the spring and summer of 1863, Grant staged a daring rear assault and siege on the Confederate fortress at Vicksburg that closed the Mississippi River and cut the South in two. News of the Vicksburg surrender on July 4 outshined the bloody, stalemated battle of Gettysburg, fought the same week.

In March 1864, faced with the failure of his military establishment, Abraham Lincoln gambled. He entrusted his entire army to the obscure general from Illinois who hated giving speeches. In the same month Congress passed a law making Grant a lieutenant-general, the highest military rank in U.S. history up to that time. Not everyone approved. "Saints are not canonized until after death," argued Representative Thaddeus Stevens, noting that Robert E. Lee could make a fool of Grant yet.

Awesome power now rested in the hands of this single man. Grant's army numbered 533,000 troops, the largest force yet assembled in modem times, with the possible exception of Napoleon's 1812 Russian invasion army of 675,500. Napoleon, however, took only about a half-million troops over the border with him. "In all purely military questions [Grant's] will was almost supreme, and his authority usually unquestioned," explained his devoted aide General Horace Porter. "He occupied the most conspicuous position in the nation, not excepting the President himself, and the eyes of all the loyal people in the land were turned to him appealingly as the man upon whom their hopes were centered and in whom their chief faith reposed."

General Grant now charged ahead, leading his Army of the Potomac across the Rapidan River in May 1864 on a crushing invasion of Virginia to capture Richmond and kill the Confederacy. For ten months, Grant pursued Robert E. Lee from battlefield to battlefield: the Wilderness, Spotsylvania, Cold Harbor, Petersburg, and finally surrender at Appomattox.

Afterward, the general's popularity was immense. The war had touched almost every American family. Some 3.3 million men had served in the Union and Confederate armies—about one out of every ten citizens. Over 500,000 soldiers—husbands, brothers, and sons—died, and countless others were wounded. For years after the war, impoverished, crippled veterans whose legs, arms, and feet had been amputated in battlefield hospitals swarmed cities North and South by the thousands, begging for handouts. The financial cost of the war was also enormous. The U.S. national debt rose from $64 million to over $2.8 billion between June 30, 1860, and September 1, 1865.

Fame brought changes to the conquering general. Ulysses Grant became the constant center of adoring crowds. The murder of Abraham Lincoln six days after Appomattox only magnified the popular affection for the shy commander.

On his tours across the country, people jammed parade routes to cheer the "Savior of the Nation." On speaker's platforms, Grant drew louder applause than senators and even President Andrew Johnson. Social invitations poured in. Rich, powerful men sought to befriend the soldier and opened their bankrolls to him. When Philadelphians learned that General and Mrs. Grant wanted a home in their city, local businessmen presented the couple with a fully furnished mansion. Grateful citizens in Galena, Illinois, gave the Grants a gift house in their city. "Fifty solid men of Boston" presented Grant with a library valued at $75,000. New Yorkers gave the general a check for $105,000.

Grant's popularity inevitably carried him into politics. Postwar Washington was deadlocked in a conflict between ambitious radical Republicans in Congress and Andrew Johnson, the embattled President and former Tennessee senator who favored "moderate" reconstruction of the South. By May

1868, as Republicans gathered in Chicago to choose a presidential candidate, Johnson was a political dead duck, impeached by Congress and standing trial in the Senate on the "high crime and misdemeanor" of firing his secretary of war, Edwin Stanton.

Someone was needed to restore stability.

Henry Adams compared Grant's situation with George Washington's. "Grant represented order ... ," Adams wrote. "[A] general who had organized and commanded half a million or a million men in the field, must know how to administer. Even Washington, who was, in education and experience, a mere cave dweller, had known how to organize a government, and had found Jeffersons and Hamiltons to organize his departments."

Grant had defeated Robert E. Lee and a rebel army a million strong. Certainly he could clean up the politicians' nest in Washington.

In early 1868, as commander of the army, Grant watched Andrew Johnson's presidency crumble under pressure from congressional enemies. Grant broke with his commander-in-chief over the Stanton firing and suggested that Johnson had lied about the affair. Grant resigned from his post, destroying Johnson's credibility. He actively lobbied for impeachment of the unpopular President and called him a liar and traitor in meetings with undecided senators.

Intentionally or not, Grant had launched his political star. He emerged from the mud as the darling of the congressional radicals and to the public as a man of unblemished integrity. The Senate ultimately acquitted Johnson of "high crimes and misdemeanors" in a parliamentary cliff-hanger, but Republicans had embraced U. S. Grant as their unanimous choice for the White House.

Once he was nominated, Grant hardly campaigned. Despite his obvious advantages, however, he won a surprisingly narrow victory over Democrat Horatio Seymour, the six-term New York governor who had been nominated in Tweed's newly built Tammany Hall and was known for his role in sparking the bloody 1863 New York antidraft riots. Republicans spent over $250,000 on Grant's campaign—an unprecedented sum, almost twice the amount the Democrats spent on Seymour. The money came from the rising class of robber barons, Ulysses Grant's wealthy friends. Commodore Vanderbilt, William Astor, and Hamilton Fish all donated sums from $5,000 to $10,000. Lawyer Edwards Pierrepont reportedly gave $20,000.

As President, the middle-aged Ulysses cast an image far different from that of the iron-willed Civil War leader. It took only days before the congressional oligarchs collared him with a choke-chain.

On his second day in office, Grant announced a list of Cabinet appointments without consulting even his closest advisors. The list set the politicians howling. His own special friends dominated all important positions. His choice for secretary of the Treasury was A. T. Stewart, a wealthy New York dry-goods merchant who had contributed heavily to Grant's Philadelphia house, New York stipend, and campaign war chest. For secretary of the navy he chose Adolph Borie, the Philadelphia businessman who had headed the fund drive for Grant's Philadelphia house. For secretary of state—Elihu Washburne, Grant's Illinois congressman and champion during his rise to Civil War prominence. For secretary of war—General John Rawlins, Grant's loyal chief of staff from the war years.

Except for Washburne, none of these men had any experience in government or politics. Totally absent from the list were any radical Republicans from Congress.

The radicals trained their guns on A. T. Stewart. They dredged up a 1792 statute that forbade commercial importers from serving in the treasury post. Grant asked Congress to change the statute, but Congress said no. Stewart then offered to donate his $100,000-plus annual income to charity to satisfy the legal restriction. Congress balked again. Stewart had no choice but to resign, having been blocked by the same hard-line Republican clique that had ruined Andrew Johnson's presidency.

To replace Stewart, Grant bowed to the radicals by choosing George Boutwell, a radical Republican congressman from Massachusetts and a manager of the losing 1868 Senate impeachment trial against Johnson.

Grant's "surrender to the politicians" set the tone of his new administration as it settled into office. He surrounded himself with army cronies in high government posts and appeared to be blind to the subtleties of personal influence. Greedy men in government and business—including some of Grant's closest confidants—observed these signs of weakness.

Now, three months into his presidency, General Grant, once commander of all Union forces, steamed across Long Island Sound on the *Providence* as the honored guest of former draft-dodger Jay Gould and war profiteer Jim Fisk, Jr.

· 8 ·
PROPAGANDA

J AY AND JIM PLANNED TO SPRING their trap at dinner. There they'd have the President relaxed with a drink under his belt, puffing a good cigar, surrounded by friendly rich men. Any lobbyist knew the routine. Politicians always spoke more easily with their appetites pampered and their egos stroked. The *Providence* served a lavish meal for its illustrious passengers that night. Grant's party occupied a private table and included such distinguished guests as inventor Cyrus Field and capitalist William Marston.

Waiters served the ship's best wine and whiskey, although the President surprised others by not drinking. After dinner, they smoked cigars. The conversation turned to finance.

That prominent businessmen would talk about money could hardly have surprised President Grant. Debate on the economy dogged him wherever he went. Even his staunch allies questioned his performance in addressing the problems of currency, debt, inflation, and other mysteries far removed from the mind of a soldier. Grant's "hard-money" rhetoric aside, the gold price since his mid-March inauguration had risen from $132 to over $140 in mid-May and still hovered at $138—despite the fact that Treasury Secretary George Boutwell had been selling government gold into the market regularly since April.

These "embarrassing and injurious fluctuations [were] anything but pleasing," grumbled the *Times*, "and anything but what the public expected" from a Republican administration.

Little did the *Times* or even Grant suspect that the unexpected blip in the gold price bore the fingerprints of speculator Jay Gould, the President's dinner host.

Jay, the youngest man at the table and fourteen years the junior of the forty-seven-year-old President, guided the after-dinner talk to the question of gold. Each of the older, better-known men around the table voiced his opinion before Jay made his own pitch. He showed no shyness face to face with America's most famous personality. Calmly and politely, using his soft persuasion to best advantage in the small group, Jay told how the government could help producers—mostly farmers—sell their goods overseas by letting gold prices rise and the value of greenbacks fall.

The argument had political appeal. Not only would farmers and factory workers benefit from scarce gold and cheap money, but so would railroads like the Erie that carried their produce to market (and that shared their good fortune with Republican politicians).

Ulysses Grant listened but kept his lips buttoned; he smoked his cigar and fidgeted with a piece of bread. A commander of armies knows the need for reticence. Any forewarning of change in government gold policy could tip off Wall Street speculators and allow them to profit. That would be unconscionable, though it was exactly what Fisk, Gould, and others around the table wanted.

Frustrated by Grant's inscrutability, the never-bashful Jim Fisk asked the direct question: What did the President think?

"There is a certain amount of fictitiousness about the prosperity of the country, " said Ulysses Grant. "The bubble might as well be tapped in one way as another." Nobody misunderstood the oblique message: The President thought that paper money was too cheap already, poor farmers notwithstanding. Grant did not buy Jay Gould's argument, did not care if his "hard-money" stand caused a financial panic, and was not about to use the government's clout to prop up gold.

The mood changed. Jay, a flash of color in his face, challenged the President. He waxed melodramatic. If the government let gold prices slip, he said, "it would produce great distress, and almost lead to civil war." Threatening Ulysses Grant with civil war took no small amount of brass, but Jay charged on. "It would produce strikes among the workmen," he said, "and their workshops, to a great extent, would have to be closed, the manufactories would have to stop."

Jim Fisk, energized by the clash, backed up his partner. "You see, General," he said, addressing the President like an old railroad buddy, "Gould isn't entirely disinterested in this business. He and I have got the responsibility of running the Erie Railroad. We've got about forty thousand wives to look after and we can't do it if our sidetracks are full of empties."

Grant stroked his whiskers, unmoved by the appeal on behalf of helpless women and children.

The conversation lasted over three hours, until well past midnight. Grant kept his sphinxlike reticence. He was a "contractionist"; he favored shrinking the supply of paper money and returning to the gold standard. The government had no interest in propping up gold prices to help farmers, Wall Street speculators, or the innocent wives of the Erie Railway. His oblique negatives struck like a "wet blanket," Jay later said.

When the *Providence* docked at Fall River the next morning, on Wednesday, June 16, Jay left early and headed to the nearest Western Union office to telegraph Wall Street to sell gold. William Marston, a co-owner of the Narragansett steamship line who had sat with Gould and Grant at dinner the night before, was already there selling his stocks.

Jim probably chided Jay after the debacle, saying "I told you so," that the gold plan would never work.

Jay rode the morning train back to New York, but Fisk stayed with the presidential party for the trip to Boston and President Grant's reception at the Boston Peace Jubilee, a special week-long affair of patriotic music, fireworks, and celebrations.

Over 200,000 people waited for hours to see the hero of Appomattox parade from the statehouse to the legislature to a review of militia troops and finally make an appearance before the standing-room-only crowd of forty thousand at the Boston Coliseum. Grant's entourage included senators, governors, admirals, and even poet Ralph Waldo Emerson. On his arrival, a deafening cheer rose from forty thousand voices. Thousands of women waved white handkerchiefs. The President, wearing a black broadcloth coat, a black vest and trousers, a black silk necktie, and a gold watch chain, acknowledged the crowd by rising and bowing several times.

The only dark spot on Grant's hero's welcome was his public shyness.

Appearing with Governor Claflin in front of fifty thousand people at the Massachusetts Statehouse, Grant was choked with stage fright and could barely utter a two-sentence stump speech without stumbling. At the Coliseum, his anxiety became acute. "If General Grant had been about to go on stage and sing a solo he couldn't have been more nervous as he was under the gaze of the ten thousand opera glasses that were instantly leveled at him," wrote a *Boston Post* reporter. "His bashfulness is painful to the beholder and is evidently unconquerable."

Grant shrank from the spotlight, but Jim Fisk adored it. Marching into the Coliseum with Grant's entourage, Jim's ornate "admiral's" uniform drew as many eyes as the unassuming President did. The mustachioed Prince Erie took in the crowd's deafening cheer as if it had been aimed at himself. When the President took off his hat to the masses, so did Jim Fisk at his side.

The egotistical display took Bostonians by surprise. Many in the crowd thought the conspicuous fat man with the animated gestures was the President. They wondered who the nondescript man in the black suit at his side was. Jim's New York friends thought it a grand joke and starting calling him "Jubilee Jim." Fisk loved the nickname and added it to his collection.

◎ ◎ ◎ ◎ ◎

Whatever leverage Gould and Fisk had lost in their dinner with President Grant aboard the *Providence*, they more than recouped it back in New York on Friday night. Once again, Abel Corbin cemented the arrangements.

President Grant returned to New York from the Boston Jubilee by train on Thursday, June 22, to spend three days of "private" family visiting with Abel and Jennie Corbin. Julia Grant spent her afternoons shopping the finest Gotham stores, including A. T. Stewart's giant emporium on lower Broadway. The President rode horses through Central Park with friends like Edwards Pierrepont, who had been August Belmont's lawyer against Fisk and Gould in the November money lock-up.

During the day on Friday, Corbin relayed an invitation from Jim Fisk for President and Mrs. Grant to share his box at the Fifth Avenue Theatre. Jim had an excellent box, since he owned the theater. He personally produced the performances, and New York gossip buzzed about real and imagined affairs between Fisk and tantalizing actresses.

Certainly the President should accept, Corbin advised.

That night's opera bouffe production featured Mlles. Desclauzas and Irma singing *La Perichole* and the Morlacchi Ballet troupe "dancing their peculiar Can-Can." The audience rose and cheered loudly as the President and his family entered the theater. Grant bowed and took his seat in the owner's box. Sharing his company that evening for all New York society to see were Abel and Mrs. Corbin, Jay Gould, and "Jubilee Jim" Fisk.

Grant might disagree with Jay Gould's theory on gold prices, but that hardly mattered to the popular mind of New York, which identified the President with his hosts. The performance onstage dimmed next to that in the presidential box: Jay chatted easily with Grant and Corbin, Jim made small talk with the First Lady, as if they were good friends. The social interplay between the masters of Erie and Washington's highest authority was amiable.

Whatever the reality, New York would now *think* that any Erie Railway operation in the Stock Exchange was backed by the White House.

The only person missing from this portrait of togetherness was Josie Mansfield. She sat in her own private theater box, watching from a distance as the President and her lover hobnobbed before the public. Jim would have enjoyed introducing Josie to the President; she mixed so well with Tweed and his other political friends. Jay Gould had doubtless put his foot down. Jay had never liked Josie in the first place, and it is easy to picture him telling Jim not to risk their fragile new relationship with the White House by dragging an adultery scandal into the presidential box.

To ride Jim Fisk's steamboat, to take his liquor, to eat his food, and to share his dinner company, all in private, had done little damage to Ulysses Grant. Presidents had a duty to hear out controversial businessmen like Fisk and Gould on important economic issues. But to be seen sharing the social graces of Fisk's private box at the opera—the most public of places—crossed the line. Did Grant know he was being used? Perhaps he wondered; but Abel Corbin had told him that Jay Gould and Jim Fisk were all right.

· 9 ·
A NEW STOOGE

WHETHER HE KNEW IT OR NOT, Ulysses Grant left New York that June having sealed the most unlikely political alliance for a Republican war hero. He had handed a virtual blank check to Gould, Corbin, and Fisk to tout his name on all matters of money and politics. Gould and Corbin, demonstrably the President's closest confidants in Gotham, wasted no time drawing on the account.

First they planted a pliable stooge in the vacant post of assistant U.S. Treasury secretary for the New York SubTreasury. After Robert Catherwood, Corbin's son-in-law by marriage, turned down Jay's proposition to take the job and leak government secrets, they turned to Corbin's second choice, General Daniel Butterfield. The thirty-eight-year-old son of American Express Company organizer John Butterfield, he was a Civil War hero who had commanded a division at Fredericksburg, had served as army chief of staff at Chancellorsville and Gettysburg, and had helped General Sherman march on Atlanta.

Butterfield was also, incidentally, a Corbin family friend.

Abel Corbin had known Daniel Butterfield since about 1855, having been close with his father. Tall and handsome, with dark wavy hair and moustache, Daniel had invested money with Corbin after the war in stagecoaches running from St. Louis to San Francisco. Abel and Jennie often entertained the Butterfields at their New York brownstone. Corbin had recommended Butterfield to then-President Andrew Johnson when the SubTreasury post opened in 1866. In a private 1866 letter to Johnson, he contrasted his friend to the swarm of political parasites then parading in soldier's uniforms. He portrayed Butterfield as one of the few "Grant men" he could trust, "a gentleman of rare education and talents .... everybody knows that he is honest, honorable, & *has brains*—he has the confidence of the community."

Butterfield had excelled at doing kindnesses for Ulysses Grant. In January 1866, when A. T. Stewart decided that General Grant deserved a pecuniary prize for winning the Civil War, he asked Daniel Butterfield, then the chief army recruitment officer and military commander of New York harbor, to raise money among wealthy New Yorkers. Within days, Butterfield had sold subscriptions of $100 to $5,000 apiece to 156 leading bankers, brokers, and merchants, totaling $105,000. Even Uncle Dan'l Drew gave $1,000. Butterfield presented the stipend to Grant "as a testimonial of their appreciation of your services."

Grant used this money to buy the Washington, D.C., house of Abel Corbin.

Butterfield had showed the same helpfulness to Grant's staff. In January 1869 two of Grant's closest army aides, Generals Horace Porter and Orville Babcock—both of whom planned to join the President-elect on his White House staff—wanted to invest money in New York real estate. They turned to Daniel Butterfield, who found three underpriced lots on 185th Street, advanced $5,000 in down payments, and secured mortgages before transferring the deeds to Babcock and Porter. Whether the two ever repaid the loans is unclear. Daniel Butterfield didn't seem to care.

Corbin threw his weight behind Butterfield's nomination, arranging letters of support from A. T. Stewart, banker-broker Harris C. Fahnestock of Jay Cooke & Company, and half a dozen other New York cognoscenti, although he covered his tracks by sending no letter himself. Unlike lesser-knowns, Butterfield never had to promise Corbin anything in return for help; Butterfield's nomination looked like a shoo-in with or without the old political fixer's support.

Robert Catherwood later claimed that he, Corbin, and Gould had arranged a pool to invest in government bonds based on Butterfield-supplied inside information but that nothing came of the plan. Whether this was true or not, for the time being Corbin and Gould could congratulate themselves on having put a reliable ally in the SubTreasury.

Jay Gould had hardly known Daniel Butterfield before Corbin introduced them that spring of 1869. Anxious to strike up a friendship, Jay visited the new assistant treasurer on July 1, two days after Butterfield had moved into his Wall Street office, to offer his services. Jay found a useful way to help Corbin's young friend: by giving him a check for $10,000—an amount bigger than Butterfield's $8,000 annual government salary. Butterfield later portrayed the money as an innocent "real estate" loan, albeit interest free with no documentation or repayment date.

Whatever the truth, Butterfield now understood that it paid to be nice to the president of the Erie Railway.

Jay planted one more important seed that summer. He bought a bank. In late July, he collected $500,000 from Tweed ring friends—the Boss, Peter Sweeny, and Henry Smith, among others. On August 5 he used the money to buy a controlling interest of 5,010 shares in New York's Tenth National Bank, a Wall Street "broker's bank" with a purple reputation. Only months earlier, federal auditors at the bank had found that out of fifteen randomly selected drafts put up by stock and gold traders to back certified checks, only three had been good. The rest represented the bank's sweetheart arrangements with favorite customers.

Jay offered Daniel Butterfield a share in the pool, but the assistant treasurer declined.

Jay and Boss Tweed could not install their own directors and officers in the bank until the next January, but bank owners nonetheless had ways to throw weight in their own houses. Every employee knew who was going to sit on the incoming board of directors. Smith, Gould, Martin & Company, Jay's brokerage house, opened an account at the Tenth National and started enjoying its new VIP treatment.

For most wealthy New Yorkers, summer meant vacations at Saratoga, Newport, or the countryside. Abel Corbin, Commodore Vanderbilt, Jay's brokerage partner Henry Smith, and even President Grant all left home for travel and relaxation. Only Fisk and Gould seemed to work overtime through the hot summer of 1869.

Jim's Narragansett Steamship Company opened daily service to Long Branch, New York's favorite resort on the Jersey shore for summer city dwellers wanting a getaway to the beach. Jim often joined the nightly boat rides, using the commutes to rub elbows with political cronies and enjoy the high life at Long Branch's Continental Hotel. Josie Mansfield usually came along for the glittery fashion scene, an opportunity to parade the gowns and jewels she collected as Jim Fisk's kept woman.

Less of a social lion, Jay's mind buzzed all July and August with money-making schemes. Every one of them had the same bottom line: gold.

Jay's obsession with the yellow metal fermented with age as Gold Room prices slumped to $135 in early August, the lowest since April and far below the mid-May high of $144. Not since 1862, when gold and greenbacks were first decoupled, had gold stood below $140 going into the fall harvest season. Ignoring President Grant's cold shoulder to his crop theory, Jay plotted every action around his plan to bull New York gold. If Grant refused to help, then maybe Jay could go it alone or find a way to force the President's hand.

As part of the grand design, Jay concentrated on pushing the Erie Railway westward. He opened talks with the Lake Shore and Michigan Southern to build compatible-gauge tracks for direct trains from New York to Chicago. This would top any service offered by Vanderbilt or anyone else. Should rising gold prices ever send oceans of western grain flooding east for export, Jay's railroad would be ready to handle the business.

In August 1869 this mania for expansion set the stage for Jim Fisk's biggest public embarrassment yet: his battle to capture the 142-mile Albany Susquehanna Railroad, which connected Albany and Binghamton, New York. Beyond the usual crooked stock deals and injunctions from Judge Barnard, including one probably signed in Josie Mansfield's parlor, in this bizarre battle Jim Fisk personally led a platoon of fifty-odd hired goons to try to occupy the company's Albany offices.

Unfortunately for Jim, the Albany-Susquehanna, led by its feisty president Joseph Ramsey, fought back. Ramsey found his own friendly judge to neutralize Barnard's decrees, and he hired his own city toughs to block Jim's.

The affair turned ugly one mid-August night when both sides resorted to large-scale mob violence. Jim Fisk ordered a trainload of almost eight hundred Erie vigilantes to occupy the rail line by force, starting at its southern terminus in Binghamton. Ramsey countered with his own trainload of four hundred odd men, headed south from the line's opposite end in Albany. The two trains met in a head-on collision at a desolate mountaintop near the Harpersville tunnel, about fifteen miles north of Binghamton.

The ensuing brawl lasted well into the night before heavily armed state militia reached the scene and restored order. Dozens were injured. Amazingly, nobody died.

Jim himself was arrested twice by outraged Albany magistrates before being forced to retreat red-faced and empty-handed to New York by overnight steamer from Albany. The upstate press touted the affair as a victory of rural virtue over the "Money-bags, swagger and braggadocio, and eleven thousand dollar [diamond] pins" of Wall Street, New York.

· 10 ·
THE PLUNGE

J AY GOULD COULD WAIT no longer. On Thursday morning, August 12, 1869, as newspaper readers across America gasped at the details of Jim Fisk's Albany-Susquehanna monstrosity, Jay placed an order through Smith, Gould, Martin & Company to buy $375,000 in gold specie at the dirt-cheap price of $135 (per $100 gold). Henry Smith filled the order through Henry Enos, a long-time independent Gold Room floor hack.

Enos had no idea that this modest purchase for an anonymous customer would start a snowball rolling downhill that would grow bigger and faster and eventually smash Wall Street to smithereens.

More than blind hope pushed Jay to jump at this precise moment. Time was running out on his crop theory. The fall harvest would begin in weeks, and gold prices sagged $10 below the mid-$140s level that Jay hoped would spark an export boom. Gold-selling by the U.S. Treasury, on Secretary George Boutwell's orders, had continued all summer, weighing down the market. Somebody had to act fast to save American farmers and railroad speculators. There was no time to wait for a green light from the White House.

Jim Fisk had no patience with Jay's babble about gold that morning on his return from Albany. Newspaper reporters were swarming the Opera House trying to question Jim over the Harpersville tunnel brawl, but they heard only that Prince Erie was "laying low" inside his marble castle. Jim must have choked at disclosures in the *Tribune* that an unseen Albany assassin, later discovered by police, had nearly ended Jim's parade and his life on the steps of the Albany-Susquehanna offices. Judge Barnard's writs would not have stopped a lead bullet aimed at his corpulent body.

Work crews spent the day repairing damage from Binghamton to Alton caused by the railroad battle—cut telegraph wires, broken bridge trestles, raised tracks. Jim tried to laugh off the affair at a meeting of the Erie executive committee: himself, Gould, and Boss Tweed.

But Jay had bigger fish to fry. Having started his gold-market bandwagon, he needed to win over Ulysses Grant to the crop theory as quickly as possible.

He turned to his instrument in the First Family, Abel Rathbone Corbin.

Henry Adams once compared Jay's "disposition to silent intrigue" to a spider's. "He spun huge webs, in corners and in the dark, which were seldom strong enough to resist a serious strain at the critical moment. ... He seemed never to be satisfied except when deceiving every one as to his intentions." Now, with money on the line and Corbin in tow, Jay began to tighten the web around the highest authority of the U.S. government.

@ @ @ @ @

The White House was unlivable that summer. Workmen were rearranging rooms, fixing furniture, and freshening the paint. So President Grant decided to take his family on an extended vacation, touring American fashion spots, visiting old friends, seeing the countryside, and mending fences with local politicians. They spent July at Long Branch, New Jersey, enjoying the beach and high society. Early in August they visited Glenclyffe, New York, for three days of horse riding, hobnobbing, and gracious dining at Secretary of State Hamilton Fish's elegant ninety-seven-acre country estate.

When President Grant returned to Washington to visit the Oval Office in mid-August, his wife Julia stayed in New York with Abel and Jennie Corbin.

Now, on August 12, the day Jay Gould bought his stake in the gold market and Jim Fisk returned from Albany infamy, the President passed through New York to continue his sojourn with a trip through Pennsylvania and West Virginia. This time Grant's party included not only his wife, children, and private secretary General Horace Porter but also his New York sister and brother-in-law. For seven days of travel, the President's ear would be Abel Corbin's to bend with Jay Gould's crop theory on how scarce gold would save the economy.

Grant began his odyssey in remarkable fashion. On Friday morning, August 13, he left New York in an Erie Railway car—provided gratis, of course— and headed west to Elmira, stopping en route at Binghamton, Oswego, and Waverly to greet well-wishers crowding the roadside. Not seventy-two hours after the Harpersville tunnel riot, President Grant stood saluting his admirers from an Erie Railway train at Binghamton, the southern terminus of the

Albany-Susquehanna line and flashpoint of the battle. Dozens of "Erie guer-rillas" must have jammed the train station to cheer their company's favorite patron.

From Binghamton the presidential party traveled past a dozen small towns to Kanesville, Pennsylvania, where the President spent three peaceful days trout fishing and riding through the countryside with his old friend Gen-eral Kane. All the while, they made a charming picture—Ulysses and Julia Grant, Jennie and Abel Corbin. For seven days they ate together, slept in ad-joining cars or rooms, rode together along endless miles of track, and talked and talked and talked.

Corbin relished a role as senior family statesman, and he worked hard to win over his in-laws, smothering the Grants with kindness and gifts. In July, Abel joined Jennie for two weeks in Kentucky with Jesse Grant, Jennie's and Ulysses's cantankerous father, and he brought the old man back to their New York house for a week-long visit.

Still, Abel preferred giving cash. Later that July he offered Julia Grant a free half-interest in $250,000 worth of bonds that he had purchased for Jen-nie. The President's wife declined, but she appreciated the thought. "My de-sire was to please her," Corbin later explained. "She was my sister-in-law."

General Horace Porter, Grant's private secretary, listened to the endless conversation and recalled that the subject often turned to gold. Corbin did most of the talking. "Grant, after his custom, sat silent," wrote a Porter biog-rapher.

By Thursday, August 19, when the presidential entourage returned to New York, Ulysses Grant, the darling of the "hard-money" Republicans, was starting to change his mind.

Instead of staying overnight in New York, President Grant, Julia, and General Porter bade the Corbins good-bye at the train station. They rode a carriage across town to the Chambers Street pier and caught the overnight steamer to Fall River, Massachusetts, to continue their odyssey for another week through New England. Abel Corbin, meanwhile, had lots to report to his ally, Jay Gould.

By now Jim Fisk had calmed down enough for Jay to tell him about his plunge into the gold market.

Jim had disliked Jay's gold-market scheme from the first time Jay had mentioned the idea the previous April—particularly after President Grant cold-shouldered it on the boat to the Boston Peace Jubilee. In every major adventure so far Fisk and Gould had acted as a team. Jay's intellect and Jim's bravado gave their operations a double whammy; in every tight corner, they trusted each other totally.

But Jim's deepest instincts warned him against touching gold. Jay probably never asked his friend outright to get involved, not wanting to put Jim on the spot. Still, Fisk took the hint and agreed to reconsider.

Late that afternoon, Jim headed down to the Chambers Street pier, where the Fall River steamer was scheduled to cast off any minute. He asked to see the President. Without an appointment but armed with a letter from Gould, Jim bypassed the presidential gatekeepers—General Porter and the secret service guards—and sat face to face alone with Grant.

Doubtless surprised to see his Fifth Avenue Theatre host of two months before, Grant greeted Fisk cordially. But any good will must have disappeared when Jim skipped the small talk and got down to business. Fisk urgently told the President that, according to Gould's latest reports, three hundred Russian ships had set sail on the Mediterranean from the Black Sea loaded with grain for the Liverpool market. With gold down to $132, American farmers could not compete. Their harvest would be ruined.

Grant might have been sympathetic toward the crop theory after a week of Abel Corbin's badgering. But he had no mind to interrupt his vacation for some fast-talking Wall Street sharper. He cut Jim off curtly. "He then asked me when we should have an interview, and we agreed upon the time, " Jim later explained. "He said, 'During that time I will see Mr. Boutwell or have him there.' " So ended the conversation.

Months later, Grant told a more self-serving version. According to the President, Jim came on board saying that Jay Gould had sent him to ask if Grant would share "a little intimation" of his gold policy. Giving private tips "would not be fair," Grant replied, and any change in government plans would be announced by Treasury Secretary Boutwell "through the newspaper as usual, so that everybody might, at the same time, know what it was, thus excluding any possible charge of favoritism."

Jim left the brief shipboard meeting having gotten nowhere with the Chief Executive. He rode back to tell Jay the bad news. "I did not think the skies looked clear enough" for a gold operation, he said. For now, Jay would have to go it alone.

All this backroom sparring left Jay on a shaky limb. With Jim out and Grant changing colors daily, his gold investment looked weak. The gold price fell like a rock from $135 on August 12, when he had bought his $375,000 worth, to $131 on August 21, just nine days later. If Jay's propaganda were true, these low prices would have devastated grain exports for the harvest season, meaning meager profits for the Erie Railway. To stay above water meant getting in deeper—buying more gold in big enough quantities to support prices.

The next morning, Jay raised the stakes.

Jay Gould was not the only gambler on Wall Street willing to bet on rising gold prices in August 1869. Without much trouble, he found two others: William Woodward, a rich private investor, and Arthur Kimber, who represented the foreign bankers J. Stern & Brothers. Both of them agreed to meet in Jay's Opera House office and listen to a business proposition. Jay suggested a classic "bull pool," with each agreeing to buy $3 million in gold—$9 million all together—to be held jointly until gold prices rose. Woodward, a long-time stock and gold operator, already owned $2 million in gold from his own speculating that August and stood to profit enormously from the plan.

Kimber too agreed, though reluctantly.

On Friday, August 20, as gold sagged at $132, they started buying massively. Soon their joint account held over $10 million in gold specie.

Any Wall Street amateur could have thought to start a bull pool to buoy a sagging market. But it took Jay Gould to conceive of the second prong of his late-August assault: scamming *The New York Times*.

Over a dozen daily newspapers competed for New York readers at that time; each had its own slant and personality. The *Herald* by far dominated circulation, followed by the intellectual favorite, Horace Greeley's *Tribune*, and the smaller, more colorful tabloids, the *Sun*, the *World*, the *Post*, and the *Ledger*. The *Times*, a relative newcomer organized in 1852 by Henry J. Raymond, a former Greeley apprentice, proudly bannered its political bias. The *Times* spoke for Republicans and was staunchly pro-Grant, anti-Tammany, pro-banking, and anti-South.

On Monday, August 23, with Ulysses Grant safely in Rhode Island, Jay asked Abel Corbin to write an article on "Grant's Financial Policy." The article would show his brother-in-law to be a believer in the crop theory. Whatever Grant really felt, New York speculators would assume that the President would not kill a bull movement in gold; they would read it in the *Times*. Grant might even enjoy seeing praise heaped on his phantom policy and decide to adopt it.

Corbin did well. He put pen to paper and produced a moving tribute to a Grant policy that was "wisest and best ... honest, simple, and statesman-like." To plant the article in the *Times*, Jay enlisted Sir James McHenry, a noted British economist and owner of the Atlantic and Great Western Rail-road, an Erie Railway offshoot. McHenry took Corbin's draft to John Bigelow, a personal friend and former U.S. minister to France who had recently been appointed *Times* chief editor.

McHenry told Bigelow that the anonymous article had come from a pres-idential intimate. Bigelow accepted the scoop and had *Times* typesetters pre-pare it for printing.

Caleb Norvell, the *Times's* financial editor, smelled a rat. Looking over the typeset galleys, Norvell noticed that the article's central point—that Ulysses Grant was opposed to selling gold during the harvest season— con-tradicted earlier White House statements and seemed well designed to serve the "sinister purpose" of some gold-bulling clique. With Bigelow's blessing, Norvell took his red pencil and changed the article's title from "Grant's Fi-nancial Policy" to "The Financial Policy of the Administration" and crossed out the most blatant pro-gold passages.

The *Times* ran the piece as an editorial the next morning. Even with Norvell's editing, New Yorkers read in the city's Republican oracle that "until the crops are moved," the President "will not send gold into the market and sell it for currency to lock up in the Treasury vaults"—a step that would "ben-efit nobody but usurers and speculators."

Satisfied with his handiwork, Jay wrote a letter to Treasury Secretary George Boutwell enclosing the *Times* editorial and complimenting Boutwell on choosing such a smart policy. "I think the country peculiarly fortunate in having a financial head who can take a broad view of the situation," Jay wrote, stroking the secretary's conceit.

Boutwell saw the trap and refused to admit or deny the authenticity of the *Times* story. He acknowledged Jay's letter with a terse, formal response.

Slowly but surely, Jay's work bore fruit. Gold prices stopped their sickly decline at $131 and nudged over $134 on August 27. But nothing was safe as long as the Hero of Appomattox remained a loose cannon on gold.

After leaving the Corbins in New York, President Grant and his en-tourage—Julia, their son Jesse, their daughter Nellie, General Porter, and a small band of newspaper reporters—had headed to Newport for a beachfront clambake at Governor Morgan's villa with ten to thirty thousand well-wishers. Treasury Secretary Boutwell, who was spending the summer in Groton, Massachusetts, came down to the affair and doubtless heard a bellyful from Grant about the constant haranguing he suffered on the gold question— prompted largely by Boutwell's own gold-selling policy. From Newport, which Porter found "not nearly as nice a place as Long Branch," they headed north through Boston, Concord, Nashua, and Manchester, where, according to the *Herald*, "[a] large crowd lined the streets, cheering and waving flags and handkerchiefs."

In northern New Hampshire, they visited rugged Mount Washington, the highest summit in the Northeast, where Grant et al. rode the "sky" railroad—a special train that climbed the 4,500 vertical feet to the mountain's breathtaking precipice—and dined at the Tip Top House.

On Saturday night, August 28, tired and ragged, the travelers reached Saratoga, New York, in a drenching rainstorm for a weekend of rest, horse racing, and posh receptions at the Union Hotel. Greeting them on their arrival were Abel and Jennie Corbin.

Saratoga, home of mineral waters and horses, bubbled with New York society during August and September. Luminaries like Vanderbilt, August Belmont, and A. T. Stewart crowded the elegant hotels and spas. Ulysses Grant, the soldier from Galena, Illinois, stuck out like a sore thumb as Saratoga dignitaries ushered the First Family through their round of parties.

A society reporter for the *Evening Mail* had good sport mocking the Chief Executive's bumpkin ways. "Like all great gentlemen, [Grant] disdains the assistance of the tailor and the 'gentleman's furnishing' establishments, and appeared among the immaculate neckties in a paper collar which looked considerably the worse for wear, and a frock coat decidedly mildewy and suggestive of innumerable campaigns," he wrote. Still, he found Ulysses "more attractive than his pictures, has a genial smile, apparently native to his features, and the unassuming manner in which he submits to the intolerable bores who crush his digits and jeopardize his ribs, [is] very prepossessing."

Later that night, after a private dinner, the President and Julia attended a reception at the Union Hotel and received a royal welcome. "General Grant entered the ballroom about eleven o'clock, and on his appearance whole battalions of dancers 'broke ranks' and fairly hemmed him in," wrote the *Evening Mail* reporter. "For once the hero of Vicksburg was compelled to surrender at discretion."

The family reunited, Abel Corbin could now resume propagandizing his brother-in-law on the gold issue. This time he had help from an unexpected source.

Grant stole away from the "intolerable bores" of Saratoga society Sunday night for a private talk with A. T. Stewart, who had been Grant's original choice for Treasury secretary. The graying Stewart, a seventy-year-old bachelor, held strong sway over the President. Ulysses still resented the radical Republican autocrats who had bumped the "Merchant Prince" from his Cabinet. Besides the political embarrassment—congressmen and senators openly joked about Grant's "bungling piece of business" in the affair—Grant had wanted Stewart to epitomize his vision of the country.

In the age of Horatio Alger, the public admired business giants like Stewart, Vanderbilt, and even Fisk and Gould—men who had started penniless and accumulated fortunes by their own wits. America was the land of opportunity, where anyone could succeed on his merits, be it on the western frontier or in business. Grant viewed himself as of the same mold.

Able to unburden himself to an unbiased friend and money expert, Grant took Stewart aside for a marathon thrashing-out of the whole gold issue. Stewart, flattered by Grant's attention, gladly obliged. "That is the only time I ever heard the President speak unreservedly on the subject," Abel Corbin recalled. For whatever reason—bitterness toward Boutwell, sympathy for American farmers, or political calculation—A. T. Stewart opposed Boutwell's selling of Treasury gold. Any intervention by Washington in the gold market would help one group of speculators over another, Stewart argued. Charges of favoritism would be inevitable. Grant should keep his hands clean and his gold in the Treasury, where it belonged.

As the President and Porter left Saratoga early Monday morning for a two-day stopover in Washington, the long-teetering balance in Ulysses Grant's mind seemed to tip.

On Wednesday, Grant and Porter rode the overnight train back from Washington again to Saratoga. In New York the President stopped en route for breakfast at Abel Corbin's house.

Sitting in Corbin's kitchen, Ulysses told his brother-in-law a secret. While in Washington, Grant had heard that Treasury Secretary Boutwell had issued orders from his Groton, Massachusetts, summer home via Washington for the New York SubTreasury to sell an extra $4 to $6 million of gold during September—triple the amount sold in July and August. The President, having seen the light, wrote Boutwell a letter chastising his decision. To sell gold during harvest season would embarrass western farmers with low crop prices, he said.

Boutwell canceled the order.

Corbin's eyes lit up. This was the signal for which he and Jay had waited weeks—a presidential commitment to withhold government gold from the market. Jay's day-dream had come true. Boutwell's hands were tied.

Word of the breakthrough moved fast. In fact, Corbin and the President were not alone in the house. Corbin had invited Jay Gould that morning, just in case Ulysses wanted to speak with the guru of scarce gold. As Grant was revealing his secret conversion to the scarce-gold crop theory in the kitchen, Jay sat just down the hall in Corbin's living room.

At his first opportunity, Abel slipped away from the breakfast table to tell Jay the good news. Having got what he'd come for, Jay left the elegant brownstone as quietly as a church mouse. Grant never knew he was there.

In ten short weeks Jay Gould and Abel Corbin had done the unthinkable: they had maneuvered "Unconditional Surrender" Grant into a 180-degree retreat from his "hard-money" gold policy. Fisk had been wrong, Jay told himself. The gold plan would work. Even Washington, D.C., could be bought.

True to his word, Jay arranged for Corbin's handsome pay-off. That day he bought first $500,000, then another $1 million in gold—$1.5 million altogether—for Corbin's account at Smith, Gould, Martin & Company. For every dollar increase in gold prices, Corbin would profit $15,000. Corbin accepted the gift on behalf of his wife Jennie.

Jay also tracked down General Daniel Butterfield at the SubTreasury and told him the news. Overcome by generosity, Jay bought a second $1.5 million block of gold and credited it to a Butterfield account at Smith, Gould, Martin & Company. "I did it as a friendly thing," Jay later told congressional investigators, "an anchor thrown to the windward" to keep his allies in tow.

PART IV

Shoulder to Shoulder

· 11 ·
COMING
UNDONE

GEORGE BOUTWELL VIEWED HIS JOB as Treasury secretary differently from the way his boss, the President, viewed it. In the melee surrounding Grant's March 1869 inaugural, Boutwell had stood high on everyone's list for a Cabinet post—even Grant's. A fifty-one-year-old former Massachusetts governor, overseer of Harvard College, organizer of the Internal Revenue Service, four-term congressman, and chairman of the House Judiciary Committee, Boutwell matched his resume with a physical presence that the *Times* described as "prepossessing. He is of medium height, has black hair and whiskers, and a countenance indicative of an educated gentleman .... one of the ablest men in the House—a fluent, impressive debater, and a conscientious worker."

More important, Boutwell was a leader of the congressional radical Republicans. He had been an early abolitionist, an advocate of Negro suffrage, a member of the Committee on Reconstruction, an architect of the postwar Constitutional amendments, and a manager of Congress's impeachment trial against former President Andrew Johnson.

Ambitious to the gills, Boutwell played a shrewd game of hard to get. In February 1869, when Grant invited Boutwell to become his secretary of the interior, Boutwell had declined, saying he enjoyed Congress too much to leave. More to the point, Grant had refused to accept Boutwell's terms for the job, which included "radical changes in ... *personnel*" and full policy control. Later, when congressional radicals torpedoed Grant's appointment of A. T. Stewart to head the Treasury, they had urged the President to name the Massachusetts congressman to the vacancy. Boutwell again played coy, asking Grant's friend Elihu Washburne "to say to the President that I was unwilling to accept the place."

Finally, according to Boutwell, "My nomination was sent to the Senate and confirmed, and as there seemed to be no alternative for me, I entered upon the duties of the office."

Whether the shotgun had been aimed at Boutwell in this awkward marriage or at Ulysses, the new Treasury secretary cloaked himself as the reluctant bride and flaunted his independence. "[T]he President accepted the idea that the management of the Treasury Department was in my hands," he claimed. George Boutwell took orders from nobody, he said, and only rarely consulted his President or Cabinet colleagues.

After all, Boutwell's radical friends in Congress held the whip hand in Washington. Just ask Andrew Johnson, back home in Tennessee.

Other Grant appointees resented Boutwell's haughty attitude. In an 1870 diary entry, Secretary of State Hamilton Fish described a typical Cabinet meeting where Grant raised a financial policy suggestion. "Boutwell says 'he does not think that would be wise,' and there it rests. Boutwell gives no reasons, and rarely indicates or explains his policy."

Boutwell even attacked the President's family. When Judge Lewis Dent, Grant's brother-in-law, embarrassed the family by becoming a "conservative" (anti-Yankee, pro-Ku Klux) Republican candidate for Governor of Mississippi in August 1869, Boutwell openly criticized Dent for betraying the Union. Dent threw a tantrum. "Who constituted you the infallible Pope of Republicanism? Who gave you authority to hurl the political anathemas of the party?" he asked Boutwell in an open letter to the *Tribune*. Dent accused the "ungrateful and unscrupulous" Treasury secretary of promoting his own White House ambitions.

With the federal purse at his command, Boutwell set about one great task for his term at the helm of U.S. finance: repaying the nation's Civil War debt.

Treasury had suffered years of mismanagement before Boutwell took control, due partly to wartime chaos and partly to the long stalemate between Congress and President Johnson. In the accounting branch alone, Boutwell counted "about one hundred persons on the pay rolls who had no desks in the department, and who performed but little work at their homes." Widespread fraud among tax collectors, especially whiskey revenuers, cost the Treasury millions of dollars each year.

Most damaging, Boutwell felt, was the huge war debt, which undermined government credit and prevented the country from returning to a gold-based currency. The numbers staggered financiers; its pre-Civil War loans had never topped $100 million, but by Appomattox the federal government had borrowed the unheard-of sum of $2.1 *billion*, mostly through selling U.S. bonds payable with interest in gold. This was in addition to floating $428 million in unredeemable greenback dollars.

Could the Union pay its bills? Would it renege? Or would it pay back its bonds in cheap paper money instead of specie?

European bankers hardly viewed the United States as a model credit risk after four years of civil strife. Fears of default abounded. The debt had to be repaid, said George Boutwell and Ulysses Grant, even at the risk of shrinking the money supply and causing a depression. The nation's honor depended on it.

To do this, Boutwell—without asking the President, the cabinet, or anyone else—sold gold from the Treasury's hoard of $100 million specie and used the proceeds to buy back U.S. bonds. Grant backed his secretary's controversial policy and gave Boutwell latitude to set the course. But only ignorant outsiders would think "that the President was taking any part in the operations of the Treasury concerning the price of gold," Boutwell wrote.

The secretary placed all his orders to buy or sell gold and bonds through Daniel Butterfield in New York, who executed them through local brokers like Joseph Seligman or Harris C. Fahnestock of Jay Cooke & Company. To minimize any chance of foul play, Boutwell followed Butterfield's advice and announced his orders publicly through the Associated Press simultaneously with telegraphing them to New York.

Treasury gold flooded the market as Boutwell sold $1 million in April, $6 million in May, $8 million in June, and $2 million each in July and August, all the while buying back wartime bonds. By September 1 the secretary reported that though this process he had reduced the national debt by almost $50 million during his first six months in office. Horace Greeley's *Tribune*, among others, liked Boutwell's program: "We do n't object to buying up bonds with Greenbacks; we only insist on buying still more of them."

Greeley and Boutwell both saw gold prices as falling in mid-1869 and thought it best to sell gold then at a good value.

For September, Boutwell planned to accelerate his gold sales. From his summer home at Groton, he telegraphed his assistant, William Richardson, in Washington on September 1: "I think it will be necessary to sell four to six millions of gold during this month—the latter sum probably—and I think you had better give notice, say Sunday." This amount was on top of Boutwell's standing order to sell $1 million in gold every second Wednesday, bringing the September total to $9 million, the biggest monthly sale yet.

How irritating for George Boutwell now to have his orders questioned by that interloper in fiscal policy, the President of the United States!

That week Boutwell had received President Grant's letter from Washington, castigating his gold-selling plan. Perhaps he saw a connection between that letter and one he had received at about the same time from Jay Gould—a stranger except by reputation—touting a *Times* article that pretended to represent *his* policy at the Treasury.

Boutwell saw little merit in either Gould's or Grant's arguments. True, rising gold prices might help farmers move their autumn crops, but Boutwell did not see it as his job to manipulate gold prices for anyone's benefit, be they farmers, bankers, or speculators. Most Americans wanted gold prices to fall so that the country could return to a "hard-money" currency.

But politics was politics. Rather than annoy the President, Boutwell backed down and telegraphed Richardson to disregard his prior instructions: "Send no order to Butterfield as to sales of gold until you hear from me."

On Thursday, September 2, Daniel Butterfield was surprised to see Jay Gould appear suddenly at his side as he was walking alone down Twenty-third Street. Butterfield hadn't seen Gould since the Erie magnate had dropped by his Wall Street SubTreasury office the previous June with a $10,000 gift. Now Jay, in that soft enticing voice, asked Butterfield if he had time to chat.

Jay told Butterfield a delectable piece of office gossip: that his boss, Secretary Boutwell, had ordered bigger gold sales for September and that President Grant had vetoed the order. Butterfield had seen neither the order nor the retraction. Daniel marveled at Jay's knowledge of the secret leanings of his Washington superiors.

Jay then made an unusual offer. "I think he said: 'Had I not better buy some gold for you,' or 'I will buy some gold for you,' " Butterfield later told investigators. "I made no answer whatsoever." Why didn't the assistant treasurer just say no to the bribe? "I thought it unnecessary to offend anybody, " Butterfield explained, adding that Gould might take the rejection as a hint of inside information—as if Jay needed tips from Daniel Butterfield instead of vice versa.

Jay remembered the conversation differently: "[Butterfield] believed the policy of the government was pretty well settled, and he thought gold would go up. He asked me to go in and buy some for him."

In any event, after talking with Jay, Butterfield was confused. Who was running U.S. fiscal policy? Boutwell? Grant? Or Jay Gould? Butterfield wrote a letter to Boutwell via Washington that day asking whether he had misunderstood his standing orders to sell gold on alternate Wednesdays. He cited the fact that "the newspapers have been talking of my order being in error. I presume it is correct, or I should have heard to the contrary."

Butterfield heard back from Washington within twenty-four hours that no, there was no mistake: "As the month commenced on Wednesday, I see that you make one more purchase of bonds and one more sale of gold than you would had it begun on a different day of the week," wrote William Richardson, "but that is not very material."

◎ ◎ ◎ ◎ ◎

With a green light from President Grant, Jay Gould bought gold like nobody's business. His joint account with Woodward and Kimber swelled from $10 million to $18 million specie. Jay bought $2.4 million through Gold Room brokers Henry Enos and Edwin Chapin on September 2 alone. Disguising his market forays, Jay placed the orders with Henry Smith at Smith, Gould, Martin, & Company. Smith then purchased the gold through Chapin and Enos under his own name. Jay's identity never went beyond his brokerage partner.

Other Gold Room traders saw Chapin and Enos buying heavily, a clue that something might be afoot. Who they bought for, whether they bought together, or why, not even Enos and Chapin knew.

To finance these enormous gold trades, Jay instructed Henry Smith to lend out every gold dollar at market prices. The borrower of each $1 million in gold at $135 would pay Jay a cash collateral of $1,350,000—the same amount as the purchase price—which Jay would use to pay the upfront cost. This buy-lend strategy was so common that brokers transacted sales and loans side by side on the Gold Room floor. Jay could spark a crisis anytime by "calling" in the loaned gold, but then he would have to repay the collateral—an expensive proposition.

Despite the tiny upfront cost, Jay's massive gold holdings saddled him with huge risk. The $18 million gold in Jay's pool with Kimber and Woodward gained or lost $180,000 in value for each $1 rise or fall in the price.

By Monday, September 6, Jay's buying spree had helped push the gold price to $137¾—a huge $4.50 jump since President Grant had sat in Abel Corbin's kitchen just four days earlier. The move hardly amounted yet to a "corner." By loaning all his gold back into the market, Jay had avoided creating a shortage.

Most analysts blamed the price hike that week on outside forces—rumors from Europe about French Emperor Napoleon III's bad health, which did cause gyrations on markets from London and Frankfurt to the Paris bourse. The *World* reported heavy buying by "some secret French societies of the Red-Republican order" who plotted to put Prince Napoleon on the throne over the objections of the Empress Eugenie. "[T]he death of Emperor Napoleon means a revolution in France, which would probably convulse the whole of Europe," reported the *World*.

Then as now, political turmoil favored gold.

Smart New Yorkers saw shadows of speculators behind the gold boomlet. Why should gold rise when "there is no commercial, financial, nor any other good reason why it should not have fallen to [$125] or lower"? asked the *Herald*. "All the fluctuations are the result of gambling by a few individual capitalists or stock jobbing firms."

The Gold Room buzzed with rumors of cliques and rings.

But success, however sweet, bred dissent within Jay's alliance. His partners, satiated by the week-long rally, decided to cash their chips and leave the game. Woodward went first, telling Jay that the $18 million three-way pool—$6 million apiece, or twice the original target—was bigger than he cared to support. Woodward asked Jay to take $2 million off his hands while he kept his remaining $4 million. Jay agreed.

That same day, Abel Corbin, counting his profits on his fingers with gold at $137, asked Jay to sell off $500,000 of his $1,500,000 account and pay him his profit. "I should like to have this matter realized," Corbin said.

Jay obliged the President's brother-in-law by producing a $25,000 check drawn to cash and endorsed by Jay himself, which kept Corbin's name off the paper trail. Corbin deposited the check in his Bank of America account. Corbin rode off the next morning with Julia Grant, the President's wife, on a day trip to Danbury, Connecticut. Coincidence? Maybe—or perhaps this was Corbin's way of planting ideas in Jay's mind.

The final indignity came on Tuesday, September 7, when Arthur Kimber, the third member of Jay's three-way pool, reversed his stand and sold his entire $6 million interest. The Gold Room rally halted. The price tumbled from

$137 on Tuesday to $134½ on Wednesday, September 8. Jay's losses for the two days easily topped $100,000.

With Kimber gone and Woodward backing away, Jay found himself alone.

"All these fellows deserted me like rats from a ship. Kimber sold out and got short," he later explained. Prices fell, and losses mounted. Even with President Grant's backing, Jay could not support the New York gold market on his own scrawny shoulders. True, he could sell off, take his losses, and go home, but Jay Gould was no quitter.

After so much progress, Jay knew his gold plan was too good to put aside.

He saw only one answer to his predicament. He needed Jim Fisk to throw in a hand. Unfortunately, Jim was away in Albany that week seeing to unfinished business—a grudge match for control of the Albany-Susquehanna Railroad.

SHOULDER TO SHOULDER

JIM FISK HAD NO MORE SUCCESS corralling the Albany-Susquehanna annual stockholders' meeting in Albany that week than he had had at Harpersville tunnel during the August brawl. Jim and lawyer Tom Shearman, accompanied by fifty-odd thugs posing as honest shareholders, managed to tie the shareholders' session into legal knots with a barrage of writs from Judge Barnard's learned pen, but to no avail. In the end, rival shareholder factions elected two rival boards of directors—one representing the Fisk-Erie raiders, the other the Albany management defenders.

In the confusion, New York Governor John Hoffman had ordered the railroad kept under military control until his own attorney general could sort out the mess. Jim departed empty-handed again, his tail between his legs, shrugging and telling friends, "Nothing is lost save honor."

In no enviable mood, Jim returned to New York on Wednesday, September 8, to find his partner Jay Gould worried and depressed, a bundle of nervous tics. Jim recognized Jay's preoccupation with gold, which had kept Jay at home instead of with him in the Albany trenches. "I could see by the way [Jay] was tearing up little pieces of paper—every man has his peculiarities, you know—that he was pretty well up to the handle," Jim later said.

Whether Jim broached the subject or waited for Jay to raise it, the two friends found themselves talking about Jay's predicament. Jim put it simply: "He (pointing to Gould) had gold enough to sink a ship," and the gold market was going to the dogs.

Jay Gould never easily admitted failure or asked for help. To show weakness went against his education from the school of hard knocks. Now he sat on a pile of at least $14 million in gold: $10 million from the former Woodward-Kimber pool, plus $2 million held for Corbin and Butterfield, and at least $2 million more for himself. Every dollar price drop cost Jay at least $140,000 out of pocket. The fact that Jim Fisk had turned him down twice on joining the scheme only worsened the hurt.

"[Jay] was a little sensitive on the subject, feeling as if he would rather take his losses without saying anything about it," Jim later explained. "There had been a little coldness between us, which did not often exist, for the reason that [Gould] had taken upon himself a pretty heavy load, which he did not want me to share, and, therefore, he was not in the habit of saying anything about it … ," he said. "When one day he said to me, 'Don't you think gold has hit bottom?'"

Alone in the Opera House, Jim asked his partner how far into the quicksand he had sunk. Jim fretted as Jay recited the depressing numbers. He told an old Vermont tale about a farmer who was trying to yoke his two oxen, Brindle and Star. "Putting the great elm bow on the neck of Brindle, he undertakes, by main force, to carry the yoke and draw Brindle over until he can yoke Star." Gould, in Jim's story, was Brindle. "If I had as much gold as you have got," Jim told his friend, "I should think you would invite all your able-bodied friends in to help bear the yoke."

Friendship aside, Jim saw Jay's gold plan as downright "scary." Every indicator showed that the price was falling, he argued. The minute he and Gould started buying, the federal Treasury would kill their corner by selling, just as they had busted up the November money lock-up. Jay could save himself better by getting out and taking his lumps.

This time, Jay had an answer. No, the government would not sell gold. President Grant had converted to the crop theory and had tied Boutwell's hands, and half the White House was on Jay's payroll. "This matter is all fixed up; Butterfield is all right; Corbin had got Butterfield all right, and Corbin has got Grant fixed all right," Jay said.

Jim was at once appalled, impressed, and beguiled. Certainly he and Gould had hoped that Grant might be fooled by a diversion like the crop theory. But who could have imagined that the President or his family had money in the gold till? It sounded too good to be true. If they went ahead and cornered gold, their millions of dollars would depend on Grant and Boutwell standing aside while every banker in New York, Boston, and Philadelphia cried for help. With Abel Corbin their only direct link to the White House, Jim wanted more proof.

Not that he didn't believe Jay, but Corbin was a different matter.

Here the story becomes murky. According to Jim, at this point Jay took pen to paper and wrote Corbin a letter explaining that Jim had now joined the Ring and that Corbin should tell their new partner everything. The next night, Jim rode his carriage to Corbin s mansion and hand-delivered Gould's letter.

Corbin acted "very shy" at first with Prince Erie, a man not known for discretion, but finally he blurted out the whole arrangement. "[Corbin] told me that everything was all running nicely," Jim said, "that he had received a check for $25,000, which he had forwarded to Washington; that everything looked bright, and he was confident we were doing a great national good, (laughing,) … ; that he saw more money in the transaction than he had seen in all his life."

Corbin, his wife, Julia Grant, and Butterfield all owned gold, Corbin said, according to Jim. The government would never ruin their plan.

At a second meeting at Corbin's house, Jim said, Corbin dragged out his wife, Jennie, who made the same claim. "I know there will be no gold sold by the government; I am quite positive there will be no gold sold; for this is a chance of a lifetime for us," Jim recalled her saying. "You need not have any uneasiness whatever."

Jim was convinced. Who would know better about the President's plans than his own sister, who had spent most of August closeted with the President and First Lady?

Abel Corbin later denied that any of these conversations had ever happened, or that James Fisk, Jr., had ever graced his home until weeks later after the explosion. Fisk's story was "absolutely untrue; it is all coined," Corbin insisted. No evidence has ever been shown that President Grant's wife owned even a nickel of gold. To Congress, Corbin and Jay Gould both later claimed total ignorance of any purchases for the President or First Lady.

Was Corbin lying to Fisk? Was Gould lying to Fisk? Was Corbin lying to Gould? Did everyone lie to the congressional committee? Whoever actually perjured himself, somebody clearly cheated the jailor.

In any event, seeing how the land lay, Jim decided to help Jay. He joined the gold movement with a flourish, buying $750,000 of gold on Saturday, September 11, and upping his stake to $7 million.

The assault on the Gold Room had begun, with Fisk and Gould marching shoulder to shoulder.

• PART V •

Bears

• • • • •

• 13 •
BANKERS

J AMES BROWN'S SEVENTY-EIGHT-YEAR-OLD LEGS moved with a quick, nervous step. He walked out in the late-summer breeze from the Brown Brothers bank building at 59 Wall Street on Monday morning, September 13, followed by his young assistant, Kruger. They made their way down Wall past the New York Customs House toward Trinity Church, whose steeple towered over New York rooftops. Narrow brick buildings crammed with banks and brokerage offices lined both sides of the cobblestone street. Gas lamps and wooden poles strung with telegraph wires studded the sidewalk. James and Kruger threaded through clusters of dignified men in black frock coats, mingling with messengers, clerks, building guards, and occasional ladies in bright-colored dresses.

The scent of money permeated the air, along with the pungent odor of manure from horse-drawn carriages. The marble-columned Federal Building, where George Washington had taken the oath of office as first President of the United States and which now housed the federal SubTreasury under General Daniel Butterfield, stood across from the New York Stock Exchange's new one hundred-foot-tall marble edifice.

Just past the Stock Exchange, James Brown and his assistant entered a doorway facing New Street. Inside was a maze of hallways; a back entrance to the Stock Exchange, a causeway to Broad Street, and endless doors opening into small dank offices. They took the second door to the left. The guard inside recognized the senior partner of Brown Brothers & Company and allowed James and Kruger into the parlor where throbbed the heartbeat of American finance.

The Gold Room dripped with splendor. Traders entering the high-ceilinged chamber gathered around a circular iron railing at the center of the thirty-foot wide hardwood trading floor. The railing enclosed a large bronze fountain, with "a Cupid playing with a dolphin, from which microscopic streamlets of water fell harmlessly to the basin beneath," wrote speculator James Medbery, calling it "an ineffable vision of ugliness." Inside the basin swam a school of tiny goldfish.

Outside the railing, the floor rose in concentric terraces toward the outer walls, like a trading "pit" in a modem commodity futures exchange. Chandeliers illuminated the room; light flooded in from the high windows. The exchange chairman presided from a raised desk at the far end of the chamber toward New Street. Galleries for telegraph operators and spectators ringed the walls above the trading floor.

Operating the electronic "gold price indicator"—a variation on the newly invented "stock ticker" machine—was twenty-two-year-old Thomas Alva Edison, who had been hired that summer; he enjoyed tinkering with the hardware and held patents on his own telegraph innovations. The indicator flashed gold prices instantly onto a large scoreboard in the rafters, to brokers' offices throughout the city, and to another gilded indicator outside on New Street for passersby.

Crowds gathered in the street sometimes to bet small change on whether the next gold tick would be up or down—a way to pass time until the cock-fights and farot tables opened across town.

Hundreds of traders swarmed the Gold Room floor on active days. They drifted back and forth between the stock and gold markets, following the hottest action. The Gold Exchange had 485 members who paid annual dues of $25 and a $1,000 initiation fee. All but 185 also belonged to the Stock Exchange. Nonmembers could pay $100 per year to watch the goings-on from a balcony and pass notes to brokers on the floor below.

James Brown rarely came to the Gold Room or the Stock Exchange these days; normally he left the footwork to younger partners. For a week, though, gold had been acting strangely, and pandemonium ruled the Gold Room. Prices whipsawed as the Street bubbled with rumors of cliques and lock-ups. How bad was the crisis? How real were the lock-up rumors? Nobody really knew, and James Brown wanted to see with his own eyes.

James had run the Brown Brothers banking house in New York for almost half a century. He had joined the firm on his twentieth birthday in 1811 as an apprentice to his older brother William in Liverpool. When the Erie Canal opened in 1825, making New York the gateway to the American West, his father Alexander—the firm's founding patriarch—ordered James to set-tle in Gotham and open a branch there.

In the late 1860s, James, balding with short gray whiskers and thick glasses, was Wall Street's elder statesman. His bank's customers included big cotton exporters and major banker-brokers like Jay Cooke & Company and William Heath & Company. James's firm owned acres of prime city real es-tate and a Louisiana plantation; it controlled the Pacific Mail Steamship Company; it had ties to the British Cunard shipping line; and it supported dozens of charities.

James lived modestly, unspoiled by his mountains of money. The father of eleven children by two wives, James rode about town in a one-horse coupe. "He was the quietest, most polite old gentleman you ever saw," said a Brown Brothers clerk. James dressed like an old-fashioned merchant, with black trousers, swallowtail coat, wide black stock, low open waistcoat, and linen shirt.

Family members worried whether James still had the vigor to manage the family business. "The truth is ... father's advancing years are beginning to tell on him," wrote his son John Crosby Brown in mid-1868, "altho' his mind is as clear & his judgment as sound as ever."

The revolution that had swept New York banking in the 1860s and made young men rich by Civil War bond drives had eclipsed James Brown's gener-ation.

Henry Clews, another Gold Room regular, was young enough at thirty-three to be James's grandson. Born in Staffordshire, England, and brought to America as a child, Clews had elbowed his way into the aristocratic pre-Civil War Stock Exchange by sheer brass. For decades Stock Exchange members had refused to buy or sell stocks for customers on a commission of less than 1/8 of 1 percent. Clews, an outsider, had refused to play along. Shortly after the 1857 panic, the twenty-one-year-old Clews had started charging new cus-tomers a commission rate of 1/16 of 1 percent—half the Exchange members' price. Even at these discounts, he profited by trading on the Open Board, an informal curb exchange, paying lower commission rates.

Customers abandoned the "old Fogies" for Clews. The Exchange had no choice but to welcome young Henry to the establishment.

The ringleader of the younger bankers was Jay Cooke, the imposing, white-bearded Philadelphian whose firm dominated business with branches in New York and Washington, D.C., headed by Harris Fahnestock and brother Henry Cooke.

Early on in the war, Treasury Secretary Salmon Chase had turned to bankers like Cooke and Henry Clews to float enormous government debt issues. Older Yankee money men doubted that the Union could beat the Confederacy on the battlefield, let alone pay its debts. They hesitated to buy bonds from Uncle Sam. Secretary Chase turned instead to Cooke's Philadelphia house, naming it lead Fiscal Agent in 1862 along with three New York banks—Clews's, Fisk & Hatch, and Vermilye & Company.

Together, they sold U.S. bond issues totaling almost $2 billion, an unheard-of sum that was almost twice the national money supply. Cooke led the heroic effort, selling out each bond issue with orders to spare.

After the war, Cooke, Clews, and other rising bankers like Joseph Seligman steeped themselves in politics. Cooke and Clews raised money for Ulysses Grant's presidential campaign; Clews and Seligman cultivated friendships with Treasury officials in Washington and New York.

Jay Cooke took the cake for wooing opinion. He had approached Ulysses Grant after Appomattox and offered to invest $15,000 for Grant in profitable railroad ventures. Cooke gave money to newspaper publishers like Horace Greeley and donated $15,000 in stock to the Reverend Henry Ward Beecher to publish favorable articles in his newsletter, the *Christian Union*.

During Andrew Johnson's presidency, Cooke made fortunes handling secret Treasury gold and bond sales. Brother Henry in Washington wined and dined politicians on Capitol Hill, the White House, and in the Treasury, following Jay Cooke's order to "Give us promptly and in advance all the information you can about the feeling of the President & Congress."

Speculating on inside government tips was "old Rothschild's way," Henry explained.

When Ulysses Grant became President in March 1869, insiders considered Jay Cooke a sure bet to be appointed Treasury secretary. Grant ultimately chose George Boutwell, but Henry Cooke assured his brother that Boutwell too was a "good friend" and "feels kindly" toward the House of Cooke.

But if the rumors about a new Gold Room clique were true, bankers like Cooke and Henry Clews would feel the crunch.

A normal day in the Gold Room saw $70 to $90 million in gold traded. Recently, volume had surged though. The total topped $160 million every day from September 4 through 10 and hit $199 million on two days. New York banks fueled lock-up fears with their weekly statements for Saturday, September 11, which showed a huge drop in bank gold reserves, from $17.4 to $14.9 million.

Except for bear and bull speculators who delighted in making money from fast markets, these sporadic gold shortages sent shivers through most businessmen. They squeezed commerce and made bad business for bankers and their merchant customers.

International trade, a big item even in the 1860s, felt the biggest bite. U.S. producers exported over $470 million in merchandise in 1870, mostly farm goods and crude materials moving to Europe. Imports that same year topped $475 million. The health of virtually every economic sector depended on trade.

The fact that greenbacks and gold circulated as competing forms of money domestically and overseas made trade highly vulnerable to Gold Room lockups.

Any merchant who imported goods from Europe needed gold to pay his overseas supplier and to pay U.S. customs duties. When gold became scarce, import costs soared.

An even bigger risk fell on exporters selling U.S. cotton or grain abroad. Exporters paid their U.S. suppliers in greenbacks but received gold as payment from their European customers. They could lose their shirts if gold values fell sharply after they paid for the goods but before shipments could cross the Atlantic and return with payment—normally a thirty- to sixty-day gap.

Import-export merchants relied on bankers like James Brown to handle these financing arrangements. Banks would advance cash to exporters today and guarantee them a fixed price on the gold that they anticipated receiving from overseas in the future. The banks, in effect, shouldered the gold fluctuation risk.

Banks charged for this service. Scarce, erratic gold prices made export costs high, too.

The banks, in turn, relied on the Gold Room to manage these tremendous risks by taking large "short" positions in gold. They borrowed gold and sold it, then used the income from the sale as collateral for the loan. Like any other short-seller, the banks profited when gold prices fell but lost when the prices rose. Ideally, these paper gains and losses meant little since they would offset losses and gains on gold in transit from Europe.

In effect, bankers used the Gold Room to shift the commercial risks of the import-export trade to speculators who thrived on such risk.

In the late 1860s, with most U. S. gold coin locked away in the Treasury, short-selling gold could be dangerous, however.

Sooner or later, short traders had to repay their loans with actual physical gold coin or with gold certificates. If supplies dried up, they could have trouble buying or borrowing gold at any price. Gold prices could skyrocket if panicking bears bid against each other for scarce supplies.

Some bankers went beyond their commercial business and took pure speculative positions — selling gold they didn't own, not backed by any pending export loans, and betting on a price drop. One partner at Jay Cooke's New York office, Edward Dodge, had taken an enormous flier in "short" gold that year. An anonymous Brown Brothers account, "Gold Account #2," sold $136,000 in gold during the first two weeks of September while borrowing $155,000 in gold. The *World* reported that George Opdyke, another banker with Republican political ties, was "largely short at 131 to 132" as gold hovered over $135.

Gold borrowers had to pay their lenders a cash collateral or "margin" equal to the gold's day-to-day value. When prices rose, their creditors could demand more margin to keep the collateral accounts current. For a banker to default meant shame, bankruptcy, and possibly jail.

Now, thousands of dollars in margin calls had already slipped from the bankers' and merchants' pockets into the hands of the faceless "ring."

Two unidentified merchants who had "suffered by the recent locking up of gold"—probably James Brown's customers—had brought criminal conspiracy charges against unnamed "gold gamblers" before a New York grand jury.

James Brown had clamored for the federal Treasury to sell off its gold surplus to avoid periodic shortages. After a similar squeeze in 1866, Brown had organized an open letter, signed by thirty-three commercial firms, to then-Secretary Hugh McCulloch, urging him to stop Treasury "hoarding of gold coins" in order to avoid "inordinate speculation" and "embarrassments" to business. Horace Greeley, in a *Tribune* editorial that week, had echoed Brown's arguments. "Money in the Treasury will always be regarded with suspicion," said the *Tribune*. "No Secretary, however incorruptible, can escape the arrows of calumny."

Washington had dismissed Brown's and Greeley's approach as foolhardy. If the Treasury sold off its gold, they argued, the gold would only end up in Europe. They ignored the pleas.

If it seems strange that a vital economic organ like the Gold Room, with its pivotal role in world trade, could be so easily threatened by anonymous rings and lock-up cliques, it should.

It would be more than five decades before the first federal regulation of commodity exchange trading and more than six decades before President Franklin D. Roosevelt pushed Congress to adopt federal securities laws. In 1869 nobody really had the power to police Wall Street. For all its eastern glitter, the Gold Room, like most 1860s exchanges, had more in common with Dodge City and the O.K. Corral than with financial markets of the 1980s.

If Fisk and Gould were to try their gold spree today, they would be required to file daily reports with the federal Commodity Futures Trading Commission in Washington, D.C. The exchange would keep hourly watch on their margin accounts, and at the first sign of trouble, a flock of auditors would demand to inspect their books. In an emergency, the exchange or the government could close or limit trading, raise margins, or force a liquidation.

As if that weren't enough, exchange rules today set ceilings on how much gold a trader can hold for speculation—a reform adopted after the 1979-80 Hunt silver experience. Federal statutes bar price manipulation.

But in 1869 the only real law on Wall Street was the barrel of a gun or the power of one man's fortune against another's. Nobody in New York knew who was buying gold or whether a lock-up was underway in September 1869 because nobody kept records or had the authority to demand information.

The Gold Room's checkered history gave even more reason to worry. Ever since organized gold trading had first started in New York in 1862, corners, squeezes, and abuses had riddled the Exchange. As a freelance speculator, young J. P. Morgan pulled off a minicorner in October 1863 by arranging with another broker to send $2,150,000 gold coin off on a ship to Europe. Prices jumped from $146 to $156 in four days. Instead of damning this assault on government finance just three months after the bloody Gettysburg and Vicksburg battles, the *Times* barely yawned. "Though shrewdly conceived, this *manoeuvre* is not wholly new to the market, having been tried, but with no satisfactory result, last spring," it said.

Worse still, there was outright theft. The original 1864 rules required Gold Room traders to deliver physical coin the day after a sale. The Wall Street neighborhood buzzed with delivery boys early each afternoon carrying canvas sacks loaded with gold. They were often followed by complaints of robberies, missing coins, and lost bags.

To avoid this, the Exchange changed its rules to allow traders to deliver bank certificates instead of coin. But then a forgery epidemic rocked the Street in August 1865. One trader circulated $1.5 million in fake bank gold certificates before he was discovered and skipped town.

Necessity being mother to invention, the gold traders produced an innovation: a clearinghouse. Beginning in mid-1865, after each day, traders sent a list of all their buys and sells to the Gold Exchange Bank, a corporation separate from the Exchange. The Bank's clerks worked all night calculating each trader's net gain or loss and checking it against other brokers' statements. Then, if, say, James Brown traded gold with four other men one day, buying a million from one and selling a million to another, buying half a million from a third and selling $50,000 worth to a fourth, he would pay the bank a single check the next day and take his $450,000 in gold. Every other Gold Room trader would also settle with the Bank in one lump payment or collection.

Moralizers denounced the clearinghouse system as a sinful temptation to gambling. A man with $500 in his pocket, they said, could buy and sell millions, as long as he broke even at day's end. But on the whole things worked smoothly after the war years. Speculative fever in gold ebbed as the excitement in Wall Street turned to railroad stocks and convertible bonds.

Now, in September 1869, old James Brown, squinting through his thick glasses, surveyed the frantic scene on the Gold Room floor. He stood aside as his young Mr. Kruger sold and borrowed amid the crowd of noisy brokers. New York bankers had been fighting rising gold prices all week by selling huge amounts into the market. Somebody had a big appetite. Gold Room regulars knew that two floor hacks, Henry Enos and Edwin Chapin, and the better-known speculator William Woodward, had done most of the buying so far, but they might be fronts for bigger players behind the scenes.

James had heard rumors of quarreling among gold bulls, but he took little comfort.

On paper, the prospects for cornering the gold market looked far-fetched. Ever since the Gold Rush to California in 1848, U.S. mines had produced 50 million ounces of gold, worth over $1 billion at then-current prices. Europeans had bought most of this, but over $62 million in minted gold coin and another $30 million in gold certificates was circulating in the United States in 1869, not counting the Treasury's $80 million stash.

"[G]old is like air," wrote James Medbery. "London or San Francisco can transfer millions upon millions by flash of telegraph. The immense ocean of the Sub-Treasury may overflow. All the small sums of gold scattered throughout the banks of the United States may be tributary. " Medbery compared cornering gold "to the pumping out of the New York Bay by a grand combination of steam-engines."

Hyperbole aside, James Brown knew that the Gold Room operated on a thin safety margin. It took weeks to bring gold by ship from Europe. California gold stayed in California; any trainload of gold headed east across the frontier risked being waylaid by Jesse James's or some other outlaw gang. In a crisis, New Yorkers could count only on the gold in New York banks—barely $14 million by latest count—and a few million more in private hands.

The younger New York bankers—Henry Clews, George Opdyke, Jacob Vermilye, and Harris Fahnestock—all complained to Daniel Butterfield at the SubTreasury about the danger of a Gold Room clique. They plotted to use their political muscle. The government would never sit still for a gold market corner, they thought, not as long as bankers paid the bills for Republican politicians.

· 14 ·
THE BOLD AND BRILLIANT PLAN

ENRY SMITH SPENT THREE WEEKS that summer vacationing at his small ranch near Trenton, New Jersey. When he came back to the office in late August, he discovered Jay Gould dabbling in gold again. Jay might reign supreme over Erie, but Smith still gave orders at Smith, Gould, Martin & Company, their joint brokerage firm since 1862.

From their cramped rooms at 11 Broad Street, Smith, whose sharp eyes gave him what Henry Clews called "a decidedly Hebrew aspect," ran a network of operations covering the Gold Room and the Stock Exchange. Henry Martin, their third partner, kept the firm's books along with half a dozen clerks. Smith's customers included speculators like William Woodward and Arthur Kimber, but all others paled next to the firm's biggest account: Jay Gould and the Erie Railway. Jay's stock action during the Great Erie War and the November money lock-up alone had given Henry Smith enough business for ten houses.

For special occasions, the firm kept a direct telegraph wire from its Broad Street office to the Erie Railway Opera House uptown on Twenty-third Street—quite a luxury seven years before Alexander Graham Bell invented the telephone.

Henry Smith had heard Jay talk for months about "bulling" gold, and he had even placed his orders to buy gold last April. But Jay's latest predicament alarmed his long-time broker. Checking the numbers, Smith said, "I found Mr. Gould engaged in this speculation until he had about $9,000,000 of gold on hand, with a loss against us of eighteen hundred thousand dollars"—that is, $1.8 million.

So far, the red ink was only on paper. Jay owned the gold, and the price could rebound. But that kind of debt would have crippled most Wall Street houses in the late 1860s if forced to pay, no less a big firm like Smith, Gould, Martin & Company.

All through early September, as Jay maneuvered Ulysses Grant, Daniel Butterfield, and Jim Fisk into his Gold Ring, Henry Smith had borne the brunt. He bought hoards of gold for Jay through the Gold Room to buoy prices and then loaned it out to bankers and short speculators.

Not wanting to give his hand away, Smith had rarely shown his own face on the Gold Room floor. He covered his tracks by using agents and anonymous accounts.

Some time around Saturday, September 11, Jay called a strategy meeting at the Opera House to plot the operation. Four men took their places around a gilded table on plush velvet chairs under the Garibaldi ceiling frescoes: Gould, Fisk, Henry Smith, and William Belden.

Belden, a wiry, erratic man with spectacles and moustache, had once been Jim Fisk's partner in a brokerage firm called Fisk & Belden. Now he did Jim's bidding on Wall Street from a small office a few doors down from Henry Smith's. That summer, the Stock Exchange's membership committee had twice voted down Belden's application for admission because of his ties to Fisk.

Belden never wavered. Who needed a Stock Exchange seat for income when you had "Jubilee Jim" Fisk as a customer?

At the meeting, Jay laid out his gold plan like a mathematics teacher explaining an algebra problem. He isolated each variable, drawing diagrams on sheets of paper and in the air with his nervous hands, making complex puzzles look simple. Everyone would buy gold in huge quantities—$20 or $30 million altogether. Like any good bandits, they'd mask their faces by using an outside brokerage firm, William Heath & Company, for most of the purchases. Jay would keep his accounts separate from Jim's, Jim's separate from Jay's, and Belden's separate from both.

The goal, Jay said, would be to nudge the gold price up from $135 to, say, $145 and hold it there for about two months until they could sell at a profit and spark a wave of U.S. grain exports.

To keep down costs, they'd lend out as much of the gold as possible.

Jay's game was all mirrors. He had no intention of paying $14 million plus cash to acquire all the gold that was then circulating in New York banks. By loaning out all that they bought, Jay's clique could buy all the gold in New

York, lend it back to other traders, then buy it back again from the borrowers, loan it out again, buy it back again—all without pulling a dime out of circulation.

The same gold could be lent and borrowed again several times over, sometimes to the same people.

Along the way, Jay would acquire a chokehold over New York gold by "owning" two or three times as much as actually existed. If he needed to, he could tighten the vise anytime by calling in the gold loans and creating a citywide shortage, making prices snap to his whip. As long as the federal Treasury minded its business and kept its vaults shut, the "shorts" had no escape.

Abel Corbin and Daniel Butterfield would warn them ahead of time of any breakdown on the political front.

The price tag would be tiny. Under common Gold Room practice, merchants or bankers borrowing gold paid collateral equal to the gold's market price, which Jay could use to pay the upfront cost. If the price held steady, the Ring's only expense to "carry" gold would be interest on the cash collateral. In 1869 neither the government nor the Exchanges required brokers to collect initial margin from their customers. Big customers like Fisk and Gould paid none.

True, under the awkward buy-lend system, they might get stuck paying outright for any gold they failed to lend out. Also, if things turned sour and prices fell, Jay's Ring could get clobbered. With $20 million in gold on their books, each dollar price drop would cost them $200,000. Losses could mount quickly under those rules.

But money was no object for now. Jay and his friend Tweed owned New York's Tenth National Bank, which would gladly issue certified checks on demand to its favorite Wall Street customers.

The scope of Jay's plan must have dazzled his partners. The staging of the meeting heightened Jay's impact. Jim Fisk had decorated the Grand Opera House in a bold style that encouraged bold thoughts. Visitors to the Erie offices passed through a main hallway with a marble floor and walls of polished black walnut. Looking up, they saw the ceiling painted "blue, carmine, lilac, and gold in Pompeian designs with intertwining vines and flowers half-hiding naked cupids and rosy nymphs," wrote Robert Fuller. "In the four corners were highly-colored portraits of [Samuel F. B.] Morse, who invented the telegraph, [Benjamin] Franklin, who discovered electricity, [Robert] Fulton, who made steam boating practicable, and [James] Watt, who invented the steam engine."

These four giants stood as mere doormen to Jim Fisk and Jay Gould, the brassy inventors of the money lock-up, the watered stock ploy, and now, last but not least, the gold corner.

What was more, the gold scheme was only part of Jay's even larger ambitions for his railroad empire. All summer, Jay had secretly negotiated with LeGrand Lockwood, the owner of Lockwood & Company, one of Wall Street's leading brokerage houses. Lockwood held the key to expanding the Erie Railway westward to the Pacific.

Like other dreamers of his day, Jay Gould saw his future in the West. Just four months earlier, on May 10, 1869, dignitaries had hammered in the golden spike connecting the Union and Central Pacific Railroads at Promontory Point, Utah, completing America's first transcontinental line. Jay understood that his Erie Railway could survive only temporarily by carrying passengers and freight from New York merely to the eastern tip of the Great Lakes. The future lay beyond, in Illinois, Missouri, and the Great Plains.

After months of delicate talks, three key western lines had consolidated into a single corporation that July. It called itself the Lake Shore and Michigan Southern and provided a direct steel link from Buffalo across Pennsylvania, Ohio, and Indiana to its terminal in Chicago. LeGrand Lockwood, the company treasurer and a long-time Vanderbilt ally, had emerged as the Lake Shore's dominant figure.

All July and August, Jay and Commodore Vanderbilt's agents competed in wooing Lockwood for his support for merging his railroad into their own.

The stakes were enormous. Whichever line won, Erie or the New York Central, would control an uninterrupted route from New York to Chicago and would dominate transportation to the West and California. The loser could end up marooned as a local New York line with no connection past Buffalo.

Vanderbilt used his proxies to elect two friends to the Lake Shore board of directors, but Jay took a more direct approach. After hours of haggling over a dinner of oysters, wine, and steak at Delmonico's one late-August night, he promised LeGrand Lockwood that Erie would build a special third rail from Buffalo to Jersey City for the Lake Shore's narrow-gauge cars. Lockwood agreed.

On Thursday, September 10, Erie's executive committee sealed the deal by issuing $5 million in "narrow gauge [sic] sinking fund bonds" to unleash on their creditors and start the work crews.

Success in the gold corner, which under Jay's crop theory would bring a flood of Illinois grain east for export, would make the Lake Shore agreement pay from the start.

With so many pieces on the chessboard, Jay could hardly take chances. On Wednesday, September 15, he ordered Henry Smith to open fire in the Gold Room. Shattering an early-week lull, Henry directed Edwin Chapin and Henry Enos to buy almost $2.7 million gold in two days, which pushed the price from $135 to almost $137. At the same time, James Ellis, a broker from William Heath & Company, bought heavily for Fisk's account.

Meanwhile, Jay couldn't help noticing that New York bankers rumored to be "short" in gold were showing signs of fighting back. Lately, they had bared their political teeth.

As early as Tuesday, September 14, Horace Greeley's *Tribune* had run editorials railing against the "locking up of gold" in Wall Street. Greeley, the odd-looking, moralistic, fifty-eight-year-old publisher, had deep Republican ties and probably parroted whatever the bankers told him. His opening salvo had a chilling tone. "And now, Messrs. Gold-gamblers! A word with you!" it said, pointing its rhetorical finger. Holding up the much-abused New York State conspiracy statute with its draconian prison terms, it promised to deal with "Your next conspiracy to lock up gold … as the law directs."

Treasury Secretary George Boutwell planned to visit New York that week. Everyone knew that the city's well-connected Republican bankers would try to twist his arm on selling Treasury specie. Jay Cooke, Henry Clews, or some other bear had likely tipped off Greeley's editorial writers, hoping to use the *Tribune's* clout to push Boutwell's thinking or at least warn the bull clique that they too could play hardball.

How could Jay help but be nervous when the success of his financial venture depended on politicians under pressure keeping their word?

· 15 ·
A DONE DEAL

THE PARLOR OF ABEL CORBIN'S HOUSE looked like a busy train station on Monday afternoon, September 13, 1869. President Grant had arrived in New York on Friday for one last trip before ending his summer sojourns and settling into a long winter at the White House. Ulysses, Julia, their two children, and General Porter planned to travel west from New York to Pittsburgh Friday afternoon and spend a long weekend visiting family friends in tiny Washington, Pennsylvania, before coming home to Washington, D.C.

The First Family would travel on a private Erie Railway car, provided gratis, courtesy of Jay Gould, of course.

President Grant's traveling had become a national joke that summer. Even the *Anti-Slavery Standard*, a Republican organ, observed that Grant "recreates excessively" and had allowed a "pilotless drifting" of the White House.

Friends like the *Times* tried to brush aside the issue. "Happy is the President of whom the worst thing grumblers can say is that he travels too much," it quipped, "for grumblers, like disease, always attack a man's weakest point."

Grant, by now well versed in Gould economics, had heard an earful about gold since he left Washington three days earlier.

On Friday, the President and his family had taken a boat ride up the Hudson to West Point. While watching the pretty tree-covered New Jersey Palisade cliffs glide by, he had had a long talk with Daniel Butterfield from the SubTreasury about the current state of New York finance. Butterfield briefed the President on "all matters pertaining to the Treasury," he said, including the raging battle between bulls and bears in the Gold Room.

Having taken money from Jay Gould put Daniel in a ticklish spot. Butterfield must have assumed that Grant had spoken with Gould and Corbin about his gold policy. He knew that Grant had backed Jay's crop theory argument over his own Treasury secretary's objections. Did Corbin, Julia Grant, or even Ulysses all have secret gold accounts like his own, courtesy of the Erie Railway president? To make things worse, since July, Butterfield had bought $1.37 million in bonds through banker-broker Joseph Seligman for a personal account in his wife's name, mostly through European markets in Frankfurt and London. The foreign-bought bonds, denominated in gold, rose in value in harmony with Gold Room prices. It was a clever side bet that Jay's Gold Room scheme would succeed.

On the other hand, Republican bankers, staunch Party backers, had been complaining to Butterfield for almost two weeks that the latest Gold Room shenanigans were squeezing legitimate merchants.

Almost anything Butterfield said to Grant as they rode upstream that day would violate some ulterior loyalty, either to his bear Republican banker friends or to his bull benefactor Jay Gould. If Daniel admitted his own personal stake in gold, Grant might think him corrupt. At the same time, Daniel felt responsible to tell the President as much of the truth as he safely could. Daniel was no coward. As a wartime officer, he had earned the Congressional Medal of Honor for gallantry under enemy fire. He had a formidable sense of duty.

"I think I said to the President that the people in Wall Street were all apparently very patriotic, but that most of them wanted to make money," Daniel explained tactfully to Congress later on, "and that whatever they said on either side had to be pretty carefully weighed." Probably, he said a lot more—about Jay Gould, Abel Corbin, Jay Cooke, and other bears and bulls.

Ulysses Grant, as usual, listened quietly to the whole story and then gave no hint of an opinion.

Gold talk stalked Ulysses again on Sunday night when he had dinner with A. T. Stewart at his Fifth Avenue mansion. Big importers like Stewart suffered badly from gold run-ups like that underway on Wall Street, but Stewart stood by his advice to the President of two weeks earlier in Saratoga. Ulysses should keep his nose and the Treasury's gold out of the tight market. Otherwise, people would accuse him of helping one group of speculators against another.

Jay Gould made a point to visit Corbin's house twice a day these days, once in the morning and once at night. Now on Monday afternoon, as a dozen aides and family members scurried about ironing out last-minute details for the President's Pennsylvania trip, Jay sat patiently in the foyer waiting to see Grant.

Corbin "was very anxious that I should come around," Jay recalled. Jay felt perfectly comfortable by now rubbing elbows with the highest figures in U.S. politics. Grant perhaps had less flair and less magnetism than his other political friend Bill Tweed, but politicians at heart were all the same. "When the Legislature is Republican, I am a Republican. When it is Democratic, I am a Democrat, but I am always an Erie man," Jay once said, explaining his pay-offs to law makers on both sides of the aisle. After a few minutes, Corbin's face peeked out from a back room, and he signaled for Jay to come.

They only had a few minutes together: Jay, Corbin, and Ulysses Grant. Jay noticed the fruits of Corbin's salesmanship on the Chief Executive. "The President had changed his views [on gold policy], as I at once discovered, " Jay later said. "He seemed to take a very deep interest in it; it seemed to have been a matter of study to him. " The President repeated what Jay already knew—that he had countermanded Secretary Boutwell's order to sell gold and that Boutwell now agreed with the President's policy.

What could Jay have thought after all these weeks as he listened to Ulysses Grant's quiet voice, fixed on the general's weathered eyes, and weighed his every gesture? Surely they had a deal. Why else would Grant, the most important, sought-after man in the United States, rushing through meetings with luminaries like Secretary of State Hamilton Fish, trying to catch his family's Pennsylvania-bound train, deliberately find time to pull Jay aside and tell him his feelings on gold?

If Ulysses Grant suspected Jay, Corbin, Fisk, or anyone else of gambling in the Gold Room on the President's inside tips, he hardly seemed to care. And if Grant didn't know, if Corbin, Grant's sister, and perhaps even his wife had not told him, if the shrewd battlefield commander could not figure things out for himself, then all the better.

Jay might have thought differently had he heard the President change his tune after Jay had left the room. As Corbin recalled, Grant acted "a little peevishly," telling an aide that "he was a little too easy in allowing Mr. Gould to have an interview …. Thus indicating annoyance." Turning to Julia, Ulysses remarked, half ejaculatory, that Gould was always "trying to find something out of him."

But to Jay's face, Grant had given no hint of suspicion.

Even Boutwell, the last big gun, now seemed to be silenced. Before leaving town, Ulysses had taken paper and pencil and written a note on the subject to his Treasury secretary, not unlike the terse battlefield dispatches he had written to Sherman and Sheridan years before. Boutwell would pass through New York later in the week, and Grant wanted no misunderstanding. Without showing the letter to Corbin, Grant sealed it in an envelope. Would Abel please take this to Daniel Butterfield at the SubTreasury to give to Boutwell? the President asked. Certainly, Corbin agreed.

The President never said it directly, but Abel Corbin drew the logical inference that the letter contained an order for Boutwell against selling gold. The first person Corbin told was Jay Gould.

◎ ◎ ◎ ◎ ◎

Some people have a bad habit when things are going right. They tempt fate, push their luck, make one last adjustment that doesn't come out quite right. While waiting in Corbin's parlor to see the President, Jay Gould should have quietly counted his lucky stars. Everything looked bright for his gold designs. Through perseverance and skill, he had transformed a far-fetched vision into reality—a remarkable accomplishment.

But instead of leaving well enough alone, Jay struck up conversation with young General Horace Porter, the President's aide.

Porter, son of a Connecticut governor and a West Point honor student before the war, looked every bit the straight-arrow, bright-eyed, eager spearcarrier. A true Grant devotee, he had joined Ulysses's military staff just after Grant's promotion to General of the Army in April 1864. Porter, a dashing officer with his neatly trimmed goatee, had ridden at Grant's side as aide-de-camp throughout the bloody Virginia campaign, carrying messages to the front lines, taking Grant's dictation, sharing endless personal moments with his commander. Porter even tended Grant's migraine headache on the morning of his final triumphant meeting with Robert E. Lee at Appomattox Courthouse.

After the Confederate surrender, Porter followed Grant to Washington. When Grant became secretary of war during the Andrew Johnson impeachment imbroglio, he made Porter his assistant secretary. On road trips, when crowds demanded a few words from the shy war hero, Ulysses often would nudge his young protégé onstage to speak for him.

Now, as the President's secretary, Horace Porter acted as his gatekeeper.

He opened the President's mail and screened all his appointments; he accompanied Grant on personal trips. Even Cabinet members often communicated with the President through his secretary. Some congressmen and newspaper writers criticized Grant for surrounding himself with military cronies like Porter and Orville Babcock, another wartime aide-de-camp now serving as Grant's military secretary. But Grant felt comfortable around the army comrades who had shared his military achievements.

Outside his family, Ulysses had few advisors or friends closer than Babcock or Horace Porter. Upon the recent death of General John Rawlins, some Washington pundits even speculated that Grant might name Porter to take Rawlins's place as secretary of war.

Jay took advantage of the quiet moment in Abel Corbin's living room to take Porter aside for a private talk. There, Jay startled the President's aide with a blunt proposition. "I purchase and sell immense sums of gold in New York," Jay said, "and I have means of knowing just when gold is going up, and I sell when it is going down and buy when it is going up. Do you ever purchase or sell gold or stocks?"

Porter shook his head, and Jay charged on.

"You had better let me get you some gold; gold is going to rise before long, and suppose I purchase some for you."

Porter, aghast at the bribe offer, had no trouble figuring out the right answer. No, he said, "I have neither the inclination nor the means of purchasing gold; and if I had, I am an officer of the Government, and cannot enter into anything that looks like speculation, It may be perfectly proper for you to do it, but it would be manifestly improper for me."

Jay could hardly believe his ears. Who ever heard of a government employee—a politician's aide, no less—turning down free money? It had to be a mistake. The conversation returned to pleasantries. Porter dismissed the entire incident as an innocent faux pas. Jay did the only logical thing. He took Porter's coy no for a yes and that afternoon asked Henry Smith to open an account for Porter at Smith, Gould, Martin & Company and to buy $500,000 gold in Porter's name.

Horace Porter would certainly thank him later, Jay thought—at least if Porter were like everyone else Jay knew in politics.

• 16 •
TWISTING ARMS

G EORGE BOUTWELL NEVER KNEW he had so many friends in New York. After decades in Boston and Washington politics, Ulysses Grant's Treasury secretary considered himself a stranger there. Now it seemed that every banker, broker, and money-worshipper in Gotham wanted to visit him, shake his hand, pat his back, and bend his ear.

Boutwell knew that a political crossfire waited to greet him in New York after his day-long journey on the afternoon of Wednesday, September 15. The bankers had sent an emissary, Frank Howe, to Boston to buttonhole Boutwell on the gold issue before he even reached New York. The newspapers that morning buzzed with talk of the gold contest. The *Times* flatly predicted a "*corner* in Gold when the *Bull* combination get ready for its preconcerted squeeze." The *World* and *Tribune* both featured Boutwell's visit in their columns.

"We are credibly informed," the *Tribune* announced, "that certain financiers of our City, in combination with European capitalists, have conspired to buy and withdraw from use Thirty Millions of Gold, with intent to compel those who must pay at the Customs-House or elsewhere to buy of them at exorbitant rates." Greeley had the details wrong; Jay Gould had no "European capitalists" in his Ring. But the story rang true. "Mr. Boutwell can surely ascertain that such conspiracy does or does not exist," Greeley's editorial insisted. "If it does, we submit that his duty is plain and imperative—to sell gold as long as the market will take it, and to invest the proceeds in bonds."

The *World* shouted an opposite warning, claiming that certain "influential parties who are heavily short of gold … are bringing a pressure to bear upon the Secretary in order to induce him to sell about $10,000,000 of gold. "Boutwell should resist the appeals, the *World* argued, and not "run his department to suit either 'bears' or 'bulls' in Wall Street." Selling gold at this point would "place money in the pockets of the 'bears' in gold, at the expense of the United States Treasury."

Jay Gould could have conceived the *World's* government-stay-out-of-gold story himself. Maybe he did.

Boutwell approached his New York visit with lawyerly caution. Two days before leaving Boston, he telegraphed Daniel Butterfield to meet him alone for dinner first thing for a report. "Will you dine with me at 6½ p.m. Wednesday next, at the Astor House, where I then expect to be? No one else. I wish to see you before I see others in New York," the message read.

Boutwell had never met Daniel Butterfield face to face before, although he certainly knew of Butterfield's reputation as a political friend of Grant's military circle and of New York figures like A. T. Stewart.

Down in the financial district, meanwhile, as Boutwell stepped off his train at the Twenty-seventh Street station, the bulls and bears continued their gold war on two fronts. In the Gold Room, Ring brokers under Henry Smith and William Belden bought heavily and loaned out gold while banker-brokers Henry Clews and Harris Fahnestock and the export-import merchants sold, sold, sold. So far, the damage was contained. Despite massive trading in phantom "short" and "long" interests by speculators, gold coin still flowed freely. Merchants had no trouble buying or borrowing specie for their businesses.

Even the U.S. government could barely sell the $1 million in gold that Butterfield had put up that day under his regular biweekly schedule. Bidders asked for only $500,000 worth; the rest wasn't sold until Thursday. "The Bankers and Importers are not particularly exercised by the forced advance" in gold prices, reported the *Times*.

Jay Gould, after all, had planned it that way. He would keep loaning his gold back to the market to create a false sense of security, then snap the whip at the right moment.

The real struggle now switched to political backrooms. Both sides knew that the U.S. government could decide the Gold Room contest on its own. Boutwell might have preferred to stay neutral, but that option had long ago disappeared. By intervening to sell gold, he would back the bears. By staying on the sidelines, he would back Jay Gould's bulls. After hoarding gold in the SubTreasury for almost ten years, Washington was the biggest factor in Wall Street's calculus. Bears and bulls alike wanted Uncle Sam in their clique.

The stakes in the Gold Room struggle involved more than local Wall Street speculators. The "public interest" as a concept barely existed in 1869. William H. Vanderbilt, the Commodore's son, would not utter his famous "The public be damned" remark until 1882, during a railroad rate war. Politicians did recognize, though, the danger of playing favorites among competing business interests: bankers versus railroaders, importers versus exporters, bears versus bulls.

Boutwell knew that scarce gold could cripple the U.S. export-import trade, Jay Gould's crop theory aside. Without gold, foreign trade could dry up, causing farm prices to collapse and the prices of imported goods to skyrocket. A steep gold price hike would mean a sharp devaluation of every greenback dollar held in every American pocket or bank account. What was more, the spectacle of gold gamblers manipulating the national currency could destroy confidence in U.S. finance. Foreign creditors would see the United States as a sick joke, a "banana republic." Selling U.S. bonds overseas would become impossible.

Even worse for Boutwell, his hands were tied. Horace Greeley might want him to "investigate" Gold Room conspiracies, but legally the secretary had no police power. He had no right to issue subpoenas, take testimony from witnesses, or seize a broker's books and records.

Politically, Ulysses Grant had taken away his strongest market-moving tool by opposing any more gold sales in September.

Since leaving Corbin's house on Monday afternoon, President Grant's traveling band had passed through Altoona and Pittsburgh, the "City of Soot," where Grant had spent the day visiting a German-American picnic and hobnobbing with local politicos. Hours before Boutwell's train pulled into New York on Wednesday afternoon, Grant had bid farewell to Pittsburgh and retired with his family and General Porter to visit a cousin of Julia's near Washington, Pennsylvania, an outpost thirty miles from Pittsburgh and reachable only by horse-drawn carriage through rugged mountain terrain. The town had no rail or telegraph connections.

For almost a week, the President would be virtually *incommunicado*.

Alone at dinner that night at the sumptuous Astor House, Daniel Butterfield finally met Boutwell personally. He gave him the sealed letter that Grant had written at Abel Corbin's house two days earlier.

Butterfield must have been impressed by his bureaucratic superior. For all his faults, Boutwell carried himself with distinction. A *Sun* reporter described the fifty-year-old secretary that week as "wiry and muscular, with a stoop in his broad shoulders. His height is five feet eight inches; his features bold, cheek bones high, cheeks hollow, and his complexion is well tanned by the sun. His beard and straight hair are dark, and are becoming grizzly."

Boutwell took the letter from Butterfield and doubtless opened it right away, reading the President's message by candlelight as his deputy looked on:

New York City, September 12, 1869

Honorable George S. Boutwell, Secretary of the Treasury

Dear Sir: I leave here tomorrow morning for Western Pennsylvania and will not reach Washington before the middle or last of next week. Had I known before making my arrangements for starting that you would be in this city early this week, I would have remained to meet you. I am satisfied that on your arrival you will be met by the bulls and bears of Wall street, and probably by merchants too, to induce you to sell gold, or pay the November interest in advance, on the one side, and to hold fast on the other. The fact is, a desperate struggle is now taking place, and each party want the government to help them out. I write this letter to advise you of what I think you may expect, to put you on your guard.

I think, from the lights before me, I would move on, without change, until the present struggle is over.

If you want to write me this week, my address will be Washington, Pennsylvania.

I would like to hear your experience with the factions at all events, if they give you time to write. No doubt you will have a better chance to judge than I, for I have avoided general discussion of the subject.

Yours truly,
U.S. Grant

The President's point came across crystal clear: The gold impasse had become a brawl. Grant wanted no change. Do not sell gold—at least, not yet.

As Boutwell digested his marching orders, Daniel Butterfield gave his own firsthand report on the Gold Room battle. Without revealing his private interests, Daniel painted a frank picture of three groups at war over gold: bulls betting for a price rise; bears betting for a price collapse and selling short;

and innocent businessmen stuck in the middle. Leading the bulls was "one party of railroad men," Butterfield said.

It takes little to imagine the names Gould, Fisk, and perhaps Corbin passing his lips in hushed tones, spilling whatever truth he actually knew.

Boutwell knew the reputations of the Erie Railway moguls but little else. For the time being, Butterfield advised the secretary to keep his mouth shut and his ears open, to listen to all sides. Daniel offered to arrange a meeting of bank presidents the next day for Boutwell to hear their squeals with his own ears. Boutwell agreed.

The hard sell started early Thursday morning. Boutwell woke up to find not only long articles in the *Herald* and the *World* on his visit but also reporters from at least five dailies—the *Herald*, the *World*, the *Tribune*, the *Times*, and the *Sun*—camped outside his hotel room waiting to dog him every step of his day in New York.

The raging Gold Room contest had made George Boutwell's visit into a media circus on this bright autumn Thursday. With so much local money tied up in speculation, many New Yorkers enjoyed Wall Street theatrics as a sporting event, much like the horse track or the baseball park.

Newspapers openly took sides. The *World* that morning blasted Gold Room bears, the "Loyal League" Republican bankers. "Why even a 'trooly loil' gold-gambler should expect the government to assist him in making money ... in his gold-gambling operations" by forcing the Treasury to dump gold on the bulls "is a question which the heavily taxed, hard working, non-gambling people may well ask," it said.

The *Herald* warned Boutwell to "hold himself aloof" from Wall Street speculators, but it also leaned against the bears. "The only people who want gold cheap at this season are the few merchants who have borrowed gold [gone short]," the *Herald* said. "Those who wish to see gold higher are the great body of produce and cotton merchants [who] desire to market their goods in Europe for the greatest sum of greenbacks possible."

Even the city's most widely read newspaper, the *New York Herald*, now openly preached Jay Gould's crop theory.

New York money men flocked to George Boutwell's hotel suite early that morning, scrounging for a few words with him out of earshot from the media. Horace Greeley dropped by for breakfast and repeated his warnings against a Gold Room bull clique. He brought along George Opdyke, a politically active banker and former New York mayor.

Greeley and Opdyke wasted no time before warning Boutwell of the latest treason. Opdyke could only guess who constituted the clique that was terrorizing the gold market, but he smelled Tweed a mile away. The so-called crop theory to justify high prices was rubbish, Opdyke argued. Any rise in gold caused by "artificial means" would soon break down. Middlemen would buy overpriced grain and other products; when "the thing collapsed," he said, "the grain would be left on their hands, and would produce bankruptcy."

George Boutwell may have sympathized, but he followed Daniel Butterfield's advice and kept a poker face.

Also among the influence-seekers fluttering around Boutwell's suite that morning was Abel Corbin. Whether Corbin came as an agent of his brother-in-law or of his gold mentor is anyone's guess. But Boutwell felt no compulsion to humor presidential relatives. Having never met Corbin, Boutwell happily let him get lost in the shuffle. Testifying months later, Boutwell pleaded ignorance of seeing Corbin that morning at all. He could only reconstruct Corbin's visit from notes.

"He probably did not stay long," Boutwell said. "[A]t the time it did not occur to me that he was Mr. Corbin. After I saw his card it did occur to me that he was the President's brother-in-law."

From the Astor House, Boutwell's carriage led a parade downtown to the New York Customs House on Wall Street, followed by press onlookers. Setting up shop in Port Collector Moses Grinnell's office, Boutwell spent the afternoon hearing a dreary parade of businessmen asking special favors from the government and delegations of steel importers, sugar importers, ship owners, et al. On every question of government policy, he kept his lips buttoned.

With the steel men, Boutwell barely hid his condescension. As the meeting started, the steel group spokesman stepped forward and "flourished before [Boutwell's] eyes a gigantic blue envelope, containing a huge statement of grievances," reported the *Sun*. "At this the Secretary qualified, and said that he had no time to receive an address, but would beg the gentleman to come to the point."

As if on cue, a messenger from Butterfield at the SubTreasury interrupted him with news that the secretary's meeting with the bankers was ready to start. Boutwell jumped at the chance to leave. Cutting off the steel representative in midsentence, he curtly promised to return immediately and dashed off.

Unfortunately for the "trooly loil types," the twenty-odd bank presidents crowded into Butterfield's office that morning could hardly bare their souls to the Treasury secretary about gold. Newspaper reporters were jotting down every syllable for publication. Henry Clews, Opdyke, Vermilye, Harris Fahnestock, and the others settled for engaging Boutwell in talk "wholly of an informal nature," limiting the subject to the recent scarcity of small-denomination bills in New York banks.

Afterward, though, Clews pulled Boutwell aside into his own office at 32 Wall Street, a door down from the SubTreasury, for a private earful on gold.

The coup de grace came at dinner. Thirty-odd New York bluebloods invited Boutwell for a strictly private get-together at the arch-aristocratic Union League Club on Madison Avenue.

Besides Daniel Butterfield, the guest list included party stalwarts like Greeley, *Times* editor John Bigelow, A. T. Stewart, William Vermilye, lawyer Edwards Pierrepont, and merchant A. A. Lowe, president of the New York Chamber of Commerce. Moses Grinnell presided at the head of a long table, with Boutwell at his left.

No reporters were allowed, though the *Sun* and the *Times* seemed to have ears at the keyhole.

As black waiters cleared the plates, the men talked politics and money. "[W]hen cigars were introduced," the *Sun* reported, "a number of gentlemen took chairs near Mr. Boutwell and held short conversations on the working of sundry revenue laws." The room grew hazy with wine and cigar smoke.

Grinnell stood up and introduced Boutwell. Boutwell, a polished speaker, gave a short, crisp oration that only touched lightly on finance. Boutwell sounded his favorite themes: the need for Uncle Sam to pay the national debt "in gold," and the need for the states to ratify the Fifteenth Amendment to the Constitution guaranteeing freed Negro slaves the right to vote.

The bland setting of woozy aristocrats made Boutwell's mild soliloquy adequate. After a full day of having his arm twisted by New York's financial heavyweights, though, Boutwell had more to get off his chest. Ever since he had taken office in March, Boutwell told the group, he had consistently denied "giving anyone opportunities of making money out of the government's operations." This policy included unpopular steps, such as eliminating Jay Cooke & Company's favored position as Uncle Sam's broker. Private enrichment "could not always be prevented," Boutwell said, "but at least it should never occur through the aid or connivance of his department," despite the fact that "bad men would sometimes get into office."

Boutwell's not-so-subtle barb threw the dinner into a frenzy.

Nobody had planned on speech-making, but one banker, probably S. B. Chittenden, took the floor and "shocked some of the gentlemen present," according to A. A. Lowe, by saying that "the country was in a high condition of prosperity, and that the true policy was to drift along"—a not-so-subtle hint for Boutwell to keep his nose out of gold.

Lowe stood up and launched into excited oratory on the need to keep gold prices cheap, but he ended up criticizing Washington's "policy of holding seven-tenths of all the gold in the country" locked away in its vaults. For good measure, he also blasted the newspapers: "the financial columns of our press ... appeared to be, very largely in the hands of speculators."

Other men rose in response, mostly taking Lowe's viewpoint. The air grew thick and noisy. Horace Greeley mumbled something about lower interest rates.

A. T. Stewart rose to give his opinion. It was a poignant moment. New Yorkers had rallied around the aging "Merchant Prince" when radical Republicans in Washington torpedoed his nomination for Treasury secretary last March. Stewart barely hid his resentment. Boutwell later explained that Stewart "gradually took on a dislike to me" after his own nomination to the Treasury post.

The details of A. T. Stewart's Union League speech are lost. A. A. Lowe recalled Stewart talking "in favor of hard money." But Boutwell, rightly or wrongly, felt a dagger twisting in his back with each word from Stewart's lips. In his memoirs, he said only that Stewart "made a speech in which he criticized my administration of the Treasury."

If the Union League crowd had planned to show Boutwell a united front on gold, they failed miserably. Jim Fisk later described the scene as "one of those self-admiration dinners. They told Boutwell that he was the greatest financier on the face of the earth, and if he would only tell them what he was going to do [on gold], they would fish a big thing out of the sea." For all they tried, though, be it in private conversations, public toasts, or backroom harangues, they got not a peep out of Grant's Treasury secretary.

By the time Boutwell left for Washington on Friday morning, he had seen more than seventy leading New York financiers. His antennae had been finely tuned to the Gold Room tug-of-war. Later, after the explosion, Boutwell could never say that they hadn't warned him.

Whatever thoughts he had, Boutwell kept to himself. Ulysses Grant had made a decision to stand aside in the struggle and keep the Treasury's gold shut tight. And Grant himself was almost unreachable in isolated Washington, Pennsylvania, holding a tight leash.

· 17 ·

RESISTANCE

I N ALL THE ACCOUNTS of George Boutwell's New York tour that week, one
name never appeared: James Brown. Brown kept to himself during most
of September 1869. His family had set sail for Liverpool, England, in June,
and he planned to join them later in the month if business allowed. Meanwhile, he lived quietly at their summer house in New Utrecht, Long Island—
now a part of Brooklyn—commuting to Wall Street by ferry every morning
and night. He busied himself with civic meetings.

But first and foremost, James kept his eye to his first love, Wall Street.
After visiting the Gold Room to see the much-ballyhooed bull clique in action, James, like most bankers, felt relieved over the chances of a panic. On
James's orders, Brown Brothers lowered its rate for buying foreign exchange
on Thursday, a reaction to weakening gold prices. The lull hardly lasted the
day, though; fresh waves of buying rocked the Gold Room on Thursday and
Friday.

James knew about the other powerful pieces on the chessboard. Jay Cooke
& Company, the biggest of the bear bankers, had borrowed $350,000 from
Brown Brothers that week. Harris Fahnestock was planning his own secret operation to exploit George Boutwell's policy of paying off the national debt, a
joint scheme with bankers Fisk & Hatch to gobble up government bonds and
make them scarce.

Fahnestock, a dapper man with spectacles and sharp eyes, had served as
Jay Cooke's chief financial lieutenant since joining the firm's Washington
branch in 1862 after starting his career as a banker in Harrisburg, Pennsylvania. "Fisk [& Hatch] is going in for a bull movement and proposes concert
of action," Fahnestock wrote to Jay Cooke in Philadelphia in a letter dated
September 17. "He is buying whatever he can get his hands on and I hope

that by next Wednesday when $3 million [in bonds] will be bought [by the U.S. Treasury] that we shall have good prices and good feeling."

During Boutwell's visit to the city, while other bankers peppered the secretary with questions about gold, Fahnestock kept his eye on his own target. "I had a brief talk with Boutwell yesterday," he reported. "He is committed unequivocally to the bond purchasing policy."

Only one thing could ruin Fahnestock's plan: a successful gold corner.

Rising gold prices would send bonds plummeting. James Brown, in the middle of these complex deals, saw Jay Cooke & Company, the country's most influential financial house, traveling on a collision course with the Gold Ring.

· 18 ·

MESSAGES

NOBODY HAD INVITED JIM FISK, Jay Gould, or Abel Corbin to the Union League dinner for Treasury Secretary Boutwell. All day long they had heard about Boutwell's comings and goings around New York, about his private chats with Republican pals Horace Greeley, George Opdyke, and Henry Clews, and all the Gold Room bears. Everyone on Wall Street had seen the lanky Treasury secretary hiking between the Customs House and the SubTreasury, surrounded by obsequious "loyal league" bankers.

Out of all the gold bulls, only Jay Gould kept his calm during the bears' obvious schmoozing of the Treasury secretary. Jim Fisk had buzzed like a bee all week since he started pouring money into the gold operation. He worried constantly about whether Abel Corbin could keep the President in line. Jim visited Corbin's house almost daily, he said; Jay visited every morning and night.

Still, Jim never felt he was getting a straight answer from the old politico. "I found after I left Corbin's office that I felt very like getting back there again," he later joked. But "old Hamlet Corbin" always gave Jim the same message: relax, don't worry, it's all right.

Jim asked Jay Gould about the Boutwell visit back at the Opera House. Not to worry, Jay told him; whatever Boutwell was up to, Jay had Daniel Butterfield shadowing the Treasury Secretary every step of the way. "If Butterfield gives any information, we will get it in time to get out" of the market.

After calming Jim, Jay took his nightly carriage ride across town to Abel Corbin's house. Unfortunately for Jay's dyspepsia, he found Corbin alarmed. Saying hardly a word, Corbin ushered Jay upstairs to the library. Jay found it strange that the lanky man, who was always so dignified, was now fidgety.

Corbin talked quickly when he was nervous. He told Jay about his dismal meeting with George Boutwell that morning at the Astor House. The secretary had barely given him the time of day. And now all these meetings with bears …

Jay tried to soothe the old man. They had no reason to panic, he said. Hadn't Grant assured them days earlier that he opposed government gold sales?

Maybe so, Corbin said, but what about Boutwell?

The more Corbin spoke, the more it bothered Jay that other people—his enemies—were monopolizing the Treasury secretary's ear. Who knew what might happen at the Union League dinner, with all the schmoozing by Republican bankers?

Corbin raised the worst possibility. What if Boutwell, taken in by the "trooly loil" crowd, decided to sell gold without Grant's permission? Could the Treasury secretary do that? Could Boutwell convince Grant to back him after the fact? Would Butterfield, their erstwhile ally, betray them if the pressure got heavy?

The idea made Jay furious. His pale cheeks flushed; his eyes glared. "I have made an honest effort to maintain the price of gold," Jay said. They must not let Boutwell and the bankers destroy the effort. Corbin must write a letter to President Grant immediately, that very night, Jay said, before Boutwell's crowd had time to act. They must make sure that Grant was onboard.

As Jay looked on, Corbin sat at his cluttered desk and started to write. His aged hand moved swiftly across the page, scratching out small, neat letters in heavy ink. Jay stood at Corbin's shoulder, reading the words as they appeared. The letter ran "page after page," Jay later recalled, intermingling arguments about the gold market with bits of family news and political gossip.

To make certain that Boutwell did not reach the President first, Jay offered to have the letter delivered directly to Ulysses Grant in Washington, Pennsylvania, by an Erie company messenger.

At about eight o'clock that night, as the Union League revelers were breaking out cigars and launching into clouds of confused speech-making, Jay Gould rode his carriage back along darkened city streets toward the Opera House, watching the flickering shadows cast by gas lamps along the way. He found Jim Fisk working in his office. Without wasting a minute, he called the troops to action.

"Who is the most confidential man you have got?" Jay asked his partner.

"It all depends upon what the mission is," Jim said.

"I want a man who is a quick traveler; says nothing, but passes right along," Jay said. "I want him to take a letter tonight from Mr. Corbin to General Grant."

Jim though only a minute. He prided himself in knowing every clerk and workman on the Erie line. How about Billing Chapin? he said.

William O. Chapin had worked as an Erie Railway "clerk" for almost a year. Long before telephones, modems, or Telex machines, private messengers enjoyed special status. They carried intimate, vital information between important people. Working around Wall Street, Chapin wore a sharp looking, vaguely military uniform with polished buttons and shiny leather boots. That night, as Chapin sat home reading a book, a man knocked on his door. He gave Chapin a message that "they wanted me at the office."

Chapin knew the drill. "I put on my boots and went down there," he said. Reaching the Opera House by special carriage, a guard took him to the company president's office. There, he found Fisk and Gould looking over maps and railroad schedules. Billy Chapin knew it was going to be a long night.

Jay Gould told Chapin his mission. The young courier was to go to Abel Corbin's house, pick up a parcel, and deliver it to the President of the United States in Washington, Pennsylvania, as quickly as possible.

Washington, Pennsylvania? Where was that? Chapin asked.

They showed him a map. It was near Pittsburgh. The first westbound train left New York at nine the next morning.

Jim Fisk added another point. After delivering the letter, Chapin should "See what [Grant] says. Go from there to the first telegraph station, and telegraph me what the reply is; that is, if you can do it without communicating any secrets."

They gave Chapin a room that night at the Fifth Avenue Hotel. Jim assigned his brother-in-law, George Hooker, to chaperone Chapin. "I was afraid [Chapin] would sleep too long, and I said to my brother-in-law, 'Go to Mr. Chapin and see him aboard the train,' " Jim later explained.

The next morning, Chapin, dressed in his sharpest Wall Street getup for meeting the President, rode with Hooker to Corbin's house on West Twenty-seventh Street, and rang the bell at about half past seven. A servant showed them into the vestibule.

After a few minutes, Corbin "appeared at the top of the stairs in his night-gown," Chapin recalled, and "gave the servant two letters to hand to me." One letter was addressed to General Horace Porter, the other, to Grant. Corbin told Chapin to hand Grant's letter directly to the President. "If the President was busy or engaged, [Chapin was] to use [Corbin's] name; that would be sure to give me access to him," he later said.

The trip from New York took Chapin more than twenty-four hours of nonstop travel. The train ride from Jersey City to Pittsburgh alone lasted six-teen hours, with stops at a dozen towns. Reaching Pittsburgh at 1:00 a.m., Chapin found everyone asleep. To wait till sunrise was out of the question. Chapin located the nearest stable and woke up the proprietor.

After an argument, the stable owner let Chapin hire out two horses and a driver. All night long, Chapin and his driver made their way through the treacherous mountain passes south of Pittsburgh. They lost the trail several times in the predawn darkness. Finally, at about nine in the morning, Chapin reached the small town of Washington and found the house where President Grant was supposed to be staying. It was the wrong address. Hiring fresh horses from the local livery, Chapin set out again for "Mr. Smith's house, some way out of town."

Finally, he knocked on the right door. Mrs. Smith, Julia Grant's cousin, showed poor, tired Billy Chapin to a sofa in the parlor of her large country home.

Out in the yard, President Grant was playing croquet with General Porter. Bill Chapin barely had time to catch his breath and brush the dust off his uniform before Porter came inside to greet him. Relieved to deliver his parcel finally, Chapin gave Porter the skinnier letter, addressed to the Presi-dent's aide. Porter read it quickly: "The bearer has a letter, which he desires to deliver to the President. Please afford him an opportunity of doing so. A. R. Corbin."

Porter left Chapin alone in the parlor and went to find President Grant. The President soon appeared and asked the messenger his business. Chapin handed him the thicker letter from Abel Corbin.

Ulysses Grant looked relaxed after two days in the country air, far from the headaches of running a country. He took the envelope, walked over to a window, opened the seal, and leaned on the windowsill. He unfolded the pages and read them quietly.

A servant came, and the President disappeared for about fifteen minutes.

"I think someone said Mrs. Grant wanted to see him," Chapin recalled, though Grant may simply have gone to sit on the porch while reading his brother-in-law's missive.

As Chapin waited on the parlor sofa, he made small talk with Porter. They chatted about the weather. Porter asked about Abel Corbin's health. Warming to each other, Chapin told Grant's aide about his adventures rushing from New York City—the long train ride, the overnight carriage drive through winding country roads.

Grant reappeared, the letter in his hand, walked over to the window, and stood silently for a minute.

Porter and Chapin eyed the President closely, expecting an utterance. "[Grant] seemed to wait so long," Chapin remembered. "I said to him, 'is it all satisfactory?' or something like that," he explained. "[Grant] says, 'yes.' I asked him if there was any reply. He says, 'no, nothing,' and he wished me a good morning."

The job done, Billy Chapin and his driver excused themselves and rode all Saturday through the same hilly byways back to Pittsburgh. They found the nearest telegraph office. Chapin went inside and sent a wire to Fisk and Gould in New York: "Letter delivered all right."

◎ ◎ ◎ ◎ ◎

As Chapin climbed into his buggy and rode off, a subtle alarm sounded in Horace Porter's mind. Something bothered Porter about the messenger, the fact that he had traveled all night from Pittsburgh in a madcap rush from New York. "Who is that man?" Porter asked Ulysses Grant.

"I do not know; why?" said the President.

"I merely asked on account of the peculiarity of the letter of introduction which he brought to me; his name is not mentioned in it," Porter said.

"Letter of introduction from whom?" asked the President. "From Mr. Corbin, of New York," Porter said.

"Is that messenger from New York?" Grant asked.

"He appears to be," Porter said.

The President sat silently. He had assumed Chapin was a local post office clerk, what with his uniform, the polished buttons, and shiny boots.

Porter's suspicions had already been raised that week by a note he had received a few days earlier from Jay Gould. The note, dated September 13, had been sealed in an envelope with markings from Smith, Gould, Martin &

Company. "Purchased to-day $500,000 of gold," it said, "which will be placed to the credit of General Porter."

Irritated and insulted at the continuing bribe offers, Porter had put pen to paper and written Gould a terse rejection. "I have never authorized any-one to buy gold for me, and I requested that no such purchase should be made on my account," it said. "I am an officer of the government, and cannot enter into any speculation whatever."

Ulysses Grant now asked pointed questions about Corbin, Jay Gould, and the whole gold business. "The letter would have been like hundreds of other letters received by the President, if it had not been for the fact that it was sent by a special messenger from New York to Washington, Pennsylvania, the messenger having to take a carriage and ride some twenty-eight miles from Pittsburgh," Porter later explained.

What had Corbin found so urgent? Grant wondered. Hadn't he already given Corbin and Jay Gould enough assurances about his gold policy? Grant had heard allusions all week to a clique of speculators running up prices in the Gold Room. Jay Gould's name always came up in this connection. If Gould were involved, could Corbin be far behind? And what about Jennie?

Ulysses Grant, as if waking up from a long sleep, put the pieces together. He walked back to the Smiths' house with Porter and summoned Julia to join them to talk about the letter from Abel Corbin.

The meaning was plain enough to Ulysses. Corbin had lied to him—he was a Gold Room bull. Grant had no direct proof; the major newspapers had all stopped short of naming names of the Gold Room "combination." The tabloids may have mentioned Corbin, but they were notoriously unreli-able.

Horace Porter blew the whistle by telling the President about Jay Gould's bribe offer. That was damning evidence, but not conclusive.

Perhaps one of the New York "loyal league" bears like George Opdyke or Jay Cooke or some other speculator had sent a private messenger to Grant that weekend connecting Corbin to the affair. In any event, if Grant's suspi-cions were true, it meant the blackest possible scandal. His enemies would waste no time claiming that the President had dabbled personally in the spec-ulation.

Ulysses must have looked back misty-eyed at his days as General of the Army, when life was simpler. He had given orders, and people had obeyed. But as President he had less power. Congress blocked his appointments and laughed at his political bungling. Wall Street connived behind his back. His own family undercut him.

Horace Porter saw first hand how Ulysses Grant recoiled from this treatment. Grant had had little to gain by running for President in 1868. As a national hero after the war, he enjoyed every luxury; people had loved him, admired him, kept him well-heeled. Julia remembered fondly the days before the White House. "Those four years [1865 through 1869] are to me a pleasant memory of dinners, balls, and receptions, of pleasant people who said kind things, and some pleasant visits away from Washington," she wrote.

The Presidency so far had been a continuation of that endless party for Julia. Until now. Someone had spoiled her parade.

Ulysses bristled with self-criticism. "I always felt great respect for Corbin and thought he took much pleasure in the supposition that he was rendering great assistance to the administration by his valuable advice," he told the others that weekend. "I blame myself now for not checking this (as I thought) innocent vanity. It is very sad. I fear he may be ruined—and my poor sister."

The "council of three," as Porter called it, agreed on a plan. Julia would write a letter to Jennie Corbin containing a special warning. As Porter recalled, Grant "suggested" that Julia tell Jennie in the letter "rumors had reached her that Mr. Corbin was connected with speculators in New York, and that she hoped that if this was so, he would disengage himself from them at once; that he (the President) was very much distressed at such rumors."

Julia's memory matched Porter's. She remembered writing this: "The General says, if you have any influence with your husband, tell him to have nothing whatever to do with [the New York gold speculators]. If he does, he will be ruined, for come what may, he (your brother) will do his duty to the country and the trusts in his keeping."

Julia wrote the sensitive document in pencil. She signed the letter "Sis." In case Corbin decided not to destroy it, she did not want the signature "Julia Grant," let alone the President's name, anywhere in sight.

At first, Grant may even have suspected Julia of being part of the conspiracy, along with Corbin and Jennie. Julia later claimed that Ulysses barged into her room that morning and started asking blunt questions.

"I sat in the library writing letters. General Grant entered and asked: 'Whom are you writing to?' I answered 'Your sister.' He said: 'Write this,' " and then he "dictated" the famous letter. Julia probably understated her own role;

she was not the type of politician's wife to sit by and take dictation without asking questions.

Whatever the exact wording, the letter's message was clear. Jennie must tell her husband to get out of whatever Gold Ring he had gotten into. The President's earlier promises to protect the New York bulls no longer held.

The warning was meant for only two people—Abel Corbin and Jennie—not for Jay Gould, not Jim Fisk, not anyone else. Ulysses gave his brother-in-law the signal for one reason only: to save Jennie from financial disaster and his family from scandal. Hopefully the world would never know that the President's flesh and blood had tried to trick the White House into helping a Wall Street gambling ring.

After Julia had finished writing the letter, she sealed it and mailed it to New York. By the usual post office schedule, the time bomb would reach the Corbin residence on West Twenty-seventh Street on Wednesday, September 22.

For now, they passed the time safely secluded in tiny Washington, Pennsylvania, far from the political swirl. "We may not leave here till Wednesday," Porter wrote to his wife that September afternoon. "It is as stupid as can be. They dread getting back to Washington though."

Jay Gould, mastermind
of the Gold Ring.
(Library of Congress)

James Fisk, Jr.,
self-styled "admiral"
of the Narragansett
Steamship Company.
Note the finely waxed
moustache and the
diamond pin on
his chest.

New York Historical Society

James Fisk, Jr., as Colonel of the Ninth Regiment, NYS militia.

Helen Josephene "Josie" Mansfield, the Gold Ring's *femme fatale*.

New York Historical Society

Commodore Cornelius Vanderbilt, king of Wall Street until bested by Fisk and Gould.

Library of Congress

President Ulysses Grant, photographed by Mathew Brady. The Civil War battlefield hero had less success with the subtleties of politics.

William Magear Tweed,
Boss of Tammany Hall,
twisted the wheels of justice
in favor of Fisk and Gould.

New York Historical Society

George S. Boutwell, Grant's
Secretary of the Treasury,
had little symphany for either
bears or bulls in the New York
gold battle.

Library of Congress

Daniel Butterfield, Boutwell's
New York deputy, understood
that it paid to help the Gold Ring.
Here as a young Civil War hero.

Horace Porter, the only
"Grant man" to turn down
a bribe offer from Jay Gould.

Horace Greeley and George Opdyke (*see next page*)
pressed Boutwell to investigate the Gold Ring conspiracy.

George Opdyke

Jay Cooke, America's foremost financier, pressed Washington to break the Black Friday corner.

Cartoon of Jay Gould explaining his gold corner scheme to captivated Jim Fisk and William Belden. Artist should have included Jay's broker Henry N. Smith in the picture.

PLOTTING THE GREAT GOLD RING OF '69.

Below: Cartoon of organ-grinder
Jay Gould with his "monkey,"
presumably broker Henry N. Smith.

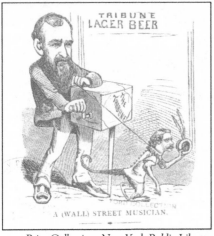

Above: Thomas G. Shearman,
the Gold Ring's legal eagle.

Newspaper depiction of Jim Fisk sipping wine with his supposed
good friend President Grant some time before the gold panic.

"Gold at 160. Gold at 130."
A *Harper's Weekly* cartoon
published shortly after Black
Friday, showed the devil's role
in Wall Street speculation.

Library of Congress

Drawing of the Gold Room at the height of the Black Friday panic from *Frank Leslie's Illustrated Newspaper*.

"The Bull and Bear Fight," a *Frank Leslie's Illustrated Newspaper* cartoon, portrayed Jim Fisk's demise at the hands of the Gold Room bears.

James Brown, leader of the bears on Black Friday.

"Scene in the Gold Exchange Bank," a *Frank Leslie's* depiction of the
chaotic scene as the gold clearinghouse falls captive to the Gold Ring
through Judge Cardozo's injunction.

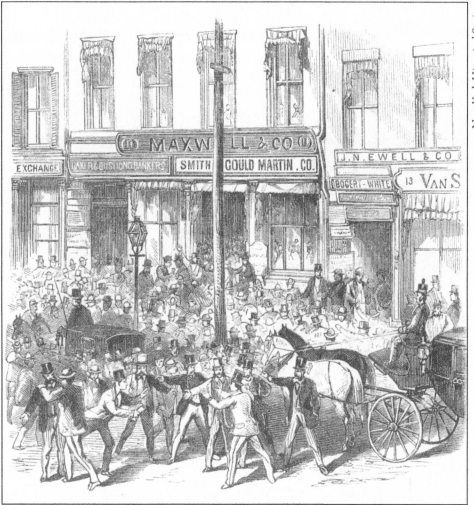

A mob of angry brokers congregates in front of Smith, Gould,
Martin & Company shortly after the Black Friday crash,
as appeared on the front page of *Frank Leslie's*.

Mug shots of Gould and Fisk from the front page
of *Frank Leslie's* shortly after Black Friday.

PART VI

Bulls

· 19 ·
SNEAK ATTACK

I N CASE ANYBODY STILL DIDN'T KNOW IT, the *Sun* announced on Monday morning, September 20, that evil people were trying to corner the gold market. "An alliance of the most powerful and influential firms in Wall Street, including notorious Erie speculators, has been effected with a view of obtaining the exclusive possession of all the gold in the market," the paper said, linking Jay Gould and Jim Fisk publicly to the operation for the first time.

After all the political foreplay and arcane maneuvering, the spotlight now shifted to the ornate chamber between Broad and New Streets in New York City, where brokers traded the "currency of the world."

With Jim Fisk now an equal partner, the operation's color changed overnight from soft pastels to bold scarlet. Jim had little patience for Jay Gould's subtlety. The man who turned the Albany-Susquehanna takeover contest into a midnight brawl at the Harpersville tunnel a month earlier now wanted to make the Gold Room strategy a blunt assault. "Boldness! boldness! twice, thrice, and four times," William Fowler wrote of Jim's approach. "Impudence, cheek! brass! unparalleled, unapproachable. He demoralized and corrupted society."

Jay Gould gave orders on the gold operation, but no one could hold back his dandified partner once his adrenalin got flowing.

Starting Friday, September 18, Jim Fisk opened full throttle on the gold assault. He, Jay, and Belden had dozens of brokers buying gold on the Gold Room floor. To heighten the stampede effect, they spread rumors that Washington was backing the operation. Over the weekend, Jim's agents told the *Herald* about "an intimation given them that Secretary Boutwell will take no part for or against the speculation in gold."

Boutwell had not even seen Fisk or Gould during his New York trip and had barely recognized Corbin, let alone signaled them any "intimation."

Jay opened a special account at Smith, Gould, Martin & Company called the National Gold Account to feed the illusion of government complicity.

On Monday and Tuesday, September 20 and 21, Ring brokers in the Gold Room raised a loud chorus from all around the trading floor: "Buy," "Buy," "Buy." James Ellis of Heath & Company, Henry Enos, and brokers Russell Hills, E. K. Willard, Charles Quincy, and Samuel Boocock all bought huge sums. Only Jay Gould knew the total. He kept no written records, but even conservative guesses started to look gargantuan.

Fueling the flames, on Saturday Jim received the wire from his courier Billy Chapin that he had delivered Abel Corbin's latest salvo to Grant. "Letter delivered all right" Chapin had said—on its face a simple affirmation that he had put the letter in the President's hands.

Somehow, a telegraph operator between Pittsburgh and New York had placed a punctuation mark in the message. The note handed to Jim read: "Letter delivered. All right." Jim took this to mean that Grant had not only received the message but had read it and answered "All right"—an "all clear" signal for the bull assault. By the time Chapin returned to New York on Sunday or Monday and corrected the error, the buying had reached a fever pitch.

Outside the Gold Room, ripples from the buying spree hit the business world like tidal waves. With a corner hanging over gold, chaos descended on the foreign exchange and produce markets. U. S. grain and cotton exporters, the very people supposed to benefit under Jay Gould's crop theory, suffered badly. The prices of cotton, flour, wheat, and corn all slipped. Exporters could no longer arrange financing for overseas shipments. Banks, anticipating a price crash, refused to loan gold for any length of time without charging prohibitive interest rates.

"[L]arge Export orders for Flour, Grain, Provisions, Petroleum, &c., are held in abeyance on account of the difficulty of negotiating Exchange," the *Times* reported. The problem would remain, it said, *"until the combination in Gold is broken down,"* either by gold imports from Europe or "by some sort of action by the Treasury" to provide bankers with "a free supply of Gold which speculation cannot lock up or control."

Any suggestion that scarce gold would help American farmers at this point sounded like a sick joke.

Meanwhile, word reached Jay Gould that his old enemy Commodore

Vanderbilt had interfered in his new alliance with the Lake Shore Railroad, Jay's long-sought link to Chicago. Vanderbilt, learning that his fair-weather ally LeGrand Lockwood had reached terms with Gould, had launched an early-September stock raid that sent Lake Shore shares plummeting from $120 to $95 and left Lockwood teetering on the brink of personal bankruptcy. To make peace with Vanderbilt, Lockwood was now planning to scrap his deal with Gould.

After losing the Albany-Susquehanna War in August, Jay had no intention of letting Vanderbilt steal the Lake Shore, too. He and Jim decided to have fun at their rival's expense. They would make Vanderbilt sweat as they dazzled Wall Street with a fireworks display.

Jay and Jim launched an assault on Wall Street on Wednesday, September 22, a simultaneous two-front sneak attack worthy of Ulysses Grant's or Robert E. Lee's finest moments of Civil War generalship. Early that morning, Jay and Jim took a carriage from the Opera House down to William Belden's cramped offices on Broad Street, a stone's throw from the gold and stock trading floors. There Fisk and Gould set up their command center in the best military tradition, complete with messengers to run orders to the Stock Exchange and the Gold Room.

At the same early hour Commodore Vanderbilt boarded a train headed north to Albany for a special meeting of his New York Central directors. Vanderbilt had announced plans earlier that month to merge two key components of his New York Central system—the New York Central and Harlem River railroads—into a single corporation. Wall Street expected the Commodore to couple the link with a big stock dividend. The price of New York Central shares had soared as high as $204 in the Long Room on Monday, September 20.

The Albany directors' meeting had been called to seal the deal.

A spy assigned to shadow the Commodore rushed downtown to Broad Street to tell Fisk and Gould.

With everything in place, the leaders signaled the attack.

That morning at ten o'clock, a dense crowd of brokers thronged the Long Room for the opening calls at the Stock Exchange. When the chairman banged his gavel at about ten-thirty to start trading in New York Central, the buyers well outnumbered the sellers. Investors rushed to grab the Vanderbilt shares, expecting the Commodore's merger to be rubberstamped in Albany that day.

Taking advantage of the bullish herd, Fisk and Gould's brokers quietly sold the stock short, poising themselves to profit from a big fall.

All was calm until eleven o'clock. At that point, with Vanderbilt safely aboard his train to Albany, Jay and Jim unleashed their torrent. A dozen brokers scattered about the room started dumping large blocks of New York Central stock. At the same time, they riddled the Exchange floor with rumors of disaster in the Vanderbilt empire. The Commodore's Albany-bound train had run off the tracks killing Cornele, they said. Everyone believed it. Judge Barnard had issued a "midnight injunction" to block the Vanderbilt merger, said others. There would be no dividend on New York Central shares.

In minutes the stock fell from $198 to $177 per share. Confusion reigned.

Brokers selling New York Central for $177 stood inches across from brokers selling for $180 or more. "It is astonishing to see how easily these manufactured stories are swallowed by the men who operate" in the Stock Exchange, wrote a *World* reporter, "and how some men, who have the reputation of being sharp, lose all control over themselves."

The crash in New York Central put pressure on other Vanderbilt-owned companies. Margin accounts vanished, and banks refused to accept Vanderbilt stock as collateral for further loans, which caused more selling waves. Hudson River Railroad shares fell from $177 to $168, and Lake Shore from $95 to $91.

By lunchtime, the Gold Ring brokers had taken their profits by buying New York Central stock at cheap prices to cover their "shorts." Like an Indian tribe on the Wyoming plains, they swooped in from out of nowhere, did their damage, and vanished, leaving only scorched earth.

After decimating the New York Central, the Erie brokers—Smith, Belden, Willard, and Woodward—moved from the Stock Exchange to the Gold Room next door. That gilded chamber now became the scene of an intense bashing contest between bears and bulls as "the *screw was turned* upon the market by the Gold Ring."

Unlike earlier days, this time the bears came well prepared. A group of "loyal league" bankers had met that morning and put together their own pool to dump gold, in hopes of breaking the Fisk-Gould combination. Harris Fahnestock, Jay Cooke's man, had probably organized the group. Fahnestock had been buying U. S. bonds heavily all week along with Fisk & Hatch, another banking firm. In the chaos, bond prices sagged. "If it were not for the deadlock in Exchange forming out of the forced gold market, bonds would be

2% higher today—and foreign trade would be brisk instead of dull," Fahnestock wrote to Cooke in Philadelphia on Monday.

Nobody liked losing money, especially to a pair of upstarts like Jay Gould and Jim Fisk. Henry Clews, also alarmed, warned Boutwell in a letter that "nearly the entire supply of gold" in New York was "under speculative control."

The men who were gathered face to face around the brass railing in the center of the Gold Room floor that morning were almost exactly the same men who had just finished gouging each other at the Stock Exchange. As the chairman prepared to gavel the session open, they quivered in anticipation of a brawl. Newspaper reporters jammed the galleries.

The bears struck first. Moments before trading began, the floor came alive with rumors that banks had ordered millions of dollars in gold shipped from England. The gold would arrive any minute to break the corner.

Then came the deluge. At the opening gavel, the banker-brokers—probably Clews, Fahnestock, and George Opdyke—raised their voices in a cacophony of offers to sell gold at $137¼. They dumped altogether $8 million worth in one fell swoop. The scale was astounding. Even assuming they could borrow that much gold, the sale placed the bankers at a risk of $80,000 for each subsequent $1 rise in prices.

Tense minutes ticked by. Jay Gould and Jim Fisk, hearing the news in Belden's office blocks away, sent back orders for their brokers to buy every penny of gold the bears offered. Henry Smith, Jay's chief lieutenant, stood on the Gold Room floor telling his brokers to hold firm. Soon bull brokers met every voice screaming to sell with an offer to buy. The price held firm at $137¼ and crept upward.

The bankers opened a second barrage, throwing out another $4 million in gold for sale at $137⅝. Henry Smith's brokers again held firm. In the firefight, broker James Ellis bought $2 million worth at $137½ and another $1.1 million at 139—a total for the day of over $5 million for Gould's account and $1.5 million more for Fisk's. Henry Enos bought $1.1 million for Gould. Belden reportedly bought $8 million for himself or Fisk, mostly through a floor hack named Albert Speyers. Broker Russell Hills received orders on the Gold Room floor "to hold the market" first at $137½ and then at $140½—that is, to buy everything offered below that price. He bought $3 million.

"[T]hey were never frightened," Jay Gould said of his well-disciplined troops. "All they know is how to obey orders. They do not know any such thing as fear."

As before, the Ring brokers loaned out as much gold as possible, mostly to the same bankers who had sold them the gold earlier.

Having withstood the attack, Jay's army unleashed its own wave of market rumors. They mixed stories about Washington complicity in the Ring with reports playing on recent tensions in U.S. relations with Spain.

"The gold room, within half an hour's time, had Boutwell buying gold, vessels of war sailing down the bay, en route for Spain, and a military force ordered to the fortifications in our harbor to defend the city against an immediate attack," reported the *World*. The roomful of shrewd Yankee traders believed the hysterical talk. "Had some person just then fired a cannon at the Battery, the cry would have been sent up that hostilities had already commenced and the Spaniards were here sacking the city."

The gold price jumped in reaction to the make-believe crisis. "The 'bears' became frightened, and large numbers cowered, their fears being heightened by reports that war with Spain was imminent, as General Sickles [the U.S. Minister to Madrid and a Civil War hero] had demanded his papers," added the *Herald*.

◎ ◎ ◎ ◎ ◎

The smoke cleared. Almost every Wall Street operator outside of Jay Gould and Jim Fisk's circle that Wednesday afternoon dreaded the coming day. The Ring had shown pity on Wall Street only by lending out its gold to let business continue. The whole city knew that Gould and Fisk could turn the stand-off into a rout at their whim by holding their gold.

The *Times* predicted that the final blow would come on Thursday. The "intense feeling against the movement on the Produce Exchange, among the merchants engaged in the Export trade, and in business and banking circles" would soon compel Washington to break the corner, it said. This "fear of sudden Government sales and the strong probability of early receipts of gold from the other side [of the Atlantic]" would make the bulls climax their operation.

Nobody doubted that Fisk and Gould had money to back their threat. Jay Gould controlled the Erie Railway treasury, and he and Boss Tweed owned the Tenth National Bank. That bank had been certifying checks on dubious collateral for Ring brokers all week, including over $14 million worth each on Monday and Wednesday.

Harris Fahnestock wrote to Jay Cooke in Philadelphia that night, "We shant have any peace until this stock and gold movement is finished, and that won't likely be long. The Treas. will do something soon." Fahnestock had reason to worry. Besides failing to kill the gold bull movement, all the bonds he had bought that week dropped another point, from $119⅛ to $118¼ between Tuesday and Wednesday—down from over $120 the week before.

The message was not lost on Jay Cooke in Philadelphia. He telegraphed instructions to his brother Henry in Washington to tell Boutwell and Grant to *do something* about the Wall Street crisis.

As the bears besieged Washington for help, Jay Gould sent his own private letter to George Boutwell that day. "There is a panic in Wall street, engineered by a bear combination," Jay wrote, turning the world on its head. "They have withdrawn currency to such an extent that it is impossible to do ordinary business." Earlier that week, Jay had warned Boutwell in a separate letter that any Treasury gold sales would cause U.S. bond prices to drop to 115, "leaving the purchases made by the government in the past few months [under Boutwell's debt-repayment policy] open to criticism as showing a loss."

Gold reached a high of $141⅞ on Wednesday afternoon, September 22, and closed at $141, up from $137½ that morning. Fisk and Gould together "owned" $50 to $60 million in gold, about triple the actual public supply around New York. Wednesday's $3.50 price jump, magnified by $50 million plus in gold, generated winnings of over $1.75 million for the Ring.

Despite all this buying, Jay and Jim had moved the market a mere $6 since September 8, two weeks earlier, when the price stood at $135. "I did not want to buy so much gold," Jay later explained, "but all these fellows went in and sold short, so that in order to keep it up I had to buy or else to back down and show the white feather."

Jay had "no idea of cornering it," he said. Those darned bears had caused the problem by trying to fight back.

"If a person desires to see excitement and bedlam confusion," reported the *World*, "he can get his money's worth by being in Wall street during one of these fierce attacks of the bears upon the bulls on a panic day."

• 20 •
BAD BLOOD

WORD CAME FROM UPSTATE late Wednesday night that Cornelius Vanderbilt had heard about the bear raid against the New York Central on Wall Street and had figured his losses. According to Fuller, "the sky over Albany was blue with the Commodore's curses." Back in New York, rumors floated that Jay Gould had orchestrated the New York Central raid to "punish" Vanderbilt for interfering in Jay's deal with the Lake Shore Railroad. With Lake Shore stock falling from $95 to $91 on that day, LeGrand Lockwood's fortune teetered closer to the brink.

Wall Street gasped at the sassy maneuver. Nobody tweaked the Commodore's nose without expecting a fight. Victims of Wednesday's raid consoled themselves that "Vanderbilt would be back in town to-morrow and punish [Gould and Fisk]," the *World* reported.

James Brown fumed at the situation. All day customers had come to his office at 59 Wall Street complaining that U.S. exporting had ground to a halt. The merchants and Brown himself had borrowed vast sums of gold to finance their short Gold Room positions. Now they paid margin as the price rose from $132 in August to over $140 that day.

If Fisk and Gould collected $1.75 million in profits on Wednesday's trading, much of it came from James's and his customers' pockets.

Totally apart from the gold business, Brown Brothers also owned vast stock holdings, including more than ten thousand shares of the Pacific Mail Steamship Company, a major West Coast sea carrier. In the stock tumble following the New York Central raid, Pacific Mail stock shares fell from $75¾ to $73, a loss for Brown of almost $30,000 within hours.

That afternoon, a messenger delivered a letter to the *Times* for its Thursday morning editions. Signed "J.B.E." (James Brown, Esq. ?), the letter detailed the impact of the Gold Room affair on trade. "The lock up of gold affects negotiations for the export of Cotton and Breadstuffs, which are wanted for shipment, but orders remain unfilled because shippers can make no contracts for their Exchange or its equivalent, Gold," it said. The Treasury should immediately buy bonds for gold to relieve the congestion, argued J.B.E.

But J.B.E. 's proposal barely matched James Brown's brewing anger toward the Gold Ring. After forty-five years on Wall Street, Brown understood that civilized behavior had its limits. Greed had a proper place in business, and love of money made capitalism work. But even so, society called stealing a crime. Fisk and Gould, with all their bravado, grated against everything that James Brown considered decent.

He especially resented their arrogance. "At no time for months have the bull clique of operators felt more sure of their ground than they were [on Wednesday]," James read in the *Evening Mail*. "They were even somewhat indifferent as to whether or not Mr. Boutwell came into the market, and boasted that they could put gold up to 150 if they chose to press matters."

James harangued his business friends about the situation. "Is this thing to be perpetuated?" he asked them. "Are we to stand and be flayed by this unscrupulous party, when there is nothing in the political or commercial atmosphere to account for any rise in gold?"

For Brown, the question answered itself. Washington so far had shown itself unwilling to break the gold conspiracy. He saw how easily Fisk and Gould had defeated the bankers' Gold Room pool that morning. Tackling the bulls would take more skill, muscle, and nerve than anyone had shown so far. But somebody had to do it.

James Brown sat back and waited for events to unfold with time. Wall Street had its own version of vigilante justice. Let the bulls laugh today, he thought. When the right moment came, he would have their skins.

· 21 ·
CHANGE OF PLANS

ONG AFTER THE STOCK AND GOLD MARKETS closed for the night that Wednesday, Jay Gould came around to Abel Corbin's house. He found the old man grave and distraught. With hardly a word, Corbin let Jay in and led him upstairs to the library. Corbin's wife Jennie had received a letter from Julia Grant that morning. She had shown it to her husband, and then he and Jennie had had a terrible fight.

Now, hours later, Abel was walking about the house on cat's paws, afraid to make a sound for fear that Jennie might emerge from a back room. When they reached the library, Corbin lit a gas lamp, closed the door, and took the letter from his pocket. Corbin never put the document in Jay Gould's hands, he claimed; he only read Jay excerpts. The letter was a private note to his wife, and Jennie had not given him permission to show it to anyone, let alone Jay Gould. "We were in my library, sitting under one of the chandeliers, in front of the table, so that [Jay] might easily have looked over my shoulder and seen it; but I think him too much a gentleman to do that," Corbin recalled.

Whether Corbin actually handed Jay the sheets of paper or not, Jay had ample opportunity to look closely at the pages covered with faint penciled words. "It was in a lady's handwriting," Jay later explained. "I had never seen the handwriting before, and could not swear that it was not a forgery."

There was no mistake about the content. "The substance of it was that: She says, 'Tell your husband,' or 'tell Mr. Corbin, that my husband is very much annoyed by your speculations. You must close them as quick as you can.' That was the substance," Jay recalled.

Coming so soon after their summer of family visits, the letter had left

Abel and Jennie Corbin smarting. "I was very much excited, and my wife still more so—such rumors were so disgraceful," Corbin explained. "I never did have a more unhappy day than I had when witnessing the distress which that letter inflicted upon my wife."

While Corbin ranted, Jay sat silent. He understood Julia Grant's point instantly. Somebody had betrayed him. Now he sat on a powder keg. Ulysses Grant, the key to the gold scheme, after months of careful cultivation, had become a problem again.

Grant had ended his near-week of isolation in Washington, Pennsylvania on Tuesday morning, September 21, and had made the six-hour carriage ride to Wheeling, West Virginia. After an elegant dinner with local politicians, the Grants had left town in a special car attached to the regular overnight express train to Washington, D.C.

Boutwell had reached Washington the previous Friday after his New York adventure and had been besieged all weekend over the gold deadlock. On Sunday, Boutwell had told a lobbyist that "he expected a decline this week in the premium on gold." As for his plans, he had said nothing. "Mr. Boutwell strives hard to keep his plans concealed from the public," wrote the *World's* Washington correspondent, "but, by Sunday next, some official statement will doubtless go out, settling all doubts for another four weeks."

By Wednesday night, with Grant and Boutwell reunited in Washington, it was only a matter of time before they got together and compared notes. For all Jay and Corbin knew Grant and Boutwell might be conferring in the White House at that moment. With every Republican banker appealing for Washington to break the gold corner, Jay had no doubt what the President would do.

"The picture of [Gould and Corbin] that night ... is a remarkable one," reported congressional investigators later on. "Shut up in the library, near midnight, Corbin was bending over the table and straining with dim eyes to decipher and read the contents of a letter, written in pencil, to his wife, while the great gold gambler, looking over his shoulder, caught with his sharper vision every word.

"The envelope was examined, with its post-mark and date, and all the circumstances which lent significance to the document. ... Corbin had the advantage, for he had had time to mature a plan."

As Jay sat impassively, Corbin talked a new line about his role in the Gold Ring. "I must get out instantly—instantly!" he told Jay. Jennie was demanding it, Corbin said. To stay in the Ring would be to risk his wife's love, his standing with the President, and his reputation in the city.

Corbin had calculated the figures in advance and now confronted Jay with a dollars-and-cents proposal. Jay owed him money, Corbin said—the profits on the $1.5 million in gold that Jay had bought for him two weeks ago. With prices at $141, Corbin figured that his winnings were almost $150,000, minus the $25,000 that Jay had paid earlier.

"[Corbin] wanted me to give him a check for a hundred thousand dollars, and just take the gold off his hands," Jay explained. Corbin had written a letter to Ulysses Grant, which he planned to mail the next morning, swearing that he had no interest in the gold movement. If Jay were to buy back his gold, Corbin's letter would become conveniently accurate.

Jay listened to Corbin's proposition, stroking his beard with his nervous fingers. Jay did not like the idea at all. If he sold Corbin's gold, he would lose any leverage he had over the President's brother-in-law. Why should he give Corbin a free pass? Weren't they all in this mess together? Jay had little choice, though. Legally he could not force Corbin to keep the gold. And Corbin had been a useful ally so far; why antagonize him now?

Jay made him a counteroffer. "I told [Corbin] I did not want to do that," he later said, "but I would give him a check for a hundred thousand dollars on account; that I did not want to throw his gold on the market at that time." In other words, Jay said he would pay Corbin $100,000 to do nothing, just to stay in the Ring and wait.

Corbin scratched his head. Let me think about it overnight, he said.

Jay agreed. As Corbin showed him to the door, Jay asked one more thing. "Will you please say nothing until you see me to-morrow morning?"

Jay knocked on Corbin's door bright and early the next morning, and a servant showed him in. He saw Corbin appear at the top of the main stairway, followed closely by Jennie. As Jay waited at the door, they argued. Jennie pleaded with her husband to bail out of the market. Beyond everything else, Jennie "was angry because I had read [the letter] to Mr. Gould," violating a family trust, Corbin later explained.

Corbin left Jennie and came down to see Jay alone in the foyer. Jay repeated his offer of the night before. "Mr. Corbin, I cannot give you anything if you will go out," Jay said. "If you will remain in and take the chances of the market I will give you my check for $100,000."

Corbin later claimed that he rejected the offer, saying, "Mr. Gould, my wife says, 'No; Ulysses thinks it wrong, and that it ought to end.' " Instead, he insisted on liquidating his gold account and being paid the full $100,000 that he felt he deserved, he said.

"Mr. Gould stood there for a little while looking very thoughtful—exceedingly thoughtful," Corbin recalled. "Then he left—about 10 o'clock—and went into Wall Street."

Walking away, Jay had one more thought. He turned back to his former ally standing in the doorway and said, "If the contents of Mrs. Grant's letter is known, I am a ruined man."

Jennie destroyed the letter from Julia Grant promptly.

◎ ◎ ◎ ◎ ◎

After leaving Corbin's house, Jay rode across town to the Opera House, where Jim Fisk was waiting to join him for another day of Gold Room bashing on Wall Street. But before he met his partner, Jay needed time to think. Probably he told his carriage driver to take a slow route through the crowded city streets.

Julia Grant's letter signaled an imminent market break. Any sharp spike in prices would prompt Grant to open the Treasury's gold vaults. To avoid disaster, Jay had to sell his gold now, fast, while the price hovered over $140. If the market crashed first, his losses could be devastating.

Trying to unload $50 million-plus in gold in a panic-driven trading room could be dangerous. If the bears sensed weakness in Jay's clique, they would refuse to buy until the price scraped bottom. Jay had to sell—but quietly, secretly, like a burglar slipping out the back of a house on hearing the owner's key in the front door.

And what about Fisk?

For all his admiration of Jim Fisk's courage and loyalty, Jay recognized his partner's biggest flaw. Jim did not have a discreet bone in his body.

It wasn't that Jim couldn't keep a secret. The bears had to remain convinced that the bulls meant business, and frightened into paying exorbitant prices until Jay could sell out. If Jim were to discover that Ulysses Grant had deceived them, he might sell along with Jay, or he might buy less aggressively. In either case, the bears would smell blood, the market would crash, and he and Fisk would lose their shirts together.

It was better that one of them should survive than neither.

At all costs, Jay told himself, he must not tell Jim about Julia Grant's letter. Jim Fisk of all people would understand.

Jay, as an young high school boy in rural Roxbury, New York, had written a school paper called "Honesty is the Best Policy." Now, as an adult, he
apparently thought he knew better.

Jay's carriage pulled up in front of the Opera House on that brisk Thursday morning September 23 1869 and Jim Fisk maneuvered himself on board
for the ride downtown. They chatted about strategy as they threaded down
Broadway toward the financial district. Jay mentioned off-handedly that he
had seen Abel Corbin that morning and that Corbin had asked for $100,000.
Jay said nothing about a letter from Julia Grant, nothing about the President's
reneging, and nothing about Corbin's quitting the Ring.

By shading the facts, Jay let his partner think that Corbin needed the
money to keep his famous family happy.

Jim saw nothing strange in Corbin's request. He and Gould had been
bribing politicians for years. "Mr. Gould says to me, 'Old Corbin feels troubled and nervous about some gold; he wants a hundred thousand dollars ....
What do you think of it?'" Jim recalled.

"Said I, 'If he wants a hundred thousand dollars to feed out to parties in
interest, he had better have it.'

" 'Well,' said [Gould], 'do as you please.' "

At this point, Jim asked the carriage driver to stop at the office of Smith,
Gould, Martin & Company. There, Jim left Jay alone outside for a few minutes as he went in and executed a check for $100,000. Jim then came back
and handed the check to Jay to give to Corbin to give to ... whomever.

Unfortunately for Corbin, in the rush of events on Thursday and Friday
Jay Gould never delivered the money. The check remained in Jay's pocket the
whole time. Corbin stopped by the Opera House on both Thursday and Friday, and Jay may have stopped by Corbin's house as well. Jay did not normally forget things, especially things involving large sums of money.

At first, Jay probably just wanted to make Corbin sweat a little before
getting his pay-off. After Black Friday, to Jay Gould's mind, Abel Corbin and
his hush money could go to hell.

· 22 ·
CENTER STAGE

BEARS AND BULLS GATHERED early on Wall Street on Thursday morning, September 23. All sides smelled blood after Wednesday's session. Traders started bidding for gold two hours before the Gold Room's ten o'clock opening, meeting in cramped offices, hallways, and street corners around the Exchange. Spectators crowded the sidewalks to catch glimpses of the financial celebrities or to watch the gilded gold-price indicator on New Street.

The curiosity seekers didn't have to wait long.

At nine o'clock an elegant carriage turned at Wall onto Broad Street, carrying the two central characters of New York's latest dizzy drama. People easily recognized Jim Fisk; he was the big man with the waxed moustache and the diamond stickpin, waving to the crowd. Scrawny Jay Gould was at his side, his eyes looking out icily from behind his full black beard, his body slouched in his seat. Sitting together, Fisk and Gould gave every appearance of being two men in harmony. They talked in hushed tones traded glances, and shared a private laugh at this or that.

Jim saw nothing unusual in Jay's behavior that morning. His partner always seemed nervous before big money action. But underneath the surface the two could have been in different worlds. While Jim enjoyed the excitement of the street crowds and the coming battle, Jay sat back, weighing his dilemma.

He and Fisk had shared every confidence about their monumental gold market plan up to now, but Jay was keeping one secret locked up tight: the news of Ulysses Grant's defection.

By the time they reached Wall Street, Jay had a plan.

After making a quick stop at Smith, Gould, Martin & Company, the carriage delivered the two speculators to William Belden's office on Broad Street. There in the front room Belden was assembling his hired brokers for the day's assault, mostly men from other Wall Street firms like Albert Speyers, Samuel Boocock, and James Ellis of Heath & Company.

By now, Belden and Henry Smith commanded fifty to sixty brokers who were buying and loaning gold for the Ring. They operated separately; Belden's brokers worked only for him or Fisk, and Henry Smith's worked solely for Jay Gould. The two camps often bristled with antagonism. "There seemed to have been two separate rings in this matter: one a ring of rascals, and the other not much better," said Charles Osborne, a broker working for Smith.

"Fisk could never do business with Smith, Gould, Martin & Co.," echoed K. Willard, another Smith broker. Nobody could predict "where Fisk might be" on a deal, Willard said. "He [was] an erratic sort of genius."

For working the Gold Room floor, Belden relied increasingly on Speyers, a fiery, German-Jewish gentleman. A Gold Room old-timer, Speyers held seats on both the Gold and the Stock Exchanges and had served as a Gold Exchange officer, which gave him a veil of respectability. "Speyers was the true type of the gold-dealer class," wrote William Fowler. "A slender, wiry man, with inflammable eyes, a face criss-crossed with wrinkles, and an impulsive, dashing style in making purchases and sales, he was a supple tool in the hands of his principals."

Edmund Stedman, the Stock Exchange maven, saw Speyers as "an elderly man of small intelligence, who was well calculated to do what he was told and ask no questions."

Speyers reached Belden's office that morning at nine, shortly after Fisk and Gould. Belden took him into the back room to meet the Erie Railway moguls. After a few pleasantries, Belden took Speyers aside and asked him to start the day's extravaganza by buying $2 million worth of gold—by far his biggest single order yet.

Speyers balked at the large amount.

Up until now, neither Belden nor Henry Smith had told their brokers whom they were buying for, even though all Wall Street understood that Gould and Fisk were directing the Ring.

Brokers normally took risks executing large orders for anonymous principals. If a customer walked away from a bad trade, the broker swallowed the loss. For Henry Smith, a trusted veteran, this was no problem. Brokers assumed that he would protect them.

But Belden had a checkered reputation. Before going into the hole for $2 million in gold, Albert Speyers wanted assurance that someone solid stood behind him.

Belden told his nervous agent, "[T]he gentlemen whom you saw this morning in my back office are equally interested." He left Speyers with no doubt that Fisk and Gould were the customers. They, if anyone, had money to back their accounts.

Belden used the same line on broker Samuel Boocock, telling Boocock that Jim Fisk "intended to make his (Belden's) house the largest in Wall street," Boocock said. Despite later claims, nobody seriously thought that William Belden, the barely reputable proprietor of a one-man broker's shop, had led what the *Times* called "the most powerful clique we have had in gold since the [Civil] war." Otherwise, no competent broker on Wall Street would have carried his orders.

On reaching the Gold Room, Speyers and Boocock found the chamber transformed. A human cauldron was pressing around the circular railing by the bronze cupid fountain. Body-to-body brokers raised a deafening noise, shouting buy and sell orders across the room, waving their hands and fists in the air. Beyond the immediate bull and bear cliques, scores of eager new gamblers who had been drawn by the prospect of a hot market swelled the ranks, hoping to buy fast while prices skyrocketed.

To a *Times* reporter looking down from the gallery onto the sea of heads and black silk hats below, the "roar of battle and the screams of the victims" filling the hall made it seem "as though human nature were undergoing torments worse than any that Dante ever witnessed in hell."

All morning, Gold Room bulls and bears fought a tense tug-of-war. The momentum passed back and forth. The price vibrated in a narrow range, reaching $142½ well before the market opened. Brokers on the floor greeted every price rise or fall "with groans and yells, and cheers and cries of exultant delight," reported the *Sun*. They "bellowed and roared with marvelous vigor of lung."

Clearly audible above the mountain of decibels, Albert Speyers's tinny voice shrieked order after order to Buy! Buy! Buy!

The excitement spread to the crowds on New Street outside, where they watched the gold-price indicator bob back and forth and bet on each tick of the market. "One man, when the Gold Room indicator marked 141¾, wagered $20 that it would show 142 within three minutes," the *Sun* reported.

"One bet of $30 to $50 that during the day the indicator would make a 'clean jump' of ½ was eagerly taken."

In early bidding after the opening gavel, the price slipped to $141 on bearish news from Washington. Daniel Butterfield had posted notice at the SubTreasury that Secretary George Boutwell had decided to prepay the November interest on the national debt in gold—a step to release Treasury gold to bondholders. A swarm of smartly dressed messengers ran from the SubTreasury to tell the stock and gold traders the news.

Butterfield had spent much of the morning in his Wall Street office being berated by bankers like Henry Clews, Harris Fahnestock, and W. Butler Duncan about the gold corner's devastating impact on trade. He passed the sentiment on to his superiors in Washington in dispatches during the day. Butterfield's office became a nerve center for gossip and news. His messengers ran notes to money houses allover town, from Cooke & Company to William Belden's and even Boss Tweed's City Hall office.

Butterfield had a private agenda that morning. Scruples aside, he planned to make his own private killing.

Besides dabbling through Jay Gould, during the week Butterfield had summoned to his office Joseph Seligman, the banker-broker who often bought bonds for the government and who took orders for Gould and Fisk. Seligman had earlier bought $700,000 in gold-denominated foreign bonds for Butterfield's personal account—in Mrs. Butterfield's name.

Now, with gold topping $141 Butterfield decided to sell. Seligman agreed. "I told him, of course, that I thought gold at [1]40 was a good sale in connection" with Butterfield's foreign bonds, Seligman later testified.

That morning Seligman was selling not only Daniel Butterfield's gold but all the gold he could find. He even telegraphed San Francisco to send shipments of gold coin to unload at bloated New York prices. Seligman feared a crash. Working through broker William Reed on the Gold Room floor, he sold $400,000 in gold for Butterfield that day at prices ranging from $141 to $143, plus another $300,000 during the week—a heavy bet that Jay Gould's jig was nearly up.

"[Butterfield] told me afterward that these operations were for Mrs. Butterfield, his wife," Seligman testified.

The Treasury announcement of the prepayment of the November interest had only a short-lived effect. Gold Room traders recognized that Europeans, not New Yorkers, held most of the coupons on the November debt.

The relief would arrive too late for the current battle. After a short dip, the price rose by fractions above $141 as the seesaw continued. At about eleven o'clock, gold hovered below $142.

Jim Fisk decided to take center stage himself and break the stalemate. Henry Clews later dated the Gold Ring's fall from that moment on Thursday when Fisk's "erratic conduct" drove him into the Gold Room "wild with enthusiasm." For a born showman like Fisk, the scene was irresistible. At about 11:30 A.M., as the mass of brokers in the Gold Room bought and sold amid the clamor, they looked up to see "Jubilee Jim" himself stroll out onto the Exchange floor, flanked by Belden and Speyers.

All eyes fixed on Fisk. Voices hushed into whispers. The mob parted before him like the Red Sea before Moses. Bears looked on horrified. Jim smiling and laughing, greeted friends and taunted enemies. His sheer presence transformed the faceless bull clique into a menacing, irresistible *force* with himself the leading persona, a flesh-and-blood confirmation of Wall Street's darkest fears.

Jim exuded arrogant confidence as he circulated through the room. In a loud voice he offered to bet any part of $50,000 that gold would reach $200. Nobody took the wager, but they took the hint: Fisk must have had the corner "fixed" with Washington. Just look at how he walked, the cocky way he held his head! Otherwise, his buying at such high prices would have been suicidal.

Wild rumors swept the Gold Room, passed along by formerly skeptical men who were now ready to believe anything. The Ring had in league with them "pretty much everybody in authority in the United States, beginning with President Grant and ending with the door-keeper of Congress," they were saying, recalled trader James Hodgskin. "The President was reported as having a large interest, as well as every member of his cabinet especially the Secretary of the Treasury, also a large number of the members of Congress." It sounded plausible.

According to another rumor, Gould and Boss Tweed planned to install Abel Corbin as president of their jointly owned Tenth National Bank at an annual salary of $25,000—the same as Ulysses Grant's.

The price leaped from $141 to $143. Jim's brokers gobbled up gold in earnest. James Ellis bought $600,000. Woodward grabbed another $2.5 million. Boocock bought $1.26 million, and Albert Speyers bought $5 to $6 million. Broker Lewis Stimson, ordered by Belden "to put gold to $144 and to keep it there," claimed he bought $7.25 million.

Endless cash backed the buying spree. The Tenth National Bank certified more than $25 million in checks for Ring brokers that day. Most were backed by flimsy or nonexistent collateral.

Sitting in the gallery for the Western Union telegraph operators, Thomas Alva Edison worked the controls of the gold-price indicator machine high on the wall above the trading floor, trying to keep pace with fast-rising bids below.

As all eyes were fixed on Jim Fisk and his bulls, nobody seemed to notice a strange cross-current. Jay Gould, mastermind of the affair, was following a different drummer. At about midday, while Jim was creating a spectacle in the Gold Room, Jay summoned his trusted broker Henry Smith to the back room of William Heath's office, where he and Fisk had set up shop during the morning. There, out of earshot from Fisk, Belden, et al., Jay gave Henry a surprising order.

Sell!

With Fisk keeping the bears on tenderhooks and prices soaring, Jay planned to sell his huge gold hoard while the getting was good. His plan demanded the tightest secrecy. Any hint of retreat could signal a panic and price collapse. "I was a seller of gold that day," Jay later explained. "I purchased merely enough to make believe I was a bull."

Smith entrusted this sensitive mission to Edwin Chapin, the independent hack who had been buying gold for him since August. Leaving Jay, Smith tracked down Chapin at the Gold Room and gave him his new marching orders. Smith told Chapin to camouflage the sales by farming out his orders to lesser-known brokers and to keep his own face away from the Exchange.

By day's end, Chapin's agents had sold $8.1 million in gold from Jay Gould's account. Most of this gold was snatched up by the Exchange's biggest buyers that day, Speyers and Belden. In effect, Jay sold his own mountain of precarious gold to his partner, Jim Fisk.

At day's end traders submitted for clearance through the Gold Exchange Bank statements for $325 million in gold sales, almost five times the usual daily amount. The Bank's clerks fell hours behind trying to calculate by hand each broker's gains and losses so that assessments could be collected and paid by two-fifteen the next afternoon.

The gold price closed at $144¼—up by over $3 from Wednesday's $141 finish. After the trading was finished, Gould and Fisk's agents visited each banker who had borrowed gold from the Ring to demand margin money.

The Gold Room jumble had devastated normal commerce across the country. With the machinery to change U. S. money into foreign gold-based currencies crippled, imports and exports stopped. Waterfronts from Boston to Savannah looked like ghost towns. Prices for wheat, cotton, and corn on the Produce Exchange all slumped. Like dominos, "the foreign trade of the United States came to a dead stop; ... goods offered for sale for export could not be sold; ... goods ready for shipment could not be shipped; ... vessels half laden could receive no more cargo; ... clerks, warehousemen, porters, draymen, stevedores, sailors, and the whole army of workingmen occupied about our export trade, were compelled to be idle," explained the *Tribune*.

As for the farmers, who made up almost half the national work force, the *Tribune* reported, "the West was warned to stop shipments [of grain] to consignees here [in New York] who could make no use of them."

In the rubble everyone—bull and bear alike—took notice of one fact. Despite their pleas and cries, the government in Washington had sat on its hands. New York merchants regarded George Boutwell's midday announcement to prepay the November interest as a meager gesture, an admission of impotence. Any hope that Boutwell and Grant were independent of the Gold Ring vanished.

Knowledge of the gold corner had been common for weeks. What was Washington waiting for? they asked. Ulysses Grant was either stupid or crooked, New York's leading financiers thought. The President and his men were villains just like Fisk and Gould, they said—accessories to the outrage.

· 23 ·
PUTTING HEADS TOGETHER

O N THURSDAY NIGHT, September 23, Treasury Secretary George Boutwell rode alone in a carriage through the muddy streets of Washington to the White House for an appointment with President Grant. Boutwell had not seen the President face to face since July, two months earlier—long before any talk of bull cliques or gold corners. Boutwell would have preferred a happier occasion to renew the acquaintance. Unfortunately, he bore bad news.

Ever since he returned to Washington the previous Friday, Boutwell had been beset by money men from New York, Philadelphia, Boston, and elsewhere across the country. They all had one word on their lips: *gold*. By Thursday their outcry had become deafening.

The New York gold crisis had reached a watershed. A stock panic or a major bankruptcy could come at any time and perhaps could trigger a national depression. Such things had happened before. The devastating panic of 1857, the worst in U.S. history up until that time, had been sparked by the collapse of the Ohio Life and Trust Company, a large eastern bank.

Boutwell's present task was unpleasant, given Grant's obstinate tie to Jay Gould's "crop theory." But he felt he had no choice but to try to convince the President to release his lock on the Treasury vaults and let him break the gold corner.

Boutwell had tracked the Wall Street crisis by a variety of channels that day, including letters and visits from a parade of New York agents. Lobbyists of every stripe had congregated in the hallway outside his Treasury office clamoring for appointments. Henry Cooke came with an urgent plea to release gold. The House of Cooke had suffered badly. Cooke partner Edward

Dodge held a huge speculative position in "short" gold; Harris Fahnestock had mounting losses on government bonds.

Boutwell had a list of "persons in New York who were supposed to be contestants" in the Gold Room struggle, both bulls and bears, he later said. To avoid being snookered, he had checked the names of his callers that day against the names on the list. Cooke's name certainly had to appear. Still, he liked one of Henry Cooke's ideas—to announce an early payment of the November gold interest on the national debt. This would be an indirect way to release government gold without opening the floodgates. He sent orders to Butterfield in New York to do it.

Boutwell also received messages from Vermilye & Company, Fisk & Hatch, and Collector Moses Grinnell. "Bull clique are defying you to do your worst," said one cable.

Henry Clews wrote of "extreme anxiety among the banks" and "numerous failures" should the corner succeed. Boutwell should act "without one day's delay," Clews said, and do so without warning; otherwise, the bulls might block Treasury gold sales with an injunction.

Duncan, Sherman & Company, the U.S. agents for Baring Brothers, the British banking firm, pleaded with the Treasury to loan it gold to ease the export-import logjam until its own shipload of gold could arrive from England. Boutwell heard news of emergency gold shipments to New York from San Francisco and Boston as well. He felt obliged to turn down the Barings' request.

The New York press barraged Washington with pointed appeals. Horace Greeley tugged at Boutwell's Republican heartstrings. "The raiders in Government credit and the old Copperheads, who opposed the Union arms in the war, and who would be quite as happy to embarrass the Government now as they were during the progress of the Rebellion, are all delighted" at the gold conspiracy, Greeley said. "Gold 141½, Government securities falling—why must this continue?"

One piece of news especially bothered Boutwell. As early as Monday he had learned that the Fisk-Gould ring had taken control of a federally chartered bank, the Tenth National, and had turned it into a brothel of certified checks for their operation. Boutwell had evidence that the Bank had certified $18 million in unsecured checks for the Ring on Wednesday and Thursday alone—a violation of federal law even in 1869 and one point on which the Treasury had clear authority.

During the afternoon, Boutwell instructed H. R. Hulburd, comptroller of the currency, to send three inspectors to New York to seize the Tenth National Bank before it opened on Friday morning, to investigate the charges, and to shut down any illegal cash flow. If Fisk and Gould were using the Bank to back their corner, Boutwell would see to it that their money spigot was closed.

Publicly, Boutwell gave every appearance of indifference to the gold panic. He answered none of the wires from the New York bears. He refused to give reporters or visitors any clue as to his leanings. When approached by his hometown *Boston Herald,* he said only that a group of "rich gamblers" stood behind the Wall Street stalemate but that he felt "confident of his ability to smash" them.

Ulysses Grant had arrived in Washington on Thursday morning and immersed himself in his presidential workload. Senators, congressmen, generals, ambassadors—all had pressing government business that had been put off while Grant toured the countryside. Each demanded the President's time. Grant spent Thursday with the postmaster general, the secretary of the navy, the secretary of war, and his good friend Henry Cooke, who had come to talk about gold.

"A large crowd of visitors were present [at the Mansion], but were unable to see the President because of important business with prominent officials here," reported the *Times.* Ulysses enjoyed the flurry of action after his long layoff.

Julia spent her day inspecting the White House renovations that painters and carpenters had done while they were traveling. Workmen had refinished chairs and sofas, replaced worn carpets, and fixed and repainted the reception rooms.

When Ulysses asked Julia about the dozens of new paintings and marble statues that were now all over the house, he learned that $60,000 worth of the decorations had been delivered free of charge from a New York art dealer while they were out of town. Grant smelled a rat and ordered the goods recrated and shipped back. Rumors reached Daniel Butterfield in New York that the statues were a gift from "the Gold Ring" to "curry favor" with Washington's elite.

George Boutwell had heard nothing of the President's views on gold since Grant's terse letter of the week before opposing government sales. Now, on Thursday night, as Grant showed him into a private White House chamber and closed the heavy wooden door, Boutwell expected a fight over his plea to abandon the discredited "crop theory." Sitting face to face with the President, Boutwell had his arguments lined up. Wasting little time, he gave Grant a crisp rundown of the Wall Street situation and then launched into his brief.

Boutwell raised the specter of economic chaos: "We thought the business of the country was endangered," he said. "[I]f banking institutions should become involved and break, we might have a repetition of such disasters as we had in 1857." He talked about Jay Gould and Jim Fisk. Nobody could discuss gold without mentioning Ulysses Grant's embarrassing choice of friends.

Whether Grant told Boutwell that his brother-in-law was also in the Ring, or whether Boutwell sensed the President's chagrin at being played a fool by a couple of New York hucksters, we can only guess.

Instead of giving Boutwell a fight, Grant surprised him by giving him full backing to break the gold corner. Ulysses agreed that a gold price of $144 was "unnatural." It took them only a few minutes to decide the question. For now, they would wait. Washington should stay out of battles between Wall Street speculators whenever possible, but they must be ready to respond if the gold corner threatened the general public ... as if it hadn't already.

Tomorrow would judge itself. Grant's view was that "if the price of gold advanced materially the next day ... it would be the duty of the government to sell gold to save the country from the disasters of a panic," Boutwell recalled.

As the secretary left the presidential mansion and rode off into the Washington night, he knew that if push came to shove, the President would back him in crushing the New York bulls. Although nobody knew it yet, the government now stood united against the Ring.

· 24 ·
FOREBODING

LONG AFTER WALL STREET MARKETS had closed that Thursday, the action moved uptown to the Fifth Avenue Hotel. There, bears and bulls, energized from the day's money-making, thronged the lobbies and barroom to trade after normal hours. Thousands of shares of New York Central changed hands in the hot, stuffy hallways as brokers with a drink or two under their belts offered prices far below Central's afternoon Wall Street close of $181.

Others bought gold, hoping that the bull rally would last forever. Financial sharpsters traded stories and wagered money until midnight, when senses dimmed from drunken fatigue and minds were lost to dreams of riches.

Commodore Vanderbilt, livid over Wednesday's devastating bear raid on his companies, had returned from Albany that morning to chair his Harlem River Railroad directors' meeting. He issued denials of yesterday's ruinous rumors. No, the Commodore was not dead. No, Judge Barnard had not issued any "midnight injunctions" against the merger. Yes, the big stock dividend would still come in November.

The damage hung over the market, though. Confidence in Vanderbilt railroads had sunk so low that one bank demanded interest of 2 percent per day—730 percent annualized—for loans secured by New York Central stock. Vanderbilt had to use his considerable clout to keep the prices of his railroad shares from slipping further in panic bidding.

The time would come soon enough to wreak vengeance upon the perpetrators of the attack.

In quieter corners that night, two separate meetings took place to conjure up the next day's machinations. The inner councils of the bulls and bears gathered in contrasting moods of glee and gloom.

Jim Fisk ordered a celebration. Buzzing from his triumphant Gold Room debut, Jim and his principal brokers—Belden, Ellis, and probably Boocock and Speyers—feasted royally. William Fowler placed the party at William Heath & Company's offices near Wall Street. "A sumptuous banquet and wine were ordered in from a neighboring restaurant," he said. Fuller claimed that Josie Mansfield hosted the happy hour at her Twenty-third Street house.

And why should she not? The clique under Fisk and Gould had achieved a financial masterpiece, a near-perfect corner in the most precious of commodities, gold. Jim later claimed that it had happened almost by accident, that Belden had come to him that night saying "evidently you have got a corner on this gold market," as if he were surprised.

In pure nuts-and-bolts terms, the gold corner rivaled the finest works of engineering or sculpture.

The Gold Ring now held "calls" that gave it the legal right to demand immediate delivery of more than six times the total amount of gold coin and certificates publicly accessible around New York. Jay Gould's "national gold account" alone had peaked at $40 to $55 million in gold calls. Jim held another $60-odd million; Belden another $20 million. Whatever the exact count, the Ring's calls certainly topped $100 million.

As a result, the Ring stood to clear at least $1 million for each $1 price increase, or more than $3 million on Thursday's trading alone.

To tighten demand, Jay and Jim had paid for and taken possession of $6 to $7 million in physical gold coin and certificates—about half the total from New York banks. For all practical purposes, the clique owned all the gold within reach. No one could buy gold except from the clique. No one could sell gold without borrowing it from the clique.

By playing their flute and tugging the demand, they could dictate the price at will and make a fortune on each step up the ladder.

At the same time, by loaning out their gold, Jay and Jim saved the "shorts" from bankruptcy and kept the government off their backs. They could inch the price up slowly, by a few dollars each day. The loan strategy also kept down costs, although the Ring could always get cash galore through the Tenth National Bank, Jay's trump card.

So far, only one Wall Street firm had failed. Van DeVenter & Company, a small house that traded gold and stocks, had informed the Stock Exchange at eleven o'clock on Thursday morning that one of its partners, a Mr. Hedley, had disappeared with the company's money and nobody knew where to find him.

Now, as the bulls toasted their own brilliance, they faced a dilemma. They could not hold the corner forever; sooner or later, the high price would draw a flood of gold into New York, and the market would break. "The vaults of every bank in the Union, in Montreal and the Bank of England had been called upon to disgorge," William Fowler noted, "and the gates of the national treasury had been stormed with prayers to let loose the coin and save the country, or at least the bears."

Buying huge amounts of a commodity was the easy part of making a corner. But cashing in the profit and selling off the mother lode while prices stayed high required supreme delicacy. Between Gould and Fisk, delicacy marked the former, not the latter.

After having their fill of food, wine, and laughter at their success, the Fiskites moved their gaggle to the Grand Opera House. Here they found Jay Gould, who had skipped the merrymaking, sitting at his desk poring over mounds of paperwork, along with Henry Smith, E. K. Willard, and other Gouldites.

Jay later claimed that he ignored the strategy session in his office that night. "I sat there transacting [Erie Railway] business," he explained, "and very likely I listened to what was said, but it went in one ear and out the other. I was all alne so to speak in what I did, and I did not let any of those people know exactly how I stood." Having secretly sold off gold during the day and having concealed Abel Corbin's letter from Julia Grant, he had deceived his fellow Ring members.

But Jay could not have hidden from the others without drawing suspicion. His partners would have wanted his opinion on their complex calculations.

Jim Fisk might have been a showman but Jay proved himself the better actor as he conversed late into the night with his closest allies closeted together in a small room, giving no hint that he had swallowed the canary.

Fisk proposed a bold plan to the hungry bulls. He and Jay held a list of every broker, banker, and speculator in New York who had borrowed gold from the Ring—over 250 bears altogether, starting with Jay Cooke & Company, the largest. Why not publish the list in tomorrow's newspapers, Jim said, with a demand that these bears "settle" with them by three o'clock the next afternoon at a fixed price of $160? If the borrowers refused to buy back the gold at $160, the Ring would squeeze them for an even higher price.

The proposition bordered on blackmail, and everyone else in the room later claimed to have disowned it instantly. Henry Smith called it "absurd." Even Belden scoffed, not wanting to make his business public. "Fisk never could do anything regular," Willard said.

For once, Jim let the law decide the question. He sent for "Tearful Tommy" Shearman, the Erie Railway lawyer, who came and calmly explained that the scheme violated not only common practice but also the New York State criminal conspiracy law. The whole group could be prosecuted if they went ahead with the plan.

As gas lamps burned low and the hour grew late, the room thick with cigar smoke, the Ring members chose a more conventional approach. Come Friday, they would bull gold to ever-higher price levels while quietly negotiating settlements from the major bears. Their own brokers would boost prices by buying gold well above the market. If other brokers offered $140, they'd offer $150.

In practical terms, instead of buying low and selling high, they would sell high and buy higher to push the price higher still. With an escalating price, the bears would then be confronted with ruinous margin calls. They would have to accept any outrageous terms that the bulls offered.

The fact that their scheme might bankrupt innocent men, destroy commerce, ruin their country's standing in world credit markets, and cover themselves with scandal never entered the conversation. To "Admiral" James Fisk, this was war, the noblest adventure, and he would fight with a flourish.

Jay Gould knew the plan's fatal flaw. By pushing prices too high too fast, Jim would provoke Grant into stepping in and breaking the corner. To succeed, Jim needed protection from Washington, but their license from the President had expired.

As his confidants prepared to charge off into oblivion, Jay held his tongue. Afterwards, Gould and Fisk went their separate ways into the New York night. Jim walked only a few steps from the Erie offices to where Josie Mansfield awaited him. Jay hailed a carriage to spend the night with his wife Helen at their stately Fifth Avenue home.

Parting in the street, the two friends may unknowingly have saluted the end of an era.

◎ ◎ ◎ ◎ ◎

By contrast, the scene downtown that night was anything but merry. After the market deluge that day, James Brown, who had been driven to distraction by the gold corner, brought together an odd covey of financiers. They probably met in the Brown Brothers building at 59 Wall Street. No records exist from this meeting, and nobody besides James has ever admitted to being present; but the faces that appeared around the room are easy to guess. They doubtless included big exporters like William E. Dodge and A. A. Lowe. These exporters-importers had reached desperation; their business was at a standstill.

If Harris Fahnestock came, he dragged his tail between his legs. The $12 million pool designed to bury the Ring on Wednesday had failed miserably. James Brown's bank had pumped huge loans into Fahnestock's bond-buying, gold-selling operations via Jay Cooke & Company. Both investments had turned sour.

Banker Henry Clews, Wall Street's biggest gossip, always seemed to show up at such backroom cabals. Based on his later actions, W. Butler Duncan of Duncan, Sherman & Company, the agent of England's Baring Brothers bank, also probably came. Baring Brothers, like Brown Brothers, handled a large import-export trade.

James Brown later claimed that he himself prodded the group into taking a strong stand. "[W]e had paid, paid, paid through that infernal combination" as prices rose to $144, he said. How many more days could they pay margin to the bulls without breaking? How could they let honorable New York merchants be bled to death by railroad gamblers like Gould and Fisk? "I myself suggested that a bold proceeding such as giving them all the gold that they would take, would probably kill the bull," James said.

He spoke for many. Somebody had to stand out in front and lead. Whether the congregation dragged James reluctantly forward or he seized the banner himself, the yoke inevitably fell onto his shoulders.

The conservative money men in James's office settled on a plan not much different from Wednesday's pool. Putting together their reserves, James would enter the Gold Room the next morning like a matador, carrying a blank check to kill the bull corner. Only James, the oldest man on Wall Street—older than Commodore Vanderbilt and Daniel Drew, old enough to remember George Washington as a living President—had the experience and skill for the job. No younger man could be trusted with the snap judgments and heavy monetary commitments needed to slay this beast.

James knew the danger. Fisk and Gould owned most of the gold in New York. To sell and deliver large additional amounts, James might have to borrow the gold from Fisk and Gould themselves to sell it back to them. Would the Ring lend him any?

And with Washington apparently in their pockets, the Ring's threats to raise the gold price to $150, $160, or higher had to be taken seriously. The bulls had already swallowed Wednesday's $12 million pool in a single gulp. If the price rose sharply after tomorrow's sales, the new pool could face huge losses. A bank or major trade house could tumble.

But what choice did they have? Nobody else was going to save them.

Washington had no credibility. Like on the western frontier, Wall Street's own posse of law-abiding citizens would have to hunt down the villains themselves and bring justice to bear.

Perhaps Vanderbilt, Daniel Drew, even A. T. Stewart or Daniel Butterfield sent agents to the meeting in James Brown's office that night. All had reason to want Fisk and Gould humbled. Or maybe they even attended in person to lend ideas and bankrolls to the holy crusade.

After leaving the secret conclave, James took a ferry across the East River to his home in New Utrecht. He slept as best he could with his family away in Europe, his friends confused, and his world in chaos on the eve of Black Friday.

◎ ◎ ◎ ◎ ◎

Caleb Norvell, financial editor of the *Times,* was staring at a blank sheet of paper late Thursday night. For days he had covered the Gold and Stock Exchange battles for the *Times,* rubbing elbows with the chief bulls and bears; he had heard all the gossip and rumors. He had never met George Boutwell, but Norvell, as a loyal Yankee, trusted that Boutwell would not have sat still for a minute if he had known the stories being told behind his back.

On Thursday Norvell had heard the "monstrous" yarn that Abel Corbin would be named president of the Gould-and-Tweed-owned Tenth National Bank. He immediately rushed over to Joseph Seligman, a bank director; Seligman denied the rumor but implied through his "manner ... that such a thing had at least been suggested."

Every major newspaper had assigned a full-time reporter to cover the Wall

Street contest: Norvell for the *Times*, Ford Barksdale for the *Sun*, and George Crouch for the *Herald*. Norvell had written a blistering editorial that night laying out the atrocities. He named Gould, Fisk, and Corbin as the conspiracy heads, tied the operation to Tweed's Tammany Hall through the Tenth National Bank, and quoted the insinuations of government involvement.

The bulls "talked freely of the warrant which they had from Washington, [though] this must have been known to be false," Norvell wrote. "The Government is scandalized by false rumors of complicity."

The article went further than anything that had yet been published in the New York press. The *Time's* financial column for Friday morning stopped short of naming names, claiming that "we do not propose to injure any man's reputation here by accusing him of being a member of the *Ring*."

Now, sitting alone at his desk, Norvell racked his brain for ideas of how to stop the outrage. He put pen to paper and wrote a note to his friend Mr. Crounse, the *Time's* Washington correspondent, asking him to "say to Mr. Boutwell that if he would come to New York and hear what was said about the streets in regard to high officials in Washington, he would see it was necessary" to act.

Norvell's letter mayor may or may not have reached the Capitol before Friday's climax, but it hardly mattered. The *Times* editors who were already irritated at having been tricked by Gould and Corbin last August into printing the fraudulent article on "Grant's Financial Policy," decided now to run Norvell's scathing editorial in their Friday-morning editions. As soon as it came off the printers' galleys, they would telegraph a copy to Boutwell in Washington to read for himself.

• 25 •

EYE OF
THE STORM

J AY GOULD AND JIM FISK rode downtown from the Grand Opera House
together early on Friday morning, September 24. The late-summer sun
warmed the city breezes to temperatures in the low 70s. It was a grand
day for conquest. With $100 million in gold calls in their pockets and backed
by Tammany Hall and the Tenth National Bank—and as far as Jim knew,
President Ulysses Grant—their Gold Ring held New York finance on a silver
platter, like a turkey ready for carving.

Jim dared anyone to stop them, even a thousand growling "loyal league"
bears.

Not all signs pointed to clear sailing that day, however. New York had
reached a fever pitch over the gold siege. Jay and Jim could hardly have
missed the bitterness directed their way. Jay pointed out Caleb Norvell's *Times*
expose of the sins of the "Gould-Fisk party" against Washington officialdom.
"[W]e made up our mind that that article would be telegraphed to Grant and
Boutwell," Jim later said. "I looked right at it, and it made me feel weak in the
knees."

Only Gould and Fisk knew what plans they made and what secrets they
shared during their private moments riding to Wall Street that morning. His-
torians would spin theories about them for the next hundred years.

On reaching the Stock Exchange, they directed the carriage to the offices
of William Heath & Company at 15 Broad Street, near Wall. The financial
district brimmed with carnival animation. Crowds of people flooded the hotel
lobbies, saloons, and shops along Broadway, growing thicker near the banks,
exchanges, and money dens of Wall Street. Bankers and brokers mingled with
apple-sellers and laborers. "Representatives of almost every class were there,"

wrote a *Times* reporter. "The great merchant stood side-by-side with the *sans culotte*—*the* gutter stripe of society; the man of law compared notes with the Wall Street 'goat,' an individual known only to brokers."

Pickpockets flocked like locusts to prey on the innocent.

Jay Gould, shrinking from the attention, ducked off the carriage a block or two early, leaving Jim the stage to himself. Colorful stories of Jim's arrival in the financial district surrounded by Opera House beauties soon permeated the Street. "A carriage wheeled into [Broad] street," wrote William Fowler. "On the back seat sat the actresses, Miss L[ucille] W[estern, who was then appearing nightly on Jim's Opera House stage as "Patrie"] and Miss P. M_____, the latter the queen of the blonde troupe.

> 'Her lips were red, her looks were free,
> Her locks were as yellow as gold.'

"A thick, blue-eyed man, dressed in magnificent costume, and perfumed like a milliner, descended from the carriage, and entered the office of William Heath & Co. It was James Fisk, Jr., 'the oiled and curled Assyrian Bull of Wall Street.'"

Financier John Morrissey also saw Miss Western and another of Jim's "lady friends" downtown during the fracas.

Why Jim would have preferred the company of Lucille Western to that of Josie Mansfield on this, the biggest day of his wheeler-dealer life, is anyone's guess. He and Josie had been arguing recently over money; perhaps the fights had grown worse. Or maybe Josie didn't want to ride with Jim's spidery partner Jay even for this special occasion.

Or maybe half-crazed financiers invented the scene from whole cloth hours after the trauma. This day, Black Friday 1869, ultimately captured the imaginations of New Yorkers for a generation.

When they both reached Heath & Company's office, Fisk and Gould commandeered the back room normally used by brokers Russell Hills and Charles Quincey and set up their command headquarters there. The small room had every convenience. Carpeted and furnished with a lounge and an easy chair, it also had a separate rear exit to the back alleyway behind Broad Street and was an easy walk from the Gold and Stock Exchanges. A platoon of Erie toughs stationed themselves as guards outside the main door as Jim rolled up his sleeves.

Jim boiled with energy that morning, consumed totally by the hour. He paced back and forth, carrying a large cane like Moses, barking orders like Napoleon.

Meanwhile, over at the Gold Room, bears and bulls jammed the floor and started shouting bids an hour before the opening. Shortly after nine, Jim opened fire. He directed broker Russell Hills to run over to the Gold Room and "put the market up to 145" by buying $100,000 at that price. Gold had closed Wednesday afternoon at $144.

Jim's troops would move in one direction only: upward!

Jay Gould studiously avoided involving himself in Jim's rambunctious carrying-on. He still held a massive pile of gold to sell before the market broke. Secrecy was essential. Sitting sphinx-like, he hardly spoke a word to the brokers and runners who crowded the room all day, except for his trusted lieutenant Henry Smith. "I had my own plans, and I did not mean that anybody should say that I had opened my mouth that day," Jay testified. "I sat in one corner of the room reading."

Whether this was play-acting or genuine deceit, only he and Jim Fisk knew for sure.

Broker Albert Speyers arrived at William Belden's office on Broad Street that morning at about nine, and the two men hurried together to Heath's. On the way, Belden told Speyers all about the Ring's plan for its final gold assault, the fruits of the Opera House strategy session the night before.

"This will be the last day of the Gold Room," Speyers remembered Belden saying. "We have got over $110 million of calls and we have an immense amount of money, and we can buy all the gold the government dare to sell. We are all one family—Smith, Gould, and Martin and others, and my partner is Mrs. Fisk's brother-in-law."

Belden later denied saying all this, but other sources back up Speyers's memory. Samuel Boocock remembered Belden telling him that morning that gold would sell at $200 and that Fisk and Gould were his customers. Boocock claimed that another Belden customer, a Mr. Newcome, repeated Belden's warning that Friday "was his last day in Wall street."

The *Sun* quoted a "leading operator of the ring" as saying, "We have it in our power to put gold up to 200, and we mean to do it."

On reaching Heath's office, Belden brought Speyers into the back room with Fisk and Gould. There he turned his lackey over to the wolves. Belden gave Jim a blank check to use Speyers as he pleased. "Mr. Speyers will execute any orders of mine, any orders that you may give him," Belden said.

Then, turning to Speyers, he said, "When you have executed these orders, you will report to me."

Jim decided to break in his new servant right away. He told Speyers to rush over and "buy all the gold I could get at 145." He "spoke loud in the hearing of everybody," Speyers recalled.

The buying by Speyers and Hills sent gold flying to $145 within minutes.

Then Jim decided to up it to $150. Sitting in the cramped command center, delighting in his bold advance, Jim took paper and wrote out a simple, direct message: "Put it to 150 at once." He gave the note to a messenger to deliver to Speyers on the Gold Room floor. He also sent one of Heath & Company's clerks to find C. C. Allen, a broker with Livermore & Company who had been hired by Heath for trading that day, and to tell him to buy $500,000 gold at $150.

Broker Henry Enos came into Heath's back room at about nine-thirty. He also took an order from "Gould & Fisk jointly," he later said, to "put gold to 150." Enos was struck by Jim Fisk's early-morning zeal. "Mr. Gould, as I was going out of the door, came up to me and said, 'Enos, go and put gold to 150.' As I went out of the door, Mr. Fisk, in a rather gesticulating way, told me to hold it there. Using some rather emphatic expression he told me to hold it here—rather in a decisive manner."

It didn't take long. Within ten minutes Enos had bought $430,000 worth of gold.

Speyers ran back from the Gold Room to tell Jim that gold had reached 150. Jim, amused at the spectacle of Albert Speyers running around at his command, immediately told him, "All right; go back and take all you can get at 150," and a bit later, "Go back and take all you can get under 150."

At such moments, Jim bragged that there was "nothing the matter with my old tin stove."

◎ ◎ ◎ ◎ ◎

That Friday morning, James Brown awoke early and took the ferry back to New York. He had seen none of his business allies since the previous night's meeting. As he was walking from the boat pier to his Wall Street office shortly after nine o'clock, he passed a banker friend who told him that gold had already reached $150. James quickened his pace and proceeded directly to the Gold Room, where he met his apprentice, Kruger.

In the Gold Room, James found a "considerable gathering" of men al-

ready absorbed in trading well before the Exchange's formal ten o'clock opening. He sought out other bears from the last night's meeting and pulled them
aside one by one to compare notes. Then he decided to test the waters.
Shortly before ten, James threaded through the storm of humanity to the circular brass rail at the center of the Room, where he could best see through his
thick spectacles. There he recognized another old-timer, Albert Speyers, the
wily German gentleman. Brown marveled at the strange abandon with which
Speyers was conducting himself.

Waving a hand in the air, James offered to sell $500,000 in gold at the
market price, then at $150. In the blink of an eye, Speyers answered James's
bid and bought the gold.

His job done, James stepped back toward the perimeter of the Room for
a better view of the gathering storm.

Henry Benedict, chairman of the Gold Exchange and president of the
Gold Exchange Bank, was worried about the frenzy escalating so early in the
day. His clerks at the Gold Exchange Bank, working around the clock, still
had not finished sorting through the $300 million-plus in gold transactions
that had been submitted for clearing after Thursday's record-breaking day.
Brokers still had not been assessed their gains or losses.

Another high-volume day could overwhelm the Bank. If the market exploded, Benedict wanted at least to protect the Exchange and clearinghouse
systems themselves.

Minutes before the Gold Room's official opening, Benedict left the Exchange and walked over to Heath & Company's office. He made his way past
the beefy guards and knocked on the backroom door.

If Jim was surprised to see the Exchange chairman come to sermonize
him at this early hour, he didn't show it. Benedict, who was aware that the
Ring held "calls" on immense amounts of New York gold, got straight to the
point. He took Fisk aside and asked him "whether this was to be the settling
day for closing these gold contracts."

Jim "hesitated at first," according to Benedict. Then he conceded the obvious. "I might as well tell you that this is the day."

Benedict then laid out his problem. He "did not propose to get between
the upper and the nether millstone in this movement," he said, and suggested
that Jim and Gould settle their gold trades outside the clearinghouse.

Jim couldn't have cared less about humoring the stodgy bureaucrat. He
gave Benedict an adroit brush-off, telling him not to worry, that he had come

"down to do business, expected no trouble." Benedict, as Exchange chairman, had no real authority to support his plea. No effective self-regulation by stock or commodity exchanges would come into being for decades.

Benedict left Fisk and Gould empty-handed and walked back across Broad Street to gavel his gold-grubbers' association into session for its day of destiny.

Barely had the Exchange chairman gone when another knock on the backroom door brought Mr. Dickinson, president of the Tenth National Bank, into the busy room. Dickinson had bad news. He could not certify checks for Gould and Fisk that day. Three bank examiners from Washington had shown up that morning with orders from George Boutwell and were plowing through the books, Dickinson said.

Dickinson had no desire to push his luck with them.

By the time Henry Benedict took his seat at the raised dais and banged his gavel, three hundred sweaty brokers were jamming the Exchange floor, immersed in capitalistic fervor. The cast included almost every major financier in New York: Arthur Kimber, Henry Clews, Speyers, James Brown, William Woodward, "and dozens of others hardly less famous," wrote James Medbery. The galleries swarmed with newspaper reporters.

Sketch artists from *Harper's Weekly* and *Frank Leslie's Illustrated* worked their pencils to capture the bedlam visually.

The fevered pace strained the Exchange's physical plant. The gold-price indicator machine that hung high above the traders' heads lagged minutes behind the turbulent floor action. "The indicator was composed of several wheels; on the circumference of each wheel were the numerals; and one wheel had fractions," explained Thomas Alva Edison later. "[O]ne wheel made ten revolutions, and at the tenth it advanced the adjacent wheel; and this, in its turn having gone ten revolutions, advanced the next wheel, and so on."

Electrical signals from buttons at Edison's fingertips ran three hundred indicators throughout the city. The Ring "had run up the quotations faster than the indicator could follow," Edison said. Working feverishly in his booth above the fray, Edison rigged the machine with paperweights to speed the gears as prices moved up and up. Still the machine could barely keep pace with the overheated human engine below.

At about eleven o'clock, Jim Fisk turned to Albert Speyers and told him "to go to the gold room and raise the price of gold to [1]55. It was then [1]50."

Speyers hopped to attention and rushed from the command headquarters back to the Exchange. He elbowed his way to the middle of the floor and shrieked forth his latest bid.

The roomful of men gasped. Each dollar rise in gold meant millions in losses for brokers, bankers, and merchants. There were no government or exchange rules in 1869 that required brokers to keep cash reserves for emergencies. Most had none. Unpaid margins meant bankruptcy.

"A hundred fists were shaken at each other over the little fountain, and an infernal series of yells filled the room," wrote the *Sun* reporter. Like magic, the price jumped at Speyers's command. The numbers on the gold price indicator hurried to catch up.

As gold hovered at $155, James Brown, having consulted his mysterious bear pool, walked into the knot of traders again and sold another $500,000 worth to Albert Speyers.

While Fisk was leading his charge toward gold heaven, Jay Gould tended his own affairs. He continued his secret unloading of $40-odd million in gold. Henry Smith operated autonomously, checking with Jay only a handful of times during the morning. Jay had given Henry a free license to sell gold at any price over $143.

To mask the sales, Smith laundered his orders through layers of faceless agents. E. K. Willard, one of his field captains, told his troops to "Sell, sell, sell; do nothing but sell." They sold $5 million. Broker Charles Osborne, also working on orders from Smith via Willard, sold another $5 million.

Less visibly but far more brutally, Henry Smith instructed his brokers to press bears into backroom settlements.

Edwin Chapin, one of Smith's agents, turned the screws on one firm Friday morning by calling in $780,000 in gold that the firm had borrowed earlier that week at $142. The price had by then hit $150. The victim borrowed gold at $150 to return to Chapin but gagged at the steep margin calls as the price surged toward $160. The bears begged Chapin to sell them gold outright at $150 for a handsome commission rather than risk further losses.

Chapin agreed, although the complicated deal later ended up in an arbitrator's courtroom. Inevitably, Jay's brokers sold oceans of gold to Albert Speyers and other Fiskites.

By all accounts Jim Fisk had no idea that morning that Jay, sitting just across from him, was systematically undercutting his corner by selling gold willy-nilly. The image of Jay Gould on Black Friday coldly cheating his partner by silent winks and whispers has been a popular piece of Americana ever since, but it is unfair. Jim Fisk, if anyone, appreciated Jay's role as master puppeteer in their financial ventures, even with himself as the trusting marionette. Maybe Jim knew exactly what Jay was up to; maybe he didn't. But by his silence, Jay forever placed the blame for Black Friday on himself and gave his friend a cunning alibi.

At midmorning, both Jay and Jim saw signs of the corner starting to crumble. They discovered that Joseph Seligman was selling gold furiously and knew that Seligman was "intimate" with Daniel Butterfield. Jim had ordered messengers to stop at Butterfield's SubTreasury office throughout the morning, but so far they had heard nothing. The presence of federal examiners at the Tenth National Bank raised further doubts about the political front.

As the price of gold streaked skyward, the New York financial system writhed. The city's leading bankers unleashed a torrent of appeals to Washington. Harris Fahnestock rushed to the Franklin Telegraph office shortly after ten and wired Jay Cooke in Philadelphia that "immediate interference in this gold market is imperative to avoid disgrace of administration. Boutwell's policy has brought gold and bonds within 10 percent of each other. Gold now fifty & bonds eighteen [and a] quarter. Exchange of few millions gold for bonds immediately done would change current at once. Otherwise advance is indefinite."

Jay Cooke bristled at the spectacle. Cooke had prepared an appeal that he now wired to his brother Henry in Washington. "If I were Geo. S. Boutwell, Sec 'y of Treasury, I would not allow pride or any fear of 'changing of front or policy' to influence me but should at once" act, Cooke said. Cooke suggested a radical departure: Washington should fix a ceiling price for gold and use its market muscle to enforce it. "[T]he gamblers should have someone stationed above them. " Without a gold standard, the government had a "*duty* to keep things steady for the benefit of the honest interests of the country."

On Black Friday, more than a half-century before Federal commodity price controls or Wall Street regulations, this radical suggestion sounded like the essence of reason from a consummate conservative. "I want you to go over & see Secty Boutwell & read him *this*," Jay Cooke directed Henry. "As *we* have no interest in the rise or fall of gold, I feel we can coolly advise in this matter," he added, apparently ignorant of the gambling by his own New York satellite office.

Henry Clews and Moses Grinnell also sent telegrams to Boutwell and Grant that morning, telling them to sell gold without delay. Grinnell argued that without government help a "large proportion" of "reliable merchants and bankers" would have to close their doors permanently by three o'clock.

Closer to home, fifty-odd bankers, speculators, and messengers crammed Daniel Butterfield's office at the SubTreasury. Clews, William Vermilye, and Fahnestock demanded that Butterfield inform his Washington superiors of the looming debacle. They repeated the accusations that Boutwell himself had a hand in the corner.

Daniel Butterfield's position in the affair had become a mush of conflicting motives. As a civil servant, he had a duty to report the situation truthfully to his superiors. Having taken money and gold from Jay Gould, he also had an obligation to the bulls. Having sold gold through Joseph Seligman, he also had selfish reasons to see the corner fail and prices crash.

Fortunately for Butterfield, his control over events was nonexistent. All he could do was ride the storm, keep track of messages, and avoid the fallout as best he could.

At about ten-thirty, Butterfield sent Washington a blunt dispatch:

Franklin Telegraph Company, September 24, 1869

To Hon. G.S. Boutwell.

I am requested to represent to you condition of affairs here. Gold is 150; much feeling, and accusations of government complicity. The propositions of Weatherspoon, Duncan, Sherman & Co., and Seligman [to release Treasury gold in anticipation of shipments from England or San Francisco], if accepted, would relieve exchange market and be judicious. Should be done by telegraph.

Dan'l Butterfield.

News of the worsening Wall Street battle swept uptown, drawing thousands of New Yorkers from every walk of life into the narrow lanes around the Gold and Stock Exchanges. The streets became impassable to traffic on foot, carriage, or horseback. "The Gold Room was the magnet of attraction; all else was abandoned," said the *Herald*.

New Street, where the gold-price indicator faced out onto the sidewalk, bubbled with crowds that cheered each tick in the market like blood-wounds in a cockfight. "Here the silk-hatted importer jostled elbows with the shoe-string gambler, the gamins supplemented the babel from the Gold Room with their jests, and the pickpocket covertly plied his calling," wrote Edmund Stedman of the scene.

"In and out through the [sidewalk] tumult an enterprising peddler went crying his timely little gimcracks, a Bull and a Bear," noted Meade Minnigerode, "and men incomprehensibly stopped long enough to smile and buy them, guerdons of the forthcoming battle."

◎ ◎ ◎ ◎ ◎

George Boutwell had been following the New York market all morning by telegraph. Outside his Treasury department office, a throng of visitors, lobbyists, reporters, and agents for New York and Philadelphia banks crowded the hallway. They were watching for any sign of government action.

At about eleven o'clock Boutwell left the Treasury and walked briskly to the White House to see President Grant. He brought with him a sheaf of cables from New York, dispatches from Daniel Butterfield, editorials from the *Times* and the *Tribune*, and wires from Henry Clews and other bankers all begging Washington for relief. As he passed through the gate, Boutwell understood that his worst fear had come true. Gold had gone haywire, and Wall Street was blaming him and the President.

The chaotic scene in New York was being repeated from coast to coast that morning. Bostonians followed the New York struggle from the Merchants' Exchange Reading room. Crowds on Philadelphia's Third Street bordered on panic when the gold-price indicator in one major bank, operated by telegraph from New York, suddenly went blank. "Boys had therefore to be employed to run from the telegraph office to one broker's office after another, and cry out the premium" said *The Philadelphia Ledger*, "This added to the Babel." Baltimore businessmen jammed the streets around McKim's Banking House.

Banks in San Francisco, where gold was plentiful, were swamped by appeals from New York for wire gold transfers, but they refused to sell at any price, fearing a West Coast shortage.

President Grant had scheduled a Cabinet meeting for noon that Friday to discuss a host of long-ignored issues, particularly a political dispute between rival Republican factions in Texas. He put aside his work as an aide announced Boutwell's arrival. He ushered the secretary into a private meeting room.

They had "very little conversation," Boutwell recalled. Grant probably re-frained from taking out a hunting knife and whittling while listening to Boutwell's report as he had done on battlefields from the Wilderness to Cold Harbor, but the situation must have recalled the war years to Grant's mind. As commander-in-chief and a seasoned fighter, Ulysses recognized the time to blast away.

Boutwell suggested that the government sell $3 million in gold from the New York SubTreasury to break the corner.

Grant raised the stakes. "I think you had better make it $5,000,000." Without nailing down a figure, Boutwell wrapped up the interview, left the President, and hurried back to the Treasury, where platoons of lobbyists lurk-ing in the hallway studied his every coming and going. Boutwell sidestepped the hall vultures and ordered his office cleared of outsiders. The secretary would see nobody for the next thirty minutes, he announced.

"Those waiting in the corridor presumed he wanted to prepare for the Cabinet meeting," wrote a *Times* correspondent among the Treasury hallway hangers-on.

Alone and out of sight, Boutwell summoned an aide and dictated a brief dispatch to Daniel Butterfield, to be sent immediately in uncoded form over both the Western Union and the Franklin Telegraph Company lines.

Treasury Department, September 24, 1869

Daniel Butterfield, Assistant Treasurer, U.S., New York:
*   Sell four millions ($4,000,000) gold to-morrow [Saturday], and buy four millions ($4,000,000) bonds.*

Geo. S. Boutwell
Secretary Treasury

Boutwell's clerks ran the message to the Washington telegraph operators for transmission over the two lines, stamped in at 11:42 and 11:45 A.M.

By selling gold the next day instead of right away, Boutwell risked burst-ing the gold bubble before the government could profit from the current high prices. Still, even at the height of the crisis, the secretary cringed at the idea of government intervention in the market. He knew he was playing with fire in the New York Gold Room. Dumping U.S. gold could very well be like dropping a lighted match on gasoline.

Whether cold feet or good sense stood behind this squeamishness, Boutwell wanted as much flexibility as possible. If New York protested his announcement, the day's delay would give him a chance to cancel his gold sales before Saturday. If it approved, Boutwell would be an instant hero.

The deed done, the secretary opened the doors to his office, invited the lobbyists and other onlookers from the hallway, and told them his decision.

Daniel Butterfield received Boutwell's parallel dispatches in New York at 12:05 and 12:10 P.M., respectively.

◎ ◎ ◎ ◎ ◎

At about eleven-thirty Jim Fisk decided to capture the next line of trenches.

Gold, now trading at $155, must be raised to $160. Jim sent orders through his network of runners and messengers.

C. C. Allen of Livermore & Company received word on the Gold Room floor to bid $160 for $1 million in gold. Allen, who had thought he was buying for William Heath all morning, not Fisk, sent the messenger back for clarification. Jim responded by ripping the corner off a *Herald*, scribbling out the order, and signing it. Allen, getting the new instruction, dashed from the Exchange back through the sidewalk crowds to Heath & Company. He found Fisk et al. in the back room.

Who would stand behind the audacious order? Allen asked.

"Go ahead, and put down what you buy to Belden & Co.," Jim told him.

Allen still balked, saying he did no business with Belden.

"G-d d—n, it, then, put it down to this concern," Jim said. Satisfied, Allen hurried back to the Gold Room to join the battle in progress.

◎ ◎ ◎ ◎ ◎

Albert Speyers also received the new orders from Heath's back room.

"Go and bid gold up to 160. Take all you can get at 160," Jim told him. He added, "But you will be too late, for I have given orders to other brokers already to buy at 160." Speyers saluted and dashed across the street. On reaching the Gold Room, he wedged himself mouse like through the crowd of bears and bulls. He cleared his throat like an opera singer and sent forth from his prodigious larynx his boldest demand yet.

"160 for any part of five millions."

Having started the day at under $145, gold at $160 meant a more than

$15 price rise in little over three hours. With over $100 million gold in its coffers, that meant profits for the Ring of more than $15 million. This money would not come from thin air. Bankers, merchants, and lesser bears all faced steep margin calls. Many feared default, failure, or bankruptcy. Under the harsh laws of the 1860s, this could mean destitution, the destruction of their businesses and their families, and perhaps even civil imprisonment.

A pall set over the frightened men in the chamber.

"160 for any part of five millions," repeated Albert Speyers.

Every sign pointed in the Ring's favor. It appeared that nothing would prevent gold from reaching even $200, observed Edmund Stedman, as "it seemed unlikely that the Treasury, which had permitted these excesses, would interfere now."

"When gold was $160 it was not for a moment anticipated that it would descend," said the *Herald*.

William Heath, the respected proprietor of Heath & Company, appeared personally on the Gold Room floor at this point and likewise bid $160 "with his finger poised high in the air," wrote William Fowler. C. C. Allen across the room bid $160 as well.

But Speyers's shrill voice sounded above the others.

Sitting in the gallery overlooking the drama, a reporter for *The Nation* described how "the noise was hushed. Terror became depicted on every countenance. Cool, sober men looked at one another, and noted the ashy paleness that spread over all. Even those who had but little or no interest at stake were seized with the infection of fear, and were conscious of a great evil approaching.

"And from the silence again came forth the shrieking bid, '160 for five millions,' and no answer; '161 for five millions;' '162 for five millions,' still no answer."

The eerie silence pounded at a thousand eardrums. Endless seconds passed as Speyers's challenge stood unanswered. Nobody could speak. Nobody dared question the grip that "Jubilee Jim" Fisk through *his* diminutive puppet, held on the economic hub of the nation.

Finally, a voice spoke up.

James Brown had not checked with his partners, but he understood the moment. In any movement of men and events there comes a pivot, a singular instant when one's opponent grasps just beyond his reach and leaves himself vulnerable. A small, accurate thrust at that point can redirect the entire momentum of an affair. If missed, the chance is lost forever. The beast becomes unstoppable.

"Sold one million at 162," James said.

Time stood still. All eyes gazed on the two men standing at the railing.

The sound of water dripping into the tiny pool from the dolphin in Cupid's arms was clearly audible at the farthest corner of the gallery.

Speyers repeated his bid, this time a notch lower. Sold, a million at 161, said James Brown.

"160 for five millions," Speyers said.

Sensing the tide turning, James unloaded a full blow. "Sold five million at 160."

Suddenly, bears found courage where they had none before. Color returned to a hundred cadaverous faces. A broker for Hallgarten & Company, a German firm, offered his own bid to sell a million at $160, which was snapped up. Duncan, Sherman & Company sold Speyers $1 million at $160. Orlando Joslyn, a private broker, sold him $500,000 at $160; Dzondi, another $1 million; Parks, another $2 million.

The price may have touched $165 in one corner of the Room, but never again did Speyers's shrieks ascend beyond $160.

Meanwhile, a chilling rumor circulated around the fringes of the Room. Washington had made its move. Ulysses Grant had ordered the Gold Ring crushed.

Across the street at the SubTreasury, Daniel Butterfield, tired and bemused, sat down at his large desk across from a roomful of bankers and messengers. The crowd grew silent as Butterfield closed his lips and silently read the message from Washington. Without uttering a word he took pen to paper and wrote in longhand: "Notice: By order of the Secretary of the Treasury, the assistant treasurer will sell, at 12 o'clock noon to-morrow, four million gold and buy four million of bonds." He signed the paper and instructed a doorkeeper to post it on the SubTreasury's bulletin board.

Butterfield then lifted his face to the assemblage, cleared his throat, and read aloud the text of Boutwell's telegram.

The men in the room applauded.

Before Butterfield could finish his announcement, the crowd had dispersed. Squads of messengers carried the news to the Gold Room that George Boutwell had taken a stand. In the confusion, word of mouth magnified the government's planned $4 million gold sale to $15 million. Others said that

Duncan, Sherman, & Company had borrowed $10 million in gold from the SubTreasury to break the corner.

The news hit the market like a ton of bricks. "The moral effect of this Government action was to strike terror to the holders of gold, and a general rush was made to sell out," wrote Henry Clews. Prices galloped like mad; from $160, gold crashed down to $140, rebounded to $150, fell to $133—all in minutes.

"Possibly no avalanche ever swept with more terrible violence," reported the *Herald*. "As the bells of Trinity [Church] pealed forth the hour of noon the gold on the indicator stood at 160. Just a moment later, and before the echoes died away, gold fell to 138."

In ludicrous contrast Albert Speyers, who looked to one observer "like a goblin rather than a man, with dim eyes and face as pale as ashes," continued offering to pay $160 for gold while brokers inches away sold for $135. Sellers refused to accept Speyers's inflated bids for fear that the old man had lost his sanity or his solvency.

A Western Union telegraph operator turned to Tom Edison in the operators' booth and said: "Shake, Edison, we are O.K. We haven't got a cent." Edison wrote, "I felt very happy because we were poor. These occasions are very enjoyable to a poor man; but they occur rarely."

PART VII

Outlaws

· · · · ·

• 26 •
HIGH OLD TIMES

EWS OF THE BREAK reached Fisk and Gould instantly. Terrified messengers and brokers poured into the back room of William Heath & Company and asked for instructions. Speyers himself burst through the door to report the disaster. He bordered on idiocy, according to Jim. "Mine Got, mine Got! The whole thing is gone up! Mine Got! I have got sixty millions, and it is now 141!" Jim later recalled him saying.

"If you don't know anything better than to be out there buying gold at 160, you had better be out of it, " Jim claimed that he shot back.

Speyers' memory of the scene differed completely. "Mr. Fisk, in spite of my objections, told me always that I was perfectly safe" and should "keep up that status, (that was the elegant language he used) to keep up that status of 160," he aid. Remarkably. Albert Speyers followed this order. On Jim's command he charged back to the Gold Room to beat his head some more. He would buy $26 million in gold on Black Friday before it was over.

Jay Gould's brokers continued to unload his gold, trying their best not to sell it to Speyers or to other busted Fisk brokers. Henry Smith raced from Heath offices into the street to find his agent Edwin Chapin outside the Exchange and told him to "sell five millions of gold, not below [1]35, but not to Belden or Speyers." Chapin sold $2,825,000 at prices ranging from $135 to $138 in less than an hour, scattering the transactions among dozens of smaller buyers.

An agent for E. K. Willard, another Smith broker, reported selling $2 million to Speyers by mistake. " [I]t was not worth a damn," Willard fumed, crossing it off his books.

James Brown, delighted by his handiwork, used the opportunity to buy $7 million in gold at about $140 to deliver to Speyers at $160. By simple arithmetic, that neat trick would profit him by $1.4 million—at least as long as Speyers and Fisk stood behind their contracts.

Resentment against Speyers grew dramatically. Jostling elbows and shoving hands escalated into death threats. A colleague grabbed Speyers and told him that "people were accusing me of putting up the price of gold, and. that they threatened to shoot me if I did not stop," he said. Speyers claimed that he rushed instantly to the Stock Exchange, mounted the podium, and bared his chest. "I am here; I am a good target; shoot me if you dare," he said. "Any man that wants to shoot can have a chance now; and any man that said he would shoot me is a poor miserable coward."

The Room responded with loud hisses.

A *Sun* reporter in the Gold Room gallery reported a less flattering version of the event. At about twelve-thirty, the reporter wrote, Speyers "rushed about the little [Cupid's] fountain as if in terror," then raised his hand and shouted hoarsely to the heated, struggling mass below him that someone was trying to kill him. " 'He is after me now with a big knife' shrieked Mr. Speyers. 'Look, look!' he continued 'don't you see the knife?' "

Tom Edison, sitting in the gallery above, recalled that Speyers "went crazy" and "it took five men to hold him; and everybody lost their heads."

Saved from assassins, Albert Speyers's problems had only just begun. He found himself standing at the center of the Gold Room face to face with James Brown, who was intent on protecting his investment. Having sold Speyers $7 million in gold at $160, James wanted a margin deposit to cover the price drop.

Speyers did not have a dime; he was only a broker carrying orders for customers.

"Speyers, I want to know who your principals are; I want you to make a deposit," James shouted above the din.

"My principals are the clique," Speyers said.

"I want names."

"Come with me." Like old friends, Speyers and Brown strolled together off the Exchange floor. "He put his arm in mine and led me across the street" to the Ring's headquarters, James later said.

James knew the way very well. William Heath was a long-time Brown Brothers customer. James had loaned Heath & Company large sums as recently as August, before the gold corner business.

On reaching the now-famous back room, James found his way blocked.

Three muscular guards allowed Speyers to enter the narrow doorway, but they halted James Brown. "You cannot go through there," one of them said.

"I have business with these gentlemen," James responded. The guard repeated his orders.

Speyers ended this indignity to James after a few minutes by opening the door to let him in. Jim and Jay knew they could not put off a confrontation with the senior partner of Brown Brothers bank forever.

Once inside, James enjoyed a rare outsider's view of the Gold Ring's inner sanctum. Fisk, Gould, and Belden all looked frazzled and disheveled. Speyers made the introduction. "Gentlemen, this is Mr. Brown, of whose firm I bought seven millions of gold on your account. He has demanded a margin of me; you have not given me any, and, therefore, I refer him to you."

Brown added only that the Exchange's rules gave him power to collect the deposit.

Fisk and Gould barely acknowledged James's presence, let alone his request. James described their evasions as being like those of schoolboys caught red-handed. "Jay Gould replied and stated that they could not say what they would do in reference to it just at that time," James recalled. "Mr. Belden, who was in a corner of the room on his knees looking over some statements, shouted out that they could not attend to that just now. Fisk had his coat off, and looked like a bull badly baited, puffing and blowing at a great rate; he did not appear to make any remarks."

"If you do not make the margin to-night, I will have your heads," James said. With that, he turned and left to find satisfaction elsewhere.

As the market descended into chaos, hundreds of furious, ruined gamblers, merchants, and brokers swarmed out of the Gold Room into the streets around the Exchange. Squads of New York police, who had been alerted to the crash, raced to Broad Street and stood guard in front of the main Ring offices—Belden & Company, Heath & Company, and Smith, Gould, Martin & Company.

Confusion reigned supreme. Rumors of bankruptcy swept the street. Nobody knew where they stood in relation to vast sums of money. The Gold Exchange Bank had not yet paid a penny for Thursday's trades. Had it gone bust? If the Bank could not pay, could anyone?

Streams of creditors visited the Ring brokers demanding restitution, but they were turned away empty-handed. Afterward, they joined the desperate men congregating outside.

The mood turned ugly. The street crowd appealed to "Judge Lynch." If Jim Fisk and Jay Gould refused to repay their stealings in cash, they should pay in blood. If the Ring leaders had shown their faces at that point, wrote Henry Clews, "the chances were that the lamp-post near by would have very soon been decorated with a breathless body."

In one spirited moment someone in the crowd recalled that Jay Gould had reputedly cheated his first New York business partner years before. "Who killed Leupp?" shouted a voice. "Jay Gould! Jay Gould!" responded the street chorus, along with cries of "lynch, lynch."

A rumor circulated that the sheriff's deputies who were now on the street had been sent by the order of Judge George Barnard, the well-known tool of Tweed, Fisk, and Gould. Cries to lynch Barnard flowed freely.

General James McQuade of the New York State Militia, who was already familiar with Jim Fisk's handiwork from the battle of the Harpersville tunnel, sensed an impending riot. He wired an order to Major Bush in Brooklyn to hold the Fifty-sixth Regiment in readiness for possible duty. Hundreds of Brooklyn volunteers then gathered at the Court Street armory waiting for orders to march.

As the minutes passed, the small back room at Heath & Company became uncomfortably warm. The mob out front grew impatient. At one point several men stormed the office's barricaded doors. A gun-toting guard held them off by threatening bloodshed.

"These are high old times," Jim blabbered.

The time had come to find another nest. At that moment broker Lewis Stimson happened to have been standing in the alleyway outside Heath & Company's back door. He saw Jay Gould creep outside. Jay "look[ed] around sharply to see if he was watched," Stimson said, and then "slunk off through a private rear passage behind the buildings." A minute later came Fisk, looking "steaming hot and shouting. [Fisk] took the wrong direction at first, nearly ran into Broad street, but soon discovered his error, and followed Gould through the rear passage.

"Then came Belden, with hair disordered and red eyes, as if he had been crying. He called: 'which way have they gone?' and, upon my pointing the direction, he ran after them. The rear passage led into Wall street."

The gold bandits hustled themselves through the back door of Smith, Gould, Martin & Company, just half a block down from Heath's at 11 Broad Street.

The maneuver accomplished little. News traveled through the mob out front that Jim and Jay had changed venue and were now hiding in the other building. A swollen crowd gathered outside the barricaded doors of Smith, Gould, Martin & Company, flooding the sidewalk and half the street.

One gambler offered to bet $1,000 that the firm was solvent. He found no takers.

James Brown and Kruger, still looking for a responsible person to post margin for the $7 million gold sale, joined the crush outside Jay's brokerage firm. Maybe Henry Smith could help, they thought. Assuming his own priority, James pushed through the crowd behind Kruger and demanded entrance into the building. Other frustrated creditors shouted their encouragement.

As they reached the door, one of Henry Smith's clerks standing guard gave Kruger a hard shove. Kruger, "a robust young man, and very good tempered," according to James, turned and threw a punch that knocked the clerk to the pavement. Police intervened and arrested both Kruger and the clerk. They dragged them to the New Street station house; there, James helped to get them released.

Kruger and Henry Smith's clerk eventually "shook hands and were discharged," reported the *Times*.

Locked inside Smith's cramped office, Jim and Jay heard the angry chanting. They must have felt chills as they contemplated the frailty of their necks. A hundred men swinging bricks and fists could easily trample a few guards and break down a wooden door. Did Henry Smith keep guns in the building? Could Jay or Belden shoot straight in a firefight? No injunction from Judge Barnard's court could save them if the mob decided to demand justice.

Maybe they drew straws to see which of them would go outside and face the mob: Fisk, Gould, Belden, or Henry Smith. But Jim volunteered. Jim gave the best speeches, and after all, who would want to hang good old Prince Erie?

The crowd on the sidewalk by the Smith, Gould, Martin & Company storefront on New Street was suddenly startled to see Fisk, hailed hours before as the "well oiled Assyrian bull of Wall Street," slowly unlocked the door and step out alone onto the sidewalk. His fancy clothes were wrinkled and sweaty, his diamond stickpin was shining less brightly, his eyes were red but clear, and his hands were held firmly at his sides.

Jim stood inches from the rabble, close enough to see individual twisted mouths shouting catcalls at his face. He tried to get the mob's attention for a speech. Before he could utter a word, one overexcited spectator stepped forward and "dashed his fist in the face of the portly Managing Director of the Erie," wrote a *Sun* reporter standing nearby.

A scuffle broke out. Policemen scrambled to catch the assailant. In a flash Jim retreated back indoors, blood streaming from his nose.

It would be nightfall before Jim, Jay, Belden, or Smith dared venture outside again.

FALLING OUT

A BEL CORBIN SPENT THAT FRIDAY MORNING in New Jersey tending his real estate investments. When he arrived in New York at midday, he picked up a newspaper and learned that the bottom had fallen off of Wall Street. He summoned a carriage and rushed to the Grand Opera House, where he asked to see Jay Gould. A clerk told him that Jay and Jim were downtown. Corbin hadn't seen Jay since the morning before, when Jay had promised to close his $1.5 million interest in the Ring.

Corbin had called at the Opera House on Thursday afternoon but had missed its chief denizens then, too.

Fishing for news, Corbin now struck up a conversation with two of Fisk's aides, Charles McIntosh and messenger C. W. Pollard. Corbin "appeared to be greatly excited," Pollard later claimed, "and he feared *we* would lose a great deal of money."

To McIntosh, Corbin said that "he hoped they would come out all right as he (Mr. Corbin) was deeply interested."

Abel Corbin's "interest" in the Gold Ring had as many facets as Jim Fisk's shirtfront diamond. For one thing, Jay Gould owed him at least $100,000. If Gould and Fisk had lost badly in the crash, Corbin's investment had vanished as well. More important, having been stung once before by political scandal, Corbin smelled danger. The *Times* had connected his name with the conspiracy. His brother-in-law Grant had already expressed irritation at his rumored involvement.

The fact that it was Grant who had ordered the Ring crushed only worsened the embarrassment.

Once the details of the fiasco unraveled, Corbin would inevitably be tied to the Wall Street bulls. Political enemies would hang him like an albatross around Grant's neck. Corbin's reputation, his influence, and his family honor all stood exposed. The Ring—himself, Gould, and Fisk—had to stick together to avoid disaster.

Unable to learn anything, Corbin left the Opera House to spend the afternoon at home with Jennie waiting and worrying. He'd come back later to try again.

After nightfall, Jim Fisk and Jay Gould themselves traveled uptown in a fast carriage with blinds drawn tight over the windows. "I was in no enviable state of mind," Jim later said, not unreasonably, having just lost a fortune and having barely escaped death by hanging. Belden joined them in the carriage from Wall Street. Jay looked exhausted. Jim described his partner that day as having "sunk right down. There is nothing left of him but a heap of clothes and a pair of eyes."

On reaching the Opera House, Jim stationed guards at all the doors. Like the barons of a medieval fortress, the Erie managers put alligators in the moat and pulled in the drawbridge for a long siege.

If Jay hadn't told his partner about his massive gold sales and about the mysterious "Dear Sis" letter to Jennie Corbin, he did so now.

Trying to think straight amid the chaos, Jim and Jay, along with Belden and Smith, pieced together a rough picture of their post-crash finances. Jim's position was dreadful. If held responsible for his enormous gold purchases that morning at prices ranging from $140 to $162, his losses could be astronomical—big enough to swamp himself, Jay, and the Erie Railway, too. Wall Street gossip pegged his exposure at up to $30 million, a figure that rivaled Vanderbilt's entire fortune. Speyers alone had bought $26 million in gold on Friday, mostly at prices around $160, which alone was enough to produce over $5 million in losses for Jim—besides the oceans' worth he had bought at Thursday's top dollar. Belden's total approached $70 million in high-priced calls.

Jay stood a chance of coming out better. His brokers had sold nearly all his $40 to $50 million in gold during the melee at prices from $140 to $150, plus several million more above $135. If these contracts held, Jay could reap a harvest big enough to save them both. If they could somehow enforce Jay's sales but wriggle out of Jim's buying, wealth could still ultimately be had.

Scrupulous men might have found this hot-and-cold juggling act difficult. Jay Gould and Fisk suffered no such disability.

First they needed breathing space. All the Ring brokers suspended business on Friday afternoon. Smith, Gould, Martin & Company, Heath & Company, Speyers, E. K. Willard, Belden & Company, and Dornin & Boocock all announced that they could not pay their debts until further notice. Their creditors hoped that the firms would survive, but for now everything hung in the air.

After closing their doors, the brokers streamed uptown to "Castle Erie" and asked Fisk and Gould to stand behind their trades. If they should not, Jim's brokers would absorb huge losses and probably go bust.

Few, not even the most loyal, got past the Opera House doors.

To answer their direct question, Jay put word out through Henry Smith that, yes, his credit was good. Jay's brokers—Willard, Chapin, Enos, and Osborn—would be paid. They had made him lots of money on Black Friday. Jay worried only that the Gold Exchange Bank, buried under gold paperwork, might annul the sales.

Jim Fisk sent out an equally clear message: His brokers could all hang themselves.

Jim's excuse, which he now espoused as gospel, was that he himself hadn't bought a dime's worth of gold on Friday. Every order he had given to Speyers, Boocock, et al. had been for William Belden's account, not for his own. If Belden and crazy Albert Speyers had not driven the market to ridiculous heights, Jim said, the whole disaster would not have happened.

Belden and Speyers were the villains, not innocent Jim Fisk, who had only happened to advise them on strategy as a favor.

Fortunes hung on this technicality. Without Jim's deep pockets, Belden would never be able to pay the losses for Black Friday. By going bankrupt, he'd bury the corpse with himself. Broker after broker turned to Jim Fisk for support, but Jim hid in his grand marble fortress, silent and unapproachable.

Jim had taken the refuge of a scoundrel: repudiation.

Traders submitted more than $500 million in transactions to be cleared through the Gold Exchange Bank on Friday. That much gold—a thousand tons—would require a string of horse-pulled carts eight miles long to move it, one writer figured. By 1980s standards, with gold valued at about $450 an ounce, the total would amount to at least $14 billion.

During the panic, the Franklin Telegraph Company alone had sent over 5,000 messages from New York, and Western Union's three New York outlets had sent another 5,700—including 900 transmitted from the Gold Room itself. Telegraph wires from the Gold Room melted from the heat of electrical signals, causing news blackouts across the Northeast.

Philadelphians placed a black shroud over their broken public gold-price indicator on Third Street to mark the disaster.

Wild scenes continued on Wall Street through the night. Brokers congregated at the Gold Exchange Bank at 29 New Street, still waiting to be paid for Thursday's clearings, let alone for Friday's flood. "I have made $50,000 on the fall," one operator told Edmund Stedman, "and would take a quarter of it to-day rather than run the risks of tomorrow."

Bank clerks sat up all night sorting through complex brokers' statements by hand under light from candles and gas lamps. Bank president Henry Benedict, the twenty-year veteran who had organized the gold clearinghouse system four years earlier, posted notice late Friday afternoon that the day's balances could not be paid, "owing to the failure of several dealers" to submit statements.

At about eight that evening a mob of "eager-eyed, half-crazed men" crowded the Gold Exchange Bank to check on their money. "The crowd were struggling, and in some instances fighting," reported the *Sun*. Police used billy clubs to keep order.

A few compulsive gamblers congregated in the barroom of the Fifth Avenue Hotel late Friday to bet whatever money they had left on gold, hoping that gold might yet rise from the grave as the clock ticked away toward midnight. But most men there drank their whiskey in quiet desolation, bitter, angry, and fearful.

The price slumped to $131 in the pointless trading.

That night, after hours of being closeted with Fisk, Belden, and Smith in the inner confines of the Opera House Jay Gould, his frail body drained by the long day's journey through fiscal purgatory, sent a messenger for Abel Rathbone Corbin.

◎ ◎ ◎ ◎ ◎

Jay, Jim, and Abel Corbin met at least twice that weekend to confer about the gold market disaster. The meetings degenerated into finger-pointing, shouting, and quibbling. His partner Gould had deceived him outright that week, but Jim Fisk held nothing against Jay. Whatever venom he felt, he directed solely at the odd man of the threesome, the politico who had married the President's sister.

Corbin and Fisk first butted heads on Friday afternoon, hours after the crash. Their respective portrayals of the meeting differ diametrically. Both stories, given in sworn testimony months later, reek with internal contradictions and self-serving innuendoes.

Corbin put the tête-à-tête at the Grand Opera House; Fisk put it in the dining room of Corbin's residence. Corbin said he had received a note from Jay Gould late on Friday to come by the Erie Railway office. He had left Jennie at home, since the Opera House "was no place for a lady; it was a public business office." There, an usher had taken Corbin directly to Jay, who looked "sedate" and "depressed—quite depressed," he said. After their short talk, Jim Fisk had entered the room and launched into a manic monologue on his drubbing, how "his sister, or his sister's son, was ruined, and [he] made a few general declarations relative to his losses."

According to Corbin, Jim uttered not a word of complaint against himself personally.

Jim, on the other hand, recalled throwing a full-blown temper tantrum, complete with ranting, raving, and wailing.

Jim claimed that he had known exactly who the villain was. After returning uptown from Wall Street that afternoon, he had "started round to old Corbin's to rake him out." In Jim's own words, on reaching the house,

> I was too mad to say anything civil, and when [Corbin] came into the [dining] room, said I, "You damned old scoundrel, do you know what has happened?" This was, of course, after everything had blown up. Said I, "Do you know what you have done, you and your people?"
>
> He began to wring his hands, and "Oh," he says "This is a horrible position; are you ruined?"
>
> I said I didn't know whether I was or not; and I asked him again if he knew what had happened.
>
> He had been crying, and said he had just heard; that he had been sure everything was all right; but that something had occurred entirely different from what he had anticipated.
>
> Said I, "That don't amount to anything; we know that gold ought not to be [1]31, and that it would not be but for such performances as you have had this last week; you knew damned well it would not if you had not failed." I knew that somebody had run a saw into us, and said I, "This whole damned thing had turned out just as I told you it would; I consid-

ered the whole party a pack of cowards;" and I expected that when we came to clear our hands they would sock it right into us. I said to him, "I don't know whether you have lied or not, and I don't know what ought to be done with you."

He was on the other side of the table weeping and wailing, and I was gnashing my teeth. "Now," he says, "you must quiet yourself."

I told him I didn't want to be quiet; I had no desire to ever be quiet again.

He says, "But, my dear sir, you will lose your reason."

Says I, "Speyers has already lost his reason; reason has gone out of everybody but me." I continued "Now what are you going to do; you have got us into this thing, and what are you going to do to get out of it."

He says, "I don't know; I will go and get my wife."

I said, "Get her down here." The soft talk was over. He went upstairs and they returned, "tottling" into the room, looking older than Stephen Hopkins. His wife and he both looked like death. He was tottling, just like that. (Illustrated by a trembling movement of the body.)

The tense trio met again on Saturday at the Opera House. Jim again took the offensive as each portrayed himself the victim and blamed the others for the disaster. Any hope Corbin had of ever seeing his $100,000 from Gould vanished in the cacophony of voices. According to Corbin,

[Fisk] began to say: "How is this, how is this? I have been deceived by somebody!"

"Not by me," said I, "for you and I never exchanged a word on this subject. You have not been deceived by me!"

"Well," said [Fisk], "if we had not had confidence in you, do you suppose we would have gone in?"

"I do not make any supposition about it," said I, "only that I never attempted to inspire you with confidence," and so on, interspersed with sharp passages.

Among other things [Fisk] said: "Where is that $100,000 that Gould gave you?"

I turned upon him and said: "Mr. Gould never gave me $100,000, and he will tell you so."

Mr. Gould, showing a good deal of excitement, said: "That is accounted for."

*"Accounted for or not accounted for," said I, "I never have even seen
any $100,000."*

*"Well," said Mr. Fisk, "where is the $25,000 for Mrs. [Julia]
Grant?" "Stop that," said I, "Mrs. Grant's name never has been mentioned in that connection by any human being, and you shall not mention
it. It is as false as anything can be, and it is not to be named to me." Mr.
Gould sat there perfectly quiet. I should have lost my self-possession had
the subject been pursued.*

Beneath all their recriminations, the three shared a common problem.
Fisk and Corbin could argue all day about who had first dragged the President's wife into the mud, but someone in Washington—either Boutwell or
Grant—had sold them down the river. After hours of diatribes they agreed on
a plan. Corbin would travel to Washington immediately, visit his brother-in-
law, and make a final plea for the gamblers.

Jim later claimed that this idea had grown out of his confrontation with
Corbin and Jennie Friday night. Jennie had come downstairs to join Jim and
her husband in heated debate and had thrust herself into the discussion, he
said. She insisted either that Washington had gotten cold feet or that
"Boutwell had sold the gold without consulting" her brother. "[S]he could
not think this had been done with the President's consent," Jim said.

Reluctantly, Corbin yielded to Jennie's urging and agreed to confront the
family face to face, according to Jim's story. "The old man straightened up in
front of the table and said, 'I will go to Washington, and lay it at the door; I
will fathom this thing.' "

Neither Jay nor Jim had much hope for Corbin's last-ditch mission.
Corbin's influence with Grant was "pretty well played out," Jim later ex-
plained. He had agreed to the plan for only one reason, he said: "the further
off [Corbin] was the happier I should be." Later suggestions that Fisk and
Gould had "browbeat the terrified old man" into the mission seem far-fetched.
Of the three, only Corbin himself still thought he had influence with Grant.

The innermost circle of the Gold Ring—Gould, Corbin, and Fisk, a tight
den of thieves who had performed political miracles during the past month—
had busted up. From now on, Jay and Jim would fight their own battles.
Corbin could fend for himself.

In Jim's words, "It was each man drag out his own corpse."

William Belden led Albert Speyers up the grand stairway of the Opera House late one night shortly after the panic into the upper quarters, where the top executives of the Erie Railway were holding court. They passed beneath the ceiling portraits, past the black oak walls, the marble columns, and the stained glass dividers; the building was deserted now except for a handful of ushers and clerks.

When they entered the Erie suite, Belden showed Speyers into the sumptuous private office of Jim Fisk, who had requested the meeting.

Jim was sitting behind his raised polished walnut desk. He looked up and greeted Speyers warmly. In sugary tones Jim asked Speyers about his family. How was his health? How had his business fared in the crash?

Speyers, now much reposed after his earlier Gold Room hysterics, stared back quizzically at the fat man with the waxed moustache and the patronizing look. He answered in monosyllables.

"Mr. Speyers, can you ask anything of us—money, capital, or service?" Jim asked, leaning across the desk. "What do you care about the brokers? You have a family of children. The brokers are all rascals."

Speyers, the most visible symbol of the Ring, knew plenty about Jim's comings and goings on Black Friday. It would be a lot easier for Jim to renege on his gold contracts if he had Speyers's help. Scenes like Speyers's dragging James Brown into his private command center hurt badly. Speyers could give damaging testimony about who had ordered him to buy the oceans of gold at stratospheric prices, and for whose account.

The law might call what Jim was doing now "subornation of perjury," but Jim treated this whole scene as a figment of Speyers's mad imagination.

Whether stupidly or honestly, Speyers had no desire to be bought. "All I want ... " he said in his German accent, "is that [you] should place me where I was on Wednesday," before he had gotten mixed up with the Ring, "when my credit was good, when my name was good, and when I had a good business."

Fisk had little claim to Speyers's loyalty, so he decided to sweeten the pot. At Jim's command, lawyer Thomas Shearman threw a number on the table. Referring to Speyers's lawyer Charles Rapallo, Shearman said offhandedly, "He will not give you two hundred thousand dollars to get you out of this scrape." Jim, by implication, had his checkbook ready for action.

Two hundred thousand dollars went a long way in 1869, farther than $2 million or even $10 million goes today. As pay-offs go, Speyers could not have dreamed of getting better. All Jim wanted was for the sprightly little broker to back up his and Belden's story that Jim's orders on Friday had been for Belden's account, not for Jim's.

"You know, Speyers, that you did it all for me," Belden said, speaking as one who had already sold his story to Fisk.

"Mr. Belden, and Mr. Fisk, that is all nonsense to talk to me so," Albert Speyers said. He shrugged, then ended the meeting.

He had turned down a fortune. Speyers ultimately would get nothing—not his margins, not his commissions, not his legal fees, not his name, reputation, nor business—for sticking to his story.

· 28 ·
WRECKAGE

WORD OF THE GOLD CRASH reached Washington shortly after Ulysses Grant gaveled his Cabinet to order for their Friday afternoon meeting. The news prompted rounds of back slapping and congratulations. The luster from the victory faded on Saturday morning, though, as the dimensions of Wall Street's devastation became clear. Critics aimed their fire at George Boutwell, the secretary whose gold sales had crushed the Ring. Greeley's *Tribune* hailed Boutwell's "magnificent rout of the [gold] gamblers" but criticized his action as "tardy and maladroit." The *Herald* echoed the initial praise. It said on Saturday that Boutwell "came to the rescue with promptness, and wisely, we think." On Monday it called for Boutwell's dismissal.

Critics like the *Sun* and the *World* accused the secretary of favoritism, of using public money to aid bears over bulls. The *Evening Post* saw the gold corner as a "mere struggle between gangs of gamblers," a "contest of nerve and confidence 'backed' by large purses." By elevating it to national importance, Boutwell had "surrendered [the Treasury] to the gold gamblers" and "abandoned … all principles of public policy."

Given Boutwell's cold shoulder to the bears all week, many believed that he had acted under protest. The *Evening Mail* reported late Friday that Grant had "directed" his Treasury secretary to burst the gold bubble. A "member of the firm of Jay Cooke & Co. " had appealed to the President that morning, it said, after which Grant had "sent for Boutwell," resulting in the decision.

Boutwell himself fell into shock. Talking with visitors at his Treasury office on Saturday, he waxed hot and cold. With Henry Cooke, Boutwell acted "astounded at the suddenness and terribleness of the result of his action" and complained of "terrible pressure" to "reconsider." Cooke wrote his brother in Philadelphia that "if [Boutwell] had to do the thing over again, with a full knowledge of the consequences," he doubted he "would have nerve enough to do it."

On the other hand, Boutwell boasted to a *World* reporter that same afternoon that "he had not done with the New York gold-gamblers yet, but would deal them still heavier blows."

At one point Boutwell authorized Daniel Butterfield in New York to cancel the promised $4 million government gold sale altogether. "I am not anxious to sell gold," he cabled his deputy. "If business will be injured omit sales for today. If you do not sell gold, you must not buy bonds."

But Washington's problems after the panic paled next to Wall Street's.

Even after the corner was crushed, panic still reigned. Oceans of wealth sat locked up in the banks, stock and bond values had slumped, and trade barely existed. Worst of all, nobody knew where they stood.

Thousands of demoralized speculators and curiosity-seekers milled around the financial district Saturday trying to fathom the debris. They strolled from office to office and clustered in groups on the sidewalk, groping for news. The Gold Room, the now-empty stage of yesterday's drama, drew dozens of tourists. The Exchange board met at ten that morning and voted to suspend trading at least until Monday.

"Dirt, a vast litter of scraps of paper, and the sort of gloom which always seems to settle down on the theatre of any exciting event, made the place look excessively disagreeable," wrote an observer of the eerie scene. "It smelt of the fray, too; and we think some good disinfectant would be found a good commodity in that region."

Violent talk against the manipulators, especially against Jim Fisk, could be heard all along the Street. A broker who had lost $48,000 in the crash swore to "spend $10 on a revolver and go to blow h—l out of him."

First he would have to find the bull maestro. Fisk, Gould, Belden, and Smith all knew better than to show their faces. Albert Speyers's office reported him as "seriously ill." Guards outside the Erie Railway Opera House told visitors that Fisk was "not in town" or was "in the country."

Several creditors offered cash bounties to anyone who could find the gold renegades and hijack their margins.

Jim's repudiation of his own brokers fed the bitterness. Wall Street knew no worse sin. Speyers announced from the podium of the Stock Exchange that all his gold purchases on Thursday and Friday had been for Belden and Fisk but that Belden had refused to give him a penny's margin. Broker Samuel

Boocock told how he had rushed to Belden's office on Friday afternoon, only to be turned away empty-handed, and that Belden had denied outright that Fisk was his customer.

C. C. Allen, who had bought $2 million in gold for the Ring on Friday at prices up to 160, marched to Heath & Company's office Saturday to collect a deposit. "What gold?" Heath's clerk said, as if surprised. "I gave no orders to purchase gold. You may have bought some for Mr. Fisk."

Allen, furious, threatened legal action. "If that is your little game, and you intend to repudiate our transactions, I have nothing further to say."

One speculator, Solomon Mahler, a husband and the father of six children, had suffered heavy losses; he had gone home to Williamsburg on Friday night and shot himself dead with a revolver. Brokers who heard this story took up a collection for Mahler's family; they grumbled that Fisk and Gould could just as well have pulled the trigger.

Even the biggest bears suffered. "I never want to see such a day again," Harris Fahnestock wrote to Jay Cooke on Saturday. The victory over the Ring meant nothing because his money still sat tied up in the banks. But Fahnestock made the best of the bad situation. He turned a quick profit on Saturday by unloading U.S. bonds when the Treasury implemented Boutwell's Friday order to sell gold and buy bonds. Cooke & Company sold Uncle Sam $867,000 worth of bonds at 118.07—the choicest market price.

Like other New York firms, Fahnestock ordered his clerks to sort out their Friday gold trades, to give the winners to Cooke & Company in-house accounts, and to assign the losers to customers. "All the banks here take the position that gold is borrowed for *ale* of our customers & at their risk," Fahnestock reported, "& henceforth we charge all to our customers." With minimal nineteenth-century record-keeping, most customers would never guess that they had been cheated.

"Market is over and we are lovely," Fahnestock reported. I "am a little tired but have a *level head.*"

Perhaps the only person who derived pleasure from the havoc was Commodore Cornelius Vanderbilt. He was at home in New York with his young bride Frank, a thirty-year-old beauty whom he had married that summer in a surprise elopement. At the height of Friday's panic, friends pleaded with Vanderbilt to appear at the Exchange and calm the hysteria. Cornele had declined. He preferred to let his enemies Fisk and Gould stew in their own pot and "carry it through to their heart's content."

Vanderbilt rode his carriage down to Wall Street on Saturday morning to tour the battle scene. He inspected the row of busted brokers on Broad Street, the desolate bankers, the sad Exchanges. Observers found the Commodore "calm, quiet, and serene—the very picture of self-satisfaction." Whatever vengeance Vanderbilt still planned for the Erie ruffians who had plundered his railroad stock that week, he enjoyed seeing what asses Gould and Fisk had made of themselves by their own devices.

Beyond his smug glee, Vanderbilt shared the concern that the gold crash might spark a stock panic and threaten his own fortune. When prices slipped in Saturday trading on the Stock Exchange, Vanderbilt threw his clout behind his companies. Financier John Morrissey saw Vanderbilt all day Saturday at the Bank of New York directing his brokers to buy vast quantities of New York Central, Hudson River, and Harlem River railroads to support values. "Had Vanderbilt not come to the rescue, I don't know what would have become of the street," Morrissey told a reporter.

The most immediate concern on Saturday was for the banks. Banks runs were far more common before the 1930s, when Congress adopted federal deposit insurance programs. Beyond the potential losses to customers, the collapse of even a single bank, especially a federally chartered institution, could turn crisis into calamity. Banks tended to fall in groups. One run could set off a chain reaction as confidence dwindled. When banks failed, investors hoarded their money, which made credit tight. Economic depression followed close behind.

The equation rang as true in 1869 as it did in 1857 or 1929.

Two banks became lightning rods on the morning after Black Friday, both of them heavily implicated in the panic: the Gold Exchange Bank and the Tenth National Bank.

The Gold Exchange Bank closed all its customer windows on Saturday except for one teller who handled routine savings accounts. Early that morning, dozens of creditors crowded the lobby seeking appointments with Bank president Henry Benedict. Sitting in a small side office, Benedict's worst fear from Friday had come true: The gold gamblers had screwed up the works and then dumped the whole mess on his lap. As the clearinghouse for the Exchange, the Bank still had not calculated the settlements for Thursday's hectic Gold Room session. Its clerks were choking on the $500 million-plus in trades submitted for Friday.

Some of the biggest players—brokers representing Fisk, Gould, and James

Brown—had failed to submit statements for Friday's debacle altogether. And statements from cooperating firms drawn by hand during the excitement contained errors and illegible markings.

But the danger ran deeper than a mere paperwork backlog. The Gold Exchange Bank was obligated as legal agent to stand behind every purchase and sale on the Gold Room floor. A broker who had sold gold to Jim Fisk for 160 could deliver the gold to the Bank and demand payment. To break even, the Bank had to collect the debt from Fisk directly. If Fisk defaulted, the Bank ate the loss.

Bank reserves usually covered any shortfall. Friday's enormous transactions and price swings, though, had created debts far exceeding the reserves. A default by the biggest bulls could topple the clearinghouse itself.

Starting early Saturday, traders who had sold gold to Belden, Speyers, et al. delivered gold by the cartload to the Bank to fulfill their contracts—over $12 million worth altogether, an amount more than three-fourths the total public supply in New York City. All had been committed for sale at high prices. One Bank cashier alone had $10 million in gold certificates on his desk. Bank rules required a distribution of the wealth by two-fifteen that afternoon.

But since it had not yet calculated the clearances or even received statements or payment from a dozen major firms, the Bank could not pay a penny. A king's ransom sat idly in its vaults, tempting burglars, jurists, and other highwaymen, waiting for Benedict and his clerks to figure out whom the money belonged to. Brokers claimed staggering amounts. William Heath said the Bank owed him $1.1 million in cash, proceeds from Jay Gould's large sales. Joseph Seligman claimed $651,000. The Bank also had debts to other New York banks of almost $2 million on Saturday morning, which it paid in gold.

Benedict summoned police and private detectives to patrol the building against outright theft as creditors milled about the lobby. "Every person who gained access to Mr. Benedict was instantly seized by the crowd as he emerged from the office, and was firmly held until pumped of all information that could possibly be obtained of him," reported the *Herald*. Little news came out.

While the Gold Exchange Bank hid behind closed windows, the Tenth National Bank faced customers on Saturday by opening for business. In minutes it was confronted by a stampede. Wall Street bubbled with reports that the Fisk-Gould ring had ravaged the Tenth National in its gold run-up. With Boss Tweed and Gould controlling the Bank's stock, depositors dreaded the worst. They had lined up on the sidewalk at Broad and New Streets by nine o'clock to withdraw their money, hoping the Bank's assets hadn't vanished in the Gold Room wreck.

That morning, three rival city banks had refused to honor checks certified by the Tenth National, feeding the fears.

The stream of creditors became a torrent. Police set up patrols inside and outside the Tenth National Bank to guard against rioting. With only $1.1 million in cash on hand, the Bank could easily fail by lunchtime. President Dickinson, desperate for money, called in all the Bank's day-to-day loans to gold and stock brokers. "Greenbacks were piled upon the counter like a haystack" as messenger boys carried back proceeds from the neighborhood firms, wrote Matthew Smith.

Jay Gould heard about the run from the sanctuary of the Opera House.

He ordered his brokers to help his beleaguered Tenth National. At Dickinson's request, he wired Henry Smith to withdraw a claim for $1 million by Smith, Gould, Martin & Company, which would free the funds for other customers. Heath & Company also relented on two smaller checks.

The Tenth National normally closed its doors for the day at three o'clock.

But at that hour five hundred depositors and spectators still crowded the sidewalk and streets, many still hoping to get to the tellers' windows. Dickinson considered closing down but decided against it. Locking up would only inflame public antagonism and bring a worse storm the next day.

Dickinson stepped outside into the brisk afternoon sun and mounted the stairs in front of the Bank's marble entranceway. "Gentlemen, if any of you have claims against this bank, if you walk in and present them they will be paid," he announced to the streets-side congregation in a loud, raspy voice. "The run on this bank today had been a most iniquitous one, and there are few banks in the city that could have stood it as we have done."

The doors stayed open until six that night. The Bank's tellers had satisfied every customer demanding payment. Of the $1.1 million in cash that had been on hand that morning, only $100,000 remained. Dickinson had honored every check presented except for the three withdrawn by Jay Gould and William Heath.

By then, the storm clouds had dispersed.

• 29 •
BEHIND THE BARRICADES

OUTSIDE THE COZY CONFINES of the Grand Opera House, the world pulsated with charges and threats. Accusing fingers pointed from Boston to San Francisco to Jay Gould and Jim Fisk as the outlaws who had crippled and humiliated the nation's economic center. New York streets crawled with creditors, assassins, and process servers.

Jim's sore nose reminded him constantly of the dangers of going out unguarded in daylight.

Inside, though, the Opera House offered its inmates comforts galore; it was the swankest private jail money could buy. A fully enclosed passage connected Jim's office with Josie Mansfield's townhouse just a few doors down Twenty-third Street. He used that convenient escape route at least once over the weekend. While New Yorkers searched for the renegades on Friday and Saturday, Jim cheered himself with a night of drama, sneaking out for the performance of *Leah* at Booth's Theatre.

Closer to home, he also took in Lucille Western's nightly outings on his Opera House stage as *Patrie*, which was accessible without risking his neck.

Josie took the disaster in stride, standing by her man like a good politician's wife. But Jim must have talked plenty when Josie confronted him with stories published Saturday morning about Lucille Western, his Opera House starlet, sharing his carriage to Wall Street on Black Friday. Josie now had a new gripe to hang over Jim the next time they argued about money.

Despite their creature comforts, Jay and Jim seethed inside their palace prison. The wrangling with Abel Corbin had struck a sore nerve, reminding Jay that he had paid good bribes to other Grant men, too. Take Daniel Butterfield, assistant secretary of the Treasury. Maybe Butterfield wasn't responsible for Washington's betrayal, but Jay had suspicions. What had Butterfield told Boutwell anyway, in all their private talks? Why hadn't he warned them of the deluge? Jay knew that the assistant treasurer had sold gold before the crash through broker Joseph Seligman; he had made his own profit while deceiving the Ring.

Butterfield was Corbin's friend. Skunks of a feather, Jim Fisk might have said.

Now on Saturday, as Jay struggled to survive the cyclone, Butterfield was preparing to drive in the final dagger by implementing Boutwell's order to sell gold from the SubTreasury. Had Jay showered Butterfield with gifts, given him a $10,000 loan and a treasure in gold, for this? Talk about bad investments ...

Early Saturday morning, Jay sent lawyer Frederick Lane to the assistant secretary's office in the SubTreasury Building on Wall Street.

Butterfield had been running in mad circles ever since Friday's panic. Alarmed at how quickly the word of Boutwell's message to sell $4 million in gold had broken prices, Butterfield suggested that someone had tapped the telegraph wires from Washington—one of the earliest "wire-tapping" charges on record. Experienced telegraph operators "laughed heartily" when asked about the charge.

When Lane came by on Saturday, Butterfield was arranging the infamous $4 million gold-bond sale for Uncle Sam. The process required him to conduct a silent auction. Buyers would send written bids to the SubTreasury, and Butterfield would accept the best prices. George Boutwell in Washington took a hands-on management approach as he had not in earlier months. During the day Boutwell sent his New York deputy at least eight telegrams and three letters directing his every move. "Report to me prices bid for gold before awards are made," Boutwell said. "Gold must be paid for on delivery in all cases. Acknowledge receipt of dispatch immediately, " he wired. "Do not deliver gold except for money. Have you received my letter of last evening?"

At each command Butterfield jumped like a good soldier. By mid afternoon New York bankers had bid for almost $10 million in government gold, more than twice the amount offered. But after all the hullabaloo, the Treasury had sold only $2 million worth at prices from $132½ to $134.

Frederick Lane got right to the point. He said that Jay Gould had sent him to ask about Butterfield's account at Smith, Gould, Martin & Company, which contained $1.5 million in gold. With the steep price drop, Butterfield now owed Jay a great deal of money. The total dollar debt, not mentioned directly in documentary records, staggered the assistant treasurer.

Butterfield acted surprised. What gold? he said. There must be some mistake.

Lane watched impassively as Butterfield's boyish face slowly reddened.

Lane reached into his pocket and pulled out a note from Jay, written that morning, which he handed across the desk:

> Sir: I am carrying $1.5 million gold, being your interest in the pool. Please provide a place to-day for the same, or give Messrs. Smith, Gould, Martin & Co. a satisfactory margin this morning, and let the bearer know, or they will be compelled to sell it out for your account under the rule.

Jay had scribbled a postscript on the note, an instruction for Lane: "Tell him if he don't, we will sell it publicly in his name."

Butterfield gasped. Certainly he remembered Jay's offer to buy him gold weeks before. But, he insisted, he had never accepted the offer, although he had never declined it either. If Jay had gone ahead and bought gold on his account, he, Butterfield, never knew, he said. For Jay to finger him as a dues-paying member of the bull clique that had devastated Wall Street—that was blackmail! His career, his reputation, his fortune could all be ruined.

Butterfield became upset. "[H]is conversation was so interlarded with profanity that no gentleman would repeat it," Lane recalled.

But squirming on the line as he was, Butterfield spoke circumspectly. He had signed no papers for the gold. Gould could prove nothing. Still, Butterfield said he felt "honor bound" to pay, according to Lane. Maybe he could talk things over with Gould, Butterfield suggested, but Lane demurred that Jay was very busy. Butterfield had another problem, too, he said. Despite his millions in real estate holdings, he had no cash and could not possibly pay the whole debt right away.

Seeing the assistant treasurer, a handsome, decorated war hero, reduced to pleading ignorance and begging poverty softened the heart of Jay's henchman. Lane agreed to compromise. He would trust Butterfield to pay a $10,000 down payment by two-thirty that afternoon and a second installment Monday. He'd ask Jay to give Butterfield time to mortgage one of his houses before paying the rest.

Lane returned to Butterfield's Wall Street office at two-thirty to collect the first $10,000 installment. He found Butterfield rushing to the door "with his hat on ready to go out." His wife was ill, Butterfield said, and he had to go see her right away. As for the money, he again pleaded poverty. "But you tell Mr. Gould that I will pay all that is due, and he shall not lose by me."

Pay or not, on hearing Lane's report, Jay could smile knowing that he and Jim Fisk were not the only speculators in New York with sweat on their palms.

◎ ◎ ◎ ◎ ◎

Late Saturday afternoon, Abel and Jennie Corbin left their comfortable New York home and rode by carriage across town to the ferry that would take them to their train to Washington. Gould and Fisk stepped out into the daylight world perhaps for the first time after Friday's crash to see them off. The threesome—Jay, Jim, and Corbin—had little to talk about. "You telegraph us tomorrow if the government will forbear, " Jim said politely. Gould gave Corbin the number of his Fifth Avenue house so that Corbin could reach him day or night.

Corbin dreaded the journey. Having to confront his angry brother-in-law was bad enough, but his health had also deteriorated. "[I]t was a serious thing for an old man to make a night journey of 250 miles," Corbin complained. It would take Abel and Jennie till dawn to reach Washington and ride by carriage to the White House for their graceless family reunion.

◎ ◎ ◎ ◎ ◎

Sunday brought no rest for the Opera House inmates. Jay and Jim sat cooped up with lawyers and brokers all day sorting out their hideously complex finances. Their plan to escape ruin had unraveled. To get around Jim's repudiations, Friday's bears now claimed that they had sold gold to Jay Gould instead. Henry Benedict's gold clearinghouse remained clogged. Gold Exchange officials encouraged traders to settle their transactions directly with individual brokers outside the usual system.

What would happen to the fortune in Henry Benedict's Bank vaults? Would Friday's trades be thrown out? Would Jay's profitable gold sales be canceled?

The endless scenarios ran in circles. As long as the Gold Exchange Bank dilly-dallied over settling Friday's trades, no one could make heads or tails of the situation.

Not even the Opera House fortress was safe. James Brown himself, perhaps the Ring's biggest single creditor, managed to sidestep the guards and penetrate "Castle Erie" that weekend to try to enforce his $7 million Black Friday gold sale.

Two very different versions of James's foray exist. James had given up on the Gold Exchange Bank by Saturday morning. Knowing that Jim Fisk had repudiated, James planned to bring a lawsuit. But for the legal record he needed to tender delivery of the gold to Jim Fisk formally before he could claim breach of contract.

With Kruger as witness, James wandered inside the Opera House on Saturday afternoon and reached an upstairs lobby. He came to a screen door by the company president's and comptroller's offices and suddenly faced "a dozen big fellows" who were standing watch. By his own account, after he was refused admission he cursed out the guards left the building, and noted the fact for his lawyers.

But Wall Street gossip painted a more animated picture. By one version, James got his wish that afternoon and bumped into Jim Fisk roaming the Opera House hallways. There he confronted the renegade by tendering him immediate delivery of $500,000 in gold.

That much coin would literally weigh a ton; Jim decided to call Brown's bluff. "Certainly, Mr. B[rown], we will take that gold. Here, John (calling an attendant), go down and help Mr. B[rown] to bring up his gold."

James, of course, had left his treasure chest at home. Empty-handed, in this version James could only look sheepish and retire.

The idea of James Brown being outsmarted by Jim Fisk's sharp repartee stretches credulity. James, who was still "very angry," according to Henry Smith, would have been more likely to whack Fisk with his walking stick than to put up with smart talk.

Fisk and Gould had other bears nipping at their heels, too. The situation at the Gold Exchange Bank was deteriorating hourly. The Bank's president, Henry Benedict, kept in constant touch with Jay's broker Henry Smith over the weekend. In the four years since Benedict had organized the Gold Exchange Bank and managed its daily clearings, he had never before missed a deadline. Now he sat on a time bomb. With more than $12 million in gold and another $5 to 6 million in greenbacks under his roof, Benedict controlled possibly the biggest single pile of money in the United States outside of the SubTreasury .

That much gold was "more than a man's life was worth," Benedict said, especially when "the whole public were straining for money."

Benedict saw threats everywhere. On Saturday a friend warned him to "be cautious" that a New York judge might soon issue injunctions to block his settlements. Ignoring his own attorneys, Benedict turned for help to Henry Smith and through him to Jay Gould, the only man in New York who anyone believed could still influence events.

Late Saturday night, Smith took Benedict to the Stevens Hotel, west of Broadway near Bowling Green. There, waiting to meet them, sat Jay himself; he had traveled downtown in a carriage with the curtains pulled shut. In a hushed voice Jay hurriedly introduced Benedict to William Morgan, an Erie Railway lawyer who Jay said could handle the Bank's legal problem.

Benedict hired Morgan on the spot; then Jay withdrew to the Opera House.

On Sunday Benedict contacted Henry Smith again. Several of the Fisk-Gould brokers were teetering on bankruptcy. Their failure could saddle Benedict's Bank with losses approaching half a million dollars—enough to cripple the institution. Again, he wanted Jay Gould to intervene.

Other dark rumors reached Jay about Benedict's foundering Gold Exchange Bank on Sunday. Benedict had been seen cavorting with bears, huddling with bankers like Harris Fahnestock and Henry Clews. Gossips told of Benedict secretly taking money from the Bank's vaults and hiding it with favored customers. Benedict had removed $3 million in gold from the Bank that weekend and he and two guards had hand-carried it to friendly banks in New Jersey, out of reach from New York judges.

Jay knew that the outcome of the Wall Street mess depended on how Benedict ultimately distributed his mountain of money. These reports made his skin crawl.

Late Sunday night, Jay decided to see for himself.

Near midnight, in the quiet darkness, passersby on Twenty-third Street saw a macabre spectacle. On the sidewalk outside the Grand Opera House, a dozen grim-faced men stood under black umbrellas in the hard rain. They climbed into a line of shiny black horse-drawn coaches. As New York slept, the procession rolled through the damp, darkened streets, the silence broken only by the footfalls of the horses and the creaking of the wooden wheels and axles.

On reaching the Gold Exchange Bank on New Street, Jay and his allies confronted a scene of ghastly confusion. Private detectives patrolled laconically back and forth inside as up to two hundred clerks sat cloistered at long rows of desks swamped by oceans of paper. They strained their eyes at end-less columns of handwritten numbers and notes under the hazy, flickering light of gas lamps.

A reporter for the *World* who was also poking around the Bank that night described a "staff of thirty clerks," their desks "covered with ponderous ledgers and exchange sales-books, piles of pass-books … heaped on the floor, coats off and shirts turned up, seeing by candles, stuck into bottles, that grew dimmer with passing hours. "[T]he clerks call[ed] their rolls and check[ed] their ac-counts as busy as clockwork." They had "labored without intermission, since Friday at 1 o'clock."

Lawyer Tom Shearman claimed that he saw a bottle or two of champagne being passed around the sweatshop to amuse the clerks.

Henry Benedict, tired and drawn after wall-to-wall meetings with nerv-ous creditors, led Jay's entourage to his largest conference room. There, be-hind closed doors, they could talk frankly. Jay, flanked by Jim Fisk, Belden, Henry Smith, Shearman, and brokers E. K. Willard and Charles Osborne, laid his cards on the table. Speaking softly, his eyes cold and steady, his hands and fingers knotted together, Jay "expressed greatest anxiety" about the clear-ances. The Bank had a responsibility, Jay said, to distribute its money fairly and quickly. Its delay and doubt threatened the entire city and country.

Benedict, sharing his side of the table with lesser Bank officials, listened quietly to the oration. When his turn came to speak, though, he bluntly chal-lenged the diminutive gold manipulator. Whose fault was it that the system had broken down? Benedict asked. Nine firms, including Belden's, Albert Speyers's, and those of other Ring brokers, had refused to submit statements. Still others teetered on failure. Who would stand behind them?

If the Gold Exchange Bank was gagging on Friday's workload, Benedict argued, Jay and Jim Fisk were to blame.

Despite their differences, Jay and Henry Benedict shared a common prob-lem. Both wanted the Bank to survive and to finish its work. Benedict sent his clerks to fetch statements for the fifteen-odd firms who had failed so far to pay their debts. Jim Fisk's brokers dominated the list, but Jim tonight let Jay do the talking. For over an hour they discussed each firm. Jay agreed to take responsibility for "five or six" of them. Using money from broker E. K. Willard's account, Jay told Benedict to put aside $75,000 as a cash guarantee to pay their losses.

The meeting lasted until well past 1:00 A. M. Beyond the complex guarantee deal, Jay and Henry Benedict reached a deeper understanding. Neither man trusted the other. Benedict could never end the bureaucratic mess and release his millions of gold and currency, Jay concluded. And Benedict saw Jay Gould as desperate and trigger-happy, willing to sacrifice the entire city to save himself.

At 2:20 A.M. long after Fisk and Gould had disappeared into the night, the reporter for the *World* made one last stop at the Gold Exchange Bank before his final deadline for Monday's edition. Henry Benedict oddly chipper, gave a wistful report. Despite the hurdles, he said, "all balances can be settled tomorrow." The long siege would end. Nine brokerage firms still had not submitted statements from Friday, he said, including James Brown's, Belden's, Albert Speyers's, and Boocock's, but the Bank would break the logjam.

How? At whose cost? The reporter did not ask, and Benedict did not volunteer an answer.

After scribbling a quote or two into his notebook, the *World* reporter ran off into the darkness to finish his story and then collapse for a long night's sleep.

• 30 •
FAMILY

IT SEEMED LIKE OLD TIMES sitting around the breakfast table with the Grants on Sunday morning, September 26, two days after Black Friday. The whole family was together: Ulysses, Julia, the children, and Julia's father Colonel Dent. Even General Horace Porter joined them. Then, surprise of surprises, in came Abel and Jennie Corbin from New York. They looked exhausted, Abel and Jennie; they dragged themselves into the White House foyer with just a few small bags. Ulysses and Julia hugged Jennie warmly; and Ulysses shook his brother-in-law's hand. Abel and Jennie went upstairs to freshen up and then joined the family and Porter in the parlor for coffee.

Grant had said nothing publicly about the gold panic since he had authorized his Treasury secretary to drown the bull corner with government gold on Friday. So far, his family secret had stayed shut tight. The press hadn't breathed a word since Friday connecting Corbin or himself to the Fisk-Gould cabal. Treasury Secretary George Boutwell deflected any political heat that was directed at Washington.

Before his brother-in-law showed up for breakfast that Sunday, Ulysses had already received separate letters from Abel and Jennie. Both denied any hand in the Gold Ring. Certainly his sister wouldn't lie to him, Ulysses thought. And maybe he had misjudged Corbin. Maybe his brother-in-law was a victim of vicious gossip.

"I got your letter yesterday," Grant told them, "and you can imagine how much relieved I felt … to know that you were not engaged in that disgraceful speculation."

Abel and Jennie said nothing to shake Ulysses's faith in their innocence. It was a fact that on Thursday morning, when they signed their letters, they had owned not a penny's stake in gold. That was true enough.

Sitting in the parlor, the old travel-mates made small talk about the family and the White House renovations. Then someone asked how things were in Gotham.

Talking politics around ladies might have been considered boorish, but Abel Corbin nonetheless took his cue. "There had been trouble since in New York," he said. As the family members leaned in closer to hear, Corbin drew a grim first-hand picture of Friday's wreckage. "A great many people are ruined. The bulls and the bears have both suffered very severely," he said, speaking in a thin, plaintive voice. His pale expression and fidgety hands bolstered his tale of woe.

If Corbin had planned to tug Ulysses Grant's heartstrings, he made a big mistake. Far from regret, the news brought a sparkle to Grant's crinkled face. "I am not at all sorry to hear it," the President said. "I have no sympathy with gold gamblers."

Corbin shifted his eyes from face to face but found no allies. Porter and Julia shared the President's evident pleasure at Wall Street's debacle. Jennie forced a weak smile. Having no retort, Abel Corbin said nothing. Ulysses noticed that his offhand sarcasm had brought icy silence from his New York relatives, Jennie as much as her husband. It "stopped the conversation," Porter recalled.

As Jennie and Julia eased the talk back to trivialities, Ulysses took full measure of his silver-haired, smooth-tongued New York kinsman. No, he thought, Abel Corbin was no victim. Hatred had little place in Ulysses Grant's repertoire, but any warm feelings he had for Corbin evaporated. From now on he would extend his in-laws the respect and kindness due a family member but no more.

The parlor session broke up after coffee. Horace Porter left for his small White House office, and the womenfolk took to private chatter. Corbin decided to try his pitch with the President once again. He pulled Ulysses aside into a private White House chamber during the afternoon. Alone with the door closed, Corbin gave the President a more detailed account of how his New York speculator friends had suffered from Friday's panic.

Grant must intervene to settle the chaos paralyzing finance, Corbin told him. The Treasury could help both bears and bulls settle their accounts and revitalize commerce by rescinding its order to sell gold, he argued. Grant could win many friends and do much good.

Ulysses listened politely, stroking his beard, puffing his ever-present cigar.

Corbin's insistence and urgency set off familiar alarms. Rising from his chair, the President cut his brother-in-law off in mid speech.

"This matter had been concluded," Grant said brusquely, "and I cannot open up nor consider the subject."

· 31 ·
BEARS
REGROUP

WALL STREET CAME TO ITS SENSES on Monday morning and tried to wrestle its fortunes back from the Gold Ring. The Gold Room opened its New Street doors at ten o'clock to a flood of brokers, bankers, and gamblers who had blood in their eyes. Exchange President Townsend Cox had to bang his gavel repeatedly before he could silence the mob. The fountain still spewed water droplets within the well-worn circular railing, but all but one of the goldfish in the basin below had mysteriously died over the weekend.

Most of the men in the room faced disaster. Besides the Gold Ring itself, they blamed the Gold Exchange Bank. The Bank still had not settled either Thursday's or Friday's gold transactions. More than $800 million in trades hung in doubt—an amount bigger than the nation's total supply of gold and greenbacks. The delay was crippling business and pushing interest rates to over 1 percent per day—300 percent per year—even for loans backed dollar-for-dollar by reputable stocks. Foreign trade had ceased.

The shadow of an approaching depression loomed over manufacturing, agriculture, and every other industry.

That morning Henry Benedict raised their hackles again by announcing yet another Bank foul-up: the gold clearinghouse had "rejected" statements from nine key players from Friday's trading, including Fisk brokers Albert Speyers, Samuel Boocock, and William Belden, and banker James Brown.

Before they could even think of reopening for buying and selling the "currency of the world," the Gold Room meisters had to resolve last week's transactions. Paper profits and losses meant nothing when dozens of firms teetered on bankruptcy. They prepared to argue, scream, holler, and bicker until they forged a plan to switch the noose from their own necks to those of New York's blackest scoundrels, Jay Gould and Jim Fisk.

Wall Street's senior victim came early and posted his body up front for the pow-wow. James Brown took the floor as soon as Cox had quieted the crowd. He launched into a furious tirade against the Gold Exchange Bank, the government, and the bulls. Henry Benedict's announcement that morning had been "grossly inaccurate," James fumed, pacing on his stout old legs, his face red with excitement. Brown Brothers had submitted no statement at all to Benedict's Bank, he said, and he offered $100,000 to anyone who could prove otherwise. James roused the warriors by blasting Friday's clique as a band of "ruffians and thieves."

William Heath, the only Ring broker who dared to show his face, stood up after Brown's speech and tried to soothe tempers. His firm would stand behind its Gold Ring trades, Heath said, but it could only pay after it had collected from Jay Gould. The Gold Room crowd sympathized with Heath, a respected man, but they turned viciously against William Belden. Fisk's wiry henchman had gone underground; no one had seen Belden's face in New York since Sunday night, and rumors had him hiding from creditors in New Jersey or Boston.

Questions about Belden pummeled the dais. Why was he hiding? Which trades would he stand for? Which would he deny? Somebody shouted that Belden had given a statement to the Gold Exchange Bank on Friday. The Exchange sent a delegation across the street to get it from Henry Benedict, who reluctantly handed over the private document. The Exchange members found it useless; unsigned, incomplete, and incomprehensible.

Belden owed millions that he could never pay.

Someone suggested taking a collection to keep Belden's bankruptcy from spreading to other firms, but they disagreed over how and how much.

Gold trading relied on trust. Deals struck in the Gold Room had no value unless the traders kept their word. If a trader broke faith, the law could do little.

Dozens of traders turned to the New York courts for protection. Within hours judges were pumping out a flood of orders and decrees. On Monday, Thomas Clerke, a senior justice on the Supreme Court who was holding regular chambers that month, issued injunctions in six separate cases against the Gold Exchange Bank. Two suits fingered Fisk broker Samuel Boocock for ducking out on trades. On Tuesday, Clerke issued orders against William

Heath and against Belden. Sheriffs deputies searched Broad Street in vain on Tuesday afternoon to serve Belden with attachment papers.

Henry Benedict, meanwhile, was sitting on a fortune of more than $12 million in gold and greenbacks at the Gold Exchange Bank. The responsibility scared him to death. Hundreds of cash-starved dealers were breathing down his neck. What if disaster struck, in the form of burglars, injunctions, or whatever tricks Jay Gould had up his sleeve? Every hour that he kept this wealth under lock and key, he pushed Wall Street closer to collapse.

Strict Bank rules made it almost impossible for Benedict to empty his vaults. He could not hand out a penny for Friday's trading until he had first calculated exact balances for every one of the hundreds of brokers who had sent in barely intelligible statements.

Desperate situations called for desperate actions. While working with his clerks through the weekend, Benedict decided to scrap the rulebook. Instead of demanding paperwork perfection, he would pay "approximate" balances to any firm that had given him a "tolerably" accurate statement. Early on Monday his tellers circulated through the neighborhood handing out checks to nearly one hundred different houses, totaling over $2.5 million in gold and $8 million in cash. "Loyal league" bankers dominated the list of lucky recipients. Trevor & Colgate took in $600,000; Cooke & Company collected $168,000; Duncan, Sherman & Company got $100,000; Seligman, $575,000; James Brown, $56,000 (for a customer); Dzondi, $114,000; and Vermilye & Company, $300,000.

In the rush, clerks made mistakes. More than $150,000 of the Bank's wealth ended up enriching a handful of firms beyond what they deserved. This money was lost forever; Benedict could not force the firms to return it. But not one penny went to Smith, Gould, Martin & Company, to Heath & Company, or to any other known agent of Fisk and Gould.

Word of Benedict's cash giveaways hit the Street in the form of ugly rumors of favoritism and graft. "Friends" of the directors had pillaged the clearinghouse, screamed the grapevine. Gold Room members bristled at this sloppy practice; they trembled at the thought of other perversions Henry Benedict might commit against their money. The paralyzed Gold Exchange Bank must be sidestepped. But how?

On Tuesday morning a plan emerged from the nonstop meetings in the Gold Room. The Exchange sent a delegation to ask the Bank of New York to handle the immense clerical burden of clearing Friday's trades. Optimism soared when the Bank of New York agreed. Brokers submitted new paperwork by the bushel, ignoring Benedict's clearinghouse altogether. But the experiment lasted barely two hours. Finding itself neck-deep in red tape, its lobbies jammed with frenzied gold gamblers, and its clerks drowning in reams of illegible brokers' demands, the Bank of New York threw up its hands by two-thirty.

The Gold Room would have to clean up its own mess.

Discouraged but undaunted, the Gold Room regulars reconvened and concocted an even better plan. Forget the banks, they decided; they could figure the clearings themselves. Who understood the complexities of gold trading better than the traders, the ultimate experts? They appointed twenty volunteers who were to take the fresh brokers' statements from the Bank of New York and work through the night to calculate a settlement. Worried that Benedict's mismanagement could prompt a repeat of the 1857 panic, Harris Fahnestock invited the Committee of Twenty to set up shop in his own basement counting rooms at Cooke & Company's offices at 20 Wall Street. The Committee agreed.

By midnight, working around a large circular wooden table, the Committee had analyzed statements from just about every solvent broker on Wall Street except one—Smith, Gould, Martin & Company. Henry Smith, hemming and hawing as Jay Gould's emissary, promised to deliver his firm's paperwork by early Wednesday morning.

If all went well, the quagmire could be resolved in twenty-four hours. But few outside the Gold Room shared this rosy view. Panic had swept the Stock Exchange minutes after the Bank of New York abandoned its gold rescue effort. Stock prices tumbled as banks and speculators dumped oceans of shares, fearing a prolonged gold stalemate that would keep credit costs high. The worst hit were Commodore Vanderbilt's railroads. New York Central shares fell from $177 to $150 as Cornele stood helplessly by.

A reporter tracked Vanderbilt to his Fourth Street home after the closing and found him in "horribly bad humor," pacing about his yard, smoking a cigar, waiting impatiently for his wife to meet him for a carriage ride.

Vanderbilt feigned ignorance as the newsman shouted questions. Asked who had caused the Wall Street debacle, he volunteered only "a combination of damned thieves to put money in their pockets. " Privately, the Commodore steeled himself for battle. Riding off in their private coach, Frank Vanderbilt got a quick education on the saltier side of her famous husband's vocabulary and temperament.

· 32 ·
LAWYERS

NOBODY OBSERVED THE METHOD in Wall Street's unfolding madness better than Jay Gould, watching like a hawk from the Erie Railway Opera House. What he saw was that Henry Benedict had cheated him, had sneaked away from his Sunday night commitments. The Gold Exchange Bank had run amok. The Gold Room's Committee of Twenty was an outrage. "Loyal league" bears controlled both operations. Just look where the Committee was holding its meetings—at Cooke & Company's offices, where Harris Fahnestock could peer over their shoulders!

Given half a chance, they'd throw out Jay's gold sales from Thursday and Friday and saddle him with Albert Speyers's absurd purchases at $160. Both had to be stopped.

On Tuesday night, after a day-long parade of brokers and lawyers through "Castle Erie," Jay convened his inner circle: himself, Jim Fisk, Thomas Shearman, and a handful of brokers. They had already wasted too much time, Jay told them. Wall Street's barons could not be trusted to work things out. Jay and Jim saw power lying in the streets, waiting for a strong hand to take it. They had the instrument—Boss Tweed's judges.

Jay gave orders to unleash the lawyers.

William Magear Tweed had spent the week leading up to Black Friday attending the State Democratic Party convention in Syracuse. When he came back to New York on Thursday, September 23, he marveled at the commotion that was besetting his city. The gold market had crashed, threatening his friends Fisk and Gould. His Tenth National Bank had been hit by a run. Newspapers were openly fingering him as a member of the Wall Street clique and had accused his henchman Peter Sweeny of backing the gold corner with the city treasury.

Tweed intervened personally to arrange for police protection for the Opera House hours after Friday's crash.

Irritated by the muddle, Tweed nonetheless had no doubt about his loyalties. He, Fisk, and Gould shared bonds that ran deeper than pay-offs or extortion. They were partners. Jay Gould had treated Tweed well since they had joined forces a year ago, making him an Erie Railway director and a richer man. Jim Fisk and Tweed had become genuine friends. A political ring only survived when members stood behind each other.

The risk that a smart investigator might connect Tweed to Fisk and Gould's scheming hardly bothered the Boss. The mob that had bloodied Jim Fisk's face on Friday would never dare confront Tammany's Grand Sachem. Fear played no part in his calculation.

But what use was power if not to protect your friends?

Nobody knows exactly how Jay communicated with Tweed that week. The possibilities are endless. They could have traded notes or telegrams, sent intermediaries, or even met face to face in a private place—perhaps Tweed's yacht (the *William M. Tweed*), Tweed's hotel (the Metropolitan), or Tweed's Connecticut estate. Jay needed help. He and Fisk faced ruin from the gold panic. Creditors were banging at their doors. The crisis threatened the whole city. All commercial activity was suspended. If the lock-up lasted much longer, ruin could spread to dozens of banks and businesses.

Somebody had to take responsibility, to seize control of the Gold Exchange and the clearinghouse and settle the matter. A minor functionary like Henry Benedict of the Gold Exchange Bank had no business managing such a grand affair. Bureaucrats had checked his every move, Jay must have said. If things got worse, he might soon need a judge to restore order.

Tweed could understand Jay's point perfectly. Who ran New York City, anyway? Certainly not some arrogant Republican bankers on Wall Street. The right message to the right judge could turn the whole situation to his liking, just as it had last November in the heat of Jay's money lock-up. Whether he made money was almost beside the point. Boss Tweed would not be abused by anyone on his home turf, New York.

Whatever their deal was, money began to flow from the Erie Railway's slush funds via Tweed toward the politicians. Ledgers show disbursements from Jay's "India Rubber Account" of $195,000 for September and another $25,000 in "legal expenses" earmarked specially for Tweed in December 1869. It was time for the politicos to play hardball.

For this sensitive job, Jay knew that George Barnard, their favorite judge in a pinch, would not do. Barnard was so tainted by previous scandal that the Street would laugh at any order that arrived over his signature. Tweed doubtless suggested Albert Cardozo, a justice of the New York Supreme Court and one of his oldest friends. Jay agreed. Cardozo, the studious, punctilious jurist and long-time Tammany stalwart, would be perfect.

Lawyer Tom Shearman had worked nonstop since Jay summoned him from his home in Brooklyn on Sunday afternoon. His firm's biggest clients were facing their most dire crisis yet.

Shearman, who normally transformed himself on Sundays into "Tearful Tommy," clerk of Reverend Henry Ward Beecher's Brooklyn Plymouth Church, found himself alone in the office. His three law partners dabbled at their long summer vacations. David Dudley Field was busy arranging his daughter's early-October wedding. Shearman fired off a wire to young John Sterling, who had joined the firm as junior partner last December, to cut short his holiday and hurry back to New York.

"Tearful Tommy" had interviewed dozens of Black Friday survivors and had drafted a stack of documents for the inevitable crush. On Tuesday night he got orders to sue. It was a lawyer's dream: an immensely rich client was demanding endless litigation. A paradise of billable hours would be earned in a purgatory of grinding labor.

The cleanest way to capture the Gold Exchange Bank, Shearman figured, would be to convince a judge to hand the Bank over to a friendly receiver. To do this, Shearman had to demonstrate that the bank was insolvent, was violating state law, or was wasting its assets. But even if he did, politics could dissuade a judge from taking such a bold action. The gold corner was New York's darkest scandal, a powder keg that could destroy careers, fortunes, and reputations. Few magistrates would tempt fate by seizing the city's biggest store of cash, handcuffing Wall Street's most powerful magnates, and thereby possibly bankrupting major firms or stepping between warring factions—especially on behalf of the villains Fisk and Gould?

Jay dared not put his own name on the lawsuit. He chose a stand-in for plaintiff—Charles Osborne, a loyal hack who had sold gold for Jay during the panic. Osborne claimed that the clearinghouse owed him $60,000 in profits, giving him legal standing to sue. His story was actually malarkey: Henry Benedict had paid Osborne his winnings on Monday, along with other "approximate" balances. No matter. From where Shearman sat, any name would do as long as it was Jay Gould who was paying the bills.

Derailing the Gold Room's Committee of Twenty took even less imagination. Shearman drew up a second, separate lawsuit by Smith, Gould, Martin & Company in its own name, asking for a straightforward injunction against the newfangled clearing rules. It was a request that even an honest judge could agree to.

Shearman started dictating affidavits and pleadings to his junior partner Sterling late Tuesday night, and they worked in shifts until nearly dawn, sleeping in turns in a corner of a darkened Opera House office. Shearman himself plugged away until four in the morning drafting complex legal papers before turning things over to Sterling and dozing off.

To pick the most friendly judge to hear their case, Shearman sent for expert help that night in the form of lawyer Aaron J. Vanderpoel. Jay Gould had doubtless suggested him. Vanderpoel dropped everything and raced right over, as if he'd been expecting the call.

Vanderpoel, an accomplished trial lawyer, knew a great deal about New York's judges from his vantage point. He was a partner in Brown, Hall & Vanderpoel, the law firm of Mayor A. Oakey Hall, a charter member of Tweed's Tammany machine. Vanderpoel and Mayor Hall had been classmates at New York University in the 1840s and law partners for twenty years.

If Shearman really did not know that Jay Gould and Tweed had fixed things with Albert Cardozo, he seemed to be the only one who did not. In any event, the lawyers now performed a strange ballet that made Shearman's ignorance conveniently irrelevant.

Shearman and Sterling both claimed exhaustion after the night's labor and asked Vanderpoel to carry the papers for the Osborne lawsuit to the city courthouse early Wednesday morning to get them signed. Few lawyers would have given up control over a major case at this critical point, but neither Shearman nor Sterling fancied himself a trial lawyer; neither spoke well; and Shearman often came across as dour with his thick glasses and odd black beard. Had Jay Gould told Shearman to stand aside for the more articulate Vanderpoel? Or did Oakey Hall's law partner carry a special message for a special judge?

Shearman and Vanderpoel had a long talk that night. Shearman had argued that Judge Clerke would be best to issue the Osborne decree. Clerke bad been signing hostile decrees against the Ring all week, so he had the most credibility. On the other hand, Clerke rarely opened his chambers sessions before ten o'clock. To be most effective, the Gold Exchange Bank receiver had to be picked early, so that he could take control before the clearinghouse opened for business.

No, they decided, Vanderpoel should not wait for Clerke. He should apply to any judge he could find in the chambers at nine o'clock.

They both knew that one judge always came to work an hour earlier than the rest. He was the most diligent jurist on the New York bench. Vanderpoel was looking forward to a private chat with Tweed's friend Albert Cardozo.

◎ ◎ ◎ ◎ ◎

While orchestrating these great affairs of men and money, Jay remembered one other small detail. Daniel Butterfield, his fair-weather friend in the New York SubTreasury, still owed him money. Jay sent his lawyer Frederick Lane over to harass Butterfield at his Wall Street office. But this time, unlike Saturday's awkward brush-off, Butterfield was prepared to stand his ground. He refused to pay. It was "absolutely impossible," he said. Besides having no cash, the assistant treasurer questioned Jay's very right to bill him at all for losses in his $1.5 million gold account at Smith, Gould, Martin & Company.

Jay's note from Saturday had mentioned an "interest in the pool." Butterfield had seen no accounting for a "pool." Why should he carry the burden for a group of speculators, he argued, without knowing what the others had paid?

Then Butterfield made a strange suggestion. If Jay wanted to push his claim, why not arbitrate it before the only power in New York who was able to impose justice? Daniel "would leave it to his friend Tweed" to decide the issue.

On its face, the proposal made sense. Jay and Daniel Butterfield both bowed before the altar of Tammany's Grand Sachem. Butterfield had brokered real estate for Tweed and often sent messages from the SubTreasury to Tweed's Park Place office. Only last March he had sold the Boss an eleven-acre estate near Fort Washington for $275,000. Tweed might be in the gold "pool" as well as Butterfield but the Boss could judge any gripe fairly and discreetly. No one would dare accuse him of anything else.

Jay had to laugh at Butterfield's presumption. He would have this sniveling, faithless bureaucrat for breakfast one day and spit him out before lunch.

· 33 ·
COUP D'ETAT

ALBERT CARDOZO ARRIVED at the courthouse building punctually at nine on Wednesday morning, September 29, and walked briskly to Room 13, his judge's chambers. Slender, with dark hair and a touch of gray, the forty-year-old Cardozo hardly looked Tweed's type. Soft-spoken, courteous, and scholarly, Cardozo belonged to one of America's oldest Jewish families, tracing his roots back to Aaron Cardozo, a London merchant who settled in New York around 1752. His family fought in the Revolutionary War, and Moses Sexias, his wife's grandfather, called George Washington a friend.

The vice president of his Spanish-Portuguese synagogue, Albert Cardozo kept his home kosher and filled with Jewish books.

Cardozo had known Bill Tweed since at least 1846, when both belonged to the Odd Fellows Lodge, a less exclusive social club that admitted Jews and aspiring young firemen like Tweed. Cardozo joined the Tammany Society in October 1859, just one month after Tweed did. Tammany, looking to outpoll the better-established political groups, opened its arms to immigrants and ethnics—Irish, Germans, and Jews—especially men like Cardozo, who had obvious talent. Cardozo, Tweed, and George Barnard had all marched with Abraham Lincoln's coffin during the martyred President's procession through New York in April 1865. Cardozo had represented Tammany at New York's postwar constitutional convention to adopt the Fifteenth Amendment.

Tammany had made Cardozo a judge by nominating him to the common pleas court in 1862 and in 1867 to the Supreme Court. Cardozo repaid the debt in ways big and small. In 1868 and 1869, Cardozo had opportunities to fill 227 refereeships, choice patronage plums. He gave 63 of these to Tweed's son Richard, a lawyer, and another 176 to his nephew Gratz Nathan. Cardozo had joined Judges Barnard and McCunn in naturalizing thousands of fresh-off-the-boat immigrants as voting Democrats before the 1868 election. Earlier that month he had stood shoulder to shoulder with Tweed at the state party convention in Syracuse.

Cardozo craved a seat on the United States Supreme Court and hoped that someday, if Governor John Hoffman ever became President, Tweed could produce it. "Courteous but inflexible, subtle, clear-headed, and unscrupulous," Cardozo "conceals the iron hand beneath the silken glove," wrote Charles F. Adams.

On this Wednesday morning, Aaron Vanderpoel reached the Chambers Street courthouse shortly after nine. He found that Judge Cardozo was the only magistrate present. Cardozo greeted Vanderpoel warmly and led him to a comfortable chair in his chambers. Vanderpoel and Cardozo knew each other well. Both had come of age together within New York's legal subculture and were active in Tammany circles. They traded friendly chatter for a few minutes, and then Vanderpoel handed Cardozo his papers in the Osborne suit.

Neither Vanderpoel nor Cardozo ever testified about their private *kaffeklatsch* that morning. We can't be sure that Vanderpoel was Tweed's secret go-between. But the outcome of the conversation speaks volumes. Cardozo signed Vanderpoel's papers, granted the decree against the Gold Exchange Bank, and then went them one better. As receiver, he chose Augustus L. Brown, Vanderpoel's and Oakey Hall's law partner at Brown, Hall & Vanderpoel. With no notice, hearing, or chance for rebuttal, Cardozo summarily surrendered the Gold Room clearinghouse and its mysterious fortunes into the hip pocket of the Tweed Ring and its patrons at the Erie Railway.

Tom Shearman still hadn't heard the good news about Cardozo's early morning order when he woke up that Wednesday morning. He looked over the final papers for his second lawsuit—the one targeted against the Gold Room's Committee of Twenty—and then shared a carriage downtown to Chambers Street with his partner John Sterling at about nine-thirty to get them signed. Shearman had no plans to see Albert Cardozo that morning, he later claimed, but fate nonetheless led him to Tweed's friend.

Shearman left Sterling outside and entered the courthouse alone. He walked directly to the chambers of Judge Thomas Clerke, hoping the well-respected justice would sign the papers without a fuss. Clerke, a frail man almost seventy years old, invited Shearman into his office and took his pile of affidavits and motions. Settling into a comfortable chair, Clerke glanced through the handwritten pages. He shifted uneasily and handed them back to Shearman.

What was wrong? Shearman asked.

Clerke frowned. He pointed to the heading on the lawsuit papers. It listed the plaintiffs: Henry Smith, Jay Gould, Henry Martin, and James Bach, the firm's fourth, junior associate. Bach was his wife's nephew, Judge Clerke said. He could not issue orders in a lawsuit involving a family member. That would be a conflict of interest, God forbid.

"I think you are mistaken about that," Shearman said, caught off guard.

"I am not sure, but I have an impression that this Mr. Bach is a nephew of my wife or my wife's relatives, and I had rather not do it," Clerke said. Shearman apparently knew more about Clerke's family than the judge himself. Bach was in fact no relation at all to Judge Clerke or his wife. The whole fabrication was a dodge—and it succeeded.

After failing with Clerke, Shearman moved down the hall to Judge Ingraham's chambers. Ingraham, another long-time Democrat, asked Shearman to come in and sit down. He too took his lawsuit papers just as Clerke had done, and then he studied them carefully. After several long minutes, he too handed the documents back. Ingraham's problem? A missing affidavit. Shearman offered to fix the technical flaw right away, but Ingraham balked. "I am going away, and I don't see why I should be troubled with it anyway, … it is Judge Clerke's business."

After striking out with both Clerke and Ingraham, Tom Shearman was faced with a dismal choice. He could try George Barnard, but Barnard was worse than nothing. Then there was Cardozo.

Shearman hesitated before resorting to the quiet Jewish magistrate. "I had reason to suppose that Judge Cardozo did not like me," he later explained. We can only guess what that grudge was about. Shearman, an active Republican, had written a scathing attack against corruption in the Tammany controlled New York bench for the July 1867 *North American Review*, which predated his own dealings with Barnard et al. Judge Barnard had never held it against Shearman, but Cardozo may have had a thinner skin.

By the time Shearman reached his office, Judge Cardozo had gone home for lunch. Shearman, undaunted, took a carriage to Cardozo's home on West Forty-seventh Street. He knocked on the door. Cardozo, ever gentle and polite, greeted Shearman warmly and led him to the library, where they could sit quietly. Cardozo took Shearman's legal papers and read them carefully. He asked whether Judge Clerke had seen the lawsuit documents, and Shearman told Cardozo the whole story of his frustrating morning.

Cardozo, nonplussed, turned his eyes back to the legal minutiae. He took a pen and made a technical change, lessening Shearman's decree from permanent injunction to temporary restraining order.

Then he signed it.

◎ ◎ ◎ ◎ ◎

Wall Street learned only slowly of Jay Gould's legal coup d'état. During the morning, the gold traders were meeting once again around the fountain. Their hopes that the "Committee of Twenty" would be able to fix Friday's morass had disappeared. A Committee spokesman mounted the dais and announced that their work remained incomplete for lack of a single statement: that of Smith, Gould, Martin & Company. A Committee delegate had sat for half an hour in Henry Smith's waiting room that morning, but Smith had refused to show his face. Smith's promise of Tuesday night to produce a statement wasn't worth a damn.

Friday's lynch-mob frenzy reemerged. Shouts of "hang them. Hang them," and "pull down their houses" echoed in the stuffy chamber.

The bombshell exploded when Augustus Brown, who was a dignified-looking man with crisp sideburns, arrived at the Gold Exchange Bank. Accompanied by sheriff's deputies, he took formal possession of the clearinghouse. The crowd of brokers who loitered eternally in the Bank's marble lobby erupted in disgust. "Curses, groans, trampling of feet, shouts, screams, shrieks, and whoops resounded through the building," reported the *World*. Minutes later, a deputy served Shearman's second injunction against the Gold Room.

The Street instantly recognized the impact of this legalese. They saw the names on the lawsuits: one was Osborne, and the other was Smith, Gould, Martin & Company. Jay Gould and Jim Fisk once again held Wall Street like a dog on a leash. No one doubted that receiver Augustus Brown took orders from Tweed and Jay Gould. Not a dime could pass in or out of the Bank without orders from the Opera House. Any chance to settle the financial imbroglio had gone out the window. A receiver, starting from scratch under legal strictures, could take weeks to complete an accounting. "Smith, Gould, & Martin have beat us black and blue," said one trader.

As rioters raised havoc in the lobby, Augustus Brown took control of the clearinghouse assets. Flanked by lawmen, he found an employee to open the vault where the gold and money were kept. Instead of the expected mountains of wealth, Brown found only scattered remains. His inventory that afternoon counted precisely $170,375 in currency, $132,720 in gold certificates, $75,000 in gold coin bags, and other odds and ends totaling about $500,000.

Resentment turned to panic in the Stock Exchange. Confidence, which was already shaken after Tuesday's slide, crumbled completely. New York Central and the whole Vanderbilt list melted in wild selling.

Then yet another monkey wrench entered the works.

All week long, firms had been lining up at the dais of the New York Stock Exchange to announce their failures. On Wednesday the biggest domino fell. LeGrand Lockwood, owner of Lockwood & Company, an emblem of Wall Street stability for twenty-five years, had held huge blocks of Lake Shore Railroad stock. Prices had fallen from $120 in August to $74. In barely a week, Lockwood had lost $1 million down the gold rat hole and millions more on Lake Shore and Pacific Mail shares. These had pulled his head underwater.

Word of the failure stunned the street. Lockwood was Vanderbilt's broker. Like lemmings, they began to sell stock desperately.

Two men had particularly big stakes in Lockwood's demise: Vanderbilt and Jay Gould. Jay and the Commodore had been tripping over each other for months trying to win Lockwood's support to merge his westward railroad to their own competing lines. Now Lockwood dumped his controlling interest of 70,000 shares. Lake Shore stock flooded the market, and prices dropped to bargain levels.

Jay Gould was paralyzed by his gold straitjacket; the brass ring was Vanderbilt's to pluck.

But taunted by this opportunity, old Cornele too found himself hamstrung. New York Central, his flagship company, had tumbled from $150 to $147 in the excitement. Vanderbilt stationed himself at the Bank of New York's downtown office to command his troops. He fought New York Central back up to $158 but soon lost his grip, and the stock broke down again to $150. Brokers whispered that Jim Fisk had somehow sabotaged the Commodore's companies from his Opera House hideaway, having "sworn" to "break Vanderbilt."

Vanderbilt's stockpile of mammon had finally run dry. Even at rock bottom prices, he needed cash to buy Lockwood's 70,000 Lake Shore shares, but banks shuddered to lend money to anyone right now. What with the lockup by the gold clearinghouse and the sudden stock break, dealers were lucky to borrow money at interest rates of 3 to 5 percent per day—over 1,000 percent per year—or more.

Vanderbilt called in his reserves. He sold off his interests in small western railroads and drained his cash accounts. He alone was keeping U. S. finance from sliding into the abyss, yet bank after bank refused him credit. If Vanderbilt was a bad credit risk, could anyone pass muster? He turned to the British, tracking down W. Butler Duncan of the firm Duncan, Sherman & Company, American agents of the London Baring Brothers. The Barings agreed to lend Vanderbilt an immediate $10 million in cash, secured by Hudson River Railroad shares.

In a flash, Vanderbilt took this fresh new war chest into the Street. He used half to snatch up Lockwood's company and the rest to buoy the market.

Without this infusion at that precise moment, it might have been Wednesday's stock crash that dominated the history books instead of Friday's gold epic. But with it, by day's end the panic abated. Bargain hunters now began to pick over the new low prices. "This whole stampede is going to turn to the advantage of fast hands," wrote Cooke's agent Harris Fahnestock, who was working his own hands fast as he could.

Henry Clews reported that orders were flooding into his office "from every State in the Union" to buy stock. A collective sigh rose from the Exchange. Wall Street's dark moment had passed.

Jay Gould could only wring his hands and watch helplessly as the Lake Shore, his dreamed-of gateway to the West, fell to his bitter enemy. To save himself, Jay unloaded more than $4 million of his own fast-depreciating railroad stocks onto the Erie Railway. He signed the account statements for the shares as "T.R." (for company treasurer) instead of J.G.

◎ ◎ ◎ ◎ ◎

Jim Fisk was tired of being caged up and stained with public villainy. He hungered to burst from his Opera House prison onto the public stage and rewrite the record his way. A great public sin had been committed. Jim wanted all the guilty parties to pay equally for their deeds, not just himself and Gould. Jay, having spun his legal webs, now turned center stage in the affair over to his flashy partner.

Together they had subverted Wall Street, the courts, and the U.S. Treasury. Now it was time to subvert the press.

• PART VIII •

Dirty Laundry

· 34 ·
ASTOUNDING REVELATIONS

"Y OU HAVE SENT FOR ME and I am here," said George Crouch, the *Herald's* veteran financial writer, sitting in a "fawn-colored" Moroccan armchair beneath the ceiling frescoes of the Grand Opera House. Every reporter in New York would have sold his mother for an interview with the notorious gold bandits after Friday's panic, especially with showy Jim Fisk. Late Wednesday night, September 29, a messenger from Fisk had appeared at the *Herald's* offices with the special invitation. Savoring a journalistic coup, the delighted editors had sent Crouch chasing across town to "Castle Erie." After days of barring his way, a sultry guard had let Crouch pass.

Now, at nearly midnight, Jim Fisk's portly figure appeared from behind a sliding panel, bedecked in "costly velvet" and "priceless diamonds" that shimmered in the flickering golden glow of gas lamps. Jim sat at Crouch's side—close enough, the reporter said, "to pour his more or less 'round, unvarnished tale' into the very drum of the listener's ear without spilling a single word."

"I have a most astounding revelation to make," Jim Fisk said. "I can make Rome howl at somebody besides me."

Crouch readied his pencil. He set his eyes on the jovial man with the big belly and waxed moustache who had just swindled Wall Street out of millions. "Everybody lays the blame [for the crash] on me," Jim said. "I am threatened with assassination. I'm caged up here like a tiger in a menagerie, enjoy just about as much liberty; can't go out even at night … without running pretty considerable risk of getting shot for the doings of other people."

What "other people"? Crouch's eyes lit up. For weeks, Wall Street had been buzzing with rumors of high-level Washington complicity in the gold corner. Now the truth could be *his* story.

Before he answered, Jim laid a condition on the table. He wanted Crouch's promise that the *Herald* would publish his terrible secrets. No guarantee, no story. After all, Jim said, he could just as easily spill his beans to the *Tribune*, the *World*, or any other paper.

Why was Fisk so nervous? Crouch wondered. He—Crouch—had no power to bind his paper to printing any wild accusations without solid proof.

Then again, Jim Fisk was the hottest news in town.

Crouch decided to pull in his big fish. Sure, he told his eager whistle-blower. The *Herald* will definitely print your story. Luckily for Crouch, Jim never thought to ask him *when* the article would appear.

Satisfied, Jim charged ahead. "Now, do you or does anyone else imagine that we should have risked millions, as we did, unless we had positive assurance that the government would not intervene?" Crouch shook his head. "Of course we should not. Anyone can see that," Jim said. He now unmasked his stellar accomplices. "Members of the President's family were in with us," he said, watching Crouch's face for a reaction. "The President himself was interested with us in the corner. This astonishes you, does it not?"

"Well, I must confess it does, slightly."

"Slightly! Ah! you suspected it, then?" Jim said. "Well, won't that be sufficient to make Grant tremble in his boots?" Jim filled the room with a careless laugh.

Crouch, who was truly startled, took careful notes as Jim laid out the "secret history" of the great gold conspiracy—the meetings with Ulysses Grant over the past months, the letters, the pay-offs. "It was planned by Jay Gould and Abel Corbin, the President's brother-in-law," Jim said, zeroing in on his favorite target. "Why, damn it! Old Corbin married into Grant's family for the purpose of working the thing in that direction. That's all he married for this last time."

But why was Jim now exposing his allies? Crouch asked.

"Because they went back on us and came near ruining us," he said. It was simple revenge. "Grant got scared," he said. The rest were cowards and deserved their share of public disgrace.

George Crouch nodded as he took down every word. Jim's account dripped with enough mud to incriminate a whole gallery of luminaries: the President, his wife, Corbin, and a slew of lesser officials. For such an explosive article, Crouch told Jim, his editors would need evidence, more than just one man's word. If it were true, the story could impeach the most popular President since George Washington.

Jim certainly understood. The *Herald* was the "leading paper," he said, the only "independent" voice. Just come back tomorrow, he told the reporter. You'll have all the proof you can use.

Crouch's editors back at the *Herald* must have crowed as their reporter described his strange encounter with the kingpin gold gambler that night. Could Jim Fisk really prove that Ulysses Grant was involved in his caper? Or were he and Gould trying to manipulate the *Herald* as they bad manipulated Wall Street to trick them into libeling their enemies? Newspaper editors stood to face jail like anyone else in a defamation lawsuit.

Whatever game Fisk was playing, the *Herald* editors decided to go along. If Prince Erie were bluffing, they could always back out later.

The *Herald* held its presses for Thursday morning's edition as Crouch wrote an oblique story that suggested the full extent of Jim Fisk s *gold* conspiracy but without the promised evidence. Neither admitting or denying anything, Crouch's article asked "why the carriage of the cool-headed, sharp, keen President of the Erie road has been seen morning and night in West Twenty-seventh Street at the residence of the brother-in-law of the President." He also mentioned secret interviews between the "shrewd Prince of Erie" and General Grant in New York City, at Saratoga, and on Long Island Sound steamers and a trip by Jim Fisk's special courier to Grant's vacation retreat in Washington, Pennsylvania. He hinted at pay-offs going to the capital and checks being handed to "a member of the President's family." He implied a shady "bargain" for the appointment of the New York SubTreasurer.

"A few days will reveal the mystery," Crouch told his readers, stringing them along in the best pulp tradition.

On Thursday morning the article caused a sensation. Crouch returned to the Opera House that day for more. This time Jim took him on a field trip. "You come with me, and I will show you something," he said. Jim led the reporter through the empty Opera House theater to a backstage door, where a carriage waited to drive them to 37 West Twenty-seventh Street—Abel Corbin's house.

Jim left Crouch outside in the carriage and walked briskly to the door, knocked, and then stepped inside. He was gone for a full hour. While waiting, Crouch saw a curious event. A rival reporter, Ford Barksdale of the *Sun*, appeared on the street. He too knocked at Corbin's door and disappeared within. The *Sun* reporter left after a few minutes; later so did Fisk.

Jim Fisk's ready access to Ulysses Grant's brother-in-law that morning may have impressed George Crouch as Jim's initial proof of his bold accusations, but Crouch's editors got cold feet. Friday morning came, and the *Herald* published not one word of Jim's "astounding" truths. Jim accused the *Herald* of breaking its deal and blasted Crouch for making sly half promises Wednesday night. The reporter explained, half apologizing, that the *Herald* could not indict Ulysses Grant in the gold scandal without better evidence. Jim groused and grumbled. The exclusive deal was off; he would find a more pliable outlet.

In the meantime, Jim said with a wink, he and Crouch could help each other. Why not stay friends?

Ford Barksdale of the *Sun* had visited the Twenty-seventh Street house three times on Thursday before Abel Corbin agreed to see him. During the morning, when the door had been opened to him, a servant had told him to come back after lunch. Barksdale tried again at two, but this time Corbin sent word to come back at four. Finally, on his third try, Barksdale got lucky. Corbin, the mysterious, silver-haired link in the gold conspiracy trail, greeted him personally at the door and led him inside to an elegant parlor.

Barksdale had barely opened his mouth before the gaunt old man launched into mea culpa. "I did not know I had an enemy in the world who could do me such injustice as does that false report in this morning's *Herald*," Corbin said, stinging from George Crouch's poison pen. Worst of all was the *Herald's* tying him to the notorious debaucher Jim Fisk. "Mr. Fisk may have been to my house twice since I lived here, but not since this panic began," he said. "I do not associate with such men as Fisk. He is a fast man of the city, while I am a staid, careful Methodist. I have nothing to do with any such men as Fisk." Nor would his brother-in-law Ulysses Grant ever speak "with any man such as Fisk, Jr.," Corbin told the reporter. Neither Fisk nor anybody else "has communicated with me, either verbally or by writing, respecting stock or gold operations."

Barksdale took down Corbin's ravings word for word, thanked him for the interview, then left. He rode a public horse-drawn car to the Grand Opera House. He knocked at the large, heavy-wooden doors, which resembled "the massive gates of a feudal castle," he wrote. Much to his surprise, the guard let him in. He walked down the rich hallways to the Erie Railway executive suite, where he found Jay Gould working alone in a private room.

Barksdale introduced himself, and Jay agreed to answer a question or two. For the record, Jay sheepishly apologized for the financial "depression" his gold operation had caused. "I never wanted gold above 145," he told Barksdale in a quiet, earnest voice. His only goal had been to help U.S. farmers, he said, and launched into an explanation of his crop theory.

After a few minutes the door burst open, and in came Jim Fisk from an afternoon carriage drive. Jim "whipped off" his coat and rolled up his sleeves; his famous shirtfront diamond sparkled, and his hair was combed "in exquisite style." Barksdale eagerly turned his attention from drab Jay Gould to his dandified sidekick.

Jim Fisk obliged him with a stunning performance.

Jim understood what made good print. For public consumption, he adroitly reduced Friday's panic to a joke. "A fellow can't have a little innocent fun without everybody raising a halloo and going wild," he told Barksdale, who was furiously jotting down every word. Jim harangued Barksdale that Friday's disaster was really just the work of two small-time speculators, Albert Speyers and William Belden, and certainly not his own. "Because I tell a crazy man to buy [gold at 1]60, he goes off and finds a thousand a damned sight more crazy than he is, and everybody gets sick. ... Where I suspected [Speyers] wouldn't get a hundred thousand [at 160] he took in thirty millions," Jim said. "How these fellows do squeal when they get sick." The bears had no right to complain, though. "If men will play with the cat, they'll get scratched."

Jim talked "like a race-horse, and showed no signs of nervousness," according to Barksdale. He even laughed at his own physique. Despite the siege, Jim said, "I still eat and drink, and grow fat."

Barksdale wrote up his interviews with Corbin, Fisk, and Gould, and the *Sun* ran them as front-page features on Friday morning, October 1, one week after the crash, the same morning the *Herald* backed off the trail.

The *Sun's* appetite for splashy news gave Jim Fisk an idea. If the *Herald* refused to print his charges against Ulysses Grant et al., maybe the *Sun* would play ball. The *Sun* had recently been bought by aggressive publisher Charles Dana, who had reshaped the two-penny daily into one of New York's liveliest papers. Its circulation had skyrocketed to almost 100,000 copies daily.

To seduce the *Sun*, Jim threw out the President's brother-in-law as bait.

Jim sent a message to Corbin's house early Friday morning. He said that he had seen the *Sun* interview and was "astonished" that Corbin could insult him so in public. Didn't Abel know that he, Jim, had been threatened with violence since Black Friday?

Corbin, unnerved by the publicity, wrote back a conciliatory note: "Assure Mr. Fisk that in the conversation with *The Sun* reporter yesterday, what he says regarding my imputing belittling or derogatory expressions respecting him are not true. A. R. Corbin."

"Aha!" Jim must have blurted on reading Corbin's wimpy rejoinder. "Gotcha!"

Donning his indignant citizen cloak, Jim jotted a note to Charles Dana that Mr. Abel R. Corbin had called his feature story "utterly false." If the story was really false, he himself considered the *Sun's* actions "utterly inexcusable." Jim sent the note by special courier, inviting Dana to return an explanation.

Dana, on seeing Jim's note, fumed at this blast from one of New York's wealthiest citizens. He doubtless vented his spleen on his diligent young reporter. Ford Barksdale was "dumbfounded" at being called a liar. What was Fisk so angry about? Corbin had called him a "fast man of the city." Most New Yorkers were saying plenty worse about the authors of Black Friday.

Barksdale rushed off to "Castle Erie" to defend his honor. On reaching the Opera House, he navigated the grand hallways to the executive suite. There he found Fisk, Jay Gould, and George Crouch together like three cozy birds nesting.

Jim smiled deliciously as he greeted Barksdale. He showed him a comfortable chair and offered him a good cigar and a drink from the bar. The *Sun* reporter was all business, though. Barksdale bristled when Jim showed him the note from Abel Corbin that morning denying his cover story.

No, Barksdale said, "the interview was correctly reported, and is perfectly accurate."

"Well, then it is a question of veracity between you and Mr. Corbin," Jim said, half teasing, half baiting.

"There is no question of veracity, Sir," Barksdale shot back.

Then Jim let the other shoe drop. "By the way, did you know that I was in Mr. Corbin's house when you were there yesterday?"

Barksdale shook his head.

"I was there," Jim said. "When your card came in, Mr. Corbin mentioned that a *Sun* reporter desired to see him. I told him to beware, for these *Sun* people were wide-awake men."

Wide-awake Barksdale quickly figured the score. Corbin had told him the day before at four o'clock, when he had finally been admitted, that Fisk had not been to his home in weeks; now Fisk was saying that he had been there just hours before, during one of Barksdale's own earlier attempts to talk to Corbin. George Crouch, the *Herald* reporter, vouched for Jim's story; he had seen it all from the carriage.

Abel Corbin had lied, plain and simple.

Bursting livid, Barksdale left the Erie birds and sped back across town to confront Corbin and set the record straight. Corbin "exhibited great agitation" on seeing him, Barksdale wrote. Corbin, his face flushed and drawn, led the reporter into the parlor. Barksdale got straight to the point. His story from that morning's *Sun*—was it true or was it not?

Corbin, taken aback by Barksdale's bluntness, found his composure and answered in obscure legalisms. Yes, he said, the *Sun* report was accurate, but it was also misleading. He, Corbin, had only meant to say that Jim had a "reputation" as a "fast man," not that he, Corbin, considered him a "fast man." "I did not mean to say anything derogatory," Corbin explained. He also admitted that Fisk had come to his house "late in the day" the day before but denied having any dealings with him.

All Corbin's smooth talk could not undo the damage. Ford Barksdale was convinced that Corbin was "the worst and most consummate old hypocrite I ever saw," while Jim Fisk, despite his checkered reputation, "tells the truth in this affair."

Jim, no longer tied to his exclusive deal with the *Herald's* George Crouch, now took Barksdale under his wing. Soon the pages of the *Sun* dripped with all the dirty laundry tying the New York bulls to Washington's First Family. Jim and Jay sat for twenty to thirty interviews with Barksdale, who was ready to believe any dark truth about that "hypocrite" Corbin. What the *Sun* carried, other papers repeated, as reporters clawed for scraps of news about Corbin and the Gold Ring.

A damning picture emerged in Barksdale's accounts. Corbin had acted as "cat's paw" between Washington and the clique, had bought heavily in gold, had visited Gould and Fisk three to five times every day during the panic, and had traveled to Washington with a $100,000 check right after the crash. In his interviews Jim gave Corbin "almost the entire credit for originating the grand scheme," the "bold and brilliant" plan to corner gold.

To back his story, Jim produced fistfuls of affidavits—sworn statements from coachmen, messengers, and butlers—proving Corbin's visits to the Opera House and his and Gould's visits to Corbin's Twenty-seventh Street home—including one from *Herald* reporter George Crouch. The *Sun* printed them all. Jay produced the $25,000 check he'd paid to Corbin earlier in September, and the *Sun* published it on its front page, a veritable smoking gun.

Besides tricking Grant, Corbin had also sandbagged Treasury secretary George Boutwell, the *Sun* reported. It quoted Jay Gould that Corbin "hated" Boutwell and had tried to "get him out of the way" by starting a fight between him and Grant.

Abel Corbin, despite his long years in politics as counselor to Presidents and senators, was no match for Jim Fisk's propaganda barrage. Corbin's alleged corruption became street talk not just in New York but from Chicago to Atlanta to London and Paris.

The global disgrace broke his health. George Crouch visited Corbin's house that week to hear him deny the *Sun* revelations. He found Corbin sick and bed-ridden, "suffering from disease of the heart." Corbin refused to defend himself at first, saying that "friends" would speak for him. After much browbeating, Corbin "raised himself in the bed and vowed by his God and all that he held sacred that he was in no way connected" to the Fisk-Gould Ring. The *Sun* stories were "False, every word," he said. "Fisk was not in my house that day, nor was his carriage at the door." Any affidavit to the contrary was a "lie."

After the outburst, "Mr. Corbin sank back on the bed completely overcome with emotion," Crouch reported.

George Crouch knew that Abel Corbin's dramatic outburst contained not one shred of truth. He trapped the old man by offering him the opportunity to swear his denials in a verified statement. Crouch had even dragged along a notary for that purpose. Corbin was healthy enough to remember that perjury was a crime. "I will swear to nothing," he said.

A *Tribune* reporter who visited Corbin a few days later painted the same sad picture. He found Corbin suffering from "pneumonia" and barely able to speak. With a physician standing by, the pale figure repeated his denials, calling the *Sun* reports "base and wicked falsehoods."

On Saturday night, October 2, after a fortnight of mischief, Jim Fisk rested. He left New York and the gold drama behind and rode his Narragansett steamer across Long Island Sound to Boston for a weekend with Lucy Fisk, his legal spouse. Jim had made the Boston trek routinely every few weeks, even during his steamiest passions with Josie Mansfield. He spent the weekend doing pleasant domestic chores, buying groceries, and having a barber come shave his face. Jim also may have contacted his broker William Belden, who had been hiding from creditors in Boston since the panic; he may have told Belden to go home and face the music like a man. But mostly, Jim kept business far from his mind.

POLITICS

The Fisk-Gould-Corbin-Grant combination absorbs the attention of the community at large by the developments daily made public. Corbin is seriously compromised and some others, but as far as heard from Knox, the Hatter, at 212 Broadway, had no finger in the golden pie. The aim of Knox is to keep up the quality of his hats and the price down, and he succeeds.

Advertisement in *The New York Evening Mail*
October 12, 1869

GREAT POLITICAL SCANDALS FOLLOW a ritualized path in the United States, from Aaron Burr to Teapot Dome, Watergate, and Iranscam. Public outrage gives way to carnival, and heroes and villains bask in publicity and become celebrities. Daily revelations in the press, drumbeats for heads to roll, and speculation on how high the guilt spreads all intermix with righteous indignation and moral posturing by politicians.

So it went after Black Friday.

New York District Attorney Samuel Garvin convened a grand jury to investigate the gold corner for conspiracy, usury, and other legal sins. For weeks he terrorized Wall Street with subpoenas for secret testimony. Garvin hauled in all the major bears—Harris Fahnestock, Joseph Seligman, even Daniel Butterfield and Caleb Norvell of the *Times*. The lineup included Fisk and Gould. It got nowhere, though. Bill Tweed fixed that.

Tweed tugged the wires, and like magic, the district attorney changed his approach. Garvin led the probe around in circles. He called William Belden as a witness, who demonstrated a selective memory. Garvin issued twenty-one subpoenas for Abel Corbin but not one for Albert Speyers.

Tweed left no stone unturned. He went to Albany in January and charmed the legislature into passing a crippling amendment to the state's criminal conspiracy law. There would be no jail for Jay and Jim.

The newspapers printed hot exposes on the gold conspiracy. George Crouch of the *Herald* produced his grand chronicle, pinning the debacle on a trio headed by "the great gorilla of Wall Street, the gold-gobbling Gould"; the " 'ring'-tailed financial ourangoutang" Fisk; and "that Methodistical monstrosity" Corbin, three "fellows of the same kidney."

Jay counterpunched by turning the tables on the *Times*. He disclosed that he had tricked the staunch Republican sheet last August into printing Abel Corbin's bogus column on "Grant's Financial Policy. " Stodgy *Times* editors cringed at gibes that the paper was an "organ of the Gold Ring." John Bigelow, who had accepted the Corbin piece for publication, resigned as *Times* editor-in-chief.

Beneath all the smoke and hoopla, one point struck a nerve in the body politic. The stories about Abel Corbin hardly deserved notice, but claims of complicity by Ulysses Grant shocked the nation.

In the age of Tweed and Andrew Johnson's impeachment, Americans had no lack of cynicism toward politicians. But Grant was different; Grant was a genuine national hero. Ronald Reagan's "Teflon Presidency" barely held a candle to Grant's aura as Hero of Appomattox and savior of the nation. The evidence against Corbin may have been overwhelming, but nobody—not even partisan Democrats—could believe the innuendoes of Fisk, Gould, and their newspaper pawns that Ulysses and his wife Julia had knowingly conspired in the gold corner.

The *Herald*, which was already calling for George Boutwell's scalp, railed against the "preposterous" rumors of White House complicity and found Grant "stainless" before its reporter could even probe the story. The *Albany Morning Express* called the charges "base calumnies." Grant had crushed the Gold Ring by selling gold on Black Friday. He was the hero of the story, not the villain.

Morally worse were the accusations against Julia. Only a dark coward would hide his crime by blaming a woman. The *Sun* captured a typical dialogue between Wall Streeters confused by the morality play. "It's a d—d shame," said one, "to drag a lady's name into such an affair. Gould ought to be hung for taking such a course."

"The shame is," said the other, "that a lady occupying the position of

President's wife should put herself in a situation to be made the subject of such scandal."

Grant's only sin, his defenders said, was in having corrupt kinfolk. If anything, this proved his innocence. Abel Corbin may have cavorted with the clique, argued the *Evening Mail*, but "the fact of his being a relative did not save him." By crushing Corbin along with Fisk and Gould, Ulysses Grant had demonstrated his own purity.

Ulysses Grant refused to comment at first, cloaking himself in presidential prerogative. He had a thick skin for criticism, toughened during the war years. When his 1864 Virginia campaign sent back sixty thousand dead Union soldier boys, appalled voices throughout the North had called him a "butcher" whose only strategy had been "hammering" Lee's lines with human waves.

Still, civilian politics were different. Generals could control destinies, choose battles, command troops; mere Presidents could only react, and they suffered guilt by association with vermin like Corbin, Fisk, and Gould. Ulysses had had no experience in such things.

Grant broke his silence on October 3. He told the Associated Press that yes, Jim Fisk had had at least one private meeting with him aboard his Newport-bound steamer that summer in which he asked him for confidential tips on government gold policy. Grant insisted that he had given the sly financier a stern brush-off. He also confirmed that he had ordered Boutwell to sell gold on Black Friday.

Ten days later, as new charges surfaced, Grant weighed in again. In a hastily written letter to *New York Ledger* editor Robert Bonner, he declared himself "innocent" and uninvolved in the gold corner, "except that I ordered the sale of gold to break the ring." Had Gould and Fisk succeeded in their maneuver, Grant argued, "you would never have heard of anyone connected with the Administration as being connected" with it.

Europeans laughed at Grant's awkwardness. "Too straightforward to be a politician, he bluntly denies a charge no one believed," chuckled the London *Times*. The slur of stupidity stung more than that of corruption. "Grant really thought Fisk and Gould," who had showered him with cheap gifts like railway passes, steamer trips, and dinners, "the best fellows he ever met," the *Times* said.

Grant's inner circle saw danger in the growing scandal. Fisk and Gould might be scoundrels, but they were arguing convincingly that someone in government had helped them. Grant and Boutwell could not deny this charge without appearing to cover up sin in their own house. Boutwell was still fretting about his original decision to sell gold on Black Friday. He told Henry Cooke that he "did not expect to see the whole gold board crushed to 'pie' for half a week." That same week, Boutwell received a note from New York written in red ink:

> If gold does not sell at 150 within 15 days I am a ruined man.
> You will be the cause of my ruin! Your life will be in danger.
> Wilkes Booth

To save themselves, Grant's men needed a culprit to hand the wolves. But whom? Certainly not the President nor anyone in his Cabinet. Certainly not Ulysses's immediate family or personal staff.

Jay Gould was treating Daniel Butterfield with kid gloves, considering that the assistant treasurer had walked away from his gambling debts. Early on, Jim Fisk had told the *Sun* that they had enough evidence against an unnamed "prominent government official" to "send him to State Prison." Barksdale published the threat in this anonymous form, but everyone soon guessed the name. Wall Street now buzzed with gossip about the smug bureaucrat.

Treasury Secretary George Boutwell supported his New York deputy at first but hinted that Butterfield should find another job. He sent Daniel Butterfield a note on October 8 urging him to stay in office "unless you find it necessary to resign in order to preserve your health."

Butterfield dug in his heels to defend his honor. He kept a stern profile, moralistically telling reporters that "No one has suffered" from the panic "but the gamblers." Privately, to Boutwell, he denied the attacks. Then he stepped boldly into the publicity game. Butterfield took a page from Jim Fisk's book. He hired a news writer—in fact, he hired Jim Fisk's own mouthpiece.

Ford Barksdale of the *Sun* had grown disillusioned with flaking for Fisk and Gould. It had all gotten out of control. Barksdale's personal gripe had been against Abel Corbin, but now his exposures had smeared Ulysses Grant. Barksdale, who had seen Jim Fisk's full arsenal of evidence, considered the President as pure as driven snow. He also had no scruples against playing both sides.

Barksdale hoped to collect enough material to write a "drama" about the gold corner.

Daniel Butterfield had read Barksdale's revelations in the *Sun*. He invited Barksdale to visit his Wall Street office in early October and made a tempting proposition: He would pay the reporter $100 if he would use his titillating pen to compose a strong defense of himself and the President. Barksdale agreed; it was good money. Besides, it would give him access to Butterfield's deepest secrets. Barksdale interviewed the assistant treasurer a dozen times and in the end produced a shrill tract that gave Daniel's self-aggrandizing version of Black Friday. The essay dramatically blasted the "blackness" and "criminality" of Fisk and Gould, called their evidence against Corbin, Butterfield, and Grant "worthless trash," and touted their "universal public odium."

Speaking through Barksdale's pen, Butterfield portrayed himself as the misunderstood hero of the gold drama. The Fisk-Gould ring had bypassed Butterfield's own gallant management of the SubTreasury by "tapping" the telegraph wires from Washington, he said. Of his own speculating through Jay Gould and Seligman, he revealed not a word.

Butterfield was delighted at Barksdale's handiwork and found an eager outlet for the story in the *Times*. The *Times* was keen to avenge itself against Fisk and Gould for multiple embarrassments; it snatched up the transparent attack and ran it as a front-page feature in its October 18 edition.

As Jay Gould read the *Times* blast over his breakfast he must have sneered, easily deciphering the source of the hysterical prose. He decided to lower the boom on the boyish assistant treasurer. Calling in his trusted reporter friend Ford Barksdale, Jay produced a cornucopia of documented dirt. He dug up the $10,000 check he had given Butterfield the previous June—the open-ended interest-free "loan"—complete with Butterfield's handwritten endorsement. He produced records of Daniel's real-estate dealings with Boss Tweed. He had lawyer Frederick Lane write a long, detailed account of Butterfield's welshing on his debts to the bull pool.

Barksdale, who perhaps now set Butterfield alongside Abel Corbin in his gallery of "hypocrites," took Jay's every scrap of scandal and had it printed as front page news in the *Sun*. "The Lions Devour Daniel," shouted the headline.

Daniel Butterfield's star began to fade. The New York grapevine accepted Jay Gould's heavy-handed accusations "as conclusive and unanswerable," Barksdale reported. No one doubted that young Daniel had had a finger in the Gold Ring. What was more, Wall Street had no sympathy for welshers.

Corbin and Butterfield would have taken their winnings happily if the corner had worked, one broker told the *Sun*. "Now, why don't they put up like men when the game has burst on them. D—n them, they deserve to be exposed," the broker said, "and if Mrs. Grant was in it she deserved to be exposed."

Jim Fisk iced the cake by mocking Daniel's charge that he had tapped the intercity telegraph wires. Jim had needed only "to tap Butterfield to get all the extra information required," he said.

Washington joined the chorus. If Butterfield still refused to resign, his boss in the Treasury department, George Boutwell, was ready to push him out now. Within forty-eight hours of Jay Gould's expose, Boutwell laid down the law in a private note to his tarnished assistant: "I am constrained by a sense to duty to advise you to resign. " Three days later Daniel tendered his resignation, which the President accepted.

Soon Butterfield, like Corbin before him, broke down physically. He refused to cooperate with a special Treasury department investigation, claiming he had "premonitory symptoms of an attack of congestion."

Hardly an October day passed without the media circus producing more shocking revelations. The public loved it. Retailers used the scandal to sell everything from books to haberdashery.

Susan B. Anthony and Elizabeth Cady Stanton painted the gold panic as an allegory on sexual politics that proved the "disqualification of the male man" to handle money or power. Asking "How Men Manage Money Matters?" they demanded an end to gold-based currency—a "brute force" system that gave the upper hand to "unprincipled politicians, and characterless gambling operators" to abuse weak and honest citizens, "just as man oppresses woman."

Weeks passed, but Ulysses Grant still found himself stuck in the muck. The more he struggled, the deeper he sank. Asked by a *Herald* reporter about Jim Fisk's lobbying the previous summer, Grant took a cheap shot. He would have been offended had such antics come from anyone but Fisk, "a man so destitute of moral character, I didn't think it worth noticing."

The *Herald* didn't buy it. Why hadn't Ulysses been that concerned about Jim's morals when he accepted his hospitality at the Fifth Avenue Theatre and on his Narragansett steamers?

Late in October, Jay Gould twisted the dagger a bit more. He claimed that Grant had held government bonds bought by Gould via Corbin through a small Wall Street firm called Stone, Nichols, and Stone. He had become a bull and sold out for a "handsome profit." This allegation was the most damning yet. Still George E. Stone, senior partner at the firm, waited almost a week before issuing a denial, which prompted new rounds of suspicion.

Where would it all end?

• PART IX •

Fortunes

• • • • •

• 36 •
EVASIONS

T HE SIEGE OF WALL STREET under Jay Gould's barrage of writs, propaganda, and receiverships lasted months after the Black Friday crash; any return to normalcy seemed like a far-off dream. During the siege Jay used his legal chokehold over the financial system to save his own fortune. Justice Cardozo issued eight separate injunctions and decrees for Jay that tied knots around the Gold Room, the Stock Exchange, and the Gold Exchange Bank. And once Cardozo had broken the ice, Judges Clerke and Barnard joined in with half a dozen more.

On October 21, almost a full month late, the Gold Exchange Bank receiver settled the backlog of trades from Black Friday, paying Bank creditors twenty-five cents on the dollar. By that time, individual brokers had already settled most of their open gold transactions among themselves. Also by then, Henry Benedict, the Bank's long-time president who had irritated just about everyone after the panic, had been forced out by the clearinghouse's board of directors.

In the process neither Augustus Brown—Cardozo's original receiver, who served only eleven days—nor Conrad Jordan, whom Cardozo had asked to finish the dirty work, ever challenged Jim Fisk's repudiation of his Black Friday gold purchases or William Belden's fishy bankruptcy. All trades by Belden, Albert Speyers, Samuel Boocock, and other Fisk brokers were thrown out. As a result, the clearinghouse never charged Jim a penny for his losses in the panic.

Meanwhile, Jay milked the system shamelessly. Jay asked Judge Cardozo to order the Gold Exchange Bank receiver to pay Jay's brokers first, early, and in full: a cool $400,000 for William Heath and another $75,000 for E. K. Willard. Cardozo himself joined the feeding frenzy and took special care of the lawyers. He served up a pot of $60,000 in fees, paid courtesy of the insolvent Bank. Augustus Brown got $15,000 for less than two weeks of his trouble; Vanderpoel and Shearman received $5,000 each; Conrad Jordan, Brown's replacement as receiver, took in $12,500. These sums may seem trivial by modem standards, but in 1869 such gratuities could support entire families in affluence.

By the time Cardozo ended the receivership on November 22, the Bank had lost almost $700,000 on the affair.

The Gold Room fared no better. Creditors tried to sidestep Jay's injunctions by invoking the Exchange rules to sell off Jim Fisk's gold in the open market. But Jay hardly blinked. He simply sent Tom Shearman off to get fresh decrees from Judges Clerke and Cardozo barring the Exchanges from applying their bylaws against Bill Tweed's friends.

The gold crash devastated the U.S. economy for months and even years. In one week, from September 24 to October 1, the total mass of gold and stock on Wall Street dropped in value by an estimated $100 million, an amount comparable to several *billions* today. Trading on the Stock Exchange dried up. Only 4 million shares changed hands between January and September 1870, compared with 8 million the previous year.

Stock prices rebounded after the panic and produced windfalls for Commodore Vanderbilt and other speculators who were smart enough to buy shares at the bottom. But by then a huge portion of America's wealth had vanished.

Gold Room regulars resumed trading gold, the "currency of the world," on Thursday, September 30, but damaged confidence kept volume thin and the price under $130 for months.

Virtually every Exchange member had suffered in the crash. The dozens who had sold gold to Jim Fisk at high prices thinking he would pay, the hundreds who had bought gold before the crash hoping prices would rise forever, the scores who had had accounts at the Gold Exchange Bank—all swallowed their pride and walked away poorer.

All firms felt the bite. Dozens went bankrupt or suspended. Even brokers like Speyers and Samuel Boocock, who had carried Jim Fisk's orders to the Exchange floor, were hung out to dry with the rest.

The suffering touched even big houses. Cooke & Company's New York branch lost at least $28,201 in the panic, even after Harris Fahnestock jawboned "the Fisk party" to return a $45,000 margin deposit. Edward Dodge,

Fahnestock s partner, lost almost $80,000 in gold speculation for the year and was dropped from the firm.

"We have got to find a different way to make money," Fahnestock told Jay Cooke.

Cooke himself turned cynical. He decried "the wicked want of honesty in high places & in all political circles." If Grant himself weren't President, Cooke said, he would "not hold govts at par as things now stand"—strong words from the biggest bond dealer this side of the Atlantic.

Jay Gould did lend his clout to save his own agents. Through Tom Shearman, he got an injunction from Judge Cardozo to block the Stock Exchange from expelling his partner Henry Smith. He also covered the losses on some of Jim Fisk's trades carried at Heath & Company, a gesture to keep William Heath's firm afloat. William Belden went bankrupt, but that didn't seem to affect his lifestyle; Belden got a good price selling his silence to Fisk and Gould.

Farmers, who constituted more than half the American labor force and who were supposed to benefit from Jay's "crop theory," suffered worst of all. Agriculture sank into a deep depression by year's end as tight money, overproduction and stagnant trade drove prices to record lows. Wheat dropped in value by almost one-half between August and December. The Chicago price plummeted from $1.40 per bushel to 77 cents. Com fell from 95 to 68 cents, and barley, rye, and oats all fell, too. The Chicago grain markets became ghost towns; trading volume for 1869 fell by a full one-third from a year earlier.

A few people came out ahead after the dust had settled. Bartenders at the Fifth Avenue Hotel and Delmonico's restaurant pocketed fortunes from easing the pain of broken dreams and lost treasures of New York's financial buccaneers.

Lawyers also prospered. Beyond Jay's instant, mass-produced injunctions, almost three hundred lawsuits followed the gold panic. Most charged him, Fisk, or both with fraud or breach of contract. Tom Shearman and John Sterling fought them all. Jay laid down the strategy: none of the cases must go to trial, and each must be delayed, stalled, and blocked until the plaintiffs despaired and agreed to settle.

Sterling and Shearman obstructed brilliantly. They created procedural mazes that locked up some of the cases for over a decade. Their tactics tested the frontiers of legal ethics even by loose nineteenth-century standards.

James Brown had sued Fisk and Gould in federal court to enforce his $7 million Black Friday gold sales to Albert Speyers. He got nowhere; Shearman boxed him up for years. Orlando Joslyn took a more aggressive tack and won an attachment from Judge Brady against the Grand Opera House, Jim Fisk's proudest possession. On Friday, October 1, Sheriff O'Brien interrupted Lucille Western, who was rehearsing in the theater for her upcoming role in *The Tempest*, to serve the order giving Joslyn control of Jim's property.

Joslyn's chief witness in the lawsuit was broker C. C. Allen, another victim of Jim's Black Friday repudiations.

Hit where it hurt most, Jim counterattacked viciously. Joslyn and Allen had libeled him, he charged. He filed suit with Judge Dowling. Dowling, himself a regular for dinners at Josie Mansfield's, ordered the culprits arrested. Police Captain Jourdan took Allen into custody at his Wall Street office and dragged him off to the Tombs prison. Jourdan was a policeman who took Wall Street criminals with an extra-big grain of salt; on their way uptown he stopped at the Franklin Police Station long enough to share his fine Havana cigars with Allen and give him a tour of his "rare collection of burglar instruments, and a variety of bowie knives, pistols, revolvers, pictures, &c."

After a few hours Allen's lawyer showed up with bail money. Joslyn finally agreed to settle and drop the lawsuit.

Only one case, *Davis* v. *Fisk*, apparently ever reached a jury, and that case involved only a trivial amount of money. But here, too, Jay fought to the limit. After announcing the jury's guilty verdict, the jury foreman told Judge McCunn that three of the jurors had been approached by "hirelings of the Erie ring" and offered thousands of dollars "to induce a disagreement. " Jay and his lawyer David Dudley Field hotly denied the jury-tampering claim. The district attorney felt obliged to investigate, but he never brought charges. Whether Jay or Jim ever paid the $2,333 award is unclear.

Judge Barnard won the prize for ingenuity. At one point he ordered sixteen of the gold suits pending before other judges to be moved to his own docket so that he could scuttle them personally. In one case he issued an order that checkmated broker John Bonner: it barred him from pressing his claim against Jay Gould through the Gold Exchange arbitration committee or anyplace else except as a defendant in front of Barnard's bench.

Bonner gave up.

Harris Fahnestock of Cooke & Company did not even bother to sue after he saw Fisk and Gould make legal mincemeat of other bears. He negotiated whatever settlement he could with Henry Smith and was happy to walk away with half a loaf.

For this work, Jay and Jim rewarded their lawyers well. Erie Railway ledgers show a "special disbursement" of $489,909.30 for "expenses of litigation" in September 1869 and $898,054.86 more over the next year.

Following the tumult caused by Black Friday, a transformation in public sentiment emerged. Forget Vanderbilt and his railroads, forget A. T. Stewart, the "Merchant Prince," and tycoon Jay Cooke. The status of foremost financiers in the post-Civil War United States now belonged squarely to the Erie Railway's dynamic duo, Jay Gould, thirty-three years old, and Jim Fisk, thirty-four. These *Wunderkinder*, the Napoleon of Wall Street and Prince of Erie, dominated U.S. business and the national media. Their faces peered out from the covers of illustrated tabloids. Their names clogged conversations, sermons, speeches, and news reports from Boston to San Francisco. They became emblems of a new national epoch, the Flash Age, a time of extravagant excess, of pent-up cynicism exploding after a decade of war and deprivation.

The gold corner came to be read as a social statement. Children across the land dreamed of growing up to be like the daring Wall Street bandits.

Oddly, what people most admired about them was their honesty. Fisk and Gould made no bones about their greed and corruption; they paraded it. Mark Twain fixed on the authors of Black Friday as characters for his novel *The Gilded Age*. "The people had *desired* money before [Gould's day]," he wrote, "but *he* taught them to fall down and worship it." Jim's wisecracking made him a comic antihero, a perfect foil for the pompous hypocrisy of the ruling class. He called himself a "speculator," as if that were a license to rape, pillage, and steal. He made being "smart" a virtual insult, slang for a shrewd swindler.

Even moralists defended Gould and Fisk as being no worse than their milieu. If Jim Fisk was an ethical vacuum, argued the *Herald*, "who among the gold gamblers and stock jobbers of Wall Street will be able to stand? Shall he be made the scapegoat for the whole tribe?"

E. L. Godkin's *The Nation* regarded Fisk and Gould's antics as symptoms of a public moral crisis. Why should such men "whose one passion is money making" and to whom speculation "is a delightful game" quit when "a fortune may be made in an hour ... followed by no retribution of any kind," he asked. Except for a few "fossils" or clergymen, "Few people [thought] worse of a man for having been engaged in a successful 'corner,' even though it may have carried ruin to a thousand homes," he said.

Fame had some drawbacks. Nobody had missed the dark side of Black Friday: two gamblers had twisted the national economy to fatten their own wallets and were prepared to crush thousands of innocents to get their way. If they stood above the law as pranksters, enemies waited in the wings to deal them a comeuppance. People may have envied their brass and enjoyed their showmanship, but they also recognized Fisk and Gould as common thieves in fancy clothes.

When Jim rode out to Long Branch, New Jersey, and took rooms at the Continental, his favorite hotel, respectable guests checked out and moved down the street to other lodging. Proper society shunned Jim's Opera House productions, even after *The Tempest* opened to good reviews.

These social slurs bothered Jim and Jay but not much. Each still thrived in his own way. Jim tweaked respectable noses that spring by becoming the chief patron of a state militia regiment and making himself commander. New Yorkers grew accustomed to seeing the Ninth Regiment's chubby new "colonel" parading his money-bought military rank in his splashy uniform.

Jay and Jim ran the Erie Railway as arrogantly as ever, using the company treasury as a personal piggy bank, reelecting themselves president and vice president by unanimous board votes just weeks after the Black Friday panic. So powerful were they viewed as being that two British journals refused to publish Henry Adams's biting expose of the Black Friday gold scandal for fear of transatlantic libel suits.

That November, hundreds of brakemen walked off their jobs at the Eire rail yard in Port Jervis, New York, demanding better pay and hours. Jay and Jim sent trainloads of goons to work as scabs. Jim reportedly ordered one platoon of gangsters to "shoot down" resisting strikers. Yet when Jim rode out to Port Jervis weeks later, a crowd of employees came out to meet him at the station. Prince Erie's "very appearance was greeted with shouts and hearty cheers from the very men he had ordered shot, " wrote Edward Mott.

A villain? Hardly. To his men and to many Americans, Jim Fisk was a hero and role model.

· 37 ·
LIGHT OF DAY

A NEW CONGRESS CONVENED in Washington, D.C., in December 1869 and pounced on the latest political hot potato. The gold crash had damaged business across the country, particularly for farmers and ex-port-import merchants. Voters from New York to Chicago to New Orleans had demanded answers: How could such a thing happen? Who was responsible? Democrats saw it as a chance to tarnish the Republican White House. Republicans hoped that an investigation of Fisk, Gould, and their Democratic cronies by a body outside Tammany-controlled New York would expose them.

Congress turned to its favorite fact-finding tool. On December 13 it mandated a special investigation by the House Banking Committee. Not twenty-two months after impeaching Ulysses Grant's White House predecessor, Congress wanted the answer to one central question: "whether any officers of the national government were directly or indirectly engaged in the alleged conspiracy."

In other words: What did the President know, and when did he know it? Leading the probe would be the Banking Committee's new chairman, the popular rising political star, Congressman James Abram Garfield of Ohio.

Garfield, a husky redheaded, full-bearded Civil War hero-turned-politician, had walked an independent path in Washington since his 1863 election to Congress. Unlike his weaker Capitol Hill brethren, Garfield had refused to do favors for any businessman who greased his palm. "I am trying to do two things," he wrote after the War, "viz. be a radical and not be a fool, a matter of no small difficulty."

Independence had its price. Steel industry lobbyists blocked Garfield's bid to chair the Ways and Means Committee in 1868 after he had opposed demands for protectionist legislation. The iron men "want a representative that they can own and carry around in their pantaloons pocket," Garfield wrote.

Garfield's reformist reputation made him suitable to lead the gold panic investigation. He was seen as fair. Although a party loyalist, he was yet no knee-jerk "Grant man." And if Garfield were to stray too far, he had backup; House rules stacked the Banking Committee with an 8-to-2 majority of Republicans over Democrats.

Garfield had his own clear ideas about what he called "the disgraceful scenes witnessed in Wall Street" that autumn. The main culprit, he felt, was the greenback money system that had allowed paper to float against gold. Curiously, his diary records an early encounter with the top gold gambler himself. Traveling through New York in November 1866, Garfield wrote of having "dinner with Mr. Gould in Madison Square." What the young congressman had talked about with the financial upstart, he didn't say.

Leading the two-man Democratic minority on the Committee was Congressman Samuel Sullivan "Sunset" Cox of New York. Educated at Brown University, Cox had served eight years in Congress before moving his family from Ohio to New York after the War. New Yorkers elected him to a new congressional term in 1869. How Cox had gotten himself nominated raises curious questions; New York Democrats nominated no one for street cleaner, dog catcher, or any other job who had not first paid his respects—if not something more tangible—to Tammany Hall.

No investigation has ever implicated Cox in any Tweed Ring or Erie scandals. But Cox did have a good rapport with the Boss. Tweed invited Cox to his daughter's wedding in 1870, and he made an appearance.

Far from the spectacle of modern high-glitz congressional hearings with their rooms full of reporters and photographers, Garfield conducted his Committee sessions behind closed doors. His biggest problem at first was finding witnesses. Key players from the gold panic had disappeared. William Heath had left New York for a year-long European vacation, claiming "health" reasons. Arthur Kimber, Jay's original "pool" partner, had dropped out of sight. Abel Corbin, who topped everyone's witness list, had vanished into the wilds of Kentucky, reportedly ill. Even banker Henry Clews evaded a Committee summons. And Garfield never summoned Jay Cooke or his agent Harris Fahnestock.

Even under the best of conditions, piecing together the complex story would have been a forbidding job. Garfield's Committee had to educate itself in the mechanics of New York gold trading. One biographer depicted Garfield as a gumshoe detective, visiting New York incognito, sneaking into the Gold Exchange's "private room," eavesdropping on insider talk. Many brokers kept no written records; others refused to disclose their business.

One by one the cast of characters paraded down to Washington for private confessions. Albert Speyers mesmerized the panel with his tales of Jim Fisk's wild speculations on Black Friday. Old James Brown thumped his chest, telling how he'd personally defeated the Ring. "If the bull had been as strong as twenty elephants I would have tackled him," he said. William Belden demonstrated chronic memory lapses. Daniel Butterfield gallantly admitted that his secret gold buying before the panic had been solely for his wife's benefit.

Henry Smith, George Boutwell, Henry Benedict, Horace Porter, all the key brokers, and newspaper reporters like Caleb Norvell and Ford Barksdale—each added his two cents. Even Corbin turned up and whined his story to the Committee. Fifty-seven witnesses testified in all, producing a printed transcript almost five hundred pages long that was a mass of contradictions, lies, recriminations, and gaps.

Missing from the group portrait were any sons of Tammany Hall, New York, particularly Bill Tweed and Albert Cardozo. Whether "Sunset" Cox had something to do with that is a mystery.

The high point came on Saturday, January 22, when Fisk and Gould themselves took center stage, riding down from New York to face the Committee. Jay testified first while Jim waited in the marble hallway outside; then Jim took his turn while Jay cooled his heels in the lobby. Between them, they bent the Committee's ears for six hours.

Jim gave a boffo performance. Members described his testimony as "theatrical and ludicrous in the extreme. He talked with great rapidity and illustrated his utterances with grotesque actions, and interlarded them with copious interjections and profanity."

Jim had the Committee "convulsed with laughter."

After the closed-door hearing, Gould and Fisk invited the leading reporters to their Willard Hotel suite for a press conference. As Jay sat back, Jim repeated his spirited testimony to the roomful of correspondents and stenographers. Laughing, joking, basking in the attention, he recounted the whole story of Black Friday, from Jay's original crop theory to Albert Speyers's dramatic breakdown. Along the way, he implicated Corbin, Butterfield, Julia Grant, and a parade of others.

"I said to the Committee that I had a great desire that they should examine Mrs. Grant and Mrs. Corbin," Jim told the press. "I demanded it."

The mass of evidence connecting Ulysses Grant and family to the gold scandal, especially Jim Fisk's accusations, threw the Committee for a loop. To clear the President, Democrats and Republicans agreed that they had to dig deeper. Testimony about secret meetings between Grant and Jay Gould, Grant's conversion to Jay's crop theory, the mysterious "Dear Sis" letter from Julia Grant to Jennie Corbin—all cried out for explanation.

Democrat Cox forced the issue by asking Chairman Garfield to visit Grant and invite him to answer the charges. The Committee agreed unanimously.

Garfield called at the White House one afternoon in early February with copies of the incriminating testimony under his arm. In a private meeting with the President he told Grant that witnesses had made "personal reference" both to himself and to "members of his family."

By now, Ulysses Grant had tired of the gutter contest with Fisk and Gould. He listened politely to Garfield, puffing his cigar, keeping his reticence. He decided to stand on his reputation and ignore the name-calling.

Garfield reported back to the Committee that afternoon that Grant "preferred not to see the testimony" or make any comment.

Cox, incensed at this imperial brush-off, demanded that Garfield summon Grant to testify under oath before the Committee. But the Republicans united to protect their President. They based their argument on deep Constitutional questions, the "separation of powers" issue that has come down from Thomas Jefferson to Richard Nixon.

The Committee rejected Cox's motion on a partisan tally.

Ulysses Grant carried the day. Even without his testimony, Garfield's Committee backed his innocence. The Committee's report, issued in March along with the transcript, exonerated Ulysses and Julia Grant of the" groundless and wicked" charges of complicity. The Committee relied for this on the testimony of Jay Gould and Abel Corbin, both of whom had vouched for Grant's innocence. "I am satisfied that the President has never had any connection, directly or indirectly," with the conspiracy, Jay had told the Committee, calling Ulysses "a very pure, high-minded man." Conveniently, Garfield chose to believe him.

At the same time, the Committee blasted Corbin for resorting to the "worst form of hypocrisy which puts on the guise of religion and patriotism" to exploit his famous relatives.

Garfield threw up his hands on Daniel Butterfield. It was "not conclusively proved" whether the assistant treasurer had conspired or not with Fisk and Gould, the committee said in its report, citing "conflicting" testimony.

Emerging cleanest from the muck was General Horace Porter, Grant's personal secretary. Jay had testified that he bought $500,000 in gold for Porter in mid-September, but Porter had produced his own letters turning down the offer. He was the only member of Grant's circle actually to refuse a bribe from Jay Gould.

Sunset Cox and Democrat Thomas Jones of Kentucky refused to sign the report. They would not certify Grant's "immaculateness" based solely on the "mysterious, unexplained, conflicting, and nebulous testimony" from the parade of self-serving witnesses.

Garfield's clean bill of health convinced most Americans that their President was an honest man, but Grant's standing for shrewdness fell several notches. Henry Adams, for one, balked at the result. Garfield's Committee had "dared not probe, and refused to analyze" its own reams of evidence, he said. "[T]he trail always faded and died out at the point where any member of the Administration became visible." Still, "everyone assured every one else that the President himself was the savior of the situation, and in private assured each other that if the President had not been caught this time, he was sure to be trapped the next, for the ways of Wall Street were dark and double."

E. L. Godkin's *The Nation* recited the common view that Grant's "one error" had been that he was a bad judge of character, "accepting the hospitality of, and entering into conversation with, such people as Gould, Fisk & Co. were then known to be." Henry Adams gasped at the "incredible and inexplicable lapses of Grant's intelligence" in dealing with Fisk and Jay Gould, whom he wrongly labeled "the complex Jew."

Daniel Butterfield responded to the findings by packing his bags and taking his family on an extended tour of Europe. For two years he lived off his investments, studying the London and Paris post office systems, waiting for the heat to die down before showing his face again on the streets of New York.

⊚ ⊚ ⊚ ⊚ ⊚

Garfield's Committee skipped over another pregnant question in its final report. Had Jay Gould and Jim Fisk actually gained anything from their gold
spectacular? Wall Street rumors ran the gamut from huge profits to ruinous
losses. Jim told the *Herald's* George Crouch that he had made $9 million in
winnings on Black Friday before Boutwell pulled the plug.

To this day, no one knows the truth.

Paying the losses for Black Friday could have cost Fisk and Gould $20
million. Instead, thanks to their lawyers and Boss Tweed, it cost them nothing. Jay had unloaded the bulk of his $50 million-plus "national gold account"
at high prices on Thursday and Friday before the crash, raking in profits estimated at $10 to $12 million. The Gold Room's Committee of Twenty calculated that Henry Smith's firm still held another $13 million in gold "calls"
after the panic, but Smith settled these privately with other brokers at prices
around $135—about the same that Jay had paid for most of his gold in early
September.

Take Jay's $10 to $12 million in gains selling gold at high prices; add in
his winnings on manipulating the stock market during the panic; subtract his
losses on Friday's crash—a fat zero; take out a million or two in lawyers' fees
and settlements. All in all, not bad for a few weeks' work, even after splitting
the loot with Jim and paying a well-earned tithe to Big Bill Tweed.

They were, after all, partners.

What's more, aside from the tongue-lashings by Garfield, the press, and
other respectable citizens, the law never laid a finger on the gold bandits. No
statute in America blocked two men from buying all the gold they wanted.
As for walking away from their Gold Room debts and bribing government officials—it paid to own a judge or two. Not Garfield's Committee, not the
grand jury, not the gold clearinghouse, not all the lynch mobs in New York
could reach the two speculators behind the marble fortress walls of the Opera
House.

Things could have been better for them. Ulysses Grant and George
Boutwell had stuck their noses in on Black Friday and kept Fisk and Gould
from consummating their corner; otherwise, who knows what wealth could
have been theirs? Also, Jay had lost his chance to expand the Erie Railway
westward when LeGrand Lockwood's Lake Shore line fell to his enemy Vanderbilt. And he also had lost his chance for the Erie Railway to profit from

the extra freight business from grain flowing east for export under his crop theory, if he had ever taken that seriously.

Jim Fisk best appreciated the ultimate decadence of the high-stakes game played to a dramatic standoff. Asked what had happened to the mountain of money thrown willy-nilly into the gold inferno by leading bulls and bears across the nation, Jim said simply, "It has gone where the woodbine twineth."

Where was that?

"When I was a peddler in Vermont," he explained, "I used to notice that the woodbine was generally hanging onto a spout."

· 38 ·
BYGONES

William Belden stayed on Wall Street after his Black Friday bankruptcy, but nobody would touch his business. When money ran low by 1876, he convinced Jay Gould to join him in a new brokerage venture. It turned out to be a disaster for all sides. Belden, by one account, robbed Jay "right and left," gouging him for upward of $3 million. Jay kicked Belden out of the firm and had him arrested on fraud charges in January 1879, ending Belden's career for good.

As late as 1888, twenty years after Black Friday, the Stock Exchange still considered Belden so notorious that it blackballed a member for no other specified reason than his being associated with Jim Fisk's one-time lackey.

George Boutwell became reclusive in his later years as Ulysses Grant's Treasury secretary. "The Treasury as an active influence ceased to exist," wrote Henry Adams. "Mr. Boutwell meant to invite no support and cared to receive none."

This isolation had benefits. Boutwell emerged untarnished from the later parade of Grant scandals, even the "whiskey ring" quagmire that overwhelmed the Treasury a year after he resigned in 1873 to serve as United States Senator from Massachusetts.

Boutwell held his Senate seat until 1877 , when he left to serve in a number of coveted legal positions: on the Franco-American Claims Commission, on President Rutherford Hayes's Commission to rewrite U.S. statutes, and as counsel to the governments of Haiti and Chili. He practiced law into his old age before dying of pneumonia in 1905 at the age of eighty-seven.

James Brown continued visiting his bank offices on Wall Street regularly until he fully retired in 1877 at the ripe age of eighty-six. He died peacefully two years later. As late as September 1871, New Yorkers chose the then-

eighty-year-old Brown to chair the mass public meeting on overthrowing Boss
Tweed's municipal ring. Brown Brothers' bank combined with E. H. Harriman
in 1931. It survives today as Brown Brothers Harriman & Company; its offices can still be found at 59 Wall.

Daniel Butterfield returned from Europe in mid-1872 and rejoined the
family business, a stagecoach delivery firm called the American Express Company that his father had helped organize. Butterfield prospered, branching
into ventures from steamboats to apartment houses to banks. He ran twice for
Congress on the Republican ticket and was a serious contender for the Party's
nomination for governor in the 1890s. He lived for seventy years, until 1901.

Albert Cardozo resigned from the New York Supreme Court in May
1872 after a state legislative committee recommended his impeachment,
based primarily on his controversial gold corner injunctions. Afterward, Cardozo practiced law in New York with his partner Gratz Nathan. Cardozo's
youngest son, Benjamin Nathan, born on May 24, 1870, later realized his father's dream: President Herbert Hoover nominated him in 1932 to fill the
U.S. Supreme Court seat vacated by Oliver Wendell Holmes.

George G. Barnard, Cardozo's colleague in Tweed jurisprudence, was
impeached from the New York Supreme Court in August 1872 based on
charges stemming from his Erie Railway injunctions on behalf of Fisk and
Gould.

Jay Cooke & Company went bankrupt four years after Black Friday
from over investment in railroad ventures, prompting the disastrous stock
panic of 1873. Harris Fahnestock, Cooke's New York agent, hooked his fortunes to the First National Bank of New York, becoming a director and managing vice president. Fahnestock took full control of the bank in 1877; he
forced Samuel Thompson, the previous owner, to leave and form the Chase
National Bank, a forerunner of today's Chase Manhattan.

Abel and Jennie Corbin lived quietly in Elizabeth and Jersey City, New
Jersey, for a decade after Black Friday. The scandal left Corbin a sick, broken
man. Ulysses Grant forgave his in-laws for their role in the affair and even
started asking Corbin's advice on political matters as early as in 1873. By all
accounts, Corbin never again abused the privilege. He died on March 28,
1880, at the age of seventy-two.

Jennie Grant Corbin stayed in New Jersey after Abel died. She never re-
married but moved to a small home in East Orange, where she lived until the
age of eighty-two. The last surviving Grant sibling, she died in June 1913.

James Garfield was elected President of the United States in 1880. After serving four months, he was shot by a psychopath named Charles J. Guiteau while entering the Washington, D.C. rail depot. He died from the gunshot wounds on September 19, 1881.

Ulysses Grant served two terms as President of the United States, but Black Friday ended the early optimism for his administration. "The worst scandals of the eighteenth century were relatively harmless by the side of this," wrote Henry Adams. "[E]very intelligent man about the Government prepared to go," not wanting to waste years "sweeping the stables" of Washington. Grant's presidency produced a string of scandals far beyond anything seen before. Grant's secretary of war, William Belknap, was impeached for corruption in administering the Indian territories; his first Vice President, Schuyler Colfax, sank in the Credit Mobilier swamp; his third Treasury secretary fell with the infamous "whiskey ring," along with his private secretary Orville Babcock.

In a farewell speech to Congress on leaving office, Ulysses apologized for assuming the high office "without any previous political training." Still, when he and Julia traveled around the world for two years afterward, they were received as royalty in capitals from Egypt to India to Europe. Republicans meeting in Chicago to choose an 1880 presidential candidate cast more than 300 votes on each of 36 ballots for Ulysses Grant before turning to James Garfield as their standard bearer.

Even after he left the White House, Wall Street hadn't finished with Ulysses. Settling in New York in the 1880s, Grant joined a brokerage partnership with Ferdinand Ward, a skilled con man who used the ex-President's name to run up debts of $15 million before skipping town in 1884. Grant's family lost half a million dollars in the scandal; even Jennie Corbin had invested in the firm.

Too bad Abel Corbin hadn't still been around to sniff out the rat.

Cash poor again, Ulysses wrote his war memoirs, which were published by Mark Twain for an advance of $20,000. He had barely finished the volume before throat cancer overcame him in July 1885. Grant was buried in an elaborate tomb in New York City, the most celebrated American of his generation.

Horace Porter was implicated in two well-known Grant scandals, the "whiskey ring" and one centering on frauds in the New York Custom House. In both cases, Porter testified publicly to congressional investigating committees, emerging embarrassed but unscathed.

Porter left President Grant's staff in December 1872 to become vice president of the Pullman Palace Car Company. Dabbling in railroad stocks, he emerged later as president of the West Shore Railroad and the Manhattan branch of the New York Elevated Railroad system.

President William McKinley appointed Porter U. S. Ambassador to France in 1897. Porter represented the United States at the Hague Peace Conference in 1907. After Ulysses Grant's death in 1885, Porter organized a drive to collect $600,000 for a permanent New York burial place for the Hero of Vicksburg. Porter died at eighty-four, the last surviving member of President Grant's circle, in 1921. His war memoirs, *Campaigning With Grant*, first published in 1897, portrayed his general in adoring terms.

Tom Shearman and his junior partner **John Sterling** broke away from David Dudley Field and hung out their shingle as an independent law firm in 1873. Jay Gould's continuing legal tangles over Black Friday and the Erie Railway generated plenty of business for them. Shearman also defended the Reverend Henry Ward Beecher against the charges of adultery leveled at him by Victoria Woodhull and Tennie Claflin, the scandal sensation of the mid-1870s. Up through the late 1880s, though, the firm's bread-and-butter client remained Jay Gould.

Prospering in his legal career, Shearman became known as a reformer. A founding member of the New York Reform Club, he spoke frequently on behalf of American Indians, Armenian refugees, coal miners, and tenement dwellers. He wrote several legal treatises, including a text on tort law.

Their firm survives today as a Wall Street icon. In 1987, Shearman & Sterling employed 506 lawyers—113 partners and 393 associates—making it the ninth largest in America. Its offices can still be found on Wall Street near the Stock Exchange.

Henry Smith became blood enemies with Jay Gould a few years after the gold escapade. Smith dissolved his decade-old brokerage partnership with Jay in August 1870. The firm Smith Gould, Martin & Company ceased to exist. Two years later, Smith and Daniel Drew launched a bear raid against a western railroad's stock. Jay teamed up with two prominent bulls to push prices skyward. Smith lost millions in the operation. Seeing Jay later on the street, he grew livid and shouted curses. "I'll live to see the day, sir, when you have to earn your money by going around this street with a hand organ and a monkey."

"Maybe you will, Henry," Jay said. "And when I want a monkey, I'll send for you."

Smith went bust in the 1873 panic but slowly regained his footing and emerged as one of Wall Street's leading bears. He developed an interest in horses and raised Thoroughbreds at his New Jersey stud farm, including one he named Jay Gould that he doubtless enjoyed whipping and racing in circles. The stain of Black Friday followed him for life. In 1877, even after he had broken with Jay, the Stock Exchange rejected Smith's request for membership, citing his role in the gold corner.

Henry Smith's final collapse came in 1885, when he became trapped on the wrong side of a powerful bull market in stocks created by the Vanderbilt family. Besides losing $1.4 million of his own money, Smith had also borrowed over $1 million from William Heath & Company, another Black Friday firm, to support his doomed market positions; this bankrupted Heath as well.

Albert Speyers sued Fisk and Gould to recover his losses from Black Friday, but he never got a cent. After barely surviving this one panic, Speyers was wiped out again in 1873. The Stock Exchange sold his seat for $5,000 that year to pay his debt to other brokers.

Speyers quit Wall Street altogether in 1874 and opened a real-estate shop on Cedar Street. In 1879 he was successful enough to take over the Albermarle Fertilizer Company as president. Speyers spent most of his time in courtrooms testifying in lawsuits and investigations on the gold corner. He died of stomach cancer in December 1880, about sixty years old.

William Magear Tweed was convicted on 204 counts of fraud in November 1873 and sentenced to serve twelve years in the county penitentiary on Blackwell's Island. Tweed's municipal ring had defrauded New York taxpayers of a king's ransom, estimated at over $100 million. Tweed's lawyers, including David Dudley Field and the young Elihu Root, won his release a year later in January 1875, but Tweed was immediately rearrested on civil lawsuits that had been brought to recover $6 million of stolen municipal loot. He went straight to the Ludlow Street Jail in Manhattan, where he sat awaiting trial for almost a year.

Suffocating behind bars, Tweed made a dash for freedom that December. While visiting his family on a Sunday release, Tweed bolted. He ran first to Cuba and then to Spain but was recaptured and carted back to New York by federal agents in November 1876. The jail break cost him $60,000 in bribes and destroyed any chance for legal vindication in the future.

Tweed died in his prison cell of a heart condition in April 1878, just a few days after his fifty-fifth birthday.

James Fisk, Jr.'s reign over the Erie Railway Company with Jay Gould lasted barely two more years after Black Friday. During that time he become best known for his outside indulgences. He produced ever-flashier shows on his Opera House stage; he paraded about town as "colonel" of his Ninth State Militia Regiment and "admiral" of the Narragansett Steamship line, all the while laughing off slurs from respectable New Yorkers. A social renegade after the gold affair, Jim gave extravagantly to charities and led New York's relief effort for victims of the October 1871 great Chicago fire. He helped any crippled veteran who needed a pass or a job on the Erie line.

Jim's high living, though, finally did him in. Only months after the gold panic, Josie Mansfield, Jim's live-in girlfriend, started seeing another man, a fashion plate named Edward "Ned" Stokes who had recently joined Jim in a business partnership over a Brooklyn oil refinery. Bitterly, Jim moved out of Josie's house on Twenty-third Street in September 1870 as Ned moved in.

When Josie and Ned ran short of cash, they decided to extort money from Jim Fisk's deep pockets. Over the years, Josie had studied how Jim and Jay Gould strong-armed millions out of Wall Street. Now she and Stokes unleashed on Jim a storm of lawsuits and press attacks. She demanded that he pay her a lump-sum settlement of $25,000—a forerunner of modem "palimony" actions—and tried to blackmail him with a packet of old love letters that supposedly contained damning business secrets.

Not to be outdone, Jim counterattacked by having Ned Stokes arrested for embezzling money from their business partnership. Josie then had Jim arrested for libel; Stokes sued Jim for malicious prosecution. The New York press exploited the complex ménage as a grand farce, a sex-morality play, in daily headlines.

By December 1871, Jim's reputation had suffered so badly that Jay Gould had to ask for his resignation as Erie Railway vice president, although Jim continued to run the line's nuts and bolts as company comptroller.

Unfortunately, Ned Stokes had a lower boiling point. Humiliated and infuriated by the scandal, Stokes followed Jim to the Grand Central Hotel late on the afternoon of Saturday, January 6, 1872, cornered him on a stairway, and shot him twice with a pistol. Jim died early the next morning from the bullet wounds after teary bedside farewells to his friends Jay Gould and Boss Tweed.

"Not since the memorable night that Abe Lincoln was shot was there such excitement throughout the city," reported the *Herald* after the shooting.

Over twenty-five thousand people jammed the city streets for Jim's funeral parade; well-wishers bought thousands of small photographs of the dead celebrity and Wall Street buccaneer. Clergymen like Henry Ward Beecher decried Jim as a "supreme mountebank of fortune," a man "absolutely without moral sense," but common working men sang a ballad about him called "He Never Went Back on the Poor."

Josie Mansfield moved to Paris a few months after Jim Fisk's murder. There she married a wealthy American expatriate in 1891, whom she divorced six years later. After returning to Boston in 1899 and suffering a stroke, Josie resettled in Paris and lived out her days as a popular member of the American expatriate community there until she died on October 27, 1931, at almost eighty-five years old. She outlived Prince Erie by sixty years.

Ned Stokes was tried three times for the killing but served just four months in Sing-Sing prison on a reduced charge of manslaughter. Lucy Fisk, Jim's wife, squandered her million-dollar inheritance in a few years. No Fisk fortune remains.

Jay Gould was ejected as president of the Erie Railway Company in a dramatic stockholders' uprising in March 1872, barely two months after the death of Jim Fisk. Afterward, his fortunes rose from the ashes many times before he was finished leaving his mark on nineteenth-century America.

In the 1880s Jay commanded huge portions of the nation's two most vital utilities: railroads and telegraphs. His rail system, which included the Union Pacific, the Kansas Pacific, the Missouri Pacific, and the Wabash, had six thousand miles of rail crossing the West and Southwest. Closer to home, he took over and ran New York's Elevated Railroad, the precursor of today's subways.

Jay started his own telegraph company, the Atlantic and Pacific, and captured the Western Union from William H. Vanderbilt, the Commodore's son, in another bloody takeover war. By adding to these the Baltimore and Ohio, he created an awesome combination. Even a free marketer like Henry Clews cowered at the monopoly and wondered if Washington should step in to prevent Jay from exploiting his hold over intercity and interstate communication.

Jay also branched into journalism when he bought *The New York World*. He later sold it to Joseph Pulitzer, which launched the latter's publishing empire.

When Boss Tweed was first arrested for his municipal frauds in October 1871, Jay Gould delivered his ultimate pay-off: he signed for Tweed's unprecedented million-dollar bail bond.

Despite all his wealth and power, however, Jay never seemed to find happiness. He splurged on luxuries that befit a railroad mogul—a five-hundred acre estate at Lyndhurst, New York; a fabulous yacht, the *Atalanta*; a brownstone mansion at Forty-seventh Street and Fifth Avenue. He bore a heavy stigma after the Erie days, though, which no success could erase. Jay was a marked man in the United States. The public saw him as a caricature of capitalism's evil side, even as he rubbed elbows with Presidents, senators, and captains of industry.

Jay and his wife Helen lived as social untouchables, snubbed by Astors, Belmonts, and even Vanderbilts. The New York Yacht Club blackballed Jay's membership application. He was "the most hated man in America," Jay told a reporter, although some considered him the smartest.

A haunted man at fifty-five, Jay suffered from insomnia. Often during his last years he would awaken after midnight, unable to fall back asleep. He'd step outside in front of his Fifth Avenue mansion. There, under the watchful eye of a detective, Jay would pace the sidewalk, puffing a black cigar, coughing sporadically, his stomach torn by dyspepsia.

On the morning of Jay's death in December 1892, Wall Street rallied. Western Union stock rose 2-1/8, Manhattan Elevated was up 1-1/2, and Union Pacific was up 1-3/8. He left a fortune valued at more than $70 million, which by 1980s standards was easily worth a billion or more.

The Erie Railway Company waited for three years after Jay Gould's 1872 ouster before moving its offices from the Grand Opera House back downtown. Gould and Fisk had improved the Erie line substantially during their reign. New steel rails and iron bridges, faster locomotives, more comfortable palace cars and drawing-room coaches, and stylish dining stops all had made Erie the luxury way to travel. Gross earnings for 1869 jumped to $16.7 million, from $14.3 million the year before under Daniel Drew's management.

At the same time, their chronic stock-watering, Wall Street forays, and personal extravagance left the company hopelessly broke, saddled with debts of $90 million by the time of Jay's removal. Afterward, Erie foundered from default to receivership to bankruptcy. It merged in 1878 into the New York, Lake Erie and Western Railroad Company, the first of a dozen reorganizations including its most recent marriage to the Delaware, Lackawanna & Western Railroad in 1960.

Erie, now the Erie-Lackawanna, went bankrupt for the last time in 1972. In 1976 its passenger service between New York and Chicago was absorbed under Conrail. Erie Lackawanna, Inc., still maintains offices today in Cleveland, Ohio, and its stock trades on the NASDAQ over-the-counter market, but the company's sole remaining function is to oversee the dismantling of its century-and-a-half-year-old railroad operation.

The New York Gold Room closed its doors in January 1879, when the nation returned to a gold-based currency system. With no more fluctuations between gold and paper money, gold trading was pointless and the institution obsolete. Gold was not traded as a commodity again in the United States until December 31, 1974.

The excesses of Fisk, Gould, and later speculators brought waves of government action to protect the nation's financial infrastructure. The Interstate Commerce Act of 1887 gave the federal government power over railroad rates for the first time. Congress placed agriculture futures trading under government controls in 1922, followed in the 1930s by federal securities laws. Today, both stock and commodity exchanges are regulated extensively by federal commissions and self-governing industry bodies. Laws exist banning market manipulation. The philosophy of unbridled laissez-faire capitalism has long given way to more balanced views of the public interest.

Even President Ronald Reagan's pro-free-market administration has produced crackdowns on securities fraud and insider trading on Wall Street and has kept up the network of federal controls underpinning national finance.

Laws and regulations, though, can never absolutely prevent escapades like Black Friday or the rough-and-tumble Erie wars. Rules have changed to check known abuses and protect innocent bystanders, but human motivations remain the same. The rewards for success on Wall Street have grown astronomically even after the October 1987 "Black Monday" crash. The 1980s have been littered with rapacious adventures: the Bendix-Martin Marietta war, the Penn Square collapse, the Hunt silver spree, and the Ivan Boesky insider trading scandal, to name a few.

Government rules will make the next Black Friday job more difficult. Still, every improved safe only invites a smarter safecracker. And now as then, the world is full of young Fisks and Goulds waiting to make their marks.

AFTERTHOUGHT

ISRAEL FREYER'S BID FOR GOLD*
by Edmund C. Stedman, *New York Tribune*, September 28, 1869
(four days after Black Friday)

Zounds! how the price went flashing through
Wall street, William, Broad street, New!
All the specie in all the land
Held in one ring by a giant hand—
For millions more it was ready to pay,
And throttle the Street on hangman's day.
Up from the Gold Pit's nether hell,
While the innocent fountain rose and fell,
Loud and higher the bidding rose,
And the bulls, triumphant, faced their foes.
It seemed as if Satan himself were in it:
Lifting it—one percent a minute—
Through the bellowing broker, there amid,
Who made the terrible, final bid!
High over all, and ever higher,
Was heard the voice of Israel Freyer,—
A doleful knell in the storm-swept mart,—
"Five millions more! and for any part
"I'll give One Hundred and Sixty!"

Israel Freyer—the Government Jew—
Good as the best-soaked through and through
With credit gained in the year he sold
Our Treasury's precious hoard of gold;
Now through his thankless mouth rings out
The Leaguers' last and cruellest shout!

---

* "Israel Freyer" is an allusion to Fisk broker Albert Speyers. Possibly offensive ethnic references must be read in the context of the times.

Pity the shorts? Not they indeed,
While a single rival's left to bleed!
Down come dealers in silks and hides,
Crowding the Gold Room's rounded sides,
Jostling, trampling each other's feet,
Uttering groans in the outer street;
Watching, with upturned faces pale,
The scurrying index make its tale;
    Hearing the bid of Israel Freyer,—
    That ominous voice, would it never tire?
"Five millions more—for any part,
(If it breaks your firm, if it cracks your heart,)
    I'll give One Hundred and Sixty. "

One Hundred and Sixty! Can't be true!
What will the bears-at-forty do?
How will the merchants pay their dues?
How will the country stand the news?
What'll the banks—but listen! hold!
In screwing upward the price of gold
To that dangerous, last, particular peg,
They had killed their Goose with the Golden Egg!
Just there the metal came pouring out,
All ways at once, like a water-spout,
Or a rushing, gushing, yellow flood,
That drenched the bulls wherever they stood!
Small need to open the Washington main,
Their coffer-dams were burst with the strain!
    It came by runners, it came by wire,
    To answer the bid of Israel Freyer,
It poured in millions from every side,
And almost strangled him as he cried,—
    "I'll give One Hundred and Sixty!"

Like Vulcan after Jupiter's kick,
Or the aphoristical rocket's stick,

Down, down, down, the premium fell,
Faster than this crude rhyme can tell!
Thirty per cent, the index slid,
Yet Freyer still kept making his bid
"One Hundred and Sixty for any part!"
—The sudden ruin had crazed his heart,
Shattered his senses, cracked his brain,
And left him crying again and again,—
Still making his bid at the market's top
(Like the Dutchman's leg that never could stop,)
"One Hundred and Sixty-Five Millions more!"
Till they dragged him, howling, off the floor.
        The very last words that seller and buyer
        Heard from the mouth of Israel Freyer—
A cry to remember as long as they live—
Were, "I'll take Five Millions more! I'll give,—
        I'll give One Hundred and Sixty!"

Suppose (to avoid the appearance of evil)
There's such a thing as a Personal Devil,
It would seem that his highness here got hold,
For once, of a bellowing Bull in Gold!
Whether bull or bear, it wouldn't much matter
Should Israel Freyer keep up this clatter
On earth or under it (as, they say,
He is doomed) till the general Judgment Day,
When the clerk, as he cites him to answer for' t,
Shall bid him keep silence in that Court!
But it matters most, as it seems to me,
That my countrymen, great, and strong and free,
So marvel at fellows who seem to win,
That if even a Clown can only begin
By stealing a railroad, and use its purse
For cornering stock and gold, or—worse—
For buying a Judge and Legislature,

And sinking still lower poor human nature,
 The gaping public, whatever befall,
Will swallow him, tandem, harlots, and all!
While our rich men drivel and stand amazed
At the dust and pother his gang have raised,
And make us remember a nursery tale
Of the four-and-twenty who feared one snail.

What's bred in the bone will breed, you know;
Clowns and their trainers, high and low,
Will cut such capers, long as they dare,
While honest Poverty says its prayer.
But tell me what prayer or fast can save
Some hoary candidate for the grave,
The market's wrinkled Giant Despair,
Muttering, brooding, scheeming there,—
Founding a college or building a church
Lest Heaven should leave him in the lurch!
 Better come out in the 'rival way,
Issue your script in open day,
And pour your wealth in the grimy fist
Of some gross-mouthed, gambling pugilist;
Leave toil and poverty where they lie,
Pass thinkers, workers, artists by,
Your pot-house fag from his counters bring
And make him into a Railway King!
Between such Gentiles and such Jews
Little enough one finds to choose:
Either the other will buy and use,
Eat the meat and throw him the bone,
And leave him to stand the brunt alone.

—Let the tempest come, that's gathering near,
And give us a better atmosphere!

BIBLIOGRAPHY

Newspapers

- *Albany Argus*
- *Albany Evening Times*
- *Albany Morning Express*
- *Boston Herald*
- *Boston Post*
- *Frank Leslie's Illustrated Newspaper*
- *Harper's Weekly*
- *Missouri Argus*
- *The Nation*
- *The National Law Journal*
- *New York Evening Mail*
- *New York Evening Post*
- *New York Herald*
- *New York Times*
- *New York Tribune*
- *New York Sun*
- *New York World*
- *The Revolution*
- *Springfield Daily Republican*
- *Woodhull and Claflin's Weekly*

Government Reports

United States Congress

- *Alleged Corruption in the Tariff of 1857.* House of Representatives, Rpt. No. 414, 35th Cong., 1st Sess., 5/27/1858. [cited as "H. Rpt. 414."]
- *New York Election Frauds.* House of Representatives, No. 31, 40th Cong., 3d Sess., 2/23/1869. Gold Panic Investigation. House of Representatives, Rpt. No. 31, 41st Cong., 2d Sess., 3/1/ 1870. [cited as "H. Rpt. 31 "]
- *Whiskey Frauds.* House of Representatives, Mis. Doc. No. 186, 44th Cong., 1st Sess., 7/25/ 1876.
- *Report to Congress of the Commission on the Role of Gold in the Domestic and International Monetary Systems.* March 1982.

New York State Legislature

- *Report of the Select Committee of the Senate … in Relation to Members Receiving Money from Railway Companies.* Senate, Rpt. No. 52, 3/10/1869.
- *Charges Against Justice Albert Cardozo.* Judiciary Committee, Assembly, Rpt. No. 1111, 1872. [cited as "N.Y.S. Rpt. 1111"]
- *Impeachment Trial of George G. Barnard.* Assembly, 1872.
- *Report of the Select Committee to Investigate Alleged Mismanagement of the Erie Railway.* Assembly, 1873.

Archival Materials

- Historical Society of Pennsylvania
  Jay Cooke papers
- Library of Congress
  George S. Boutwell papers James A. Garfield papers Jay Gould papers
  Ulysses Grant papers Horace Porter papers
  Abraham Lincoln and Andrew Johnson papers (Abel Corbin letters)
  Columbus Delano papers (Jay Gould letters)
- National Archives
  Treasury Department documents
  Boutwell-Butterfield dispatches and correspondence
- New-York Historical Society
  Brown Brothers papers
  Helen Gould papers
  G. P. Morosini manuscript
  Seligman papers (Wells manuscript)
  William M. Tweed papers
- New York Public Library
  August Belmont papers
  Brown Brothers ledgers
  Jay Gould papers
  William M. Tweed papers
- New York Stock Exchange Archives
  Minutes of Board of Directors; Arbitration Committee; Membership Committee; records of suspended members; clippings files.
- Pennsylvania State Archives (Harrisburg)
  Erie Railway records (Minutes of Board of Directors; Minutes of Executive Committee; ledgers and journals)
- Letters between James Fisk, Jr., and Josie Mansfield, 1868-1871, printed in New York Herald, 1114/1872. [cited as "Fisk-Mansfield letters")

Books and Pamphlets

- Adams, Charles F., and Henry Adams. *Chapters of Erie.* Boston: James R. Osgood, 1871.

- Adams, Henry. *The Education of Henry Adams.* Boston: Houghton Mifflin, 1918.

- Allen, Frederick Lewis. *The Great Pierpont Morgan.* New York: Harper & Brothers, 1949.

- Andrews, Wayne. *The Vanderbilt Legend: The Story of the Vanderbilt Family, 1794-1940.* New York: Harcourt, Brace, 1941.

- Berger, Meyer. *The Story of The New York Times, 1851-1951.* New York: Simon and Schuster, 1970.

- Boutwell, George S. *Reminiscences of Sixty Years in Public Affairs.* New York: Greenwood Press, 1968.

- Bowen, Croswell. *The Elegant Oakey.* New York: Oxford University Press, 1956.

- Boyer, Richard O., and Herbert M. Morais. *Labor's Untold Story.* New York: United Electrical, Radio and Machine Workers of America, 1955.

- Browder, Clifford. *The Money Game in Old New York: Daniel Drew and His Times.* Lexington: The University Press of Kentucky, 1986.

- Brown, John Crosby. *A Hundred Years of Merchant Banking: A History of Brown Brothers and Company, Brown Shipley & Company, and the Allied Firms.* New York; privately printed, 1909.

- Butterfield, Julia L. *A Biographical Memorial of General Daniel Butterfield.* New York: The Grafton Press, 1904.

- Catton, Bruce. *Grant Takes Command.* Boston and Toronto: Little, Brown, 1968.

- Chambers, William Nisbet. *Old Bullion Benton: Senator from the Old West.* New York: Russell & Russell, 1970, 1956.

- Clews, Henry, LL. D. *Fifty Years in Wall Street.* New York: Irving Publishing, 1908.

- Cornwallis, Kinehan. *The Gold Room and the New York Stock Exchange and Clearing House.* New York: A.S. Bames, 1879.

- Crouch, George. *Erie Under Fisk and Gould: A Comparison of the Past and Present Management.* New York, 1870.

- Earle, Walter Keese. *Shearman and Sterling: 1873-1973.* New York: Shearman and Sterling, 1973.

- *Edward S. Stokes against the People of the State of New York: Error Book.* New York: George F. Nesbitt, 1873.

- Fowler, William W. *Twenty Years of Inside Life in Wall Street.* New York; Orange Judd, 1880.

- Fuller, Robert H. *Jubilee Jim: The Life of Colonel James Fisk, Jr.* New York: MacMillan, 1928.

- Garfield, James A. *The Diary of James A. Garfield.* Ann Arbor: Michigan State University Press, 1967.

- Grant, Julia D. *The Personal Memoirs of Julia Dent Grant.* New York: G.P. Putnam's Sons, 1975.

- Grant, Ulysses S. *Personal Memoirs of Ulysses S. Grant.* New York: Charles L. Webster, 1885.

- Grodinsky, Julius. *Jay Gould: His Business Career 1867-1892.* Philadelphia: University of Pennsylvania Press, 1957.

- Hellman, George S. *Benjamin N. Cardozo: American Judge.* New York: Russell and Russell, 1940.

- Hershkowitz, Leo. *Tweed's New York: Another Look.* Garden City, N. Y.: Anchor Press/Doubleday, 1977.

- Hibben, Paxton. *Henry Ward Beecher: An American Portrait.* New York: George H. Doran, 1927.

- Holbrook, Stewart H. *The Age of The Moguls: The Story of the Robber Barons and the Great Tycoons.* New York: Harmony Books, 1953.

- Hudson, Frederic. *Journalism in the United States from 1690 to 1872.* New York: Haskell House, 1968.

- Jastram, Roy W. *The Golden Constant: The English and American Experience, 1560-1976.* New York: John Wiley and Sons, 1977.

- Johnston, Johanna. *Mrs. Satan: The Incredible Saga of Victoria C. Woodhull.* New York: G.P. Putnam's Sons, 1967.

- Josephson, Matthew. *Edison: A Biography.* New York: McGraw Hill, 1959.

- Josephson, Matthew. *The Politicos.* New York: Harcourt, Brace & World, 1938, 1966.

- Josephson, Matthew. *The Robber Barons: The Great American Capitalists, 1861-1901.* New York: Harcourt, Brace, 1934.

- Kaplan, Justin. *Mr. Clemens and Mr. Twain.* New York: Simon & Schuster, 1966.

- Katz, Irving. *August Belmont: A Political Biography.* New York: Columbia University Press, 1968.

- Klein, Maury. *The Life and Legend of Jay Gould.* Baltimore: The Johns Hopkins University Press, 1986.

- Kendall, Leon T. *The Chicago Board of Trade and the Federal Government: A Study of Their Relationship, 1848 to 1952*. Indiana University School of Business, 1956.
- Kent, Frank R. *The Story of Alexander Brown & Sons*. Baltimore: privately published for Alexander Brown & Sons, 1925.
- Kettell, Brian. *Gold*. Cambridge, Mass.: Ballinger, 1982.
- Kindleberger, Charles P. *Manias, Panics, and Crashes: A History of Financial Crises*. New York: Basic Books, 1978.
- Kouwenhoven, John A. *Partners in Banking; An Historical Portrait of a Great Private Bank, Brown Brothers Harriman & Co., 1818-1968*. Garden City, New York: Doubleday, 1968.
- Lane, Wheaton J. *Commodore Vanderbilt: An Epic of the Steam Age*. New York: Knopf, 1942.
- Larson, Henrietta M. *Jay Cooke: Private Banker*. Cambridge, Mass.: Harvard University Press, 1936.
- Levinson, Leonard Louis. *Wall Street: A Pictoral History*. New York: Ziff-Davis, 1961.
- *Life, Trial, and Conviction of Edward Stokes for the Assassination of Jas. Fisk, Jr.* Philadelphia: Barclay, 1873.
- Lynch, Denis Tilden. *"Boss" Tweed: The Story of a Grim Generation*. New York; Boni and Liveright, 1927.
- Mandelbaum, Seymour. *Boss Tweed's New York*. New York: John Wiley and Sons, 1965.
- McClure, Clarence Henry. *Opposition in Missouri to Thomas Hart Benton*. Nashville, Tenn.: George Peabody College for Teachers, 1927.
- McCullough, David. *The Great Bridge: The Epic Story of the Building of the Brooklyn Bridge*. New York: Simon and Schuster, 1972.
- McFeely, William S. *Grant: A Biography*. New York: W.W. Norton, 1981.
- Meadowcroft, William H. *The Boy's Life of Edison*. New York & London: Harper & Brothers, 1911.
- Medbery, James K. *Men and Mysteries of Wall Street*. Boston: Fields, Osgood, 1870.
- Mende, Elsie Porter. *An American Soldier and Diplomat: Horace Porter*. New York: Frederick A. Stokes, 1927.
- Minnigerode, Meade. *Certain Rich Men*. New York: G.P. Putnam's Sons, 1927.

- Morosini, G. P. *Jay Gould and the Erie Railway*. Unpublished manuscript at New-York Historical Society, 1893.
- Morris, Lloyd. *Incredible New York: High Life and Low Life of the Last Hundred Years*. New York: Random House, 1951.
- Mott, Edward H. *Between the Ocean and the Lakes: The Story of Erie*. New York: Ticker, 1908.
- Nevins, Allan. *Hamilton Fish: The Inner History of the Grant Administration*. New York: Dodd, Mead, 1936.
- Oberholtzer, Ellis Paxson. *Jay Cooke: Financier of the Civil War*. New York: Bart Franklin, 1970.
- O'Connor, Richard. *Gould's Millions*. Garden City, N.Y.; Doubleday, 1962.
- Paul, Hon. Ron, and Lewis Lehrman. *The Case for Gold: A Minority Report of the U.S. Gold Commission*. Washington, D.C.: CATO Institute, 1982.
- Pollard, James E. *The Journal of Jay Cooke or The Gibraltar Records, 1865-1905*. Columbia, Oh.: The Ohio State of University Press, 1935.
- Porter, General Horace. *Campaigning With Grant*. Secaucus, N.J.: The Blue and Grey Press, 1984, 1897.
- Redlich, Fritz. *The Molding of American Banking: Men and Ideas*. New York: Hafner, 1951.
- Ridpath, John Clark. *The Life and Work of James A. Garfield*. Cincinnati: Jones Brothers, 1882.
- Smith, Gene. *Lee and Grant: A Dual Biography*. New York: McGraw-Hill, 1984.
- Smith, Matthew Hale. *Twenty Years Among the Bulls and Bears of Wall Street*. Boston: J. R. Barr, 1870.
- Stedman, Edmund C., ed. *The New York Stock Exchange: Its History, its Contribution to National Prosperity, and its Relation to American Finance at the Outset of the Twentieth Century*. New York: Greenwood Press, 1969, 1905.
- Swanberg, W. A. *Jim Fisk: The Career of an Improbable Rascal*. New York: Charles Scribner's Sons, 1959.
- Taylor, Charles H. *History of the Board of Trade of the City of Chicago*. Chicago: Robert O. Law, 1917.
- Tilden, Samuel J. *The New York City Ring: Its Origin, Maturity, and Fall*. New York, 1873.

- Vinson, J. Chal. *Thomas Nast: Political Cartoonist*. Athens: University of Georgia Press, 1967.

- Warshow, Robert Irving. *Jay Gould: The Story of a Fortune*. New York: Greenberg, 1928.

- Wattenberg, Ben J. *The Statistical History of the United States: From Colonial Times to the Present*. New York; Basic Books, 1976.

- Wells, Linton. *The House of Seligman*. Unpublished manuscript with Seligman papers, New-York Historical Society, 1931.

- Werner, M. R. *Tammany Hall*. Garden City, N.Y.: Doubleday, Doran, 1928.

- Wimmer, Larry T. "The Gold Crisis of 1869: Stabilizing or Destabilizing Speculation Under Floating Exchange Rates?" *Explorations in Economic History*, vol. 12, number 2, New York: Academic Press, April 1975.

- Wingate, Charles F. "An Episode in Municipal Government: The Tweed Ring." *North American Review*. 119 (1874): 359; 121 (1875): 113.

- *The Youthful Days of Josie Mansfield, the Beautiful Girl from Boston*. New York, Boston, 1872.

REFERENCE NOTES

Full references to books, reports and papers cited below are found in the General Bibliography. *Press references are to New York newspapers, unless otherwise indicated.*

1. War *(pages 3–11)*

- Galveston ... the Western frontier: Story of vigilante hanging is from the *Times*, 3/2/ 1868.
- Cornelius Vanderbilt: For biographical data, see Holbrook; Andrews; Lane; and Minnigerode, pp. 101-34.
- war on ... Erie Railway Company: The best source on the Drew-Vanderbilt Erie Railway struggle is Charles Frances Adams's essay "A Chapter of Erie," published in the July 1869 *North American Review* and later in pamphlet and book forms. Grodinsky, Mott, and Swanberg were also relied on. Newspapers, particularly the financial columns of the *Herald* and *Times*, provided daily price quotations, interest rates, and gossip rundowns. The daily press also reprinted a wealth of source materials on the extensive legal battles, including texts of affidavits, opinions, and proceedings.
- Vanderbilt ... Nicaragua: For a good factual review of this affair, see "The World and William Walker, " Albert Carr's 1963 biography which is included in abridged form in *Walker: The True Story of the First American Invasion of Nicaragua,* the Rudy Wurlitzer book accompanying the 1987 film.
- Stock Exchange: See Cornwallis; Stedman for background on the New York Stock Exchange. The Stock Exchange archives also provided a wealth of detail, cited frequently below.
- "Stockbrokers are a jolly ... ": Cornwallis, p. 34.
- Daniel Drew: See generally Browder; Minnigerode; Clews, pp. 115-26; and *Tribune*, 9/19/ 1879.
- "I got to be a millionaire ... ": O'Connor, p. 64; *Tribune*, 9/19/1879.
- "two thin streaks ... ": O'Connor, p. 63. Generally on Erie, see Mott.
- Jay Gould: Many fine biographies of Jay Gould have been written, including Klein's recent excellent work. O'Connor is very readable, focusing more on Gould's character than his financial operations. Papers at the New York Historical Society and Public Library were also useful. On the Gouldsboro refinery, see *Gould v. Lee*, 44 Pa. State Rpts., 99 (1867).
- "But I'm on top ... ": O'Connor, p. 18.
- "Conscious of right ... ": J. Gould, *History of Delaware County*, quoted in O'Connor, p. 21.
- James Fisk: Swanberg's is the most entertaining and reliable Fisk biography. Fuller's is written as an historical novel, which casts doubt on his accuracy, although his eye for character was telling. Minnigerode's essay on Fisk and contemporary pamphlets were also useful.

- "No! the old man would n't … ": Many versions of this story exist. I have quoted Henry Adams, from C. F. Adams, p. 105.
- "Wall Street has ruined … ": Minnigerode, p. 195.
- "If this damned printing press … ": O'Connor, p. 67; Swanberg, p. 41; and Lane, p.247.
- "violent panic": *Herald*, 3/10/1868.
- "Buy all the stock … ": Fuller, p. 142. Dialogue from Fuller is suspect. In rare cases, I have allowed myself to be seduced. Here, Fuller has simply replaced expletives deleted from more orthodox versions of Vanderbilt's quote. See, e.g., Swanberg, p. 44; and Browder, p. 162.
- Trading in railroad stocks … : Long before the development of the modem NYSE "specialist" system, brokers traded stocks on the Exchange floor through public auction, an open outcry system like that used on the floors of commodity futures exchanges.
- Fisk and Gould … small lifeboat … : *Harper's Weekly*, 4/11/1868.

2. "Fort Taylor" (pages 12–16)

- "in the interests … ": *Herald*, 3/15/1868; quoted in Browder, p. 167.
- "Can't tell just yet … ": Mott, p. 488. See also the letter from J. Mansfield to J. Fisk, 10/31/1871, printed in the *Tribune*, 11/1/1871. For snapshots of life among the "Erie Exiles," see *Tribune*, 3/16,17/1868.
- "The wealth of Vanderbilt … ": C. F. Adams, p. 54. See N.Y.S. Report No. 52, March 1869, which draws the entertaining conclusion that, yes, Gould et al, distributed oceans of money in bribes but none ended up in the hands of the lawmakers. See also Lane, pp. 250- 52.
- "[I]t never pays to kick … ": O'Connor, p. 77.
- "of the dark days of the war … ": C. F. Adams, p. 55.
- Gould … "perfectly astounded": Minnigerode, p. 177; Lane, p. 251.
- pilgrimage to Boss Tweed.: Hastings had already introduced Gould to Tweed briefly by this point. Tweed test. to Committee of Aldermen, in *Times*, 9/22/1877; Lynch, p. 271. On Tweed generally, see Lynch; Hershkowitz; and Wingate.
- "Drew: I'm sick of the whole … ": O'Connor, p. 77; Swanberg, p. 58.
- Van Derbilt: The Commodore often preferred this misspelling of his own name.
- Fisk … Vanderbilt's bedroom … : This extract of testimony is reprinted in *Life. Trial. and Conviction; Times*, 3/18/1870.
- peace treaty … generous … : For specifics on the July 1868 Erie peace treaty. see Erie directors' minutes, 7/10/1868; Erie journals, July 1868.
- "There ain't nothin' in Airy … ": Mott, p. 161.
- "It forms an episode … ": *Life, Trial, and Conviction; Times*, 3/18/1870.

3. The Money Lock-Up (pages 17–28)

- Drew resigned … Jay president … : Erie board minutes.
- Josie Mansfield: Josie revealed most details of her comings and goings in subse-

quent court testimony, particularly her November 1871 appearance before the Yorkville Police Court, reprinted in the *World*, 11/26/1871. See also Swanberg; Fuller; and *Youthful Days*.

- "Strange you should ... ": Letter from J. Fisk to J. Mansfield, undated, Fisk-Mansfield letters.
- "James McHenry, the partner ... ": Letter from J. Fisk to J. Mansfield, *10/13/1868*, Fisk Mansfield letters.
- Stock Exchange ... SEC ... rules barring short-sales ... : The overall effectiveness of these rules, and particularly their apparent failure to stem the tide of panic selling on "Black Monday," October 19, 1987, has been a subject of substantial controversy. See "Some Watchdog! How the SEC helped set the stage for Black Monday," *Barrons*, 12/18/1987; "The October 1987 Market Break," Report at the SEC Division of Market Regulation, February 1988, pp. 3-24 *et seq.* For a run-down on recent permutations of the short-selling formula for over-the-counter stocks, see "Naked Came the Short-Sellers," *Forbes*, 2/8/1988.
- money supply: Money supply (measured as "M2"), bank deposit data from Wattenberg, p.993.
- Joseph Seligman: On Seligman's role, see Wells manuscript, New York Historical Society.
- "perhaps ... the most extraordinary feat ... ": C. F. Adams, pp. 66-67.
- Sweeny ... $3 million ... : *Herald, 10/31/1868*; *Tribune, 11/2/1868*.
- Tweed ... $20 million ... : Clews, p. 228. "There were great fluctuations in stocks while William Marcy Tweed was the power behind the throne in the government of the city of New York" as Tweed "pulled the wires at the City Hall while the puppets in several brokers' offices in the vicinity of Wall Street danced to the sweet will of the managers of the municipal building." Clews, p. 227.
- Stock Exchange ... delegation ... : C. F. Adams, p. 66; Mott, p. 162.
- "very damaging character.": *Herald, 10/28/1868*.
- "an unscrupulous crowd of speculators": *Tribune, 10/30/1868*.
- appeals ... Washington, D.C ... : See, e.g., Larson, pp. 74-75.
- "threatened to cut ... ": C. F. Adams, p. 67.
- McCulloch telegraphed word ... : *Herald; Tribune, 11/7/1868*.
- "the privilege of pulling ... .": Clews, p. 142.
- "He that sells ... ": Wells manuscript.
- Pierrepont brought together ... : See Browder, pp. 202-203.
- "Run along, Dollie ": Fuller, p. 249.
- "make a clean breast ": Fisk recounted his meetings with Daniel Drew and Jay Gould on Sunday, November IS, in a deposition presented in the *MacIntosh* lawsuit, sworn 11/18/1868, printed in the *Times* and other newspapers, 11/19/1868. See also Mott, pp. 165-66. 27 "Then if you put this stock ... ": Ibid.
- Justice George Barnard: See Wingate, pp. 392-94; *Times*, 4128179; references in Lynch; and Hershkowitz.
- lawsuit ... McIntosh ... : Court papers reprinted in the *Times, 11/19/1868*.

- "George knows ... ": Wingate, p. 393.
- "I asked [Barnard] ... ": Tweed test. to Aldermen, in the *Times*, 9/22/1877.
- "His touch ... ": Clews, p. 119; O'Connor, p. 82.
- "However questionable ... ": *Herald*, 11/19/1868.
- "The rumors in the street ... ": *World*, 11/20/1868.
- "1. Steal largely ... ": *Herald*, 11/22/1868.
- "The alliance between Tammany ... ": C. F. Adams, p. 64.

4. Alliances *(pages 31–40)*

- "The most fantastic offices ... ": Minnigerode, p. 201.
- "not infrequently opening ... ": Ibid.
- Josie Mansfield: See sources cited in Chapter 3.
- Josie ... adventuress ... : Josie saw in Jim "the man who was to gratify her love of luxury and ease, ornament and display, as well as her ambition for distinction and her uncontrollable desire to be a leader rather than a follower of all the fashionable frivolities of the day." *Youthful Days*, p. II.
- "With dark eyes ... ": *Youthful Days*, p. 5.
- Perley ... loaded pistol.: See Mansfield test. before Judge Bixby, printed in *Times*, 11/26/ 1871.
- Gould never accepted ... : G. P. Morosini writes that Jay grew increasingly irritated by "the extravagance and eccentricities of his partner James Fisk," especially Fisk's "liaisons with notorious women" and "the crowd of unscrupulous heelers by which he surrounded himself. " Morosini manuscript.
- expose ... touted Jim's adultery ... : *Springfield Daily Republican*, 11/28/1868.
- Bowles ... Ludlow Street jail.: *Times*, 12/23,29/1868.
- "[Jay] was affable ... ": Morosini manuscript.
- Tweed ... $105,000 ... : Lynch, p. 301.
- check for $100,000 ... : Tweed papers, New York Historical Society. Nobody quite knows what the check was for.
- "playboy side ... ": Lynch, p. 299.
- Bill Tweed's city: For descriptions of nineteenth-century Gotham, see Morris's excellent municipal history.
- "The streets and alleys ... ": Morris, p. 31.
- 1868 election ... fraud ... : See "New York Election Frauds," U.S. House of Representatives, 2/23/1869.
- "The ballots made no result ... ": Tweed test. to Aldermen, printed in the *Times*, 9/19/ 1877.
- "the total fraudulent ... ": "New York Election Frauds," U.S. House of Representatives, 2/23/1869; *Nation*, 3/4/1869.
- Santa Claus to the newspapers ... : Tweed test. to Aldermen, printed in the *Times*, 9/30/ 1877.
- "India Rubber Account": Mott, pp. 454-55.

5. Trial Balloons *(pages 41–46)*

- November 1868 ... corner the gold market.: *Herald, 11/17,18/1868.*
- Gold speculation in New York: See generally Kornwallis; Stedman; and Fowler.
- "General Lee's ... ": O'Connor, p. 89. Cooke's "impression was that *noone* [in New York] heartily loved their country better than their pockets," he wrote. Larson, p. 158.
- Congress had closed the Gold Exchange ... : Congressional debate on the 1864 Gold Act is well worth reading as a study in fiscal naïveté. *Congressional Globe, 4/15/1864,* pp. 1640-51.
- April 1869 ... next flier ... : Gould test., H. Rpt. 31, p. 132. See also newspaper financial reports of that period.
- "The country's against you ... ": Fuller, pp. 329, 339. 49 "in terrorem over the heads ... ": *Nation, 4/15/1869.*
- "To protect the national honor ... ": Grant inaugural, 3/4/1869, reported in newspapers, 3/5/1869.

6. The Politico *(pages 49–58)*

- Abel Rathbone Corbin: For background on Corbin, see capsule biographies in the *Sun,* 10/ 6,9/1869; the *Times,* 3/29/1880. A good sense of Corbin comes across both from *The Missouri Argus,* the tabloid he published in St. Louis, and from his letters to Presidents A. Lincoln and A. Johnson. See Lincoln and Johnson papers, Library of Congress. The *Argus* is likewise available in hard copy at the Library of Congress.
- "very tall, somewhat slender ... ": *Sun, 10/6/1869.*
- "Next came Jennie ... ": J. Grant, p. 57.
- "Mr. Corbin was a good talker ... ": *Times, 3/29/1880.*
- "It is dangerous ... ": Minnigerode, p. 55.
- *Missouri Argus:* For more on this phase of Corbin's life, including his role in local St. Louis politics, see Chambers, pp. 208-209, 261; McClure, pp. 32-40.
- Lawrence, Stone, & Company: *See* "Alleged Corruption in the Tariff of 1857," H. Rpt. 414. Corbin's test., pp. 60-76, is eye-opening.
- "$10,000 if you will carry ... ": Letter from A. R. Corbin to S. Stone, 1/8/1855, from H. Rpt. 414, pp. 70-71.
- "This was a scheme ... ": Corbin test., H. Rpt. 414, p. 73.
- "If we create ... ": Letter from A. R. Corbin to President A. Johnson, 6/26/1866, Johnson papers.
- "[A]t least [Corbin] was now no longer ... ": C. F. Adams, p. 115.
- "The furniture is Paris made ... ": *Sun, 10/6/1869.*
- "[A]s I heard that [Gould] ... ": Corbin test., H. Rpt. 31, p. 243. 58 "[Corbin] came to see me ... ": Gould test., H. Rpt. 31, p.152.
- "[Corbin] saw at a glance ... ": Ibid.'
- "I had a natural desire for ... ": Corbin test., H. Rpt. 31, p. 243.
- Robert Catherwood: Catherwood test., H. Rpt. 31, pp. 437-39.

- "operate in a legitimate way and … ": Ibid.
- "crop theory": Both H. Adams and the Garfield Committee used variations on this shorthand nomenclature for Jay Gould's argument in favor of scarce gold. C. F. Adams, p. 115; H. Rpt. 31, p. 3.
- Before 1862 … currency … : On pre-Civil War currency, see historical sections in *Report of the Commission on the Role of Gold in the Domestic and International Monetary Systems*. March 1982. Paul and Lehrman, originally written as a minority report to the Gold Commission Report, are especially useful on early U.S. currency problems. Jastram reviews gold prices back to 1800 in the United States and to 1560 in England. See also Minnigerode, p. 57.
- "The Treasury is nearly empty … ": Oberholtzer, p. 173. See also H. Adams and F. A. Walker, "The Legal-Tender Act," in C. F. Adams, p. 302.
- Wholesale prices … doubled … : Jastram, p. 212.
- "[W]e want more money … ": *The Revolution*, 6/8/1868.
- Hepburn v. Griswald: 75 U.S. 603 (Dec. 1869). On the legal-political battle over *Hepburn v, Griswald*, see C. Fairman, "Mr. Justice Bradley's Appointment to the Supreme Court and the Legal Tender Cases," *Harvard Law Review* 54 (1940-41), pp. 977, 1129.
- "If the Repub'n party … ": Larson, p. 207.
- "without material detriment … ": Grant's inaugural address, March 4, 1869; text in newspapers.
- "a railroad … stigmatized … ": Corbin test., H. Rpt. 31, p. 243.

7. Savior of the Nation (*pages 59–65*)

- Ulysses S. Grant: Of many fine volumes on Ulysses Grant, Grant's own memoirs and Gene Smith's side-by-side story of Grant and Robert E. Lee were most absorbing. McFeely's biography was useful and thorough. Bruce Catton's Civil War books, particularly *Grant Takes Command,* provided useful insight. Many Grant biographers preferred to dwell on the glorious war years rather than on the sadder story of Grant's White House and post-White House careers.
- Chambers Street pier … *Providence.*: "The Grand Rush to the Jubilee," *Herald,* 6/16/ 1869.
- "with a broad gilt … ladies in their brilliant … ": Ibid.
- "more curious than the performance of Alladin … ": *Times, 5/20/1869.*
- State legislative committee: N.Y.S. Sen. Rpt. 52., 3/10/1869.
- "Papa says I may offer … ": Grant, pp. 29-30. The hard days left their mark on Ulysses and Julia. Julia pointedly remembered people who had treated her husband badly before his rise to fame and then came forward to ask for special favors.

    She recalled visiting rich cousins of Ulysses in Kentucky around 1850. The cousins had business connections in New Orleans, New York, Liverpool, and Paris. Ulysses, then a frustrated army lieutenant who coveted a civilian career, asked their help in finding him a place in business. "[N]ot one of them offered even to introduce him to any businessmen," Julia recalled. "How these same friends petitioned for favors," she said, "and how I chafed at being *com-*

pelled to accept the hospitality of a member of the family in New Orleans on our return from Mexico. It made me ill. I spent nearly all of the time in bed while there."

- "Saints are not ... ": Catton, p. 120.
- "In all purely military ... ": Porter, p. 31.
- murder of Abraham Lincoln ... : John Wilkes Booth had planned to kill Grant along with Lincoln that night at Ford's Theatre. The general was supposed to share Lincoln's theater box. At the last minute, Mrs. Grant had insisted on visiting their children in New York instead.
- Galena ... house ... "Fifty solid men ... ": Josephson, *Politicos*, p. 59.
- New Yorkers ... $105,000.: See Butterfield, pp. 170-74.
- "Grant represented order ... ": H. Adams, p. 260.
- Republicans had embraced U. S. Grant ... : Washingtonians gossiped that strong-willed Julia had pushed her husband to seek the presidency in 1868. Julia denied it. She described in her memoirs asking Ulysses if he really wanted to be President one night before the 1868 Republican convention.

"No," he replied, "but I do not see that I have anything to say about it. The convention is about to assemble and, from all I hear, they will nominate me; and I suppose if I am nominated, I will be elected."

Julia tried to talk Ulysses out of running, she said, by reminding him of Andrew Johnson's headaches with Congress over reconstruction and impeachment. "I do not want to be President," he said again, but felt a duty to unify the badly divided country. Grant could "give to the widely separated interests and sections of the country more satisfaction than any other man," he said. The South in particular "would accept my decision on any matters affecting its interests more amiably than that of any other man." J. Grant, p. 171.

- radicals trained their guns on A. T. Stewart.: Stewart, an Irish-born self-made multimillionaire, had a record of business integrity. A Trinity College graduate, New York's "Merchant Prince' financed shiploads of food aid for his starving countrymen during the 1848 Irish potato famine and donated to Civil War fundraising drives. He dreamed of capping his career as Grant's Alexander Hamilton.
- Grant's "surrender to the politicians": Josephson, *Politicos,* p. 84. "Unquestionably the simple military man was baffled and appalled at the prospect of such a destructive internal warfare as had been waged against his predecessor Johnson," Josephson wrote. "It was a pregnant moment in the annals of party life. A President covered with 'glory' shrank from a 'constitutional' quarrel, and found it a positive relief to escape from a nightmare of party opposition, and to leave to the Senators a continued censorship (of disputed and quite doubtful legality) over the executive power of appointment and removal." (pp. 84-85)

Perhaps Grant should have listened to his friend General William Tecumseh Sherman, who had described Washington politics as a cesspool of corruption. Sherman's response to an overture for political office: "If nominated I will not run, if elected I will not serve."

8. Propoganda *(pages 66–70)*

- "embarrassing and injurious ... ": *Times*, 5/17/1869.
- Jay ... guided the after-dinner talk ... : The two principal first-hand accounts of the dinner aboard the *Providence* that night are Gould's and Fisk's test. to the Garfield Committee, H. Rpt. 31, pp. 152-53, 171-172.
- "There is a certain amount ... ": H. Rpt. 31, p. 152.
- "it would produce great distress ... ": Ibid.
- "You see, General ... ": Fuller, p. 343.
- like a "wet blanket" ... : Gould test., H. Rpt. 31, p. 154.
- Over 200,000 people waited ... : *Boston Post; Times; and Tribune*, 6/16/1869.
- "If General Grant had been ... ": *Boston Post*, 6/16/1869.
- That night's Opera bouffe production ... : *Times*, 6/19/1869.

9. A New Stooge *(pages 71–74)*

- General Daniel Butterfield: On Butterfield, see biography by Julia Butterfield; Daniel's testimony before Garfield's Committee; references in Civil War texts; and newspaper clippings such as the *Times*, 7/18/1901. Extensive Treasury-related correspondence between Butterfield and Secretary George Boutwell is available at the National Archives. Butterfield and Corbin discussed their mutual friendship in H. Rpt. 31, pp. 269, 322-23.
- one of the few "Grant men" ... : Letter from A. R. Corbin to President A. Johnson, *61 26/1866*, Johnson papers.
- "as a testimonial ... ": Letter from D. Butterfield to Grant, *2/14/1866*; text in J. Butterfield, p. 170.
- Butterfield ... Grant's staff.: Butterfield's real-estate transactions for Porter and Babcock were revealed in Congressional probes of the "whiskey ring." See "Whiskey Frauds," Mis. Doc. *186,7/25/1876*, test. of A. B. Gardner, pp. 421-37.

    These properties were later sold to Harris Fahnestock of Jay Cooke & Company, which led Treasury department officials to believe that Babcock and possibly Porter had speculated in the Black Friday gold operation. McFeely makes the same suggestion. Porter denied it. See H. Misc. Doc. 186, pp. 369, 540-50; McFeely, p. 324.
- Catherwood ... pool to invest in government bonds ... : Catherwood test., H. Rpt. 31, pp.442-43.
- Jay ... giving him a check for $10,000 ... : Butterfield test., H. Rpt. 31, pp. 317-19; Gould statements in the *Sun*, 10/19/1869.
- Tenth National Bank ... fifteen randomly selected drafts ... : Hubbard test., H. Rpt. 31, pp. 410-11; Stout test., pp. 84-85, 88.
- Albany-Susquehanna Railroad: Jim Fisk's attempted takeover of the Albany-Susquehanna is recounted most vividly by C. F. Adams's essay, "An Erie Raid," published first in the April 1871 *North American Review* and included in the *Chapters* collection. Newspaper coverage was extensive. See, e.g., *Times*, 8/14/1869. Albany papers gave the tale a provincial spin. Judge Barnard's in-

junctions were a major subject at his 1872 impeachment hearings, and that test. provided interesting details.

- "Money-bags, swagger ... ": *Albany Evening Times, 8/12/1869.*

10. The Plunge *(pages 75–83)*

- order ... to buy $375,000 in gold ... : Enos test., H. Rpt. 31, p. 105. Enos produced a full list of his purchases and sales for the Ring in test. to the Garfield Committee. Enos had moved to New York from Washington, D.C., early in 1862 and reportedly used his acquaintance with government officials to learn Civil War information that he translated into Gold Room profits. On Enos, see *Sun, 2/20/1889.*
- Prince Erie ... "laying low" ... : *Tribune, 8/13/1869.*
- unseen Albany assassin ... : *Tribune, 8/12/1869.*
- "disposition to silent intrigue" ... : C. F. Adams, pp. 103-104.
- Early in August they visited Glenclyffe ... : *Herald, 8/10/1869.* The President's day-today movements can be easily traced through daily newspapers, particularly the *Herald* and the *World.*
- offered Julia Grant a free half-interest in $250,000 ... : Corbin test., H. Rpt. 31, pp. 270-271.
- "My desire was to please her ... ": Ibid.
- Jim ... sat face to face ... : Fisk test., H. Rpt. 31, p. 172; Fisk press conference, reprinted in *Times, 1/24/1870.* Grant and Fisk were the only two in the room, so no objective version of the conversation exists.
- "He then asked me when ... ": Fisk test., H. Rpt. 31, p. 172.
- Grant ... "would not be fair" ... : Grant interview with the Associated Press, reported in the *Sun, 10/4/1869.*
- "I did not think the skies ... ": Fisk test., H. Rpt. 31, p. 172.
- William Woodward ... Arthur Kimber ... : Woodward test., H. Rpt. 31, pp. 219-20. Gould test., pp. 131, 136. Kimber dropped out of sight after Black Friday and sent Garfield his regrets.
- scamming *The New York Times.*: Norvell test., H. Rpt. 31, pp. 275-79; Gould test., pp. 164-165; Corbin test., pp. 268-69.
- Over a dozen daily newspapers ... : Journalism had changed in the 1860s. The industry ballooned, spurred by public thirst for Civil War battle news. More than 570 papers appeared daily in the United States in 1870, up from 387 ten years earlier. Postwar editors used innovative features and formats, relying on intercity, even transatlantic telegraphs for news from far-off places, fashion, society gossip, book and drama reviews, and sports. *Harper's Weekly* and *Frank Leslie's Illustrated Newspaper* hired sketch artists to draw celebrity portraits, presidential inaugurations, city street scenes, formal balls, train wrecks, arctic landscapes, and horse races. Sketches were reduced to woodcuts for ink printing, creating picture magazines. See Hudson.
- "wisest and best ... honest ... ": *Times, 8/25/1869.*
- Norvell ... changed the article's ... : For side-by-side comparison of the article before and after Norvell's changes, see H. Rpt. 31, pp. 276-78.

- "until the crops are moved ... ": *Times*, 8/25/1869.
- "I think the country ... ": Letter from J. Gould to G. Boutwell, 8/30/1869, reprinted in H. Rpt. 31, pp. 372-73.
- Boutwell ... refused to admit or deny ... : Letter from G. Boutwell to J. Gould, 9/9/1869, reprinted in *Evening Mail*, 10/7/1869.
- Newport ... "not nearly as nice a place as ... ": Letter from H. Porter to his wife, 8/22/1869, Horace Porter papers.
- "[a] large crowd lined the streets ... ": *Herald*, 8/25/1869.
- "Like all great gentlemen ... ": *Evening Mail*, 8/31/1869. 86 "General Grant entered ... ": Ibid.
- Grant ... private talk with ... A. T. Stewart ... : Corbin test., H. Rpt. 31, pp. 246, 247-48. See also Butterfield test. describing Stewart's views on gold, p. 317.
- "That is the only time ... ": Corbin test., H. Rpt. 31, p. 248.
- Corbin's kitchen, Ulysses told his brother-in-law ... : Corbin test., H. Rpt 31, p. 244; Gould test., p. 155; Boutwell test., pp. 358-59; Committee summary, p. 6. See C. F. Adams, pp. 117-18; *Herald*, 9/3/1869.
- In ten short weeks ... retreat from ... "hard-money" ... : Embellishing the story, Gould biographer Robert Warshow described how "[articles] were run in magazines and newspapers throughout the United States. Hundreds of persons of different walks in life were posted where they would come into contact with Grant and be able to give him their views on the price of gold, which were the carefully rehearsed opinions of Gould. At almost every public dinner or political meeting Grant attended, the subject was brought up and Gould's views impressed upon Grant. Everywhere he went, he heard Gould's opinion echoed [until] he began to believe that Gould was right." Warshow, pp. 99-100.
- Jay arranged for Corbin's ... pay-out.: Corbin test., H. Rpt. 31, p. 253-54.
- $1.5 million ... Butterfield account ... : Gould test., H. Rpt 31, p. 160. See also *Sun*, 10/20/1869.
- "I did it as a friendly thing ... ": H. Rpt. 31, p. 163.

11. Coming Undone *(pages 87–93)*

- George Boutwell: Boutwell's memoirs are useful for biographical data and attitudes. Nevins and McFeely reveal views of other Grant men toward the secretary. Boutwell's test. to Garfield Committee is rich in detail on his Black Friday activities.
- "prepossessing. He is of ... ": *Times*, 3/12/1869.
- Grant had refused ... "radical changes ... ": *Times*, 3/12/1869. 92 Washburne "to say to the President ... ": Boutwell, II, p. 166.
- "My nomination was sent ... ": Ibid.
- "[T]he President accepted ... ": Ibid.
- "Boutwell says 'he does not think ... .' ": Nevins, pp. 589-90. Attorney General Ebenezer Hoar compared Boutwell to a lawyer who, when consulted, always looked wise, shook his head, and said, "Well, I don't know; I don't know about that." In Hoar's story, "It is literally true in every case, for damn him, he don't know." Nevins, p. 590.

Henry Adams dismissed Boutwell as "a somewhat lugubrious joke." See H. Adams, p. 263. To Nevins, Boutwell was "as thin, acrid, and rustling as a dead elm leaf, and his intellectual poverty contrasted with the rich mind of his colleague from Massachusetts," Senator Charles Sumner. Nevins, p. 139.

- "Who constituted you ... .": Letter from L. Dent to G. Boutwell, 8/18/1869, reprinted in the *Tribune*, 8/18/1869.

- "about one hundred persons .. .": Boutwell, II, p. 125.

- Boutwell-without asking the President ... : Boutwell, II, p. 167. In his own words: "I announced my purpose to purchase bonds in May, 1869, without conference either with the Cabinet or with the President. "

- Treasury gold flooded the market ... : Data on gold and bond sales and purchases are contained in H. Rpt. 31, pp. 364-66.

- "We do n't object .. .": *Tribune*, 9/2/1869.

- "I think it will be necessary ... ": Letter from G. Boutwell to W. Richardson, 9/1/1869, reprinted in H. Rpt. 31, p. 376.

- Boutwell did not see it as his job ... : For Boutwell's views on the crop theory, see H. Rpt. 31, pp. 354-55.

- "I think he said: 'Had I not better ... .' ": Butterfield test., H. Rpt. 31, pp. 314-15. 95 "[Butterfield] believed the policy ... ": H. Rpt. 31, p. 160.

- Butterfield wrote ... "the newspapers ... ": Letter from D. Butterfield to G. Boutwell, 9/2/1869, Treasury documents. See also H. Rpt. 31, p. 376.

- "As the month commenced .. .": Letter from W. Richardson to D. Butterfield, 9/3/1869, Treasury documents.

- This buy-lend strategy ... : While mechanically different, the buy-lend and borrow-sell combinations created interests like modern "long" or "short" positions in commodity futures contracts, abstract interests in gold price movements without ever owning the gold itself.

- "some secret French societies .. .": *World*, 9/7/1869.

- "there is no commercial ...": *Herald*, 9/8/1869.

- Jay to take $2 million ... : Woodward test., H. Rpt. 31, p. 220.

- Corbin ... asked Jay to sell ... : Corbin test., H. Rpt. 31, p. 255. 96 "I should like to have ... .": Ibid.

- Corbin ... with Julia Grant ... : Ibid.

- Kimber ... sold his entire ... : H. Rpt. 31, p. 136; C. F. Adams, p. 119.

- "All these fellows ... ": Gould test., H. Rpt. 31, p. 136.

- Even with President Grant's ... : Jay may have visited face-to-face with Grant that day. Grant was rushing from Saratoga to Washington to see General John Rawlins. Rawlins was Grant's closest advisor from the War days. Doctors had given Rawlins only hours to live.

Corbin, testifying with the aid of his diary, claims that Grant did not stop at his house during this trip (H. Rpt. 31, p. 246). Gould, without written notes and with some uncertainty, recalled a meeting with the President at Corbin's when Grant "was on his way to or from" Rawlins's funeral (p. 153). McFeely, tracing Grant's footsteps that day, had Grant arriving in New York on Monday morning and riding to the Astor House, not to Corbin's, for breakfast. McFeely, though, accepts Jay's word about the meeting with Grant and places it at the Astor House (McFeely, p. 330).

In any event, Jay described this phantom meeting as almost a carbon copy of a later meeting at Corbin's house on September 13.

12. Shoulder to Shoulder (pages 94–96)

- Albany-Susquehanna annual … meeting … : See C. F. Adams, pp. 176-79; *Times*, 9/8/1869; and *Albany Morning Express*, 9/8/1869.
- "Nothing is lost save honor.": Swanberg, p. 107.
- "I could see by the way … ": Fisk news conference, reported in the *Times*, 1/24/1870.
- "He (pointing to Gould) … ": Ibid.
- "[Jay] was a little sensitive … ": Fisk test., H. Rpt. 31, p. 169.
- "There had been … coldness … ": Fisk test, H. Rpt. 31, p. 172.
- "When one day he said … ": Ibid., p. 169.
- "Putting the great elm bow … ": Ibid.
- "If I had as much … ": *Times*, 1/24/1869.
- "This matter is all fixed … ": H. Rpt. 31, p. 173.
- "[Corbin] told me that … ": *Times*, 1/24/1869.
- "I know there will be no gold sold … ": H. Rpt. 31, pp. 174-75.
- Abel Corbin … "absolutely untrue … ": Corbin test., H. Rpt. 31, p. 258.
- Jim … joined the gold movement. … : Congress later derided Jim's "singular depravity" in ignoring his better judgment. "It would appear that nothing but the scent of corruption could sharpen the appetite of Fisk for the game which his leader was pursuing," they concluded. He brought to the effort "all the force of his magnetic and infectious enthusiasm …. The malign influence which Cataline wielded over the reckless and abandoned youth of Rome, finds a fitting parallel in the power Fisk carried into Wall street, when, followed by the thugs of Erie and the debauchees of the Opera House, he swept into the gold-room and defied both the street and the treasury." (H. Rpt. 31, p. 7).

13. Bankers (pages 99–107)

- James Brown's seventy-eight-year-old legs … : James Brown's low profile in business and personal affairs makes him difficult to trace. The Brown Brothers collection at the New York Historical Society contains a "ref. sheet" confirming that "James Brown … (1791-1877)" played an "important role" in the gold episode, but no specifics-no records of family discussions of the affair, no references in letters between James and his brothers, in ledgers, or in diaries; no court documents, no notes. None of James's voluminous obituaries in 1877 mentioned a word about Black Friday.

  In his Garfield Committee test., "James Brown" gave his business as "James Brown & Co." at 54 Exchange Place instead of the Brown Brothers bank at 59 Wall. He gave his home address on Long Island instead of New Jersey.

James had a nephew who was working at Brown Brothers at the time named James Muncaster Brown. James M. was highly involved in civic affairs and was friendly with Henry Clews. Newspaper accounts often referred to James M. as "James Brown." John Crosby Brown, in his history of the family firm, noted that James M. had "special oversight" of the firm's gold-related currency business during this period, although James Sr. called the shots.

It is unlikely that James M. was the James Brown of Black Friday. Testifying before the Garfield Committee, "James" referred to his thirty years' experience in banking, starting with an apprenticeship in Scotland. James M. had had no such foreign experience. Although James Sr. had been in banking almost sixty years at this point, he may have lied about his age.

Recognizing the uncertainty, I have accepted the contemporary accounts at face value that James Brown was, in fact, "James Brown."

J. B. Brown; Kouwanhoven; and Kent provide useful background on Brown Brothers and James in particular. The extensive collections at the New York Public Library (ledger books) and New-York Historical Society (personal papers) are rife with detail but contain little on Black Friday.

- Monday morning, September 13 ... : There is no record of James's appearing in the Gold Room on any day except Black Friday. Still, as a gold dealer, he must have made occasional visits, particularly at times of concern. I have taken liberties and assumed one such visit on this Monday morning.

- his young assistant, Kruger.: Kruger's name does not appear in Brown Brothers biographies.

  Brown identified him to the Garfield Committee as "my young partner ... my son-in-law" (p. 203). Neither characterization is confirmed by family or firm histories.

- The Gold Room: Descriptions of the Gold Room are plentiful. Cornwallis provides an entertaining history. Medbery reviews the Room and its practices at length. Drawings appeared in *Frank Leslie's Illustrated*, 10/9/1869, and *Harpers Weekly*, 10/16/1869. See also Black Friday newspaper accounts.

  During the Civil War, the Stock Exchange refused to allow gold trading under its roof. Brokers met first in a dark basement called the Coal Hole to trade the "currency of the world." Later, they moved the business to Gilpin's Newsroom. After the war emotions cooled and prosperity reigned. The gold brokers rented their elaborate new quarters on New Street for $25,000 per year.

- "a Cupid playing with a dolphin ... ": Medbery, p. 232.

- Thomas Alva Edison: Edison had arrived penniless in New York in mid-1869 and gotten permission to sleep nights in the battery room of the Gold Price Indicator Company, which ran the complex Gold Room apparatus. One day that summer, the indicator stalled during a trading session causing news blackouts allover New York. Dr. S. S. Laws, owner and inventor of the machine, panicked as frantic brokers besieged his office.

  Edison, already an experienced telegraph operator and inventor, had studied the machine. In the confusion he stepped forward and found the problem-a loose contact spring. He fixed the machine in minutes. Laws put him on payroll. See Meadowcraft, pp. 119-24; Josephson, *Edison*, pp. 72-75.

- younger partners.: Other Brown Brothers partners included James's son-in-law Howard Potter, his nephew Stewart Brown, and his cousin James M. Brown.
- James ... for almost half a century.: Like the House of Rothschild, Brown Brothers started as a family business. Alexander Brown, the founder, originally sold linens in his home town of Belfast, Ireland. After a run-in with British authorities around 1798, Alexander set sail with his wife and eldest son for Baltimore, Maryland, a bustling town of twenty-six thousand people, where his older brother Stewart already lived. Two years later, he sent for his three remaining sons, including James, the youngest, born in 1791.

  Starting with a small Baltimore shop, in three decades Brown and his sons created an international commercial import-export banking operation with offices in Liverpool, Baltimore, Boston, Philadelphia, and New York and agents across the South. Alexander died in 1834 leaving an estate worth $2 million, making him "one of the three or four richest men in America." Kent, pp. 126-27.
- "He was the quietest ... : Brown, p. 232.
- "The truth is ... father's advancing years ... ": Kouwenhoven, p. 141.
- Henry Clews: See generally Clews's memoirs; *Times, 2/1/1923.*
- aristocratic pre-Civil War Stock Exchange ... : "It's members were wealthy and conservative, with a strong infusion of Knickerbocker blood, and admixture of the Southern element and a sprinkling of Englishmen and other foreigners." Clews, p. 6.
- Jay Cooke: Generally on Jay Cooke, see Larson; Pollard; Oberholtzer. The Cooke papers at the Historical Society of Pennsylvania, particularly the correspondence between Jay Cooke, Henry Cooke, and Harris Fahnestock, provide fascinating source material.
- Cooke led the heroic effort ... : "[Jay Cooke] won the war for the North, just as surely as the men in the field, and it was in the Treasury Department, a Confederate leader admitted, that the South was really defeated." Minnigerode, p. 60.
- Cooke gave ... $15,000 ... Henry Ward Beecher ... : Hibben, p. 229.
- "Give us promptly and in advance ... ": Letter from J. Cooke to H. Cooke, 11/27/1866, cited in Josephson, *Politicos,* p. 122.
- "old Rothschild's way": Josephson, *Politicos,* p. 122; Larson, p. 232.
- volume ... topped $160 million ... gold reserves ... $17.4 to $14.9 million.: Volume figures from Wimmer. Weekly bank statements were published in the *Herald* and the *Times.*

  By contrast, a typical day at the New York Commodities Exchange today would see about thirty thousand gold futures contracts change hands, each representing 100 troy ounces, worth about $45,000 per contract and $1.35 billion per day at mid-1988 prices.
- exported over $470 million ... Imports ... topped $475 ... : Wattenberg, p. 865.
- banks ... Gold Room to manage ... risks ... : This risk-reduction process, called "hedging" in modem economic parlance, is one of the primary economic purposes of commodity futures markets. Congress viewed it as a "national public interest" justifying federal regulation. See Commodity Exchange Act, 7 United States Code Sec. 1 *et seq.,* Section 3.

- taking large "short" positions ... : Even in 1869, the awkward borrow-sell and buy-lend practices were archaic. Modern-style "futures contracts' had been used for over a decade in New York and Chicago markets to create "long" and "short" positions. The Chicago Board of Trade, which experienced a boom in grain-related futures trading during the Civil War, substantially revised its rules to accommodate these transactions in 1865. The Gold Room's renegade past-it had sprung up overnight and matured underground during the War-left it peppered with anachronisms.
- Dodge ... flier in "short" gold ... : Larson, pp. 268, 270.
- Brown Brothers ... "Gold Account #2" ... : Brown Brothers ledgers.
- George Opdyke: *World*, 9/16/1869, refers to "an ex-Loyal League Mayor of the city."
- borrowers had to pay ... "margin" ... : Commodity futures traders today pay "original margin," an up-front good-faith deposit on their contracts, and "variation margin," reflecting day-to-day price fluctuations. Now as then, margin is a key to maintaining the financial integrity of the market. Margin levels in 1869 were privately negotiated between individual traders. Today, minimum margins for futures are set by exchange boards of directors. For securities, they are set by the Federal Reserve Board, a government body.
- merchants who had "suffered ... ": *Tribune*, 9/ll/1869, 9/14/1869.
- James Brown ... open letter ... : Letter from Brown Brothers & Company, et al., to H. McCulloch, 7/1866. *Commercial and Financial Chronicle*, July 1866. Brown Brothers papers.
- "Money in the Treasury ... ": *Tribune*, 9/14/1869.
- the Gold Room ... more in common with Dodge City ... : The Gold Room president and board of directors had no real authority. Henry Benedict, the Exchange chairman and president of the Gold Exchange bank, did little more than bang a gavel and preside over clerks. In 1868, when the Board of Trade in Chicago tried to expel a member for "cornering" the wheat market, the members rebelled and forced the board itself to resign. It took the gruesome Wall Street panic of 1873 to make even the better-established Stock Exchange break tradition and intervene to halt trading.
- Federal statutes bar price manipulation.: Recent interpretations cast doubt on the effectiveness of these laws in many future cases. See decision of the Commodity Futures Trading Commission in *In Re Cox and Frey*, CFTC Docket No. 75-16 (July 15, 1987), particularly the dissent by Commissioner Fowler C. West.
- J. P. Morgan ... minicorner : See Allen, pp. 27-28.
- "Though shrewdly conceived ": *Times*, 10/12/1863.
- a clearinghouse: Today the clearinghouse system is standard on every designated U.S. futures exchange and most foreign exchanges as well.
- over $62 million in minted gold ... : Wattenberg, p. 995. Seligman estimated that another $200 million in unminted gold was circulating outside New York, mostly in cotton states like Texas and Louisiana and mining states like Nevada and California. H. Rpt. 31, p. 241.
- "[G]old is like air ... London or San Francisco can transfer ... ": Medbery, pp. 260-61.

14. The Bold and Brilliant Plan (*pages 108–112*)

- Henry Smith: See generally Clews, pp. 223-29; *Times*, 10/3/1885; and references in Gould and Drew biographies cited elsewhere.
- "a decidedly Hebrew aspect": Clews, p. 223.
- "I found Mr. Gould … ": Smith gave his fullest recounting of his Black Friday role in his appearance before the Stock Exchange Committee on Admissions, *11/22/1877*. The account is self-serving and must be taken with a grain of salt. Stock Exchange Archives, p. 15.
- William Belden: Very little has been written about Belden's background, aside from references in books about Jim Fisk cited elsewhere.

  Belden's loyalty bordered on the extreme. He made Jim's brother-in-law, George Hooker, a partner in his Wall Street firm. Once during the 1868 Drew-Vanderbilt Erie takeover fight, Judge Barnard hauled Belden into his court for interrogation. Belden testified for hours on every detail of the operation. Belden and Erie Railway lawyer David Dudley Field defended with memory lapses and legal objections. Asked where he was on March 9, the day Fisk issued fifty thousand shares of watered stock, Belden answered "in various places." Six times Belden refused to answer Barnard's questions, claiming that "a truthful answer would tend to incriminate me." The evasions drove Barnard into a fit and earned Belden six separate thirty-day commitments to the county jail. Barnard only agreed to an overnight parole after Field guaranteed that Belden would come back to court the next day. See *Times*, 4/21/1868.
- Jay laid out his gold plan … : This meeting was portrayed in a contemporary cartoon. See Levinson, p. 150.

  Jay's original plan at the time he entered the gold market in August-September 1869 can only be inferred. Jay told the Garfield Committee that he had had no intent originally to "corner" gold but had rather wished to put up the price in line with his crop theory to promote exports. See H. Rpt. 31, pp. 132, 135. There is no reason to doubt this, especially since Jay loaned out all the gold he purchased. The operation escalated into a go-for-broke corner only later, when bears and bulls accelerated their selling and buying, forcing each other into more drastic measures.
- "owning" two or three times … : The idea is similar to modern commodity futures markets, where the "open interest" -the total number of outstanding contracts for future delivery often represents more of the physical goods than is available. By far, most futures contracts today are settled through "offset"-buying an equal and opposite position on the exchange floor-rather than by delivering tons of pork bellies, coffee, or grain. Concerns about corners or other market "congestions" arise only when traders start demanding delivery.
- "blue, carmine, lilac … ": Fuller, pp. 275-76.
- Lake Shore and Michigan Southern: For the story of Gould's and Vanderbilt's wooing of the Lake Shore line, see Grodinsky, pp. 73, 79-80; Lane, pp. 263-67.
- The stakes were enormous.: Jay upped the *ante* in August by buying twelve thousand shares of stock in the Wabash Railroad, a Lake Shore feeder line, plus fifteen thousand shares in the Lake Shore itself.

- "narrow gauge [sic] sinking fund bonds": Erie Railway directors' minutes, 10/12/1869.

  To raise more cash, Jay unleashed 235,000 newly issued Erie shares during the summer and fall of 1869, worth $23.5 million at par. In early September, Jay yielded to yearlong demands from the Stock Exchange and registered his Company's stock with a neutral bank. The next day, Friday, September 10, Erie traded for the first time since January in the Stock Exchange's Long Room. The price jumped from $34 to $39, sparking talk of a new speculative war. One rumor had Daniel Drew trying a comeback at the upcoming shareholders' election, set for October 13. Not even disclosures of massive new stock-watering could dim the excitement. On Tuesday, September 14, the price topped $40.

- Chapin and Henry Enos ... Ellis ... bought heavily ... : Chapin, Enos, Ellis test., H. Rpt. 31.

- "And now, Messrs. Gold-gamblers! ... ": *Tribune*, 9/14/1869. Lawyers could argue over whether the New York statute forbidding conspiracies "to commit any act injurious ... to trade or commerce," which some zealous prosecutors had used to put labor union organizers behind bars, really applied to Gold Room financiers.

15. A Done Deal (*pages 113–117*)

- Grant "recreates excessively": *Anti-Slavery Standard*, quoted by *Times*, 9/17/1869. If Ulysses needed rest, the *Standard* argued, he should "resign, that the country may have what it very much needs, a President in fact as well as in name."

- "Happy is the President ... ": *Times*, 9/17/1869. See also *Herald*, 9/19/1869.

- President ... talk with Daniel Butterfield ... : We have only Butterfield's account of his conversation with Grant en route up the Hudson that day. H. Rpt. 31, p. 314. Butterfield could not recall the date of this meeting, but Corbin pinpointed Grant's West Point trip in his review of Grant's travels during August and September. H. Rpt. 31, p. 244.

- Butterfield ... Joseph Seligman ... : Butterfield test., H. Rpt. 31, pp. 319-21, 329; Seligman test., pp. 238-39.

- "I think I said to the President ... ": H. Rpt. 31, p. 314.

- Ulysses ... A. T. Stewart ... : Corbin noted this dinner in his calendar, though apparently he did not attend. H. Rpt. 31, p. 244. Stewart's continuing opposition to government gold sales is seen from test. on his dinner with Secretary Boutwell the next week. See H. Rpt. 31, pp. 163, 317.

- Corbin "was very anxious ... ": H. Rpt. 31, p. 153.

- "When the legislature is Republican ... ": Mott, p. 454.

- "The President had changed ... ": H. Rpt. 31, p. 153.

- Grant acted "a little peevishly" ... : Corbin test., H. Rpt. 31, p. 246.

- Ulysses ... note ... to his Treasury secretary ... : Gould test., H. Rpt. 31, p. 155. For text of the letter, see Chapter 16 of this book.

- General Horace Porter: On Porter, see generally Mende. Porter's wartime memoirs are revealing of the author's affection toward Grant. Porter's papers at the Library of Congress contain letters to his wife from this period.

- Orville Babcock: Babcock, Grant's military secretary, was then busy negotiating a treaty to annex Santo Domingo, over the objections of Secretary of State Hamilton Fish.

- Porter ... secretary of war.: See *Evening Mail, 10/1869.* Grant chose General William Belknap for the position. Belknap was impeached by Congress in 1876 for corruption in managing army trading posts.
- "I purchase and sell ... ": Porter test., H. Rpt. 31, p. 447. Porter's version is unrebutted.
- "You had better let me ... ": Ibid.
- "I have neither the inclination ... ": Ibid.
- Jay ... open an account for Porter ... : Ibid., p. 445.

16. Twisting Arms *(pages 118–126)*

- bankers ... sent ... Frank Howe ... : Corbin test., H. Rpt. 31, p. 263. Howe also attended the Union League dinner discussed later in this chapter. See *Evening Post, 9/17/1869.*
- *"corner* in Gold ... ": *Times, 9/15/1869.*
- "We are credibly informed ... ": *Tribune, 9/15/1869.*
- certain "influential parties-": *World, 9/15/1869.*
- "Will you dine with me ... ": Letter from G. Boutwell to D. Butterfield, 9/13/1869, printed in H. Rpt. 31, p. 331.
- Butterfield ... A. T. Stewart.: Butterfield's connection with Stewart, Grant's first choice for the Treasury post, could have caused him initial tension with Boutwell. Grant may have relished naming a Stewart intimate as Boutwell's second-in-command, causing sour grapes. Why else would Boutwell have waited more than three months before seeing his principal deputy in New York? Even in 1869 the train ride between New York and Washington took only several hours-not much more than the Amtrak Metroliner on a bad day. Boutwell could have invited Butterfield to visit him at the capital or his Boston summer home or vice versa. But egos govern politics more than railroad schedules.

    Butterfield took Boutwell on a fence-mending mission to Stewart's Fifth Avenue mansion that week. It only made sense, Butterfield figured, for New York's biggest importer and Republican booster to get along with the Republican secretary of the Treasury. Also, Stewart had vigorously urged President Grant not to sell gold in the current crisis. Boutwell needed to hear those arguments as well.

    The mission failed, as shown by Stewart's outburst at the Union League, discussed later in this chapter. See H. Rpt. 31, pp. 313, 317.
- "The Bankers and Importers ... " *Times, 9/15/1869.*
- "The public be damned": For the full text of this famous interview, see Andrews, pp. 189-95.
- danger of playing favorites ... : Almost fifty years later, Congress would switch responsibility for some of these decisions from politicians at Treasury to an independent, nonpolitical Federal Reserve Board. Modern skeptics who argue today for a more politically "accountable" or "responsive" Fed should take note.
- the "City of Soot": Reporters in Grant's coterie cringed at the "dirty, dingy, muddy, murky, melancholy" factory town with its grimy smokestacks. "The air is

filled with smoke and soot, a white shirt is an impossibility," wrote the *World's* representative. *World*, 9/17/1869.

- "wiry and muscular, with a stoop ... ": *Sun*, 9/17/1869.
- "Dear Sir: I leave here tomorrow ... ": Letter from Grant to G. Boutwell, 9/12/1869, printed in H. Rpt. 31, p. 359.
- "one party of railroad men": Butterfield test., H. Rpt. 31, p. 313.
- reporters from at least five dailies ... : The stories in each of these papers appear to be firsthand accounts.
- "Why even a 'trooly loil' gold-gambler ... ": *World*, 9/16/1869.
- "The only people who want gold cheap ... ": *Herald*, 9/16/1869.
- Horace Greeley: Greeley's political past made him a sympathetic figure for Republicans like Boutwell. Greeley had crusaded against slavery since the 1840s and had helped found the Republican Party in 1854. Almost alone among New Yorkers, he actively supported the country-bumpkin Abraham Lincoln for President in 1860, although he surprised hard-liners by signing a bail bond for Jefferson Davis after the war.
- George Opdyke: After a freak vote split, Opdyke found himself elected Republican Mayor of New York in early 1862, on the eve of the antidraft riots. Tweed controlled the Common Council, which could override Opdyke's veto on any graft he wanted.

    At the height of the July 1863 riots, a mob carrying bricks and torches marched on the mayor's house. They backed off only after hearing an appeal from Justice George Barnard, who was already known as a Tweed mouthpiece. This heightened suspicions of Tammany's hand in the bloody affair. During the violence, Democratic Governor Horatio Seymour turned a deaf ear to Opdyke's appeals for state militia until he saw federal troops well on their way.

    Opdyke gave up politics after the war and went back to Wall Street.
- Opdyke ... "artificial means" ... when "the thing collapsed ... ": Opdyke test., H. Rpt. 31, p. 339.
- "He probably did not stay ... ": Boutwell test., H. Rpt. 31, p. 357.
- "flourished before [Boutwell's] ... ": *Sun*, 9/17/1869.
- talk "wholly of ... ": *Herald*, 9/17/1869; See also *Sun*, 9/17/1869.
- Clews pulled Boutwell ... : *Tribune*, 10/11 1869.
- Union League Club: The Union League had curious patriotic roots. It was formed in 1863 as a loyalist offshoot of the older ever-more-aristocratic Union Club, which had refused to expel Judah P. Benjamin, secretary of state to the Confederacy, from its membership. One Democratic newspaper described the young men in the original Union League as "able-bodied gentlemen, whose purpose is to induce other able-bodied men to enlist" in Lincoln's Army.
- the guest list included ... : Sketchy but informative accounts of the private dinner appear in *Times*, *Herald*, and *Sun*, 9/17/1869. See also test. of A. A. Lowe before Garfield Committee, H. Rpt. 31, pp. 294-95.
- "[W]hen cigars were introduced ... ": *Sun*, 9/17/1869.
- Boutwell ... "giving anyone opportunities ... ": *Times*, 9/17/1869.

- S. B. Chittenden ... "shocked some of the gentlemen ... ": H. Rpt. 31, p. 295. See *Sun*, 9/17/1869, which identifies Chittenden as having "ventilated" his feelings that evening.
- "policy of holding seven-tenths ... ": H. Rpt. 31, p. 295.
- Stewart "gradually took on ... ": Boutwell II, p. 205.
- "in favor of hard money": H. Rpt. 31, p. 295.
- Stewart "made a speech in which ... ": Boutwell II, p. 205.
- "one of those self-admiration ... ": Fisk press conference, 1/23/1870, reported in the *Times*, 1/24/1870.

17. Resistance *(pages 127–128)*

- James Brown ... civic meetings.: In the 1840s, James had co-founded and now presided over New York's Society for Improving the Condition of the Poor. He also served on the board of Presbyterian Hospital and helped E. L. Godkin set up the financial end of his new magazine, *The Nation*.
- Jay Cooke & Company ... $350,000 ... : Brown Brothers ledgers, New York Public Library.
- "Fisk [& Hatch] is going ... ": Letter from H. Fahnestock to J. Cooke, 9/17/1869, Cooke papers.
- "I had a brief talk ... ": Ibid.

18. Messages *(pages 129–136)*

- "I found after I left Corbin's ... ": *Times*, 1/24/1870.
- "If Butterfield gives any ... ": Fisk test., H. Rpt. 341, p. 174.
- Corbin ... ushered Jay upstairs ... : On Corbin-Gould conversation, see Gould test., H. Rpt. 31, p. 155; Corbin test., p. 249.
- "I have made an honest ... ": H. Rpt. 31, p. 249. 136 "page after page" ... : H. Rpt. 31, p. 155.
- "Who is the most confidential ... ": Except as noted, dialogue is from Fisk test., H. Rpt. 31, p. 174.
- "I want him to take ... ": Fisk news conference, *Times*, 1/24/1870.
- William O. Chapin ... "they wanted me ... ": Chapin test., H. Rpt. 31, pp. 230-31.
- "I put on my boots ... ": Ibid.
- "See what [Grant] says ... ": *Times*, 1/24/1870.
- "I was afraid [Chapin] ... ": Ibid.
- Corbin "appeared at the top ... ": Chapin test., H. Rpt. 31, p. 231.
- trip from New York ... : Details of the journey from Chapin test., Ibid.
- "Mr. Smith's house ... ": Ibid.
- "The bearer has a letter ... ": Porter test., H. Rpt. 31, p. 444.
- "I think someone said Mrs. Grant ... ": H. Rpt. 31, pp. 231-32.
- "[Grant] seemed to wait ... ": H. Rpt. 31, p. 232; Porter test., p. 444.
- "Letter delivered ... ": Ibid. See also H. Rpt. 31, p. 9. Whether the telegram referred to "letter" (singular) or "letters" (plural) is unclear from the testimony.

- "Who is that man?": Porter-Grant dialogue from Porter test., H. Rpt. 31, p. 444.
- Purchased today $500,000 ... ": H. Rpt. 31, p. 445.
- "I have never authorized ... ": H. Rpt. 31, p. 446.
- "The letter would have been ... ": H. Rpt. 31, p. 448.
- Perhaps ... bears ... sent ... messenger ... : Jim Fisk fingered Arthur Kimber as the squealer, although without any apparent evidence. *Herald, 10/8/1869.*
- Horace Porter saw firsthand ... : After weeks of traveling with Ulysses and Julia Grant, Porter had become like a family member. They shared countless intimacies. When Porter's wife wrote that she had lost a trunk containing favorite clothes, the First Lady took an interest. "Mrs. Grant expressed a great deal of sympathy and at once started to get a black silk dress of hers to send you by express which I would not let her do, and which might not have exactly fit you, but the act was very thoughtful," Porter wrote home. Letter from H. Porter to his wife, 9/4/1869.
- "Those four years [1865 through 1869] ... ": J. Grant, p. 170.
- "I always felt ... ": J. Grant, pp. 182-83.
- "rumors had reached her ... ": Porter test., H. rpt. 31, p. 448.
- "The General says, if you have ... ": J. Grant, p. 182.
- "I sat in the library ... ": Ibid.
- "We may not leave here ... ": Letter from H. Porter to his wife, 9/18/1869, Porter papers.

19. Sneak Attack *(pages 155–161)*

- "An alliance ... ": *Sun, 9/20/1869.*
- "Boldness! boldness! ... ": Fowler, p. 479.
- "an intimation given ... ": *Herald, 9/19/1869.*
- National Gold Account ... : H. Rpt. 31, pp. 8, 211.
- "Buy," "Buy," "Buy." James Ellis ... Enos ... Hills ... Willard ... Quincy ... Boocock ... : See Garfield Committee test. of individual brokers. Ellis and Enos provided detailed day-to-day trading summaries. Willard testified that he had bought a total of $10 to $15 million for the Ring that week.
- Jay ... no written records ... To Garfield's direct question, Jay responded, "No, I carried the whole thing in my head ... I never kept a book in my life." H. Rpt. 31, p. 133.
- "Letter delivered ... ": H. Rpt. 31, p. 174 ["Delivered. All right. "]. See *Times, 1/24/1870* ["Delivered-all right."].
- "[L]arge Export orders for ... ": *Times, 9/22/1869.*
- Vanderbilt ... stock raid ... : See Lane, p. 267.
- simultaneous two front sneak attack ... : Reconstruction of trading on September 22 is based on newspaper accounts and testimony of relevant traders. See *Times, World; Herald;* and *Evening Post, 9/23/1869.*
- "It is astonishing to see ... ": *World, 9/23/1869.*
- "the *screw was turned* ... ": *Times, 8/23/1869.*

- bankers had met ... "pool" ... : No records exist of this meeting. The *World* provides sharpest detail on the bears' Gold Room counteroffensive.
- Fahnestock ... probably organized ... : Fahnestock had much to lose from the runaway gold market, given his bond-buying spree with Fisk & Hatch. He was also experienced in collective tactics and took a leadership role in Wall Street affairs. Because no records were kept, there exists no list of names of leaders or participants in the bear pool that day.
- "If it were not ... ": Letter from H. Fahnestock to J. Cooke, 9/20/1869, Cooke papers.
- "nearly the entire supply ... ": Letter from H. Clews to G. Boutwell, 9/20/1869, from *Tribune*, 10/1/1869.
- Hills ... "to hold the market" ... : Hills test., H. Rpt. 31, p. 398.
- "[T]hey were never frightened" ... : Gould test., H. Rpt. 31, p. 138.
- "The gold room, within half an hour's ... ": *World*, 9/23/1869.
- "Had some person just then ... ": Ibid.
- "The 'bears' became frightened ... ": *Herald*, 9/23/1869.
- "intense feeling against ... ": *Times*, 9/23/1869.
- "We shant have any peace ... ": Letter from H. Fahnestock to J. Cooke, 9/22/1869, Cooke papers.
- "There is a panic ... ": Letter from J. Gould to G. Boutwell, 9/22/1869, printed in H. Rpt. 31, p. 377.
- U.S. bond prices to drop to 115, "leaving the purchases made ... ": Letter from J. Gould to G. Boutwell, 9/20/1879, printed in H. Rpt. 31, p. 373.
- "I did not want to buy ... ": Gould test., H. Rpt. 31, p. 135.
- "no idea of cornering ... .": Ibid.
- "If a person desires ... ": *World*, 9/23/1869.

20. Bad Blood (*pages 162–163*)

- "the sky over Albany ... ": Fuller, p. 347.
- "Vanderbilt would be back ... ": *World*, 9/23/1869.
- Brown Brothers ... Pacific Mail ... : Brown Brothers ledgers.
- "The lock up of gold affects ... ": Letter from "J.B.E." to editor of *The New York Times*, published in the *Times*, 9/23/1869.
- "At no time for months ... ": *Evening Mail*, 9/23/1869.
- "Is this thing to be ... ": Brown test., H. Rpt. 31, p. 205.

21. Change of Plans (*pages 164–168*)

- "We were in my library ... ": Corbin test., H. Rpt. 31, p. 252.
- "It was in a lady's ... ": Gould test., H. Rpt. 31, p. 156.
- "The substance of it was that ... ": Ibid., p. 157 Compare with Corbin test., pp. 251- 52.
- "I was very much excited ... ": H. Rpt. 31, p. 251.

- Grant had ended ... isolation ... : See *Herald*, 9/22/1869, for details of the Grants' return to Washington, D.C.
- "he expected a decline ... ": *World*, 9/21/1869.
- "The picture of [Gould and Corbin] ... ": H. Rpt. 31, p. II.
- "The envelope was examined ... ": Ibid.
- "I must get out ... ": Corbin test., H. Rpt. 31, p. 251.
- "[Corbin] wanted me ... ": Gould test., H. Rpt. 31, p. 157.
- "I told [Corbin] I did not ... ": Ibid.
- "Will you please ... ": Corbin test., H. Rpt. 31, p. 256.
- Jennie "was angry ... ": H. Rpt. 31, p. 270.
- Corbin ... came down to see Jay alone ... : Gould did not cover this second meeting with Corbin in his test. to the Garfield Committee. We have only Corbin's unanswered version. H. Rpt. 31, p. 256. Take it with the appropriate grain of salt.
- "If you will remain ... ": H. Rpt. 31, p. 256.
- "Mr. Gould, my wife says ... ": Ibid.
- "Mr. Gould stood there ... " Ibid.
- "If the contents ... ": H. Rpt. 31, p. 12.
- "Honesty is the Best Policy": See O'Connor, pp. 23-24, for the text of this ironic artifact.
- "Mr. Gould says to me, 'Old Corbin ... ' ": Fisk test., H. Rpt. 31, p. 175.

22. Center Stage *(pages 169–175)*

- Wall Street ... September 23: Reconstruction of Gold Room trading on September 23 is based primarily on newspaper accounts and Garfield Committee test. from key brokers. The *Sun* and the *Times*, 9/24/1869, ran extensive front-page accounts. The *Herald* also provided useful detail.
- Belden ... Smith commanded fifty to sixty brokers ... : H. Rpt. 31, pp. 8,282.
- "There seemed to have been two ... ": H. Rpt. 31, p. 119.
- "Fisk could never ... ": H. Rpt. 31, p. 217.
- Albert Speyers: Speyers holds a special place in Black Friday lore. His Gold Room antics were captured in E. Stedman's epic poem *"Israel Freyer's Bid for Gold,"* first published in the *Tribune*, 9/28/1869, and reproduced as an Appendix to this book. For background on Speyers, see *Times*, 12/24/1880. For his role on Black Friday, Speyers's test. to the Garfield Committee is vivid and largely believable. H. Rpt. 31, pp. 63-73. See also *Sun*, 9/29/1869.
- "Speyers was the true type ... ": Fowler, p. 518.
- "an elderly man of small ... ": Stedman, p. 223.
- Belden took [Speyers] ... Erie Railway moguls.: Fisk and Gould recalled Belden's first introducing them to Speyers on Friday, not Thursday; H. Rpt. 31, pp. 139, 170. See also Fisk's test. in *Davis v. Fisk*, reported in the *Times*, 11/25/1871. Belden too drew a memory blank on any Thursday-morning meeting between Speyers, Fisk, and Gould. Ibid., p. 299. Speyers remembered the Thursday encounter vividly and clearly. Ibid., p. 63.

- "[T]he gentlemen whom you saw ... ": H. Rpt. 31, p. 64.
- "intended to make his (Belden's) ... ": Boocock statement to the Gold Exchange arbitration committee, in H. Rpt. 31, pp. 109-10.

    "Belden has always struck me as a very timid man who was easily frightened," Boocock said. "He seems to be thoroughly under the influence of this man Fisk." H. Rpt. 31, p. ll2.
- "the most powerful clique ... ": *Times*, 9/24/1869.
- the "roar of battle ... ": Ibid.
- "with groans and yells ... ": *Sun*, 9/24/1869.
- "One man, when the ... indicator ... ": Ibid.
- Butterfield ... Joseph Seligman ... : On Butterfield's transactions via Seligman, see their respective test. before Garfield Committee, H. Rpt. 31, pp. 238-40 (Seligman), pp. 319-22, 329-30 (Butterfield). Butterfield ultimately acknowledged Seligman's story, pp. 22-23.
- "I told him, of course ... ": H. Rpt. 31, p. 238.
- Seligman ... selling ... all the gold ... : Wells claimed that Seligman had buttonholed President Grant in Long Branch, New Jersey, and "Grant told him just enough to warn him that it would be wise to sever relations with Gould, at least temporarily, and to sell gold instead of buy it." The story is clearly wrong. Grant had not been to Long Branch since July. Besides, the President kept his thoughts to himself on the gold matter. See Wells manuscript.
- "[Butterfield] told me ... ": Seligman test., H. Rpt. 31, p. 238.
- Clews ... Fisk's "erratic conduct" ... : Clews, p. 182.
- Jim ... offered to bet ... $50,000 000: See H. Rpt. 31, p. 13; Fowler, p. 515.
- Ring "had in league with them ... ": H. Rpt. 31, p. 35.
- Corbin ... Tenth National ... : *Times*, 9/24/1869; Norvell test., H. Rpt. 31, p. 279; Boutwell, II, p. 172.
- Stimson ... "to put gold to $144 ... ": H. Rpt. 31, p. 91.
- "I was a seller ... ": Gould test., H. Rpt. 31, p. 142. Henry Smith claimed credit for Jay's decision to unload, saying that he himself anticipated a crash and started selling without orders. See Smith test. to Stock Exchange Committee on Admissions, 11/22/1877, p. 16, Stock Exchange archives. See also H. Rpt. 31, p. 286.
- "the foreign trade ... ": *Tribune*, 9/24/1869.
- "the West was warned ... ": Ibid.

23. Putting Heads Together *(pages 176–179)*

- Boutwell ... to the White House ... : Boutwell, in his memoirs, confuses the dates of his meetings with Grant that week. He puts his first meeting on Wednesday night, September 22; the second on Thursday, September 23. In congressional test., taken under oath and nearer in time to the events, he places the meetings on the twenty-third and twenty-fourth. The congressional version is more consistent with other sources, and I have relied on it here. Compare Boutwell, II, pp. 171, 175; H. Rpt. 31, pp. 344-46.

- Henry Cooke ... plea to release gold ... : See letter from H. Cooke to J. Cooke, 9/231 1869, Cooke papers.
- list of "persons in New York ... ": Boutwell, II, p. 168.
- "Bull clique are defying you ... ": *World*, 9/24/1869.
- "extreme anxiety among the banks ... :" Letter from H. Clews to G. Boutwell, 9/231 1869, printed in the *Tribune*, 10/1/1869.
- Baring Brothers ... loan it gold ... : See *Tribune*, 10/111869; Boutwell test., H. Rpt. 31, p. 345.
- "The raiders ... ": *Tribune*, 9/23/1869. The *Herald* suggested that Boutwell exploit high gold prices and sell Treasury reserves before they fell-making a killing for taxpayers. *Herald*, 9/23/1869.
- H.R. Hulburd ... Tenth National Bank ... : See Boutwell and Hulburd test., H. Rpt. 31, pp. 355-56,411-12. See also Boutwell, II, pp. 174-75.
- Boutwell ... "confident of his ability ... ": *Boston Herald*, Extra Edition, 9/24/1869, Boutwell papers.
- "A large crowd ... ": *Times*, 9/24/1869.
- Julia ... White House renovations ... : Julia had fretted at disrepair of the presidential mansion when she and Ulysses moved in the previous March. Now she imposed her own order and style. Beyond the physical plant, Julia decreed that White House ushers, messengers, and sweepers must "appear in dress suits and white gloves," she wrote. "They must take their meals at home and would not be allowed to smoke while on duty at the Mansion." She even closed the gates to the White House grounds to gain privacy for her family. See J. Grant, 174-75.
- $60,000 worth of the decorations ... : See Barksdale test., H. Rpt. 31, pp. 418, 425-26; Porter test., p. 449.
- gift from "the Gold Ring" ... : H. Rpt. 31, pp. 426-27.
- "we thought the business ... ": Ibid., p. 344.
- "if the price of gold advanced ... ": Ibid.

24. Foreboding *(pages 180–186)*

- Fifth Avenue Hotel: During the Civil War, the nightly scene at the Fifth Avenue Hotel had become a semi-formalized Evening Exchange. Wild speculation, midnight corners, and price swings grew common as "spiritous liquors were dispensed from a bar which did a thriving business," wrote Kinehan Cornwallis. Night owls often bid recklessly and woke up the next morning penniless. Physically, they "burned the candle of life at both ends in dissipation and eager worship of Mammon," turning the scene into "a hot-bed of vice, extravagance, and fraud." The Stock and Gold Exchanges banned night hours in 1865 by a formal joint vote.

  In April 1987, the Chicago Board of Trade instituted the first formal night trading session of modern times, allowing members and customers to trade futures on U.S. Treasury Bonds, Notes, and Precious Metals on weeknights from 6 to 9 pm. The session coincides with morning trading hours in Japan as part of an industry ide push toward market globalization. So far, the new Chicago night trading, conducted under rigorous 1980s exchange regulation, has been happily free of the night owl abuses of the 1860s.

- 2 percent per day-730 percent annualized ... : *Sun, 9/24/1869*.
- "A sumptuous banquet ... ": Fowler, p. 514.
- "evidently you have got ... ": H. Rpt. 31, p. 170.
- Jay ... $40 to $55 million ... Jim ... $60-odd million; Belden ... $20 million.: H. Rpt. 31, pp. 282, 179,299.
- paid for ... $6 to $7 million ... : H. Rpt. 31, p. 180.
- Van Deventer & Company. ... : Letters from Van Deventer & Company to Stock Exchange, *9/23/1869, 11/11/1869*, Stock Exchange Archives.
- "The vaults of every bank ... ": Fowler, p. 514.
- Jay ... ignored ... session ... : H. Rpt. 31, p. 141.
- "I sat there transacting ... ": H. Rpt. 31, p. 141.
- Fisk proposed ... publish the list ... : See H. Rpt. 31, pp. 13, 178-79.
- "absurd." ... Belden scoffed ... "Fisk could never ... ": H. Rpt. 31, pp. 217, 306.
- Brown ... brought together ... : The Garfield Committee described James's "movement" as "supported by many leading bankers and merchants," (p. 15) but the Committee never asked James to identify the participants. James testified that he did no business for Henry Clews on Friday and that he visited neither Clews's office nor that of Duncan, Sherman & Company on Friday morning, but that answer provides plenty of flexibility. Clews, Harris, Fahnestock, and W. Butler Duncan did not testify to the Committee and thus have never denied taking part.

  The meeting can be clearly pinpointed at Thursday night. James Brown described lecturing the group that prices had risen to 144-Thursday afternoon's close. See Brown test., H. Rpt. 31, pp. 205-206.
- "[W]e had paid, paid, paid ... ": Ibid.
- Caleb Norvell: Jim Fisk had tried to have Norvell arrested in May 1869 in a libel suit against the *Times* similar to that against Samuel Bowles of *The Springfield Daily Republican*. Norvell narrowly escaped a night at the Ludlow Street jail. See *Times, 5/15/1869*. This incident might explain some of Norvell's bitterness toward the Gold Ring on the eve of Black Friday.
- "manner ... that such a thing ... ": H. Rpt. 31, p. 279.
- bulls "talked freely ... ": Ibid.
- "we do not propose ... ": *Times, 9/24/1869*.
- "say to Mr. Boutwell ... ": H. Rpt. 31, p. 280.

25. Eye of the Storm (*pages 187–201*)

- "[W]e made up our mind ... ": Fisk news conference, *Times, 1/24/1870*.
- "Representatives of almost ... ": *Times, 9/25/1869*.
- "A carriage wheeled into ... ": Fowler, p. 518-19. Meade Minnigerode told the same story: "Mr. Gould had slipped quietly into a back room; Mr. Fisk [arrived] not at all quietly, having driven downtown in his barouche with two ladies of the theatre, as was his not infrequent custom." Minnigerode, p. 158.
- John Morrissey also saw ... : *World, 9/26/1869*.

- Hills ... "put the market up ... ": Hills test., H. Rpt. 31, p. 401.
- "I had my own plans ... ": H. Rpt. 31, pp. 143, 144.
- "This will be the last ... ": H. Rpt. 31, p. 64.
- Belden later denied ... : H. Rpt. 31, p. 304.
- Boocock ... gold ... at $200 ... : H. Rpt. 31, p. 109.
- Friday "was his last ... ": H. Rpt. 31, p. 110.
- "We have it in our power ... ": *Sun, 1/25/1869.*
- "Mr. Speyers will execute ... ": The exact wording of Belden's delegation became significant because of Jim's subsequent repudiations. Compare various accounts: Speyers's, H. Rpt. 31, pp. 64-65; Belden's ("I told [Speyers] that if Mr. Fisk gave him an order, he might execute it for me"), p. 300; Fisk's ("Mr. Belden came into the office and said' ... Mr. Speyers will receive from you any orders for purchases or sales of gold on my account' "), p. 170; and Gould's ("Belden ... was very busy ... would like to have Mr. Fisk give [Speyers] some orders while (Belden) was engaged in fixing his clearances .... "), p. 139. I have used here the version from Fisk's news conference, *Times, 1/24/1870,* which appears consistent with the others.
- "buy all ... at 145." ... : H. Rpt. 31, pp. 64-65. 180 "Put it to 150 ... ": Ibid.
- C. C. Allen ... buy $500,000 at $150.: Allen did not testify to Garfield Committee. Accounts of his Black Friday dealings with Fisk appear in *The Sun, 9/27/1869* and *9/28/1869.* See also Fisk's test. in H. Rpt. 31, p. 178.
- Enos ... order from "Gould & Fisk jointly" ... : Enos test., H. Rpt. 31, pp. 100-101.

  Gould denied giving any orders to buy gold that day, jointly with Fisk or otherwise. Other accounts back his version. After Fisk's repudiation, brokers like Enos tried to make Gould responsible for their Black Friday purchases. Enos was one of few whom Jay agreed to back. See Gould test., p. 143.
- "All right; go back ... ": H. Rpt. 31, p. 65.
- "nothing the matter with my old ... ": Minnigerode, p. 199.
- James found a "considerable gathering" ... : H. Rpt. 31, p. 205.
- Benedict ... "whether this was to be ... ": Benedict-Fisk dialogue is from Benedict test., H. Rpt. 31, pp. 56-57. Benedict also had a similar conversation with Jay Gould later that morning. See Gould test., p. 143.
- No effective self-regulation ... would come into being for decades ... : Some reviewers of this manuscript questioned whether fully effective self-regulation has arrived even yet. Federal statutes adopted during the 1920s and 1930s have created a two-tiered system for regulating trading on U.S. exchanges under which government bodies-the SEC and the CFTC-are responsible for acting as back-up to ensure that the public interest is protected. These systems have withstood many storms over the decades, including the October 1987 "Black Monday" crash. Current proposals for stronger institutional links between futures and securities oversight bodies do not belie this fact.
- Dickinson ... bank examiners from Washington ... : The three inspectors had taken the night train from Washington and arrived at the Bank's offices at 8:30

A.M., before most Bank officers. After watching the Bank open its vaults, they physically counted its money and assets and discovered that "two or three firms of brokers were, in fact, running the bank. "

- "and dozens of others … ": Medbery, p. 265.
- "The indicator was composed … ": Meadowcroft, pp. 125-26.
- Speyers … "to go to the gold room … ": H. Rpt. 31, p. 399.
- "A hundred fists were shaken … ": *Sun*, 9/25/1869.
- Henry … license to sell … over $143.: Smith test. to Stock Exchange Committee on Admissions, 11/22/1877, p. 16.
- "Sell, sell, sell … ": H. Rpt. 31, p. 213.
- Chapin … calling in $780,000 … : See opinion of Stock Exchange Arbitration Committee in *Chapin. Bowen & Day v. Chase. McClure & Co.*, 10/19/1869, Stock Exchange Archives.
- Fisk … appreciated Jay's role … : Fowler described the modus operandi this way: Gould "was the engineer, with his hand on the engine-lever, while Fisk was the roar of the wheels, the volume of smoke from the stack, the glare of the headlight, and the screaming whistle of the locomotive." p. 480.
- "immediate interference … ": Telegraph message from H. Fahnestock to J. Cooke, 9/24/ 1869, Cooke papers.
- "If I were Goo. S. Boutwell … ": Letter from J. Cooke to H. Cooke, 9/24/1869, Cooke papers.
- "As *we* have no interest … ": I assume that had Jay Cooke known of speculative gold positions held by his New York partner Dodge, he would not have told this untruth. Fahnestock's bond hoarding, of which Cooke *was* aware, can perhaps be explained as only indirectly tied to gold, though one's nose grows longer the harder one tries.
- "large proportion" of "reliable merchants … ": Boutwell, II, p. 177.
- "I am requested to represent … ": Cable from D. Butterfield to G. Boutwell, 9/24/1869, printed in H. Rpt. 31, p. 345.
- "The Gold Room was the magnet … ": *Herald*, 9/25/1869.
- "Here the silk-hatted … ": Stedman, p. 225.
- "In and out through … ": Minnigerode, p. 158.
- "Boys had therefore … ": *Philadelphia Ledger*, printed in the *Herald*, 9/26/1869.
- They had "very little conversation" … : H. Rpt. 31, pp. 345-46.
- "I think … $5,000,000": Boutwell, II, p. 175. Boutwell, in his memoirs, places this meeting on Thursday night, September 23; his congressional test. places it at midmorning on Friday, as do newspaper accounts. See *Times*, 9/25/1869; *Evening Mail*, 9/24/1869.
- "Those waiting … ": *Times*, 9/25/1869.
- "Sell four millions ($4,000,000) … ": Telegraphed message from G. Boutwell to D. Butterfield, 9/24/1869, printed in H. Rpt. 31, p. 346, 330.
- "Go ahead, and put down … ": *Sun*, 9/27/1869.
- "G-d d-n, it, then, put it down … ": Ibid.

- "Go and bid gold up to 160 ... ": H. Rpt. 31, p. 65.
- "160 for any part ... ": Speyers's bid is immortalized in Edmund Stedman's poetic effort, "Israel Freyer's Bid for Gold," in the *Tribune*, 9/28/1869; Stedman, p. 234; and the Appendix to this volume.
- "it seemed unlikely that ... ": Stedman, p. 228.
- "When gold was $160 ... ": *Herald*, 9/25/1869.
- Heath ... "with his finger ... ": Fowler, p. 519. 189 "the noise was hushed ... ": *Nation*, 10/7/1869.
- "Sold one million at 162" ... : Ibid. Details of Brown's sales to Speyers from Brown test., H. Rpt. 31, p. 202.
- "Notice: By order of the Secretary ... ": H. Rpt. 31, p. 312.
- "The moral effect ... ": Clews, p. 182.
- "Possibly no avalanche ... ": *Herald*, 9/25/1869.
- Speyers ... "like a goblin ... ": Fowler, p. 521.
- "Shake, Edison ... ": Meadowcroft, pp. 126-7.

26. High Old Times (*pages 205–210*)

- "Mine Got, mine Got! ... ": Fisk news conference, *Times*, 1/24/1870.
- "If you don't know ... ": Ibid.
- "Mr. Fisk, in spite of ... ": Speyers test., H. Rpt. 31, p. 65.
- "sell five millions ... ": H. Rpt. 31, p. 96.
- "[I]t was not worth a damn": H. Rpt. 31, p. 214.
- "people were accusing me ... : Speyers interview with the *Sun*, 9/29/1869. See also H. Rpt. 31, p. 65; *Times*, 9/25/1869. Unlike other sources, such as the *Sun* reporter cited below, Speyers suggests that this incident occurred at midmorning before the price break. Given the flow of events and Speyers's foggy memory on some other aspects of the panic, I prefer the *Sun* version on this point.
- Speyers "rushed about ... ": *Sun*, 9/25/1869.
- Speyers "went crazy" ... : Meadowcroft, p. 126.
- "Speyers, I want to know ... ": Brown-Speyers dialogue is from Brown test., H. Rpt. 31, p. 202.
- "He put his arm ... ": Ibid.
- "You cannot go through there" ... : Dialogue between Brown and guards, Ibid.
- "Gentlemen, this is Mr. Brown ... ": H. Rpt. 31, p. 203. See also Speyers test., p. 67.
- "Jay Gould replied ... ": Ibid.
- "If you do not make ... ": Ibid.
- "the chances were ... ": Clews, p. 199.
- "Who killed Leupp?" : Minnigerode, p. 160. See also Warshow, p. 107.
- General James McQuade Militia ... : *Sun; Herald*, 9/25/1869.
- "These are high old times" ... : H. Rpt. 31, p. 92.
- Jay "look[ed] around sharply ... ": Clews, p. 199. Clews does not identify his

"eyewitness" for this account, but Stimson is the likely candidate. Stimson carried messages for Belden all morning between Heath's and the Gold Room and claimed to overhear Fisk speaking shortly before Fisk left Wall Street. Clews's source erred slightly. In describing the retreat, he said: "At its exit the conspirators jumped into a carriage and fled the street." Actually, they ducked into Henry Smith's office up the block.

- "Then came Belden ... ": Ibid.
- Kruger, "a robust ... ": H. Rpt. 31, p. 204.
- "shook hands ... ": *Times, 9/25/1869*.
- "dashed his fist ... ": *Sun, 9/25/1869*.

27. Falling Out *(pages 211–219)*

- Corbin "appeared to be ... ": Affidavit of C. W. Pollard, sworn 4/10/1869, printed in the *Sun, 5/10/1869*.
- "he hoped they would ... ": Affidavit of C. McIntosh, sworn 4/10/1869, printed in the *Sun, 5/10/1869*.
- "I was in no enviable ... ": H. Rpt. 31, p. 175.
- "Belden joined them ... : The *Sun* reported that "two ladies" also accompanied Fisk for the uptown retreat that night. *Sun, 9/28/1869*.
- "sunk right down. There is nothing left ... ": Corbin is the source for this quintessential Fiskism. H. Rpt. 31, p. 262.
- gossip ... exposure at ... $30 million ... : O'Connor, p. 107; Minnigerode, p. 168. Fowler, p. 523, cited a $20 million figure.
- Speyers ... $26 million ... : H. Rpt. 31, p. 66. Speyers estimated his total for the week at $35 million. *Sun, 9/29/1869*.
- Jim's excuse ... Belden's account ... : Jim claimed that he and Belden had worked out this plan Thursday night, perhaps as a contingency against a collapse. Jim later produced a signed letter from Belden dated Friday morning authorizing him to order sales for Belden's account. Belden refused to acknowledge the probable forgery. See H. Rpt. 31, pp. 170,301.
- string of horse-pulled carts eight miles long ... : *Harper's Weekly, 10/16/1869*. $500 million+ 16 ($ per ounce, as assumed by *Harper's*)+ 16 (ounces per pound)+ 2,000 (pounds per ton) = 977 tons or 31.3 million ounces x $450/0unce = $14.1 billion. By contrast, an estimated $20 billion in stock (608 million shares) changed hands on the New York Stock Exchange on "Black Monday," October 19, 1987.
- Franklin Telegraph Company ... 5,000 messages ... : Ibid. 204 "I have made $50,000 ... ": Stedman, p. 230.
- "owing to the failure ... ": Letters from H. Benedict to *Sun, Times*, and other papers, 91 24/1869; printed 9/25/1869.
- "The crowd were struggling ... ": *Sun, 9/25/1869*.
- "was no place for a lady ... ": Corbin test., H. Rpt. 31, pp. 261, 257.
- "started round to old Corbin's ... " I was too mad ... : Excerpt is from Fisk test., H. Rpt. 31, pp. 175-76.

- [Fisk] began to say: "How is this? ... ": Excerpt is from Corbin test., H. Rpt. 31, p. 262.
- "Boutwell had sold ... ": Fisk press conference, *Times*, *1/24/1870*; H. Rpt. 31, p. 176.
- "The old man straightened ... ": H. Rpt. 31, p. 176.
- Corbin's ... "pretty well played out" ... : Ibid.
- "browbeat the terrified old man" ... : Mende, p. 116.
- "It was each man drag ... ": H. Rpt. 31, p. 176.
- Speyers ... Jim Fisk ... : Speyers does not pinpoint a date for this meeting, but his test. to the Garfield Committee suggests that it occurred about two weeks after Black Friday. I am inserting it here, perhaps out of chronological order, for narrative coherence. H. Rpt. 31, p. 67-68.
- "Mr. Speyers, can you ask ... ": Ibid.
- Jim treated ... scene ... : Jim Fisk never directly challenged Speyers's charge that Jim offered to pay hush-money after the gold panic. In fact, in his Garfield Committee test., Jim suggested that he indeed saw Speyers two or three weeks after Black Friday. At no point, however, did Jim ever confirm Speyers's story, treating it as undeserving of a response. See H. Rpt. 31, p. 170.
- "All I want ... .": Ibid.
- "He will not give you ... " Ibid. Shearman proposed the $200,000 pay-off at a second meeting about a week after Speyers's original talk with Jim Fisk. Once again, I have combined the two for narrative coherence.
- "You know, Speyers ... ": Ibid.
- "Mr. Belden, and Mr. Fisk ... ": Ibid.

28. Wreckage *(pages 220–225)*

- Boutwell's "magnificent rout ... ": *Tribune*, 9/25,27/1869.
- "came to tbe rescue ... ": Herald, 9/25,27/1869.
- "mere struggle between gangs ... ": *Evening Post*, 9/24,25/1869. See *World*, 9/27/1869. 210 "member of ... Jay Cooke & Co." ... : *Evening Mail*, 9/24/1869. See also *Herald* 9/26/1869.
- "astounded at tbe suddenness ... ": Letter from H. Cooke to J. Cooke, 9/25/1869, Cooke papers.
- "be bad not done witb ... ": *World*, 9/26/1869.
- "I am not anxious ... ": Telegraph message from G. Boutwell to D. Butterfield, 9/25/1869, Treasury documents.
- "Dirt, a vast litter ... ": *World*, 9/26/1869.
- "spend $10 on a revolver ... ": Ibid.
- "What gold?" ... : Dialogue between C. C. Allen and the Heath & Company clerk is from the *Sun*, 9/27/1869.
- Solomon Mabler ... : See *World*, 9126/1869; *Sun*, 9/27/1869; and Stedman, p. 233.
- "I never want to see ... ": Letter from H. Fahnestock to J. Cooke, 9/25/1869, Cooke papers.

- "All tbe banks bere ... ": Ibid. Federal law today makes such bookkeeping sleight-of-hand illegal.
- "Market is over ... ": Ibid.
- "carry it through ... ": *Sun*, 9/27/1869.
- "calm, quiet, and serene ... ": Ibid.
- "Had Vanderbilt not come ... ": Morrissey interview in *World*, 9/26/1869.
- topple the clearinghouse ... : For a modem example of the financial concerns that can beset an exchange clearing organization in an emergency situation, see *Volume Investors Corporation*. "Report of the Division of Trading and Markets," Commodity Futures Trading Commission, July 1985. On the predicament of the Gold Exchange Bank, see Benedict test. to the Garfield Committee and to the Cardozo impeachment inquiry, N.Y.S. Rpt. llll.
- "Every person who gained ... ": *Herald*, 9/26/1869.
- Tenth National ... : On Saturday's run at the Tenth National, see *Herald*; *World*, 9/26/1869; M. H. Smith, 115-17.
- ravaged ... in its gold run-up: Even with Washington examiners on hand, the Tenth National had certified over $14 million in checks on Friday, mostly for Ring brokers.
- city banks had refused ... : The Bank of Commerce had posted notice that morning: "No checks on the Tenth National and Gold Exchange Banks received." The New York bank clearinghouse association, which settled interbank accounts, announced that the Tenth National owed over $700,000 in debts to other institutions. To even open its doors that morning, the Tenth National had to settle its balance by paying $400,000 in notes and another $300,000 in loans.

  By 2:30 P.M., the Tenth National had nearly exhausted its funds, and the clearinghouse association was demanding another $152,000. The Bank of New York heeded urgent pleas and accepted a certified check from the Tenth National to cover the debt. See H. Rpt. 31, pp. 407-408.
- "Greenbacks were piled ... ": M. H. Smith, p. 115.
- "Gentlemen, if any of you ... ": *World*, 9/26/1869.

29: Behind the Barricades *(pages 226–233)*

- *Leah* at Booth's Theatre.: Jim was spotted by the *Evening Mail* drama critic. *Evening Mail*, 9/25/1869.
- tapped the telegraph wires ... : Letter from D. Butterfield to G. Boutwell, 9/24/1869, Treasury documents.
- operators "laughed heartily" ... : *Sun*, 10/20/1869.
- "Report to me prices ... ": Letters, telegraph messages from G. Boutwell to D. Butterfield, 9/25/1869, Treasury documents.
- Lane got right to the point ... : On Lane's meetings with Butterfield, see letter from F. Lane to 1. Gould, 10/14/1869, published in *Sun*, 10/20/1869; Butterfield test., H. Rpt. 31, 319.
- Sir: I am carrying ... : Letter from J. Gould, 9/25/1869, printed in H. Rpt. 31, p. 330.

- "[H]is conversation was so … " Letter from F. Lane to J. Gould, 10/14/1869, op. cit.
- "with his hat on … But you tell … ": Ibid. Butterfield's account of the meeting bolsters Lane's story. Butterfield claimed that he had refused to pay the debt only "until I knew the authority and order he had, and saw the evidence in the matter, and then I would make my decision." A lawyer's denial, at best. H. Rpt. 31, p. 319.
- "You telegraph us … ": Corbin test., H. Rpt. 31, p. 263.
- "[I]t was a serious thing … ": Ibid.
- "a dozen big fellows" … : James's version of the episode is from his test. to Garfield Committee, H. Rpt. 31, pp. 204-205.
- "Certainly, Mr. B[rown] … ": The grapevine version is from Fowler, pp. 479-80. Between the two, James Brown's sworn test. must be considered the more reliable.
- "more than a man's life … ": Benedict test., N.Y.S. Rpt. 1111, p. 185.
- Benedict … Stevens Hotel … : On this meeting between Gould and Benedict, see Benedict test., N.Y.S. Rpt. 1111, pp. 286, 291.
- Benedict had removed $3 million … : Ibid., p. 186.
- Two hundred clerks sat cloistered … : Description from Shearman test., N.Y.S. Rpt. 1111, p. 228.
- "staff of thirty clerks" … : World, 9/27/1869.
- Jay … "expressed greatest anxiety" … : On meeting at the Gold Exchange Bank Sunday night, see Benedict test., N.Y.S. Rpt. 1111, pp. 182, 288-90; Shearman test., ibid., pp. 227-29. See also H. Rpt. 31, pp. 57-58.
- Jay … responsibility for "five or six" … : As Shearman recalled the Bank's attitude, "they all looked to Mr. Gould as the man who was able and willing to extricate the bank from its difficulties; they expected him to lend enough money to carry the bank through." N.Y.S. Rpt. 1111, p. 261.
- "all balances can be settled … ": World, 9/27/1869.

30. Family (pages 234–236)

- "I got your letter … ": Corbin test., H. Rpt. 31, p. 267.
- "There has been trouble … ": Porter test., H. Rpt. 31, p. 446.
- "I am not at all … ": ibid., pp. 446-47.
- "stopped the conversation" … : Ibid.
- "This matter has been … ": Corbin test., H. Rpt. 31, p. 266.

31. Bears Regroup (pages 237–240)

- Gold Room opened its New Street doors … : Accounts of the Gold Room proceedings were carried in the Times, World, Sun, 9/28, et seq. 1869.
- clearinghouse had "rejected" statements … : Letter from H. Benedict posted at Gold Exchange Bank and announced at the Gold Room; included in newspaper accounts.
- James Brown … tirade … : Ibid.

- law could do little.: Courts in the 1860s had frequently refused to recognize Gold Room sales, viewing them either as void gambling agreements or oral contracts violating the common law "statute of frauds."

  Exchange rules too gave little hope. If Jim Fisk or Belden walked away from agreements to buy gold, the Exchange could sell the gold in the open market and sue the defaulters for any loss. The process was a two-edged sword, though. Fisk's repudiation via Belden totaled an estimated $70 million. Dumping that much gold could cripple commerce by crushing prices further.

  As a final protection in such situations, traders looked to the clearinghouse system managed by the Gold Exchange Bank. The clearinghouse was designed to remove credit risks from Gold Room trading. As "common agent" for members, the Bank guaranteed Gold Room trades against default by the opposite party. If things turned sour, the clearinghouse was supposed to suffer the loss to protect the market. See e.g. *Fowler v. N.Y. Gold Exchange Bank*, 67 N.Y. Reports 138 (Oct. 1876).

  But the 1869 clearinghouse too had its limits, as seen here.

- "approximate" balances ... : Benedict test., H. Rpt. 31, p. 54. See also test. of Bank cashier Hiram Rogers, H. Rpt. 31, pp. 222-27.

  Benedict encountered problems in arranging to pay the "approximate" balances. The Bank's assets Monday were mostly in gold, not greenbacks. Benedict had to swap metal for money under panic conditions. He borrowed heavily and by Tuesday owed almost $2.5 million to the city's bank clearinghouse association. He paid this by transferring gold and demand loans. He also asked the U.S. Treasury via Daniel Butterfield to trade $2 million in gold for $2 million in greenbacks, but George Boutwell vetoed the proposal from Washington as "unlawful and unwise." See telegraph message from G. Boutwell to D. Butterfield, 9/281 1869, Treasury documents.

- Trevor & Colgate took in $600,000; Cooke & Company ... : Rogers presented a full list of these payouts to the Garfield Committee, ibid., p. 225-27.

- "Friends" of the directors ... : *World*, 9/27/1869; *Sun*, 9/28/1869; *Times*, 10/29/1869.

- "mismanagement" could prompt a "repeat ... ": Letter from H. Fahnestock to J. Cooke, 9/28/1869, Cooke papers.

- "horribly bad humor" ... : *World*, 9/29/1869. 231 "a combination ... ": Ibid.

32. Lawyers *(pages 241–245)*

- Democratic Party convention in Syracuse.: Jim Fisk had given Tweed confidant Peter Sweeny several platform resolutions for Tammany to propose at the Syracuse convention. The resolutions, drafted by Abel Corbin, denounced Treasury Secretary George Boutwell in strong terms and were designed to drive a wedge between Boutwell and the President-a sidelight to the gold conspiracy. Tweed, however, decided not to press the Fisk-Corbin resolutions in Syracuse, having been humbled on a number of other matters that week by a coalition of political enemies. *Times*, 10/18/1869; *Sun*, 10/8/1869.

- Tweed ... police protection ... : Swanberg, p. 154.

- "India Rubber Account" of $195,000 ... : Mott, p. 455. Two of the September entries totaling $94,000 were dated September 9, predating Black Friday by two weeks. These could have been backdated or the money used to prime the pumps in advance.
- Lawyer Tom Shearman: On Shearman's role, see test. of Shearman and John Sterling to the Cardozo impeachment committee, N.Y.S. Rpt. 1111, pp. 226-86, 206-21. See also Earle, pp. 71-78.

  Shearman doubtless had heard his other mentor, the Reverend Henry Ward Beecher, preaching that week against the evils of greed and avarice like other clergymen across America. Beecher took his Sunday text from Matthew VI: "Lay not up for yourselves treasures on earth."
- Henry Benedict had paid Osborne ... : Hiram Rogers, the Gold Exchange Bank cashier, provided the Cardozo impeachment committee with a receipt documenting the Bank's payment to Osborne of $58,850, dated 9/27/1869. N.Y.S. Rpt. 1111, p. 226.
- Aaron J. Vanderpoel: On Vanderpoel's relationship with Mayor Hall, see references in Bowen. On Vanderpoel's contacts with Shearman, see Shearman cites, *supra.*
- Butterfield ... refused to pay .... : Letter from Lane to J. Gould, 10/14/1869, printed in the *Sun*, 10/20/1869.
- "would leave it ... ": Ibid.

33. Coup d'Etat *(pages 246–252)*

- Albert Cardozo: Generally on Judge Cardozo, see references in Lynch; Hellman; and Wingate, pp. 386, 392, 395-6.

  Cardozo's Jewishness was a major influence on his life. One of Cardozo's first public appearances as a Columbia College graduate was at the May 1855 opening of Jews' Hospital (today, Mt. Sinai). When he first learned that he would have to hold Supreme Court Chambers on Saturday, he planned to resign rather than violate the Sabbath. He appealed to a Beit Din, a Jewish religious court. The rabbis, sitting in London, ruled that public business could sometimes take precedence over Jewish law. On Saturday mornings thereafter, Cardozo started his day at the synagogue and finished his prayers before going off to do Tweed's work in the hall of justice.
- Cardozo craved ... United States Supreme Court ... : Wingate, p. 395.
- "Courteous but inflexible ... ": C. F. Adams, p. 82.
- Bach was his wife's nephew ... : Dialogue between Shearman and Judge Clerke is from Shearman test., N.Y.S. Rpt. 1111, p. 232.
- "I am going away ... ": Sheannan-Ingraham meeting, ibid., p. 233.
- "I had reason to suppose ... ": ibid., p. 253.
- Shearman ... *North American Review* ... : The article was unsigned, but H. Adams identified Shearman as the author. See C.F. Adams, p. 109.
- "hang them. Hang them" ... : *World*, 9/30/1869.
- "Curses, groans ... ": Ibid.
- "Smith, Gould, & Martin have beat us ... ": Ibid.

- Augustus Brown ... inventory ... : H. Rpt. 31, p. 47.
- Barings agreed to lend ... : *Tribune*, 10/1/1869; *Times*, 10/1/1869; *Evening Mail* , 10/6/ 1869; and Grodinsky, p. 80.
- "This whole stampede ... ": Letter from H. Fahnestock to J. Cooke, 9/29/1869, Cooke papers.
- "from every State ... ": *Tribune*, 10/1/1869.
- Jay unloaded ... stocks ... : Clews, p. 622-23; Grodinsky, p. 79.

34. Astounding Revelations (*pages 255–263*)

- "You have sent for me ... ": Dialogue between Crouch and Jim Fisk is from Crouch's unrebutted account in the *Herald*, 10/8/1869.
- "why the carriage ... ": *Herald*, 9/30/1869.
- "You come with me ... ": *Herald*, 10/8/1869.
- "I did not know I had ... ": *Sun*, 10/8/1869. On Barksdale's account of his contacts with Corbin, Fisk, and Gould that week, see also Barksdale test., H. Rpt. 31, pp, 421-23.
- "the massive gates ... .": Ibid.
- "I never wanted gold above 145," ... : Ibid.
- "A fellow can't have ... ": Ibid.
- "Assure Mr. Fisk ... ": Note from A. Corbin, printed in the *Sun*, 10/2/1869.
- feature story "utterly false" ... : Note from J. Fisk to Dana, 10/1/1869, printed in the *Sun*, 10/2/1869.
- "the interview was correctly reported ... ": Dialogue between Barksdale and Fisk is from Barksdale's account in the *Sun*, 10/2/1869. See also H. Rpt. 31, pp. 421-23.
- Corbin "exhibited great agitation" ... : Account of Barksdale-Corbin meeting is from the *Sun*, 10/2/1869.
- "the worst and most consummate ... ": H. Rpt. 31, p. 429.
- "tells the truth in this affair.": Ibid.
- damning picture ... Barksdale's accounts ... : See *Sun*, 10/2,5,6,7,8/1869.
- Corbin "hated" Boutwell ... : *Sun*, 10/8/1869.
- "suffering from disease ... ": *Herald*, 10/8/1869.
- "Mr. Corbin sank back ... ": Ibid.
- "I will swear to nothing, ... : *Sun*, 1017/1869.
- "pneumonia" ... *Sun* reports "base and wicked ... ": *Tribune*, 10/4/1869.
- Jim ... to Boston ... : *Evening Mail* , 10/4/1869. See also affidavits in the Joslyn lawsuit over whether Boston or New York was Jim's legal domicile, printed in the *Times*, 10/23/ 1869.
- passions with Josie Mansfield.: Josie apparently took advantage of Jim's absences during this period to broaden her own horizons. It was about this time that socialite Edward "Ned" Stokes, who had recently entered into a business partnership with Jim over his Brooklyn oil refinery, started spending time with Josie during Jim's absences. Whether it was Josie who first seduced Stokes or vice versa, the seeds of a stormy lovers' conflict were soon planted.

35. Politics (pages 264–270)

- grand jury: Grand jury proceedings were secret. Information on the investigation here is from newspaper accounts. See, e.g., *Sun*; 10/27/1869; *Harper's Weekly*, 2/5/1870; *Nation*, 10/28/1869; and *Evening Mail*, 10/12/1869.
- amendment … conspiracy law.: Laws of New York, 1870, vol. I, p. 30. The amendment, designed to exempt labor unions, had been pressed for years by reformers but was never passed until after Black Friday.
- "the great gorilla … ": *Herald*, 10/8/1869.
- *Times* … "organ of the Gold Ring" … : See *Sun*, 10/23/1869.
- "preposterous" rumors … "base calumnies" … : *Herald*, 10/8/1869; *Morning Express*, 9/30/1869. See also *Harper's Weekly*, 11/6/1869.
- "It's a d-d shame … ": *Sun*, 10/23/1869.
- "the fact of his being … ": *Evening Mail*, 10/7/1869.
- Grant … a "butcher" … : Porter, pp. 179-81. Grant later conceded "regret" for ordering the fruitless June 3 assault at Cold Harbor, where rebels killed seven thousand of his troops in barely two hours.
- Grant broke his silence … : Grant's interview with the Associated Press is reported in the *Sun*, 10/4/1869.
- "innocent … except that I ordered … ": Letter from Grant to R. Bonner, 10/13/1869, printed in the *Sun*, 10/16/1869.
- "Too straightforward … ": London *Times*, 11/2,9/1869.
- Boutwell … "did not expect … ": Letter from H. Cooke to J. Cooke, 9/29/1869, Cooke papers.
- If gold does not sell … Wilkes Booth: Boutwell, II, p. 181.
- "prominent government official" … : *Sun*, 10/8/1869. Jim had also alluded to Butterfield in his first talk with George Crouch. See *Herald*, 10/8/1869
- "unless you find it necessary … ": Letter from G. Boutwell to D. Butterfield, 10/8/1869, printed in H. Rpt. 31, p. 379.
- "No one has suffered … ": Butterfield interview with Tribune, 10/1/1869.
- Daniel's self-aggrandizing version … : On Barksdale's contacts with Butterfield, see Barksdale test., H. Rpt. 31,418-19. The article text appeared in the *Times*, 10/18/1869.
- Butterfield … misunderstood hero … : Butterfield, through the *Times* article, pictured himself the victim of a fantastic gossip campaign by the Fisk-Gould Ring. According to these supposed rumors, the bulls had planned to run gold prices up to $200 on Black Friday. At that point, Butterfield was to dump $20 million of Treasury gold on the market, causing a crash. The conspirators would sell their gold at the high and then take "short" positions, making a profit from both the rise and fall.

  The story is clearly false and illogical. Butterfield, after all, had no legal authority to sell Treasury gold on his own, a fact that Jay Gould knew perfectly well.

  Having created a straw man, Butterfield proceeded to debunk it. "Nonsensical" and "preposterous," he said, via Barksdale, of the supposed allegations.

- "The Lions Devour Daniel" ... : *Sun*, 10/20/1869. See also *Sun*, 10/19,2111869.
- "as conclusive and unanswerable": *Sun*, 10/23/1869.
- "Now, why don't they ... ": Ibid.
- "to tap Butterfield ... ": *Sun*, 10/19/1869.
- "I am constrained. ... .": Letter from G. Boutwell to D. Butterfield, 10/22/1869, printed in H. Rpt. 31, p. 379.
- "premonitory symptoms ... ": H. Rpt. 31, p. 327.
- to sell ... books ... : Charles F. Adams published his lurid expose of the 1868 DrewVanderbilt Erie takeover wars that month in a pamphlet called "A Chapter of Erie" which became a best-seller, reaching the *Evening Mail* 's "Book of the Week" list in mid-October.
- "disqualification of the male man" ... : The Revolution, 9/20/1869, 10/28/1869.
- "a man so destitute ... ": *Herald*, 10/26/1869.
- Stone, Nichols, and Stone ... : Jay's allegations appeared in the *Sun*, 10/2111869. Stone's ultimate denial is from the *Times*, 10/27/1869. Jay's allegations throughout the gold affair generally had at least a grain of truth, even if slanted to his ends. If Stone's denial was truthful, then this case was an exception. Or perhaps it is the tip of an iceberg beyond our knowledge.

36. Evasions *(pages 273–278)*

- twenty-five cents on the dollar.: *Herald*, 10/21/1869.
- Cardozo ... pay Jay's brokers ... : Order of October 9, 1869. An exhaustive (and exhausting) set of legal documents from the Gold Exchange Bank receivership and related cases is contained in the Cardozo impeachment committee's report, N.Y.S. Rpt. 1111, pp. 16-157.
- Bank ... lost. .. $700,000 ... : Cornwallis, p. 16. The Bank lost $310,000 of its $500,000 capital, in addition to its surplus of $360,000. Henry Benedict cited losses of $3 to $400,000 in test. to Garfield Committee, H. Rpt. 31, p. 56.
- gold and stocks ... dropped ... $100 million, ... : *Times*, 10/111869. By contrast, the total loss of portfolio value of all stocks in the United States during the week of October 14-19, 1987 ("Black Monday") has been estimated at nearly a *trillion* dollars.
- Cooke ... lost at least $28,201 ... : Letter from H. Fahnestock to J. Cooke, 10/16/1869, Cooke papers; Larson, p. 270.
- Fahnestock jawboned "the Fisk party" ... : Letter from H. Fahnestock to J. Cooke, 10/16/1869, Cooke papers.
- "We have got to find ... ": Larson, p. 271. 267 "the wicked want of honesty ... ": Ibid.
- The Chicago price plummeted ... : See Taylor.
- Judge Dowling ... : Mansfield test., *Trial of George G. Barnard*, p. 389.
- "rare collection of burglar instruments ... ": *Sun*, 11/2/1869.
- Davis v. Fisk: For trial excerpts, see *Times*, 11/15/1871. On verdict and jury-tampering controversy, *Times*, 12/1/1871.

    See also *Peabody v. Speyers*, 56 New York Rpts. 230 (March 1874), where Speyers was separately held liable for a $40,000 Black Friday sale; and *Mills v. Gould,* 10 Jones & Spencer 119, where a court refused to dismiss a gold claim on procedural grounds.

- "The people had desired … ": Quoted in Kaplan, p. 157.
- "who among the gold gamblers … ": *Herald,* 10/26/1869.
- "whose one passion … ": *Nation,* 9/23/1869.
- Henry Adams's … expose … : H. Adams, *Education,* pp. 286-87.
- Prince Erie's "very appearance … ": Mott, p. 489-90.

37. Light of Day *(pages 279–285)*

- "whether any officers … ": H. Rpt. 31, p. 1.
- James Abram Garfield: Background on Garfield is plentiful. Ridpath; and the introductory materials in Garfield's diary collection were useful.
- "I am trying to do … ": Letter from Garfield to M. Hinsdale, from Garfield, p. xxxix.
- "want a representative that they … ": Josephson, *Politicos,* p. 113.
- Banking Committee … 8-to-2 majority of Republicans … : Besides Garfield, the Committee lineup included: Rep. John Lynch (R-Maine), Norman B. Judd (R-Illinois), John Coburn (R-Indiana), Worthington C. Smith (R-Vermont), John B. Packer (R-Pennsylvania), Israel G. Lash (R-North Carolina), Horatio C. Burchard (R-Illinois), S. S. Cox (D-New York), and Thomas L. Jones (D-Kentucky).
- "the disgraceful scenes … ": Letter from J. Garfield to H. Carey, 11/30/1869. Historical Society of Pennsylvania.
- "dinner with Mr. Gould … ": Garfield, p. 363.
- Samuel Sullivan "Sunset" Cox: See *Biographical Directory of the American Congress: 1774-1971,* U.S. Government Printing Office, 1971.
- Garfield playing gumshoe detective … : Ridpath, pp. 225-26.
- "If the bull had been … ": Brown test., H. Rpt. 31, p. 206.
- "theatrical and ludicrous … ": *Times,* 1/24/1870. One congressman told the *Herald* that Jim seemed "still as much befogged and muddled as he was with the collapse of Corbin and his bubble on that fatal 'Black Friday.' " 1/24/1870.
- "I said to the Committee … ": *Times,* 1/24/1870.
- Garfield to visit Grant … : Attempts by the Garfield Committee, particularly Democrats, to press Grant for a reponse are detailed in "Views of the Minority," H. Rpt. 31, p. 471-73.
- "preferred not to see … ": Ibid.
- "groundless and wicked" charges … : H. Rpt. 31, p. 21.
- "I am satisfied … ": Gould test. quoted by Committee majority, H. Rpt. 31, p. 20.
- "worst form of hypocrisy … ": Ibid., p. 20.
- "not conclusively proved" … : Ibid, p. 22.
- Grant's "immaculateness" … : "Views of the Minority," H. Rpt. 31, p. 470-72.
- "dared not probe … ": H. Adams, *Education,* p. 271.
- "accepting the hospitality … ": *Nation,* 3/3/1870.

- "incredible … lapses … intelligence" … : H. Adams, Education p. 272.
- $9 million in winnings … : *Herald*, 9/30/1869.
- profits … $10 to $12 million.: Hodgskin test., H. Rpt. 31, p. 39 ($12 million); Earle, p. 77 ($10 million); O'Connor, p. 106 ($11 million). See also *Sun*, 9/27/1869 ("How Much the Bulls Have Made").
- splitting the loot with Jim … : There is little doubt that Jay Gould ultimately split his gold corner winnings with Jim Fisk, although he waited before making a settlement until at least after the January 1870 Garfield Committee hearings. In his Garfield test., Jim explained that "Mr. Gould and I have never passed a word as to whether I was to be interested in his profits and losses, and there was no understanding that I was or was not. When the settlement is made in full, if there should be a loss, I should be very glad to help him to bear it, and if there are any profits I should not say no to a proposition to divide them with him; that is not my nature." Such dividing of gains and losses, Jim said, was his and Gould's "custom." H. Rpt. 31, p. 169.
- "It has gone where the woodbine … ": Molt, p. 489; *Life, Trial, and Conviction*, p. 94.

38. Bygones *(pages 286–294)*

- Belden … robbed Jay "right and left" … : Morosini manuscript.
- Stock Exchange … blackballed … : *Tribune*, 5/3/1888; Stock Exchange Archives.
- "The Treasury as an active … ": H. Adams, p. 273.
- combined with EoHo Harriman … : Stock Exchange Archives.
- Butterfield … : *Times*, 7/18/1901.
- Cardozo 000: N.Y.S. Rpt. llll; *Times*, 5/2/1872.
- Barnard … impeached … : Trial of George G. Barnard, 1872. See also *Times*, 4/28/1879.
- Fahnestock … First National Bank … : *Times*, 6/5/1914.
- Corbin 000 : Letters from U.S. Grant to A. R. Corbin, 12/28/1873, 11/19/1877, Grant papers, Library of Congress; *Times*, 3/29/1880.
- Jennie Grant … : *Times*, 7/111913.
- James Garfield … : See generally Ridpath.
- "The worst scandals … ": H. Adams, pp. 271-73.
- "without any previous … ": McFeely, pp. 441-43.
- Ferdinand Ward … : On the Grant & Ward collapse, see *Tribune*, 5/1O,1l11884.
- Horace Porter … : *Times*, 5/30/1921. While cleared of all corruption charges, Porter was known to have accepted during his White House tenure a $15,000 stock Subscription from Jay Cooke. Whether Porter paid for the stock or not is unclear. Oberholtzer, II, p. 165.
- Shearman & Sterling employed … : *National Law Journal*, 9128/1987.
- "I'll live to see the day … : *Times*, 12/3/1892. The *Times* article has this famous altercation taking place shortly after Black Friday. Klein, p. 132, more accurately places the exchange in the context of the 1872 Northwestern Railroad maneuver.

- Stock Exchange ... membership ... : Proceedings before the Stock Exchange Committee on Admissions, 11/22/1877, Stock Exchange Archives.
- Smith's final collapse ... : *Times*, 10/3/1885; *Tribune*, 11/21/1885, 3/2,3/1886.
- Albert Speyers ... : *Times*, 12/24/1880.
- William Magear Tweed ... : On the dramatic story of Boss Tweed's fall from graft heaven, see generally Lynch; Hershkowitz; Tilden; and contemporary press accounts.
- Fisk ... ever-flashier shows ... Opera House ... : For the 1869 winter season, Jim staged an extravagant production of *The Twelve Temptations*. Costing an unheard-of $75 ,000, the show, according to Swanberg, "boasted a cast of more than 200, a stage cataract with tons of real water, a rip-snorting cancan, and a truly Fiskian innovation described with admiration: A corps of beautiful blondes alternated with one of ravishing brunettes from night to night." Swanberg, p. 182.
- Edward "Ned" Stokes: On Stokes, see profiles in Willoughby; references in Swanberg; Fuller.
- storm of lawsuits and press attacks.: The law- and mudslinging contest among Jim, Josie Mansfield, and Ned Stokes is a wonderful romantic farce. See Swanberg; Fuller; and *Youthful Days* for good overall accounts. Exposes in the *World* ("Not for Josie" and "The Gallant Colonel Not a Weepist") 1/13,15/1871; and the *Herald*, ("Fiskiana") 1/18/1871; and accounts of Josie's courtroom dramatics in the *World* and *Herald* ("Magnificent Mansfield"), 1/26/1871; and the *Times*, 1/7/1872; are revealing specimens of media exploitation in its formative stage.
- "Not since the memorable night ... ": *Herald*, 11711872.
- Fisk ... "He Never Went Back on the Poor":

  Let me speak of a man who's now dead in his grave,
  A good man as was ever born;
  Jim Fisk he was called. and his money he gave
  To the outcast, the poor and forlorn.

  We all know he loved both women and wine,
  But his heart it was right I am sure;
  Though he lived like a prince in a palace so fine,
  Yet he never went back on the poor!

  If a man was in trouble Fisk helped him along
  To drive the grim wolf from the door;
  He strove to do right. though he may have done wrong,
  But he never went back on the poor!

  Now what do you think of the trial of Stokes,
  Who murdered this friend of the poor?
  If such men get free, is anyone safe
  To step from outside their own door?

  Minnigerode, p.209; Swanberg, p. 291.

- Josie Mansfield moved to Paris ... : Swanberg, pp. 292-93; Fuller, p. 561.
- Clews ... Washington should step in ... : Clews, p. 657.
- Tweed's ... million-dollar bail ... : *Times* and other papers, 10/28/1871. Jay was removed from the bail bond later when other sufficient backers were found. See Judge Cardozo's ruling on the adequacy of Tweed's bail, printed in the *Times*, 1/6/1872.
- "the most hated ... ": Minnigerode, p. 137.
- the smartest.: O'Connor, p. 83; Andrews, p. 184.
- improved the Erie ... : Between mid-1868, when they took control, and the end of 1869, Fisk increased Erie's fleet of locomotives from 371 to 444, its number of first-class passenger cars from 187 to 222, its freight cars from 6,040 to 7,447. Mott, pp. 483-84; and Smith, pp. 108-109.
- Erie, now the Erie-Lackawanna ... : Recent history is from company officials at the Cleveland headquarters and from newspaper accounts.
- Gold... traded as a commodity ... : Gold today is traded on a number of federally regulated futures exchanges, including the New York Commodity Exchange and the Chicago Board of Trade. Over 10.2 million gold futures contracts changed hands on the New York Commodity Exchange alone in 1987.
- Rules ... protect innocent bystanders ... : Government regulatory protections, for instance, are widely credited for preventing the October 1987 stock crash from producing a repeat of.the 1929 disaster. In 1987 federal regulators monitored the unfolding marker crisis; the Federal Reserve System eased credit pressures on the banking system; deposit insurance programs prevented the occurrence of old-style bank runs; capital and margin rules resulted in not a single major brokerage house going bankrupt; and with the exception of a one-hour period on Tuesday, October 20, all relevant stock and futures exchanges remained open for trading throughout. true, government regulation did Dot prevent the crash, but it helped prevent Wall Street's nighmare from spreading into an overnight national calamity. See "Report of The Presidential Task Force on Market Mechanisms" (Brady Commission), January 8, 1988.

ACKNOWLEDGMENTS

Every writer should be as lucky with their first book as I have been. At every step, I have had the good fortune to work with professional people who have treated my work with care, skill, and insight. The experience has been invaluable.

To start with, I was lucky enough to be represented by Raphael Sagalyn as my agent. Rafe worked with me to flesh out my book idea into a viable proposal, and marketed it well. Without his effort, *The Gold Ring* likely would not have progressed beyond a well-meaning magazine article. Two people at the Sagalyn Agency worked especially hard on my behalf: Anne Sleeper, who sweated out the details during the marketing of the manuscript, and Lisa Di-Mona who monitored the project during the critical stages as the book moved toward publication.

Luck struck again in the form of Cynthia Vartan, my editor at Dodd, Mead & Company. Cynthia applied her considerable skill and experience to my early drafts and helped to mold them into a readable, logical, well-structured book. Her sharp eye and demanding standards caused *The Gold Ring* to emerge from the editing process as a far better product.

Many friends did me the compliment of reviewing the manuscript during its development. Marshall Hanbury, Douglas Leslie, Glynn Mays, Fowler C. West, Betsy Wharton, and Gary DeWaal, all experts in the world of commodity futures, lent their time and expertise. Andrea Corcoran provided particularly useful comments on my descriptions of the Gold Room clearing system.

Writers, of course, need the company and encouragement of other writers to keep their sanity during the long drudgery of producing a book. The Arlington Writers' Group, sponsored by the Washington Independent Writers organization, filled this therapeutic need for me. Tere Rios, Elyse Gussow, Shelley Schwab, Pat Prendergast, and John Grady all listened to my biweekly whining and commented ruthlessly on my draft chapters.

Research for *The Gold Ring* brought me to some of America's foremost academic facilities. Like many before me, I discovered the national treasure that is the Library of Congress. The periodical reading room staff showed particular patience with my frequent barrages of requests. Steven Wheeler, chief archivist at the New York Stock Exchange, guided me through that venerable institution's invaluable stockpile of data on member firms and traders from the 1860s and other periods. Thanks also to William Sherman at the National Archives and to the people at the New York State Library at Albany, the New York Historical Society, the New York Public Library, the Historical Society of Pennsylvania, and the Pennsylvania State Archives in Harrisburg for helping me sift through their immense manuscript and photograph collections.

Futures Magazine and the *Legal Times* published earlier versions of my attempts to chronicle the Fisk and Gould story in article form in early 1985. The *Legal Times* ran my piece on the front page of its New York edition along with a clever cartoon by artist Joseph Azur.

For this new Viral History Press edition, I thank Catherine Zaccarine of Zaccarine Design, Inc., a very talented designer who has tranformed this book into an elegant new edition.

Finally, during the many months of researching and drafting this book, my wife Karen helped me to keep the whole affair in perspective. She provided humor, relief, understanding, and a cold dose of reality when it was needed. To her, for putting up with all this foolishness, this book is dedicated.

INDEX

A

Adams, Charles Frances, 13, 23, 30, 249

Adams, Henry, 55, 66, 78, 279, 285, 288, 290

Albany Argus, 42

Albany Evening Journal, 42

Albany Morning Express, 267

Albany-Susquehanna Railroad, 76, 95-96

Allen, C. C., 192, 200-201, 278
  after crash, 224

Anthony, Susan B., 59, 271

Anti-Slavery Standard, 115

Astor House, 38, 121, 122, 125

Astor, William, 66

B

Babcock, Orville, 74, 119, 290

Bach, James, 250

Bank of New York, 225, 241, 252

Baring Brothers, 179, 186, 253

Barksdale, Ford, 188, 259-263, 269-270, 283

Barnard, George G., 28-29, 30, 40, 96, 210, 245, 248-250, 275, 278, 289
  and Erie Railway, 10, 12, 13, 17

Beecher, Henry Ward, 104, 291, 294

Belden & Company, 200, 209, 215

Belden, William, 111, 121, 157, 159-161, 172-173, 183, 185, 191, 209, 211, 214, 215, 261, 265, 266, 275, 277, 283, 288
  after crash, 220-221, 223, 234, 239, 240-241

Belknap, William, 290

Belmont, August, 25, 26, 33, 37

Benedict, Henry, 193-194, 216, 275, 283
  after crash, 225-226, 231, 232-235, 239-242, 245

Bigelow, John, 82, 126, 267

Black Friday, 189-203, 207-212, 286

Bonner, John, 278

Bonner, Robert, 268

Boocock, Samuel, 158, 173, 175, 191, 223-224, 239, 240, 275, 276

Booth's Theatre, 34, 228

Borie, Adolph, 67

Boston Herald, 180

Boston Peace Jubilee, 70, 79

Boston Post, 70

Boutwell, George, 47, 51, 58, 67, 68, 77, 80, 82, 83, 89-93, 104, 114, 118, 120, 131, 158, 194, 269, 271, 283, 288
  Black Friday, 199-200
  after crash, 222-223, 229, 236
  and gold crisis, 162-163, 177, 178-181, 188
  and gold scheme, 120-128, 167, 174
  press and, 264, 266

Bowles, Samuel, 36

Brady, John, 278

Breckinridge, John, 54

Brown, Augustus L., 249, 251-252, 275-276

Brown, Hall & Vanderpoel, 249

Brown, James, 101-103, 108-109, 129-130, 164-165, 185-186, 194, 241, 277-278, 283, 288-289
  Black Friday, 192-195, 201-202, 207-208, 211
  after crash, 232, 239-240
  and gold policy, 106

Brown Brothers & Company, 101,
129, 164, 240, 289
Bush (Major, N.Y. militia), 210
Butterfield, Daniel, 73-75, 85, 91-93,
98, 109, 121, 126, 131-132, 180,
266, 269-271, 289
Black Friday, 196, 197, 199-200,
202
and Boutwell, 122-123
congressional investigation,
283, 285
after crash, 223, 229-231, 247
and gold scheme, 112

C

Cardozo, Albert, 30, 245-251,
275-277, 283, 289
Cardozo, Benjamin Nathan, 289
Catherwood, Robert, 56-57, 73, 74
Chapin, Edwin, 93, 108, 114, 176,
195, 207
Chapin, William O., 132-135, 158
Chase National Bank, 289
Chase, Salmon P., 56, 57-58, 104
Chittenden, S.B., 127
Civil War, 7, 19, 42-43, 54, 57, 64,
90-91
Claflin, Tennie, 291
Clerke, Thomas, 240, 246-247,
249-251, 275
Clews, Henry, 23, 24, 103-104, 109,
110, 121, 126, 161, 175, 179, 186,
194, 197, 203, 210, 253, 282, 294
Colfax, Schuyler, 290
Congressional investigation, 281-287
Cooke, Henry, 103, 104, 163, 178,
179, 196, 222, 269
Cooke, Jay, 23, 44, 52, 59, 103,
104, 163, 196, 277, 279
Cooke, Jay, & Company, 74, 91,
103, 126, 128-130, 174, 184, 186,
222, 224, 241, 276, 278, 289

Corbin, Abel Rathbone, 47, 51-57,
59-61, 71-75, 78-85, 187, 266, 289
Black Friday, 213-214
and Boutwell, 125
congressional investigation, 282, 285
after crash, 216-220, 231, 236-238
and gold scheme, 94, 98, 112, 115,
117-118, 131-133, 166-170
and Grant, 63, 78-79, 84-85,
134-138
and press, 82, 258-264
Corbin, Elizabeth, 51, 53
Corbin, Virginia Grant, 51-53, 56,
71, 78-79, 83, 94, 137-138, 166-169,
284, 289
after crash, 218, 219, 231, 236-237
Cornwallis, Kinehan, 4
Cox, Samuel Sullivan "Sunset,"
282-285
Crop theory, 57, 60, 76, 77, 78, 97,
114, 124-125, 158, 277
Crouch, George, 188, 257-260,
262-264, 267, 286

D

Dana, Charles, 261-262
Davies, Henry E., 29
Davis v. Fisk, 278
Delmonico's, 10, 113, 277
Dent, Col. (father-in-law of Grant),
236
Dent, Julia (Mrs. U.S. Grant), 51.
See also Grant, Julia Dent.
Dent, Lewis (brother-in-law), 90
Dickinson (bank pres.), 194, 227
Dodge, Edward, 106, 179, 276
Dornin & Boocock, 215
Douglas, Stephen, 52, 53
Dowling (N.Y. judge), 278
Drew, Daniel, 4-6, 8, 14, 15, 17,
74, 291, 295
money lock-up, 19-20, 23-30

Duncan, Sherman & Company, 179, 186, 202, 203, 241, 253

Duncan, W. Butler, 174, 253

Dzondi (broker), 202, 241

E

Edison, Thomas Alva, 102, 176, 194, 203, 208

Ellis, James, 114, 158, 161, 172, 175

Enos, Henry, 77, 93, 108, 114, 158, 161, 192

Erie Railway Company, 3-7, 8-30, 33, 76, 110, 244, 253, 286, 293-296
  expansion plans, 113-114
  Fisk-Gould management, 33, 37, 42, 280

F

Fahnestock, Harris C., 74, 91, 103, 109, 121, 129-130, 160-161, 163, 179, 186, 196, 197, 224, 242, 253, 266, 276, 278, 289

Field, David Dudley, 27, 245, 278, 291, 292

Fifth Avenue Hotel, 36, 133, 182, 216, 277

Fish, Hamilton, 33, 51, 66, 78, 90

Fisk & Belden, 8, 111

Fisk & Hatch, 104, 129, 160, 179

Fisk, James, Jr., 6-8, 18, 33-37, 68-72, 75-76, 111, 169-171, 275, 293-294
  and Albany-Susquehanna Railroad, 96
  Black Friday, 189-196, 200, 207, 209-212, 214-216, 286-287
  and Butterfield, 270-271
  congressional investigation, 283-284
  after crash, 216-220, 223, 231-232, 234-235, 243, 253
  and Erie Railway, 7-16
  and gold market, 46, 56, 62, 77, 79-80, 95-98, 131, 157-163, 175-176, 183-186

money lock-up, 22-30
  and Opera House, 112
  and press, 257-265, 269
  public opinion, 279-280
  and Speyers, 220-221
  on Union League dinner, 127
  and Vanderbilt, 252

Fisk, James, Sr., 7, 36

Fisk, Lucy, 18, 34, 36, 264, 294

Fowler, William, 157, 172, 183, 184, 190, 201

Fox, Charles, 39

Fuller, Robert, 112

G

Garfield, James A., 281-286, 290

Garvin, Samuel, 266

Godkin, E. L., 47, 279, 285

Gold Exchange Bank, 108, 176
  Black Friday, 193, 209, 215-216
  after crash, 225-226, 231-235, 239-241, 243, 244-245, 249, 275-276

Gold market, 43, 45, 122. *See also* New York Gold Exchange

Gold Room. *See* New York Gold Exchange

Gould, Helen, 18, 185, 295

Gould, Jay, 6-8, 18, 27, 33, 36-37, 55-56, 121, 282, 288, 292, 294-295
  Black Friday, 189-192, 195-196, 207, 209-216, 286
  and Butterfield, 74-75, 92-93, 247, 269-271
  congressional investigation, 283-284
  after crash, 216-220, 229, 231, 233-235, 243-247, 252, 262, 275-277
  and Erie Railway, 7-16, 253
  and Fisk, 293-294
  and Gold Exchange Bank, 245

and gold market, 43-48, 59, 75-76,
77-85, 93-97
and gold scheme, 110-114, 131-133,
157-163, 166-172, 176, 184-186
and Grant, 61-63, 68-70, 71-72,
85, 117-118, 271-272
money lock-up, 22-30
and Porter, 119, 136
and press, 261, 267
public opinion, 279-280
and run on bank, 227
and Tweed, 41-42
and Vanderbilt, 164
Gould, John Burr, 6-7
Grand Opera House, 33, 184, 213,
228, 231-232, 244, 257, 260, 278,
280, 293
Erie Railway offices, 111, 112,
220, 295
Grant, Jesse, 79, 82
Grant, Julia Dent, 51, 63, 71, 79,
82, 94, 98, 115, 138, 166-167,
180, 236-237, 267, 284, 290
Grant, Ulysses S., 40, 41, 44, 51,
55, 61-67, 284, 290
Black Friday, 198-199, 202
cabinet appointments, 89-90, 104
Corbin and, 54, 56, 290
after crash, 236-238
fiscal policy, 46-47, 57, 59-60,
68-69, 84-85, 91, 116-118,
123-124, 128
Fisk's expose, 258-259, 263-264
gifts to, 65, 74
and gold crisis, 177, 178, 180-181
and gold scheme, 134-138, 167
and Porter, 118-119
public appearances, 70-72
and scandal, 267-269, 271-272
summer travels, 78-80, 82-84,
115-117, 122-123, 167
Grant, Virginia Paine, 51. See also
Corbin, Virginia Grant

Greeley, Horace, 81, 91, 104, 106,
114, 120, 124, 126, 127, 179, 222
Gregory, Dudley S., 17
Grinnell, Moses, 125, 126, 179, 197
Guiteau, Charles J., 290

H

Hall, A. Oakey, 41, 246
Hallgarten & Company, 202
Harpersville tunnel fight, 76-77, 96
Hastings, Hugh, 13
Heath, William, 201, 208, 275,
277, 282
after crash, 240-241
Heath, William, & Company, 111,
114, 158, 183, 189, 192, 193, 201,
207, 208-210, 215, 224, 227, 241,
277, 292
Hepburn v. Griswald, 59
Hills, Russell, 158, 161, 190, 191
Hodgskin, James, 175
Hoffman, John T. "Toots," 40-42,
96, 249
Howe, Frank, 120
Hulburd, H. R., 180

I

Ingraham, Daniel P., 250

J

Johnson, Andrew, 19, 23, 52, 63,
65-66, 73, 104
Jordan, Conrad, 275-276
Joslyn, Orlando, 202, 278
Jourdan (Police Captain), 278

K

Kimber, Arthur, 81, 93-94, 95, 110,
194, 282
Kruger (apprentice to Brown), 101,
108, 192, 211, 232

L

Lake Shore and Michigan Southern Railroad, 76, 113

Lake Shore Railroad, 159, 160, 164, 252, 286

Lane, Frederick, 17, 25, 229, 230-231, 247, 270

Lawlor, Frank, 35

Lawrence, Stone & Company, 53

Leupp, Charles, 6

Lincoln, Abraham, 40, 53, 54, 64, 248
  assassination of, 65

Livermore & Company, 192, 200

Lockwood, LeGrand, 113, 159, 164, 252-253

London Times, 268

Lowe, A. A., 126, 127, 186

Ludlow Street Jail, 10, 36, 292

Lynch, Denis Tilden, 37

M

Mahler, Solomon, 224

Mansfield, Charles, 35

Mansfield, Josie, 12, 17, 26, 34, 35, 36, 72, 75, 183, 185, 190, 228, 264, 278, 293

Marston, William, 68, 70

Martin, Henry, 110

Matoon, A. C., 13

McClellan, George, 64

McCulloch, Hugh, 23, 43, 47, 106

McCunn, John, 36, 40, 249, 278

McHenry, James, 18, 82

McIntosh, Charles, 28, 213

McKim's Banking House, 198

McKinley, William, 291

McQuade, James, 210

Medbery, James, 102, 108-109, 194

Minnigerode, Meade, 34, 198

Missouri Argus, 52

Money lock-up, 17-30, 43

Morgan, J.P., 7, 107

Morgan, William, 233

Morgan (governor of R.I.), 82

Morlacchi Ballet troupe, 71

Morosini, J.P., 36

Morris, Lloyd, 38

Morrissey, John, 190, 225

Morse, Samuel F. B., 53

Mott, Edward, 280

N

Narragansett Steamship Company, 33, 61, 70, 293

Nathan, Gratz, 248, 289

The Nation, 47, 201, 279, 285

Newcome (Belden customer), 191

New York Central Railroad, 3, 5-6, 113, 159-160, 164, 182, 225, 242

New York City, 3, 40-41

New York Evening Mail, 83, 165, 222, 266, 268

New York Evening Post, 222

New York Gold Exchange, 42, 44-46, 75, 93-94, 101, 104-108, 112, 114, 121, 124, 158, 160-162, 296
  Black Friday, 191-202, 206-209, 216, 286
  after crash, 223, 239-242, 243, 275
  gold corner, 171-177, 183-184

New York Herald, 9, 23, 29-30, 62, 81, 94, 124, 157, 162, 188, 197, 201, 203, 222, 226, 257-260, 267, 271, 279, 286, 293

New York Ledger, 81, 268

New York Post, 81

New York Stock Exchange, 4, 9, 19, 44, 101, 103, 111, 223, 242, 252, 276, 277, 292
  and Erie Railway, 22, 25, 30
  New York Central crash, 159-160

New York SubTreasury, 56, 73, 84, 101

New York Sun, 51, 55, 81, 122, 124, 125, 126, 157, 173, 188, 191, 195, 208, 212, 216, 222, 259, 260, 261-264

The New York Times, 3, 52, 63, 68, 81, 82, 107, 115, 120, 121, 124, 158, 162, 164, 173, 180, 187-188, 199, 211, 213, 267, 270

Gould scam, 81-82

New York Tribune, 23, 77, 81, 90, 106, 114, 120, 124, 177, 198, 258

New York World, 24, 29, 81, 94, 106, 120, 124, 160, 162-164, 167, 222, 223, 234, 235, 251, 294

New York Yacht Club, 295

Ninth Regiment, N.Y., militia, 280, 293

North American Review, 250

Norvell, Caleb, 82, 187-189, 266, 283

O

O'Brien, James, 278

Ohio Life and Trust Company, 178

Opdyke, George, 106, 109, 124, 161

Osborne, Charles, 172, 195, 234
    and Gold Exchange Bank, 245-246, 249

P

Pacific Mail Steamship Company, 103, 164, 252

Perley, D. W., 35

The Philadelphia Ledger, 198

Pierrepont, Edwards, 25-26, 66, 71, 126

Poole, Bill, 39

Porter, Horace, 65, 74, 78, 79, 82, 83, 115, 118-119, 134-138, 236-237, 283, 285, 290

Providence (steamboat), 61, 62, 67, 70-71

Q

Quincy, Charles, 158, 190

R

Rawlins, John, 67, 119

Raymond, Henry J., 81

Reed, William, 174

The Revolution, 59

Richardson, William, 91-92

Rockefeller, John D., 7

Roosevelt, Franklin D., 107

Root, Elihu, 292

S

St. Louis, Mo., 52-53

Saratoga, N.Y., 83-84

Schell, Richard, 15, 25

Seligman, Joseph, 91, 104, 116, 174, 187, 196, 226, 229, 241, 266

Sexias, Moses, 248

Seymour, Horatio, 40, 66

Shearman & Sterling, 291

Shearman, Thomas, 27, 96, 185, 220, 234, 243, 245-246, 249-251, 276-278, 291

Sickles (U.S. Minister), 162

Smith, Gould, Martin & Company, 7, 8, 45, 75, 77, 85, 93, 110-111, 119, 135, 158, 170, 172, 209, 211, 215, 227, 229, 241, 242, 246, 251, 291

Smith, Henry, 22, 45, 75, 77, 93, 110-111, 114, 119, 121, 160, 161, 172, 176, 184, 185, 191, 195, 207, 211, 215, 227, 232-234, 242, 251, 277, 279, 283, 286, 291-292

Smith, Matthew, 227

Speyers, Albert, 161, 172-173, 175, 191-192, 193-195, 200-201, 203, 207, 208, 214, 215, 261, 266, 275, 276, 278, 283, 292
    after crash, 220-221, 223, 239

Springfield Daily Republican, 36

Stanton, B. (congressman), 54

Stanton, Elizabeth Cady, 59, 271

Stedman, Edmund, 172, 198, 201, 216
  Israel Freyer's Bid/or Gold, 297-298
Sterling, John, 245-246, 249, 277, 291
Stewart, A.T., 67, 71, 84, 116, 126, 127
Stimson, Lewis, 175, 210
Stokes, Edward "Ned," 293-294
Stone, George E., 272
Stone, Nichols, and Stone, 272
Sutherland, Josiah, 25, 27, 29, 30
Sweeny, Peter, 12, 15, 22, 37, 39,
  75, 243

T

Tammany Society, 10, 14, 16, 28,
  30, 33, 39-42, 66, 244-245, 281
Tenth National Bank, 75, 112,
  162, 175, 179-180, 183, 187-188,
  194, 196
  after crash, 225-227
Thompson, Henry, 25
Trevor & Colgate, 241
Twain, Mark, 279
  The Gilded Age, 279
Tweed, William Marcy, 10, 18, 28,
  37-42, 75, 112, 162, 243-247,
  266-267, 292
  Butterfield and, 247
  and Cardozo, 248
  and Cox, 282
  and Erie Railway, 13-17
  Gould and, 295
  money lock-up, 22
Tyler, John, 53

U

Union League Club, 126-127, 131, 132
United States Supreme Court, 59
United States Treasury, 46-47, 56, 77,
  90-92, 106, 174-175, 202-203

V

Vanderbilt, Cornelius, 3-6, 66, 113,
  158-159, 164, 182, 252-253,
  276, 286
  after crash, 224-225, 242
  and Erie Railway, 8-9, 12-16
Vanderbilt, Frank, 224-225, 242
Vanderbilt, William H., 122, 294
Vanderpoel, Aaron J., 246, 247,
  249, 276
Van DeVenter & Company, 183
Vermilye & Company, 104, 179, 241
Vermilye, Jacob, 109
Vermilye, William, 126, 197

W

Ward, Ferdinand, 290
Warren, Mr. (stepfather of Josie
  Mansfield), 35
Washburne, Elihu, 67, 89
Western, Lucille, 190, 228, 278
White House, 78, 180
Willard, E. K., 158, 160, 172, 184,
  185, 195, 207, 215, 234, 275
William Marcy Tweed (yacht), 244
Wood, Annie, 18, 35
Woodhull, Victoria, 291
Woodward, William, 81, 93-94,
  108, 110, 160, 175, 194
Work, Frank, 15, 25